# THE NEW
# NINETEENTH CENTURY

WELLESLEY STUDIES IN CRITICAL THEORY, LITERARY HISTORY
AND CULTURE
VOLUME 10
GARLAND REFERENCE LIBRARY OF THE HUMANITIES
VOLUME 1700

# Wellesley Studies in Critical Theory, Literary History and Culture

William E. Cain, *General Editor*

# THE NEW NINETEENTH CENTURY

## FEMINIST READINGS OF UNDERREAD VICTORIAN FICTION

EDITED BY
BARBARA LEAH HARMAN AND SUSAN MEYER

GARLAND PUBLISHING, INC.
NEW YORK AND LONDON
1996

Copyright © 1996 by Barbara Leah Harman and Susan Meyer
All rights reserved

**Library of Congress Cataloging-in-Publication Data**

The new nineteenth century : feminist readings of underread Victorian fiction /
    edited by Barbara Leah Harman and Susan Meyer.
            p.    cm. — (Garland reference library of the humanities ; vol.
1700. Wellesley studies in critical theory, literary history and culture ; vol.
10)
        Includes bibliographical references and index.
        ISBN 0-8153-1292-X (alk. paper)
        1. English fiction—19th century—History and criticism.    2. Feminism
and literature—Great Britain—History—19th century.    3. Literature and
society—Great Britain—History—19th century.    4. Women and literature—
Great Britain—History—19th century.    5. Sex role in literature.    6. Canon
(Literature)    I. Harman, Barbara Leah.    II. Meyer, Susan.    III. Series: Garland reference library of the humanities. Wellesley studies in critical theory,
literary history and culture ; vol. 10.    IV. Series: Garland reference library
of the humanities ; v. 1700.
PR878.F45N49    1996
823'.809'082—dc20                                                                95-52470
                                                                                              CIP

*Cover illustration*: Nineteenth-century William Morris design

Printed on acid-free, 250-year-life paper
Manufactured in the United States of America

# Contents

# ACKNOWLEDGMENTS

We are grateful to *Victorian Newsletter* for permission to reprint two articles that first appeared in its pages: Judith Mitchell's "A New Perspective: Naturalism in George Moore's *A Mummer's Wife*" (1987) 71: 20–27, and Joseph H. O'Mealy's "Mrs. Oliphant, *Miss Marjoribanks*, and the Victorian Canon" (1992) 82: 44–49. Harvester/Wheatsheaf kindly granted permission to reprint chapter two of Wim Neetens's *Writing and Democracy: Literature, Politics and Culture in Transition* (1991). Deirdre David's "Rewriting the Male Plot in Wilkie Collins's *No Name:* Captain Wragge Orders an Omelette and Mrs. Wragge Goes into Custody" is here reprinted from *Out of Bounds: Male Writers and Gender(ed) Criticism*, Laura Claridge and Elizabeth Langland, eds. (Amherst: University of Massachusetts Press, 1990), copyright © 1990 by the University of Massachusetts. Nancy Paxton's "Mobilizing Chivalry: Rape in Flora Annie Steel's *On the Face of the Waters* (1896) and Other British Novels about the Indian Uprising of 1857," *Victorian Studies* (1992) 36: 5–30, is reprinted by permission of the trustees of Indiana University.

The editors also wish to thank William E. Cain for his steady and sensible advice, as well as his intellectual and editorial guidance, throughout this project. Lindy Williamson provided invaluable secretarial support, and Maureen Paulsen and Laura Kotanchik provided expert and impeccable research assistance. We also wish to thank Phyllis Korper and Alexander Metro of Garland Publishing for their careful and thoughtful supervision of this project. Finally, we wish to thank the contributors to this volume for their patience and cooperation.

# FOREWORD: THE UNDERREAD *

*John Sutherland*

I sometimes fantasize gathering together everyone who professes knowledge about "Victorian fiction" and asking them to write down the names of as many novelists as they can think of. As I guess, scores would probably run like this: (1) well-read high school graduates would come up with three to four names; (2) undergraduates with a one- or two-semester course in nineteenth-century literature might scrape together a dozen names; (3) graduates writing a dissertation in the field could probably reel off two or three dozen names; (4) young academics with an article or two in scholarly journals might muster fifty or so. Undoubtedly the longest lists would come from antiquarian book dealers and collectors—"nonprofessionals."

As a teacher, I have frequently been struck by how much less I know (in terms of range of reference) than, say, cinema buffs know about 1940s film noir or than amateur ornithologists know about finches. Generalizations about "the Victorian novel" (which are common enough in academic discourse) are often hobbled by being restricted to the dozen writers designated as "major" by the *New Cambridge Bibliography of English Literature*—writers whose extraordinary literary distinction renders them necessarily unrepresentative. Despite fifty years of intense, academically sponsored research into the form, we still make do with only the sketchiest sense of the infrastructure of Victorian fiction—how the bulk of it was produced; who originated, reproduced, distributed, and consumed the product. Statistics are an initial area of vagueness. Bluntly, when it comes to Victorian novels and Victorian novelists, we just don't know how many there were. In his monumental *Nineteenth-Century Fiction, A Bibliographical Catalogue* (5 vols., 1982–1986), R.L. Wolff estimates that there are some 42,000 published Victorian novels of which—aiming at completeness—he contrived to collect 7,000. The annual statistics of the trade journal of *Publisher's Circular,* 1837–1901, suggest that total book production rose annually from 2,000 to 8,000 new titles over the Victorian period, and that the proportion of fiction concurrently rose from around 12 percent to about 25 percent (the increase being largely explained by the recruitment of new reading publics, particularly after the Education Act of 1870). Assuming exponential progressions for both figures over the sixty-four years, one arrives at a probable total output of around 50,000 novels. But exactness is impossible, given the fuzzy borders of fiction where it shades into religious-tract, educational, and ephemeral periodical reading matter. Around 50,000 is, however, at this stage, a good figure from which to start. When the promised "History of the Book in Britain" project has done its work we shall know more precisely.[1]

The academic study of Victorian fiction has signally failed to engage with the mass of works produced in the field. Nor, I think, is there any widespread sense of inadequacy among Victorianists about the thinness of their crust of knowledge, and the even thinner crusts we serve up to our students. Our narrow frame of reference justifies itself by two implicit theses. They boil down to (1) read one Victorian novel, and you've read them all. Thus, if a student ploughs through *Silas Marner* and *Hard Times,* that student is qualified to write an essay on, for example, "The Treatment of Working-class Women in 'Victorian Fiction.'" (2) Life (or the semester) is too short to bother with anything less than the canonical best.

The first of these strategies of economies ("Read one and you've read them all") is, I believe, both wrong and horribly condescending. There is a wealth of excellent Victorian fiction lying disused outside our conventional educational and scholarly orbits. This collection is devoted in a provisional way to mapping some of those outlying areas. The initiative of feminist publishing houses like Virago (before they came to financial grief) in disinterring for the general reading public writers such as Mary Cholmondeley and Sarah Grand proves quite conclusively that there is a vast amount of high-quality Victorian fiction awaiting critical rediscovery. This is not to say that Victorian fiction, any more than any other genre, is immune from "Sturgeon's law" ("90 per cent of science fiction is crud: but 90 per cent of everything is crud," Theodore Sturgeon.) There are Victorian novelists so bad that it's one's intellectual duty *not* to read them. I would not condemn anyone to the lower reaches of Victorian fiction. Life is too short and eternity scarcely long enough to read the 197–strong output of Annie S. Swan or all the 251 works of L.T. Meade deposited in the British Library. Nonetheless, there remain a daunting number of unread but usefully readable works in the genre that ought—over the next few years as computerized cataloguing makes them accessible—to attract more critical attention than they have in the past.

The second thesis—that life's too short—has the merit of robust realism. Logistically, our educational and research system ill equips us to deal with a field like Victorian fiction as a field. Close reading is time consuming and encourages exhaustive attention to detail. There has been, for the last two decades, a prejudice against positivism as an intellectual method and a corresponding reliance on theory. As theory enriches the quality of discourse, it has impoverished the frame of reference, as scholars concentrate more on *how* they read than *what* they read. Another inhibiting factor is the obligation at the postgraduate level to produce unaided, original work. This blocks off all sorts of shortcuts and collaborations open to scientists and social scientists, who habitually work in teams and produce joint-authored research. And, finally, there is the dominance of the monograph (literally, "writing about one thing") as the main channel of scholarly communication in English studies at the highest level. All this makes it hard and unfashionable to deal with English literature *in extenso*. Particularly, one might say, the Victorian novel, given the two material facts that it is typically very long (as much as 300,000 words) and extraordinarily numerous. Assuming five hours per novel and a 40–hour workweek, it would take something over 131 years to read every work of Victorian fiction. So there is a literal sense in which life is too short to know the subject completely.

Who, then, were the novelists, those largely invisible masses that Dickens called "my fellow labourers"? And how many of them were there? Given an average output of 17 novels per novelist (for the justification of this figure, see below), a workforce of around 3,500 may be hazarded. Given an average working life for novelists of around 32 years (see below again) and the fact that many novelists qualify with only one work of fiction, it is a fair guess that two such working forces would populate the period, with the necessary chronological overlaps and a progressive upward scaling to take account of the production increase over the 64 years. At the end of the century, Walter Besant (in his capacity as founder of the Society of Authors) reckoned that there were some 1,200 novelists at work, of whom 200 were entirely self-supporting by their writing. This seems somewhat on the low side and may be biased (especially in regard to the 200) by Besant's ineradicable gloom about the treatment of the creative writer by philistine English culture. But it is roughly in line with my estimates if one adds the amateurs and one-novel wonders who would have been beneath Besant's notice.

Most of these estimated 3,500 Victorian novelists will never emerge from the obscurity of the statistical mass. Even the most exhaustive investigations can turn up no worthwhile biographical (or sometimes even reliable bibliographical) data. The cult of anonymous authorship that persisted well into the late Victorian period is an often impenetrable screen. Another source of obscurity is the sheer inaccessibility of historical evidence about the very minor Victorian novelists. They remain as unidentifiable to us as the cabby who drove Dickens to the *All the Year Round* office, or the chambermaid who cleaned the room at the "Priory," where George Eliot wrote *Felix Holt, the Radical.*

I would guess that some bio-bibliographical profile (dates of birth, death, career details, marital status, total number of novels published) can be readily retrieved for about 1,200 Victorian novelists. For another purpose than this foreword, I have gathered such material on some 878 of them. These represent authors whose records lie close enough to the surface for one to discover salient facts using the resources of the British Library.[2] It is, I think, probably the largest database yet assembled. (The *New Cambridge Bibliography of English Literature*, for instance, has entries on fewer than 200; this will probably be rectified in the third *Cambridge Bibliography*, currently in production.) A lifetime's work could probably turn up a few hundred more, but the majority of Victorian novelists have, I suspect, sunk forever without a trace.

As a sample, 878 cases out of 3,500 is more than substantial enough for statistical analysis, if the sample is not too skewed. But, one must assume, it is manifestly skewed in favor of the "noteworthy" writer. To have left any record is, in itself, a mark of egregiousness. If the condition of the Victorian novelist is obscurity, to be known is to be in some degree exceptional and to be at all famous (either to one's contemporaries or posterity) is to be a very rare bird indeed. Nevertheless, with the necessary qualifications, 878 novelists is a solid starting point. What I intend to do here is make some preliminary interrogation of these data with the hope of arriving at a set of initially serviceable generalizations about the Victorian novelist, en masse.

Skimming the bio-bibliographies of 878 Victorian novelists yields any number of suggestive, primary observations—not least, the inadequacy of the term "novelist," implying as it does both those who merely wrote a novel and those who devoted their lives to (and won their bread by) fiction. It is said that the Eskimo has twenty words for snow. It would be useful to have a similarly discriminating subvocabulary for "Victorian novelist." As it is loosely applied, the term can legitimately cover someone like Grace Kimmins ("Sister Grace of the Bermondsey Settlement," 1870–1954), whose philanthropy expressed itself primarily in charitable work in the East End and who in furtherance of that work wrote one successful novel with a purpose, *Polly of Parker Rents* (1899). "Victorian novelist" equally covers the similarly philanthropic, but exclusively literary, Miss Evelyn Everett-Green (1856–1932), who has no fewer than 254 works of fiction deposited in the British Library (many written for the Religious Tract Society). It is hard to image that, given a twenty-four–hour day and a seventy-six–year lifespan, Everett-Green ever had time to do anything but write fiction. If quantity means anything, she was a novelist of a quite different stamp from one-shot Grace Kimmins.

One pattern that emerges is the ricochet route into novel writing that is typical of male writers, who often come to novel writing late and indirectly, and the direct route into authorship that is, by contrast, typically female. The archetypal male novelist would be William de Morgan (1839–1917), who began life as an art student, worked with William Morris, rediscovered medieval techniques for staining glass, set up a ceramics factory at Fulham, and retired in 1905. In his retirement, aged sixty-five, he began a successful career writing Victorian (in all but date) novels with *Joseph Vance* (1906). He was initially encouraged to write by his wife, who was worried by his depressed state of mind. De Morgan followed his 1906 best-seller with five more, and left two works of fiction incomplete at the time of his death. The archetypal female novelist is someone like Daisy Ashford (1881–1972), who began writing at age nine and had four novels completed by age thirteen, when she was packed off to convent school, never to write fiction again. At its bluntest, one may say that men tended to have lived, loved, and worked, before writing fiction, women often the other way around.

This is not to say that women could not turn their hand to fiction late in life, if they had to; more particularly if it was the only way they could put bread on the family table. One can cite, for instance, the case of Mrs. Trollope (1779–1863) who, finding herself let down by her bankrupt husband in the early 1830s, set to at the age of fifty-five and wrote 35 sprightly works of fiction to keep the Trollopes in middle-class respectability. As resourceful was Amelia Barr (1831–1919), whose husband dragged her off to America and then died of yellow fever (together with three of his daughters), leaving the widow Barr on the streets of New York with five dollars in her purse and three surviving daughters to support. At the age of fifty-four, Mrs. Barr set to and went on to write 64 popular novels (among them, *Remember the Alamo*, 1888, elements of which resurfaced in the 1960s John Wayne movie). A sizable band of these resourceful women can be assembled who, had the wolf not been at the door, would never have put pen to paper, or certainly not so late in their lives.

Another feature that stands out from a cursory scanning of the 878 bio-bibliographical capsules is the clear link between novel writing and certain historical conjunctions. Sea captains in the 1830s, for instance, were recruited in large numbers into the profession (the names of Marryat, Howard, Chamier, Barker, Glascock, and Neale come to mind). Clearly, peace, half-pay, and national nostalgia for the Great Victorious War all played a part. But so too did the training and discipline of the officer's life at sea, which was quite different from that of the land-based soldier. Naval service in the early nineteenth century entailed long periods of boredom unrelieved by drink or the company of women. And, unlike their military counterparts, naval commanders were expected to write as a central part of their duty, keeping the logbook being a daily ritual (soldiers, by contrast, were notoriously illiterate). This state of affairs holds up only until the mid-1850s, after which (following Crimean reforms) soldiers became better penmen (and more of them wrote novels). With the advent of steam, sailors had less time to spin yarns, in both senses of the term. Apart from the 1830s and 1840s, sea captains rarely feature as active novelists.

Suicide in the ranks of the writing profession is uncommon, but pseudonyms and anonymity, for instance, were often used to mask shame at being a novelist. Thus Julia Wedgwood (1833–1914), an offspring of the Wedgwood-Darwin dynasty, wrote one of her two novels anonymously, and one pseudonymously (as "Florence Dawson"). Evidently, her first (*Framleigh Hall,* 1858) was written without her father's knowledge; the second (*An Old Debt,* 1859) was published only after he gave her his patriarchal imprimatur, having read and censored the manuscript. Thereafter, parental disapproval inhibited Julia Wedgwood from writing fiction altogether. Hugh Stowell Scott (1862–1903) ran into similar parental opposition. His father, a prosperous shipowner in Newcastle Upon Tyne, decreed that his son should enter the family business. Ostensibly dutiful, young Hugh complied. But secretly he began writing and publishing novels, at first anonymously, then under the pseudonym "Henry Seton Merriman" (the overtones of hedonistic release implicit in this pen name—"the merry man"—are striking). The difference between Scott and Wedgwood is that he did not finally crumple into filial silence. He went on to write 18 best-selling works of fiction. (He also turned duplicity to good effect in later life by serving as one of the early clandestine agents of the British secret service.) This greater resolution and independence of the male novelist in the face of stigma attached to writing fiction is generally borne out by mass survey.

Another fact that strikes the casually inquiring eye is the dynastic effect of the great Victorian novelists on those around them, particularly close relatives. Thus, for instance, Thackeray had one daughter, Anne Thackeray Ritchie, who went on to become a considerable novelist in her own right.

His other daughter became the first wife of Leslie Stephen, father of Virginia Woolf. The woman with whom Thackeray had his (possibly) adulterous love affair in 1851, Jane Octavia Brookfield, went on after 1868 (Thackeray dying in 1863) to write 4 novels. And her son, Arthur Brookfield, went on in his turn to write 5 novels. A Thackeray cousin, Blanche Ritchie, wrote a novel, and so did her husband, Francis Warre Cornish (both narratives were pseudo-Thackerayan in tone). To have 6 novelists clustered so closely around a major novelist is a much higher-than-chance rate. The same clustering phenomenon is found among the Trollopes. There is Anthony, who wrote 47 novels, his mother, Frances Milton, who wrote 35, his sister Cecilia who, before dying of consumption, wrote 1, and a couple of cousins who wrote about a dozen between them. Finally there was Anthony's brother, Thomas Adolphus, who wrote 20 novels, and Thomas's second wife, Frances Eleanor Trollope, who wrote 60–odd. Altogether, Trollopes accounted for some 170 Victorian novels, or 0.3 percent of the Victorian total. Add his present-day descendant, Joanna Trollope, and the total on the dynastic scoreboard soars out of sight.

Frances Eleanor Trollope's maiden name was Ternan, and she was the sister of Dickens's mistress, Ellen Ternan. Dickens's son Charles Jr. did not write novels (although he commissioned many, as the editor in succession to his father on *All The Year Round*). But Angela Dickens, Charles Jr.'s daughter (1863–1946), went on to write 9 novels (all noticeably morbid in tone) and she was aunt (I believe) to the twentieth-century novelist Monica Dickens. Dickens's daughter Kate married Charles Allston Collins, author of two novels and brother of Wilkie, author of 30. Altogether, this Dickens constellation accounts for some 60 Victorian novels.

Charles Kingsley wrote 10 novels of the first rank. Only slightly less far behind in critical standing was his brother Henry Kingsley, with 20. A daughter of Charles, Mary St. Leger, whose married name was Harrison and whose pen name was "Lucas Malet," wrote 12 novels. A younger sister, Charlotte (married name "Chanter"), wrote a best-seller, *Over The Cliffs*, in 1860. Altogether, this Kingsley constellation accounts for 45 works of Victorian fiction, all of very high literary quality. Of the 11 children of Frederick Marryat, four daughters and one son wrote Victorian novels, running up a family score of around 100 titles.

One could follow these genealogical, or free-masonic, connections much further than I have done here. But it is clear that one of the main predisposing factors to writing Victorian novels was to have a close relative, or intimate acquaintance, who wrote Victorian novels.

Looking at individual cases is delightful, yielding the same kind of pleasure as turning over the pages of old photograph albums. And clearly enough it is instructive as well as perplexing to get to know the personnel behind the novels. But I want now to move to quantitative and more systematic analysis of my 878 cases. The questions to which initial answers are sought are: (1) How many Victorian novelists were seriously professional, and how many were amateur or sideline novelists? (2) Given the fact that Victorian fiction was unique in being a profession/industry/hobby in which men and women took part in equal numbers, is there any observable difference in the ways in which the sexes were drawn or recruited into writing novels? Put more simply—what made the Victorian a Victorian novelist, and was the process different for men and women?

For multifactorial research, about 40 different fields can be covered by my data, including such factors as class origin, education, religious background, illness or handicap at significant periods of life, career activities, marital status, and so on. For my purposes here, I have collected responses on the following questions: (1) When were the authors born, and when did they die? (2) How many novels did they write? (3) At what age did they start writing? (4) Was there a career previous to writing novels?

Novel writing, I have said, was unique in Victorian society in being a public and professional activity open both to middle-class men and middle-class women on more or less equal terms. Nevertheless, given the social role forced on them, women naturally tended to be more of a modestly submerged component than their male partners. There was clearly more inhibition about women revealing themselves in the public activity of publication, hence they made more use of the pseudonymity and anonymity conventions afforded by the profession. Revealingly enough, their pseudonyms tended to be sexually neutral, or trans-sexual, as in the following: "John Oliver Hobbes" (Pearl M.T. Craigie), "George Egerton" (Mrs. Chavelita Bright), "G.E. Brunefille" (Lady Colin Campbell), "Lucas Malet"(Mary St. Leger Harrison), "Lucas Cleeve" (Adelina Kingscote), "Cecil Adair" (Evelyn Everett-Green), "Leslie Keith" (Grace Johnston), "Michael Fairless" (Margaret Barber), "Maxwell Gray" (Mary Tuttiett), "John Law" (Margaret Harkness), and, most famously, "Currer," "Ellis," and "Acton Bell" (the Brontë sisters). The process is almost entirely one-way. Although men often used pseudonyms, for a variety of reasons, I have discovered only one man using even a vaguely female pen name, the obscure nautical novelist Alexander Christie (1841–1895), who wrote as "Lindsay Anderson," an amalgamation of his mother's and his wife's maiden names.

The total of 878 yields 566 men and 312 women. As I suggest above, I imagine this is a function of greater reticence about declaring identity among women writers. Altogether, these 878 authors account for 15,490 fiction titles. At first glance, this looks like an impressively large fraction of the 50,000 or so hypothetical total. But it needs to be qualified. Given the fact that Victorian authors were, regrettably enough, not all born in 1837 and overlap both ends of the period, the 15,490 figure should in prudence be reduced by as much as a third. The following graph shows the birthdates of the 878 novelists, from 1790 to 1870. Many of those born at the very end of the period continued writing, in some cases up to the mid-twentieth century.

TABLE 1.

The number of Victorian novelists born in each of the decades 1790 to 1870.

| | 1790 | 1800 | 1810 | 1820 | 1830 | 1840 | 1850 | 1860 | 1870 |
|---|---|---|---|---|---|---|---|---|---|
| 150 | | | | | | | | x | |
| 140 | | | | | | | x | | |
| 130 | | | | | | | | | |
| 120 | | | | | | | | | x |
| 110 | | | | | | | | | |
| 100 | | | | | | x | | | |
| 90 | | | | x | x | | | | |
| 80 | | | x | | | | | | |
| 70 | | | | | | | | | |
| 60 | | | | | | | | | |
| 50 | | | x | | | | | | |
| 40 | | | | | | | | | |
| 30 | | | | | | | | | |
| 20 | | x | | | | | | | |

Demographically, the sample reveals no great surprises. The average life expectancy of the male novelist was sixty-six; the female novelist slightly longer, 68.5. The average length of writing career (first novel to death) was 29.9 years for men and 35.2 years for women. The average age of starting to write was thirty-six for the male novelist, thirty-three for the female. (Given the difficulty of determining when a writer actually broke into print, I suspect this figure should be adjusted downward by about 5 years.)

The per-author lifetime total breaks down to 17.6 novels per writer.

Women novelists averaged 21 titles against men's 15.7. This is a high amount in all categories and suggests that the practice of fiction was thoroughly professionalized. At an average payment of around £250, 16 to 21 novels would make a useful contribution to a life's income and in many circumstances would constitute its bulk. Given the average career length, it gives a novel for every twenty-four months of professional activity. But the per-author output figures rise even higher if one breaks them down. Thus:

878 (100%) wrote 1 novel or more (15,490 titles, or 100%)
553 (63%) wrote 5 novels or more (14,542, or 93%)
400 (45.5%) wrote 10 novels or more (13,352, or 86%)
212 (24%) wrote 20 novels or more (10,651, or 68.7%)
141 (16%) wrote 30 novels or more (8,883, or 57.3%)
95 (10.8%) wrote 40 novels or more (7,277, or 46.9%)
67 (7.6%) wrote 50 novels or more (5,992, or 38.6%)
45 (5%) wrote 60 novels or more (4,159, or 30.7%)
29 (3.3%) wrote 70 novels or more (3,713, or 23.9%)
24 (2.7%) wrote 80 novels or more (3,334, or 21.5%)
19 (2.1%) wrote 90 novels or more (2,932, or 18.9%)
18 (2%) wrote 100 novels or more (2,837, or 18%)

It is evident from this sample that Victorian fiction was largely the product of a relatively small, active component within a fairly large, loosely participatory community (i.e., 7 percent producing a third of all titles). It is evident too that the canonical novelists could make do on smaller than average outputs (Dickens 15, Gaskell 15, Thackeray 9, Eliot 10) because their work was rewarded more highly than average. And Anthony Trollope, with his 47 fiction titles, is not—given the production rates of the profession—as fertile a writer as commonly believed. Almost half of all Victorian novels seem to have been produced by authors clocking up 40 or more titles.

I have not analyzed the class backgrounds in the sample, or other predisposing factors such as higher education. But the prior or concurrent profession field throws up interesting results. Among the male novelists, all but 57 can be allocated at least one (and in many cases more than one) previous or other gainful line of work. In over half the cases, these are lines of work in which the embryo Victorian novelist has not notably succeeded. The principal stepping-stones to a Victorian man's writing fiction were as follows:

| | |
|---|---|
| law (predominantly service at the bar) | 110 |
| journalism | 82 |
| business, civil service | 75 |
| church | 57 |
| army | 50 |
| teaching | 37 |
| navy | 21 |
| medicine | 21 |
| manual, menial | 17 |
| book trade | 11 |
| Total | 481 |

The dominance of law as an entry point into novel writing is the striking feature here. Put simply, one in five (male) Victorian novelists was a lawyer, and in the vast majority of cases a failed barrister. "Called to the Bar but never practiced" is thus the commonest prelude to a career in writing novels. And if one adds lawyer fathers (or, for women, lawyer husbands) the coincidence of a training in law with the Victorian novel is even more pronounced. Nor is it just hacks who turned from law to fiction. Among the great novelists one can cite are Thackeray (failed barrister), Dickens (articled as a solicitor's clerk in Gray's Inn), Blackmore (called to the bar but never practiced), Stevenson (studied law at Edinburgh), Charles Reade (called to the bar but never practiced), Meredith (articled to a solicitor for a while), Wilkie Collins (called to the bar but never practiced), and Harrison Ainsworth (studied law at the Inner Temple).

Some reasons for the law–fiction link may be guessed at. To read for the English bar, it is necessary to have family money, contacts, and (usually) an Oxbridge education. To practice at the bar was, and is, a top job and one from which the working classes are generally excluded. And, for complex reasons, the British aristocracy have never encouraged younger sons to follow law, directing them instead to the army and the church. None of this is, however, a convincing explanation of the wide bridge connecting Victorian law and Victorian fiction. A more likely factor is the closeness of the Inns of Court to Fleet Street—journalism often being the transitional stage between law and writing novels. But geographically, some of the main teaching hospitals are even nearer Fleet Street. Yet failed doctors did not drift into novel writing in anything like the same numbers that young lawyers did.

The critical factor was, presumably, the peculiar nature of legal training. Reading for the bar centers on two activities: reading, self-evidently, and dining, the law, even more than Parliament, being one of the best clubs in

London, with the difference that taking dinner a certain number of times is obligatory on trainee barristers. Moreover, the study and practice of law is punctuated by absurdly long vacations. Young doctors, especially during internship, are routinely overworked for fifty weeks of the year, and they do not just read up their professional expertise, which is largely a matter of manual and interpersonal skills. Unlike the newly qualified doctor, the young barrister emerged from his training without any clear next step. He waited, hopefully, for briefs. Often they were slow in coming. Typically, in this awkward interval, the lawyer would marry, incurring new debts. And typically, in this interval, the drift to writing would occur. Finally, although it is a hard link to discern, there is probably an affinity between the mentalities of jurisprudence and Victorian fiction, shaped as both were by the study of individual cases and the canons of (poetic) justice.

Only 32 of 312 women can be given alternative professional, business, or trade activities. Those with no other vocational attribution than "married woman" or "spinster" hugely predominate:

| | |
|---|---|
| married women | 167 |
| spinsters | 113 |
| journalists | 9 |
| teachers or governesses | 8 |
| actresses or artists | 6 |
| doctors or nurses | 4 |
| book trade | 4 |
| business | 1 |
| Total | 312 |

Not surprisingly, perhaps, the Victorian spinster author was the most productive single category of writer, with an average output of 24 titles.

These findings are very preliminary, and in many cases simply confirm what common sense would anyway suggest. And even where the conclusions are instructive (as in the male-professional and female-amateur finding), they should be treated with some caution. The principal uncertainty can be expressed as a question: do the 878 cases examined mirror the profession, or are they a superstructure of the most successful practitioners self-selected by being that much better than the rest? Granted that the sample is probably unrepresentative, it is less unrepresentative than the invariable dozen or so novelists who furnish the staple material for the study of "Victorian fiction" in higher education. Beneath that elite handful my 878 novelists form a reasonably sound and now fairly visible foundation. Beneath these 878 is a still invisible substratum (of several thousands) composed, one suspects, of failures, rank amateurs, third-rate hacks, and utter nonentities. Some future literary archaeological tool will have to be devised to investigate these lower reaches.

How, to conclude, do the authors represented here fit into the large categories I have sketched? Among them, the fifteen novelists written about in this collection published some 363 novels. The women have 198 titles, at an average of 24.75 per novelist:

| | |
|---|---|
| Anne Brontë | 2 |
| George Egerton | 7 |
| Sarah Grand | 11 |
| Geraldine Jewsbury | 8 |
| Eliza Linton | 26 |
| Margaret Oliphant | 95 |
| Flora Steel | 24 |
| Mary Ward | 25 |
| Total | 198 |

The men have 168, at a per-novelist average of 24:

| | |
|---|---|
| Walter Besant | 31 |
| Wilkie Collins | 30 |
| George Gissing | 29 |
| Sheridan Le Fanu | 21 |
| George Moore | 19 |
| Charles Reade | 26 |
| Bram Stoker | 12 |
| Total | 168 |

Three of the women writers here (Brontë, Egerton, Grand) habitually wrote fiction under noms de plume, two of them masculine names ("Acton Bell," "George Egerton"). The points of entry into the profession for these women more or less fit the general patterns outlined above: Anne Brontë had no previous career, and published her first novel aged twenty-seven and unmarried; George Egerton had an earlier career as a nurse and as a married woman (in a spectacularly unsatisfactory marriage) and published her first novel aged thirty-four. Sarah Grand became a professional writer of fiction after a failed marriage, aged thirty-four. Geraldine Jewsbury began professional life as a journalist, and published her first novel aged thirty-three and unmarried. Eliza Linton began professional life as a journalist and published her first novel aged twenty-five and unmarried. Margaret Oliphant was unmarried and twenty-one when she published her first novel. Flora Steel had no previous profession, and published her first novel as a married woman, aged thirty-seven. Mary Ward had a successful career in journalism before writing her first novel, aged thirty-three and married.

The average age of these eight women writers starting their careers was 30.5—in line with the norm of 33. Of the group here, three at least can be said to have been precocious girl authors. Mary Ward (Arnold as she then was) wrote her first novels aged ten (they are described and discussed in W.H. Peterson's *Victorian Heretic,* 1978). Margaret Oliphant was a professional novelist aged twenty-one. And Anne Brontë participated in the famous Angria/Gondal sagas as a young girl. Sarah Grand began writing her first novel, *Ideala,* eight years before publishing it in 1888.

What is most striking in the sample of women writers discussed here is how many of them were professional journalists: Jewsbury, Linton, and Ward. Apart from Egerton's early experience as a nurse, none can be said to have entered fiction by other than the one writing profession generally open to women—magazine work. Of the sample, three were lifelong spinsters, and three entered fiction writing with broken marriages or widowed (assuming that Oliphant's career took off after her husband died and she was obliged to write for her living). Two (Steel and Ward) qualified as writers who were also married women assertive of their marital status (both wrote under their husband's names and the "Mrs." title, Ward going to the extent of calling herself "Mrs. Humphry Ward"). Two of the women writers can be said to have had "dynastic" affiliations connecting them with other famous writers: Brontë, Ward (a member of the Arnold family).

The somewhat smaller sample of men novelists represented here can also be said to conform on the whole to the general pattern of their sex. Walter Besant was a university teacher and journalist before publishing his first novel, aged thirty-six. Wilkie Collins had false starts in trade and barristry before publishing his first novel, aged twenty-six. Sheridan Le Fanu was a successful journalist before publishing his first novel, aged thirty-one. George Moore had an unsuccessful career as an artist before publishing his first novel, aged thirty-one. Charles Reade qualified as a barrister and won an Oxford fellowship before writing his first novel, aged thirty-eight. Bram Stoker was a civil servant before bringing out his first work of fiction, aged thirty-four. George Gissing was a teacher (briefly) and part-time tutor prior to the publication of his first novel, aged twenty-three. The average age of entry for these male novelists was 31.3 years. But what is most notable, in comparison with the women in the sample, is the fact that for all but one of them novel writing was a second profession, in most cases following on a failed start in some other professional walk of life—barristry, civil service, journalism, higher education. For most of these men, authorship was a second start in professional life.

Statistical analysis does not, in the final analysis, take literary criticism very far. But in an enterprise like the present one it can, I hope, give some usefully preliminary sense of the shape and size of the "underread" and—looming beneath that category—the larger obscure mass of the "totally unread."

*Notes*

*This essay is adapted from *Victorian Fiction Writers, Publishers, Readers*, forthcoming from Macmillan.

1. This project is being undertaken by a team of scholars under the general editorship of D.F. McKenzie. Simon Eliot's *Some Patterns and Trends in British Publishing, 1800–1919* (London, 1994) usefully supplements some of my comments here.

2. The purpose for which the material was collected was *The Longman Companion to Victorian Fiction* (London, 1988).

# INTRODUCTION

*Barbara Leah Harman and Susan Meyer*

Charlotte and Emily Brontë, Elizabeth Gaskell, George Eliot, Charles Dickens, William Thackeray, Anthony Trollope, Thomas Hardy—these are the novelists we assign to our students, year after year, in Victorian novel courses. To the fact that many of our students read them with avidity, and continue, after college, to be enthusiastic readers of the Victorian novel, the long shelves devoted in bookstores to Trollope and Dickens provide eloquent testimony. But what of the *other* Victorian novelists? Given both the length of the average Victorian novel and the brevity of our academic semesters, we rarely find time to assign, or perhaps even to read ourselves, the many other Victorian novelists who were known and admired in their own day, and who were often tremendously productive both of fiction and of various forms of nonfiction. Who were these other Victorian novelists? And, perhaps more important for our purposes, who among them are worth reading and writing about, and possibly worth including in our courses?

In this volume, *The New Nineteenth Century: Feminist Readings of Underread Victorian Fiction,* we devote a new kind of concerted critical attention to these novelists, who, our contributors contend, have to varying degrees been "underread" by scholars of Victorian literature. Anne Brontë, Geraldine Jewsbury, Wilkie Collins, Charles Reade, Margaret Oliphant, Sheridan Le Fanu, Bram Stoker, Eliza Linton, Walter Besant, George Moore, George Gissing, Sarah Grand, George Egerton, Mary Ward, Flora Annie Steel—these are some of the "new" names of Victorian writers, whose work spans the years 1847 to 1896, to whom the contributors to this volume direct our attention. Each of the essays here argues, in its own way, for the significance of a lesser-known Victorian novelist or text, inaugurating the process of according these writers and their works a deeper attention and a more widespread late-twentieth-century recognition.

Why, in particular, have we chosen "feminist" readings, readings animated, in whole or in part, by an attention to the dynamics of gender? The Victorian period, and the Victorian novel in particular, has proven one of the areas of English literature most responsive to—and most illuminated by—feminist criticism. In addition to being frequently written by women, Victorian novels had an enormous female readership, and often focused on the lives of—and thus the possible life choices open to—women. Whether they are attending to a woman writer's encounter with increasingly gendered formal choices (Kucich), to a male writer's representation of possibly uncontrollable female appetites and desires (Heller), or to the expression of anxieties about the dissolution of male identity in a modern professional society (Hall), the contributors to the volume all engage with the subject of gender and its construction in the Victorian novel.

The collection, which is arranged in chronological order, opens with an essay on Anne Brontë's *Agnes Grey*. In "Words on 'Great Vulgar Sheets': Writing and Social Resistance in Anne Brontë's *Agnes Grey* (1847)," Susan Meyer discusses the first of two novels by Anne Brontë, the least known of the three Brontë sisters. *Agnes Grey*, a first-person narrative chronicling the life of a governess, has commonly been dismissed by critics as stiff and emotionally flat. But the emotional restraint of the protagonist is both deliberate on Brontë's part, Meyer argues, and important to the novel's aims: Brontë uses her self-suppression to make some important points of social critique. The novel explores the way the upper class dominates those lower in class by wielding the force of language and metaphor. Brontë's novel subtly resists this act of silencing by various strategies, among them enacting its own sly reversals of the self-authorizing metaphors of the ruling class. At the same time, by continuing its exploration of the relationship between language and social hierarchy, the novel suggests that even seemingly benign relationships between men and women have disconcerting resemblances to the relationship between the upper class and the middle class. "And if the novel seems to have come [at its end] to a solution, satisfactory in middle-class terms, to the problem of class," Meyer writes, "the problem of gender remains, at the novel's end, more submerged and unresolved."

Jewsbury, like Brontë, had an ambivalent relationship to Victorian gender ideology. In "At Home upon a Stage: Domesticity and Genius in Geraldine Jewsbury's *The Half Sisters* (1848)," Judith Rosen explores a novel about two women (the half sisters of the title) one an actress, the other a more traditional, domestic figure. Though Jewsbury was herself a professional woman of many talents—she was, among other things, a regular reviewer for the *Athenaeum*—she struggled with her own sense of the difficulties associated with women whose public energies led to their abandonment of selflessness, and thence to "unwomanliness." *The Half Sisters,* according to Rosen, is Jewsbury's attempt to reconcile the contradictions inherent in this vision of public women by reconfiguring the usual associations attached to public and private female lives. The theatrical life of the heroine borrows from the writings of domestic ideologists of the 1840s the notion that femininity is "a carefully disciplined performance, one that sets self aside to represent . . . communal values and truths endangered by the selfish competition of the marketplace." Rosen claims that Jewsbury drew on such notions to present the actress's work as an extension of domestic practice into the public sphere. The heroine's clear sense of purpose throughout the novel is contrasted with that of her married, domestic half-sister, whose "selfless modesty" and lack of an "internal sense of autonomy," make her vulnerable to what Rosen calls "promiscuous possession" by another lover. Surprisingly, domestic life in *The Half Sisters* leads to self-abandonment, but acting functions as a "moral prophylactic for lives lived in the public sphere."

Deirdre David's "Rewriting the Male Plot in Wilkie Collins's *No Name* (1862): Captain Wragge Orders an Omelette and Mrs. Wragge Goes into Custody," also deals with a writer's complex relationship to Victorian gender ideology. According to David, Collins's narrative form, which refuses omniscient narration and offers its account from multiple perspectives and in multiple styles, "challenges authoritarian, patriarchal-sited power in [its] interrogation of form," mirroring as it does so the struggle of a heroine who is both "exiled from and enclosed within patriarchal structures." David's essay focuses on the wife of one of the novel's narrators who "absolutely unconsciously" expresses Collins's critique of the dominant modes of gender politics. Deprived of her identity by the "incessant discipline of [her husband's] male directions," Mrs. Wragge, in her spectacular self-confusion, produces, according to David, an extraordinary kind of female subversion. Continually, if unintentionally, she subverts the plots and plans of her husband, thwarting the "male authorized texts or laws" with which he controls both her and others. David sees Mrs. Wragge as emblematic of the novel's effort both to represent male discursive power and to reveal the ways in which it is undermined by its very force.

In her "Silent Woman, Speaking Fiction: Charles Reade's *Griffith Gaunt* (1866) at the Adultery Trial of Henry Ward Beecher," Laura Hanft Korobkin explores both the power and the subversion of the law. She interprets Reade's sensation novel in the context of the American adultery trial of Elizabeth Tilton, whose husband sued Henry Ward Beecher for what was then called "criminal conversation." The novel became an issue in the trial both because Tilton had read and written letters about it, due to the similarity between its plot and that of the Tilton/Beecher relationship, and because lawyers on both sides used it (albeit with divergent intents) to make their cases. Korobkin investigates the difference between the view of the novel as transgressive and "sensational"—providing an extraordinary example of female autonomy and agency—and the view of it as morally redemptive and "sentimental"—evoking in readers, and in Tilton herself, the "highly respectable resolution" to reaffirm her marriage vows. As Korobkin neatly puts it, Elizabeth Tilton achieved a "sentimental" and religious reading of what remains a "scandalously sensationalist text."

Margaret Oliphant's *Miss Marjoribanks* provides a radically different reading of the operations of female power in the social world. In his "Mrs. Oliphant, *Miss Marjoribanks* (1866), and the Victorian Canon," Joseph H. O'Mealy examines what is arguably the best of this prolific Victorian writer's 92 novels in order to make a claim for the worth of Oliphant's now sadly neglected fiction. Twentieth-century critics have paid little attention to Oliphant's fiction, O'Mealy writes, because traditionalists have questioned its literary quality, often criticizing Oliphant's artistry on the basis of her enormous output, whereas feminist critics have been reluctant to champion a writer of such apparent political conservatism, a writer in whom one finds no emancipated heroines, no challenges to patriarchy. But the carefully controlled, ambivalent ironies of *Miss Marjoribanks* show a real literary sophistication, O'Mealy argues, and the novel is centrally, and sympathetically, concerned with the limitations placed on the lives of Victorian women. This novel's exploration of a young woman's self-appointed "career"—reorganizing the social life of the town of Carlingford—is an ironic comedy about the struggle for power in a world that places severe limitations on female ambition. O'Mealy says of Lucilla Marjoribanks's work that it comes "as close to a public career as a Victorian lady could hope for." Lucilla makes "impressive use of the meager resources at her disposal"—however compromised her schemes and ambitions must be. In Miss Marjoribanks, O'Mealy contends, we see a kind of "comic Dorothea, also 'foundress of nothing,' but one who is too bustling, too bourgeois, and too bullheaded to care that her life 'spent itself in channels which had no great name on earth.'"

In her analysis of Joseph Sheridan Le Fanu's tale of a female vampire who preys on young women, Tamar Heller turns our attention to the energies seething beneath female bourgeois domesticity. In "The Vampire in the House: Hysteria, Female Sexuality, and Female Knowledge in Le Fanu's 'Carmilla' (1872)," Heller argues that the vampire can be read as a figure for the hysterical woman, who drains the energies and "blood" of those about her. Le Fanu's tale reveals the anxieties about uncontrollable female appetites that similarly motivate Victorian medical discourses about hysteria, anorexia, and chlorosis, discourses with which Heller finds the tale closely linked. Le Fanu's tale encodes a parallel fear that a "devouring, sexually voracious woman lurk[s] beneath the docile surface of the devoured woman, her apparent victim." The anxieties that motivate both such tales and this medical discourse arose, Heller suggests, in response to the growth of feminism in the second half of the nineteenth century. Indeed, Heller sees "Carmilla" as a precursor of fin-de-siècle and early-twentieth-century anti-feminist narratives like *The Bostonians*. Le Fanu's "Carmilla" encodes a battle over who gets to define and control femininity and female sexuality—women themselves or the male guardians of official forms of knowledge, such as priests and doctors. The tale figures female sexuality as lesbianism, as if to underscore the threat that female desire plays to male authority, and then attempts to contain that threat, in both its narrative and epistemological structure, Heller contends, by subjecting female experience to authoritative masculine scrutiny.

"Carmilla" was an important influence on that most well-known of vampire tales, Bram Stoker's *Dracula,* a novel that has until recent years been "underread" in academic, if not in popular circles. In "Solicitors Soliciting: The Dangerous Circulations of Professionalism in *Dracula* (1897)," which we include here out of chronological order to pair it with its precursor text, Jasmine Yong Hall focuses on the novel's anxious representation of the consequences of the emergent ideology of male professionalism. As a solicitor, Jonathan Harker is the quintessential modern professional man, one whose expert services are esoteric and protean, who is replaceable and subservient to clients, who survives by eliciting the public's desire for his services. He "survives by soliciting," Hall writes, "by placing himself in the female position as object of desire." Jonathan Harker's position as a professional man makes him the catalyst for dangerous circulations in the novel—of blood, money, and power—but most importantly of male identity. The dissociation of identity with which Harker and the other men in the novel are threatened is ultimately cured by the ministrations of Harker's wife, Mina, in her role as both secretary and wife. Mina, who at first represents the potentially threatening movement of women into the public sphere, does not herself gain access to power. She is instead simply a professionalized revision of the Victorian "Angel in the House," Hall contends, whose abilities in shorthand, transcription, and typewriting are eventually used to reconstruct the endangered male identity, returning to it the "aura" of unity, of privileged subjectivity, that initially disappears under the pressures of professionalism.

Nancy Fix Anderson explores the surprising contradictions in the career and writing of Eliza Lynn Linton, the first woman in England to earn a regular salary as a journalist (for the *Morning Chronicle*). In "Eliza Lynn Linton: *The Rebel of the Family* (1880) and Other Novels," Anderson describes Linton's early novel, *Realities* (1851), as "a shocking challenge to Victorian morality," exploring as it did the polarity between a "passionate, free-spirited" young woman and her "submissive alter-ego." The daring subject matter of the novel—Linton undertook its (expurgated) publication herself after it was refused by numerous publishers—brought devastating reviews, but Linton believed in its attack on the double standard, and on "the prurience underlying vigilant Victorian moralism." Linton wrote her next novel some fifteen years later, and in the interim published the notorious antifeminist essays "The Girl of the Period" (1860s), which were considered both conservative and, in their own way, daring. Linton's 1880 novel, the *Rebel of the Family*, advanced her now *anti*feminist project and deepened as well the internal contradictions of her other works. In it she offered a sympathetic analysis of the attractions of feminism, combined with condemnation of the women's movement and its goals. The novel defends the opening of employment opportunities for women (an important subject in the 1880s) and also subverts, in the person of the novel's post office worker heroine, the notion that such employment can be satisfying. A novel that at first looks like a "forerunner to the New Woman fiction of Olive Schreiner, Sarah Grand, and others" also reveals an "anti-feminist message." It is the very ambiguities and inconsistencies of the novels, Anderson contends, that make them interesting reading today. Linton, she argues, must be seen as a writer who "both attacked and endorsed the goals of women's emancipation"; the women against whom she fought, Anderson writes, "included her self."

Like Linton's novels, Walter Besant's fiction is, according to Wim Neetens, "more open about [its] propaganda content," and not as "conversant with the art of abstraction," as the fiction of "the great tradition." In "Problems of a 'Democratic Text': Walter Besant's Impossible Story in *All Sorts and Conditions of Men* (1882)," Neetens sees Henry James's triumph in the famous James/Besant debate on "The Art of Fiction" (1884) as a moment of "division between popular, commercial fiction and more select 'literary' forms of writing," a division that would have profound implications for the study of English and the formation of the literary canon. And yet Neetens maintains that Besant was a significant figure in his own time and should be interesting to us in ours precisely because he sought to democratize culture, to make literary commodities available to an ever-increasing reading public. Moreover, because Besant is "less literary, less sophisticated" about his political aims, his work, "though far from revolutionary, throws a revealing light on the democratic pretensions of a system that thrives on inequality." In *All Sorts and Conditions of Men* culture operates "as the crucial term through which reform is realized and articulated" as the wealthy heiress Angela Messenger, in disguise as a working woman, opens a factory/ home for working girls in which their minds and spirits are, according to Besant, emancipated and cultivated. Neetens sees Besant as an advocate of reform and a believer in working-class self-government. Yet Besant's is a romantic, populist vision that requires the relinquishment of "detailed analyses of class positions" and the substitution of "romantic stereotypes of organically allied 'rich' and 'poor,' and . . . the notion of a common humanity transcendent of class antagonisms" as the only means of reconciling "irreconcilable interests in the cause of a common good." But Neetens also sees Besant's fiction as "the starting point for a bourgeois-populist tradition in the novel," which, as we have moved into the twentieth century, has become at once more popular and less critically respectable.

Like Neetens, Judith Mitchell in "Naturalism in George Moore's *A Mummer's Wife* (1884)," directs our attention to a little-known novel, which, she argues, helps to illuminate a significant but undervalued literary movement. Mitchell argues that *A Mummer's Wife,* generally considered to be the first and possibly the only true English naturalistic novel, is not the mere copy of French novels that critics have taken it to be. In his novel about female adultery, Moore modified the naturalistic formula in subtle and interesting ways, Mitchell contends, and in doing so wrote a great novel and one with an important place in the history of English fiction. Moore's modifications of the naturalism of the French novel, in the greater ordinariness of his characters and the narrator's greater objectivity toward the erring female protagonist, in fact come closer to the stated goals of naturalism and result in enhancing its realism. "In this supposed 'copy' of French naturalistic novels," Mitchell writes, "Moore added something immensely vital to the English novel of the time." Moore also showed a surprising willingness to represent hitherto unrepresentable (because traditionally unfeminine) features of the female self.

In "Joy behind the Screen: The Problem of 'Presentability' in George Gissing's *The Nether World* (1889)," Barbara Leah Harman explores the last, and arguably the best, of Gissing's exclusively working-class novels. She focuses on Gissing's presentation of characters "set on the precarious line along which the aspiration for presentability" lives. Harman argues that Gissing's interest "resides in characters who inhabit the narrow space between [the] total obscurity" of the abject poor and the "partial presentability" of those whose capacity for articulation and self presentation allows them to rise just above generalization on the one hand and obscurity on the other. At the same time, Harman argues, Gissing's suspicions about public life—about public philanthropy, effective collective action, and even public recognition—make the emergence into "presentability" a risky one even for those who desire it and have the capacity to achieve it. Gissing's minimalist vision of human presentability in *The Nether World* is problematic for characters like Sidney Kirkwood, who labors to keep some human joy alive "behind the screen" in his marriage to Clara Hewett; for a "New Woman" like Clara herself, an actress who desires a publicity that Gissing clearly considers degrading; and for Jane Snowdon, who, perceiving as another kind of degraded publicity the role of social philanthropist that her grandfather creates for her, is left, like the others, with a life "unmarked and unencouraged" by the larger world. Harman argues that Gissing's problematic vision of public experience inevitably endangers and contains the human project of self-representation both for men and for women in his novels. That Gissing is ambivalent about public experience for men as well as women adds to the complexities and paradoxes of his feminism.

John Kucich's essay "Curious Dualities: *The Heavenly Twins* (1893) and Sarah Grand's Belated Modernist Aesthetics" focuses on one of the most famous New Woman novels of the 1890s. Kucich begins by noting that Grand has suffered critical neglect because of the supposed aesthetic weakness of all New Woman fiction, hers included, and because of the apparent "middlingness" of her feminism relative to other New Woman writers. But Grand's apparent "middlingness," her evenhandedness, can help us attend to the irreconcilable contradictions within which New Woman fiction operated. Grand's fiction emphasizes the impossible choices faced by women characters and reveals a fascination with the state of self-contradiction. And in formal ways as well, Grand's fiction reveals a fascination with duality. She embodies in Evadne's "manly, scandal-braving realism" a style that disappointingly ends in the "impoverished abandonment of literary possibilities." In Evadne's twin, Angelica, Grand suggests that more creative "performative strategies" are also, problematically, identified with "feminine caprice and mendacity." Grand's *Heavenly Twins* exposes the impossible formal choices late-nineteenth-century women novelists faced, when both realist and antirealist fiction by women were read as evidence of their intellectual limitations. The disjunctive form of Grand's novels reveals her recognition that, Kucich writes, "the dawning of new literary possibilities at the fin-de-siècle had already been subjected to an insidious pattern of gendering." Grand's deliberate exploration of aesthetic discontinuities,

Kucich contends, reveals that New Woman fiction anticipated the formal experiments of modernism.

Like Sarah Grand's, George Egerton's literary project has both a decidedly feminist, and a decidedly modernist, edge. As Kate McCullough suggests in "Mapping the 'Terra Incognita' of Woman: George Egerton's *Keynotes* (1893) and New Woman Fiction," Egerton saw the work of writing about women as the work of exploring an unknown land, and of doing so "through the eyes of one's sex." What makes Egerton's writing at once complex and intriguing, McCullough writes, is the apparently contradictory view that female territory is "essentially" female, that women are unchanged essences, and, at the same time, that women adapt and are altered in subtle ways by their encounters with men—that they are reshaped, "discursive," selves. Female sexuality is a central subject—in particular, the relation of "erotic desire and love to violence and power." Egerton revises conventional plots in interesting ways: the woman in one story is at once agent and victim, passionately powerful and radically marginalized; her split, fragmented identity seems surprisingly "modern" in its conceptualization. In another story a woman is "hopelessly outmatched by the cultural codes which define her," but in the narrative structure of the story the young female listener to whom she speaks has "a transformative understanding of the storyteller's experience" that challenges our sense of the teller's powerlessness. In a third story, about a stepmother who murders her stepchildren when she is barred from nurturing her own out-of-wedlock child, the "danger and power of . . . essentialist heroines" emerges as a force that both stands in "direct opposition to, and [is] ironically complicit with, what [Egerton] views as the dangers of culture." The tension between these forces in Egerton's work is, according to McCullough, both defining and powerful.

Mary Augusta (Mrs. Humphry) Ward's novels bear an interesting, contentious relation to the New Woman writings of her predecessors in this volume. As Judith Wilt points out in "'Transition Time': The Political Romances of Mrs. Humphry Ward's *Marcella* (1894) and *Sir George Tressady* (1896)," Ward's heroine in the first novel is an ambitious young woman who recognizes in the aristocrat and (eventual) parliamentarian to whom she becomes engaged, a "still greater theater for her still mixed ambition to serve and to rule." Wilt sees Marcella's early commitments in the novel as theatrical, but she views Marcella's later "self-actualized work"—as a district nurse in London and then as a wife—as evidence of her "power not so much to lose herself in love" as to "consolidate a self, choose an identity, end the quest, and marshall its energy in specific action." Ward's heroine shares with the heroines of New Woman fiction the desire for self-actualization and the willingness to pursue it with aggressive energy, but as Wilt indicates, this desire is still, in Ward, "figured as [conventional] heterosexual desire, as the desire for the male inheritor." In the sequel novel, *Sir George Tressady,* Marcella's role develops as she seeks the political support of the title character for "the Maxwell Bill," attempting to convert his ironic distance into compassion and sympathy for "the real making of one's country [that] is done out of sight, in garrets and workshops and coalpits, by people who die every minute, forgotten." Wilt notes about Ward's project in both novels that she was "cooperating with good grace in social progress" not of her own making, and that she did so in "gingerly partnership with the history that she always kept one step behind."

The last essay in the collection, Nancy Paxton's "Mobilizing Chivalry: Rape in Flora Annie Steel's *On the Face of the Waters* (1896) and Other British Novels about the Indian Uprising of 1857," considers the work of four popular Victorian novelists who wrote fiction on this subject—James Grant, G.A. Henty, George Chesney, and Meadows Taylor—in order to provide a context for her reading of Steel's *On the Face of the Waters,* a novel, she argues, that deviates from the pattern established by other Uprising novels in some significant ways. Novels written about the Indian Uprising repeatedly organized themselves around the trope of the rape of an English woman by Indian men, and in doing so, Paxton contends, they performed the ideological work of reinforcing traditional gender roles by representing English women as victims and thus "countering British feminist demands for women's greater political and social equality." Steel's novel differs from the novels of her male compatriots in its refusal to focus on the rape of an Englishwoman: the English heroine of the novel simply strategically pretends a fear of rape at one point. But although Steel thus attempts to improve on the Englishwoman's role as sacrificial victim, and although the novel at one point suggests the possibility of an alliance between English and Indian women, the novel nonetheless, Paxton argues, ultimately asserts the superiority of English culture. "Despite her resistances," Paxton writes, "Steel's novel finally confirms an ideology of nationalism that defines chastity and social purity as signs of the evolutionary superiority of English men and women."

Together, the essays in this volume examine a set of important thematic concerns: the relation between private and public realms, between gender and social class, between sexuality and the marketplace, between male and female cultural identity, between social power and the power of language. They explore the relationship between literary texts and a variety of social and cultural discourses—medical, legal, economic—and also between different literary modes: feminism and modernism, realism and naturalism, high and popular culture. The feminisms practiced by the authors in this volume are diverse and varied.

But perhaps the central feature of this volume is its effort to assemble, from among an impossibly wide array of choices, a significant selection of important but neglected works of Victorian fiction, works worthy of serious critical attention. We hope our selection is a useful and stimulating one, though of course no group of fifteen essays can even begin to approach the task of identifying and analyzing the enormous body of writings that lie below the familiar surface. John Sutherland, in his foreword to this volume and in his magisterial *Stanford Companion to Victorian Fiction,* notes that a "work-force of some 3500" British novelists published during this period. Among those he identifies a smaller group of some 878 whose "records lie close enough to the surface for one to discover salient facts" about them. In choosing 15 from these 878, we have been governed by our desire to represent writers whose work spans the Victorian period, and also by our wish to include critical essays that illuminate not only the writers at hand but also the larger field of Victorian fiction. While some of the novelists treated in these essays are more familiar than others, many of the 15 writers represented will be new to most readers, so each essay is accompanied by a brief biographical sketch and a list of important secondary sources. Any selection from such an enormous field is bound, inevitably, to leave out many interesting writers. Our choices here are not meant to close down, but rather to open up, access to the rich and diverse body of Victorian fiction.

# The New
# Nineteenth Century

# Words on "Great Vulgar Sheets"

## Writing and Social Resistance in Anne Brontë's Agnes Grey (1847)

*Susan Meyer*

Anne Brontë is usually remembered only as the younger sister of Emily and Charlotte, but she was a talented novelist in her own right who, in the course of her short life (1820–1849), published two novels, *Agnes Grey* (1847) and *The Tenant of Wildfell Hall* (1848), as well as contributing a selection of her poetry to a collection of the poems of the three sisters, published pseudonymously as *Poems by Currer, Ellis and Acton Bell* (1846). Anne Brontë's first novel was somewhat overshadowed by the fiction of her sisters, partly because it appeared as part of a three-volume set, along with *Wuthering Heights,* which occupied the other two volumes, and partly because critics speculated that the sisters' three pseudonyms belonged to the same writer. But *Agnes Grey* has since received its own more limited acclaim, including an accolade from the novelist George Moore (quoted by virtually everyone who writes on Anne Brontë), who termed *Agnes Grey* "the most perfect prose narrative in English literature." *The Tenant of Wildfell Hall,* Anne Brontë's second novel, was both controversial and an immediate success: it was in such demand that within a month of its publication the publishers brought out a second edition. Both of Anne Brontë's novels are available in print, in various paperback editions (Oxford, Penguin, Banquo, Everyman's Classic); a selection of her poems (as well as Emily's and Charlotte's) appears in an Everyman's Classic paperback.

Late in Anne Brontë's first novel, the cultivated and diligent governess-heroine, Agnes Grey, is taken to task by her employer concerning the behavior of her hoydenish student, Matilda. "If you will only think of these things and try to exert yourself a *little* more . . . then, I am convinced, you would *soon* acquire that delicate tact which alone is wanting to give you a proper influence over the mind of your pupil," Mrs. Murray tells Agnes. It seems for a moment as if the long-suffering and much-criticized Agnes is finally going to respond to one of the many unjust attacks to which she has been subjected in the course of her employment. But Agnes is never able, throughout the events the novel narrates, to "talk back" to her employers. "I was about to give the lady some idea of the fallacy of her expectations," Agnes writes, "but she sailed away as soon as she had concluded her speech. Having said what she wished, it was no part of her plan to await my answer: it was my business to hear, and not to speak" (207).

In this novel about a heroine who is, at crucial moments, nearly speechless, Anne Brontë explores the nature of a society that makes it quite literally the "business" of some of its members "not to speak": that requires silence and acquiescence of some due to the conditions of their employment or of their social position. But *Agnes Grey* is written in the form of a first-person autobiography by this silenced heroine: in the form of the novel itself Agnes "talks back," and in the course of the novel Anne Brontë both subtly criticizes and resists the unjust silencing and disempowerment of the poorer classes by an autocratic and immoral British ruling class. At the same time, however, the novel hints that some of the same problems that characterize the relationship between classes characterize the relationships between men and women, and these problems remain more irresolvable at the novel's close.[1]

Anne Brontë's fiction is frequently dismissed in a cursory fashion as less passionate and original than the fiction of her two better-known sisters; when her fiction *is* discussed, the second, and more obviously complex of her two novels, *The Tenant of Wildfell Hall,* receives most of the attention, while *Agnes Grey* is often described as slight and emotionally flat.[2] The novel tells the story of a young woman, the daughter of a clergyman, whose family loses its patrimony due to ill-advised speculation on the part of the father. To help the family finances, Agnes, the younger of two daughters, goes out as a governess to two wealthy families, first the Bloomfields, a prosperous family whose money was earned in trade, and then to the Murrays, "thorough-bred gentry" (113). In both families Agnes is ill-treated—in the first she is required to keep several headstrong young children in check, and yet is deprived of any means of offering reward or punishment, while in the second family she deals with older but equally spoiled young ladies. The Murray daughters are frivolous and thoughtless and have lax moral standards. They treat Agnes as a personal servant, and, on a whim, the flirtatious elder daughter, Rosalie, decides to interpose herself between Agnes and the man she is coming to love, the local curate, Mr. Weston. At the death of her father, Agnes leaves her painful position with the Murrays and sets up a school with her mother in a seaside town, fearing that, in part due to

Rosalie's interference, she will never see Mr. Weston again. But Mr. Weston has taken a living in a nearby village, and, after a brief courtship, he asks Agnes to be his wife. The novel comes to a close with Agnes's report that the pair has had three children and are able to subsist happily on their modest income.

*Agnes Grey* is, as critics have noted, characterized by a quiet, emotionally restrained tone. But the coolness and restraint are both deliberate on Anne Brontë's part and important to the novel's aims, because in *Agnes Grey* Anne Brontë offers the chronicle of a life of emotional and verbal repression. And if the plot of *Agnes Grey* is simple, the social criticism it offers, through this chronicle of repression, is complex.

As a condition of her employment, self-repression and the suppression of speech are continually required of Agnes. As soon as Agnes arrives at her first place of employment, for example, and is instructed in how she is to proceed, Mrs. Bloomfield warns her that she is to tell no one but herself of the children's defects. As Agnes's mother has already warned her to mention them "as little as possible to *her,* for people did not like to be told of their children's faults," Agnes rightly concludes that she is "to keep silence on them altogether" (79). Later the Bloomfield parents indirectly reprove Agnes by discussing in her presence what they see as their children's recent deterioration, and this method of criticism makes it impossible for Agnes to respond:

> All similar innuendoes affected me far more deeply than any open accusations would have done; for against the latter I should have been roused to speak in my own defence: now, I judged it my wisest plan to subdue every resentful impulse, suppress every sensitive shrinking, and go on perseveringly doing my best. (91)

Although Agnes suggests here that against direct accusations she would find a voice, this supposition is not borne out by the novel: even when Mrs. Bloomfield fires Agnes, although she wishes to speak in her own justification, she feels her "voice falter," and "rather than testify any emotion," she writes, "I chose to keep silence, and bear all" (107). And Agnes is not only prevented from using her voice toward her employers in her own defense, she is also prevented from using it forcefully toward her young charges as she works. When Agnes needs to raise her voice in an attempt to enforce order among little Tom, Mary Ann, and Fanny Bloomfield, their father chastises her for "using undue violence, and setting the girls a bad example by such ungentleness of tone and language" (98). All this stifling of Agnes's voice, in her position as governess, makes it virtually impossible, paradoxically, for her to succeed in her task of instruction.

The same situation continues in Agnes's next position, with the Murrays, when Mrs. Murray tells Agnes never to engage in forceful remonstrance with her children, but instead to "come and tell me; for *I* can speak to them more plainly than it would be proper for you to do" (120). Agnes also finds that she is expected not to speak to the Murray girls' friends, or to anyone in their social circle: instead she is required to comport herself "like one deaf and dumb, who could neither speak nor be spoken to" (184). Both sets of Agnes's charges prevent her from engaging in communication with others: the Bloomfield children interrupt her letter-writing on her first evening with them, Rosalie Murray prevents her from *reading* a letter in one episode, and Fanny Bloomfield, at her brother's command, nearly throws Agnes's writing desk out of the window. The novel clearly demonstrates that the "business" of being a governess is one completely at odds with all healthful self-expression.

But the story of Agnes's silencing also has a larger resonance: it is about more than the problems with this particular mode of women's labor. What happens to Agnes, the novel suggests, is representative of the kind of verbal suppression to which girls and women in this era are disproportionately subjected. Although as a working woman Agnes is particularly subjected to verbal suppression, girls and women at home also experience it. Agnes is silenced, although in a gentler and more loving fashion, in her own family, long before she ever goes out to work. When she proposes seeking employment, she is told to "hold [her] tongue" and termed a "naughty girl" (69). Even among the upper classes, the girls are subjected to some linguistic control. Matilda Murray is constantly chastised by her parents for speaking as freely as the grooms do: she is not even supposed to term her "horse" a "mare" (134). Mr. Bloomfield's complaint about Agnes's raised voice is that she is setting a bad example to his daughters, not to his son. And from the first evening of Agnes's arrival at the Bloomfield's, it is clear that the son's voice is permitted more freedom, and accorded more authority, than those of the daughters. Tom stands "bolt upright . . . with his hands behind his back, talking away like an orator, occasionally interrupting his discourse with a sharp reproof to his sisters when they made too much noise" (76). Tom's verbal authority is linked to the ownership of property: he claims possession of the schoolroom and the books. Despite Mary Ann's protests (76) that "they're mine too," Tom decisively asserts the prerogative of the first-born son (like John Reed in Charlotte Brontë's *Jane Eyre*) and claims ownership of these instruments of language.

Yet if male claims to authoritative speech are boosted by men's easier access to the ownership of property, the possession of property by those of either sex is shown to be linked to linguistic authority. *Agnes Grey* demonstrates that neither gender nor social class alone is explanatory: both class and gender are significant factors in determining who wields the power of language, the power to silence others. The young ladies whom Agnes instructs in her second position, Rosalie and Matilda Murray, make charitable visits to the cottagers on their father's estate, believing themselves to be revered there as ministering angels, and they certainly use their voices freely in this context:

> They would watch the poor creatures at their meals, making uncivil remarks about their food, and their manner of eating; they would laugh at their simple notions and provincial expressions, till some of them scarcely durst venture to speak; they would call the grave, elderly men and women old fools and silly blockheads to their faces; and all this without meaning to offend.

> I could see that the people were often hurt and annoyed by such conduct, though their fear of the "grand ladies" prevented them from testifying any resentment; but *they* never perceived it. They thought that, as these cottagers were poor and untaught, they must be stupid and brutish; and as long as they, their superiors, condescended to talk to them, and to give them shillings and half-crowns, or articles of clothing, they had a right to amuse themselves, even at their expense. (144)

Toward the very end of the novel, despite all of Agnes's attempts at moral instruction, Rosalie Murray more explicitly articulates her mother's position, expressed at an earlier point to Agnes, that it is the social "business" of some to speak as freely as they please, and of others never to speak, or even to formulate an internal perspective critical of those of higher rank. Agnes points out to Rosalie that she has just said, in front of her footman, that she finds her mother-in-law detestable, to which Rosalie responds:

> I never care about the footmen; they're mere automatons—it's nothing to them what their superiors say or do; they won't dare to repeat it; and as to what they think—if they presume to think at all—of course, nobody cares for that. It would be a pretty thing indeed, if we were to be tongue-tied by our servants! (233)

In telling the story of the travails of Agnes Grey, of one woman obliged to work in the homes of the wealthy, Brontë obliquely comments on the larger problem of the unjust distribution of the power of language by gender and by class.

In answer to the problem of verbal repression, Anne Brontë posits the act of novel-writing itself. In *Agnes Grey,* Brontë narrates a tale from the perspective of a woman who works in the house but nonetheless presumes to think for herself, who refuses, at least in written form, to be tongue-tied by the social order, and who offers a scathing account of what her self-styled social superiors say and do in the privacy of their own homes. Agnes shows the people from wealthy families with whom she lives to be vain, frivolous, and unprincipled, prone to drinking and gluttony, quarrelsome, and self-centered. She recounts domestic altercations between husband and wife that have taken place in her presence, as if she were an automaton, shows a mother determined to marry her daughter to the wealthiest possible man, and displays the mutual hatred that substitutes for love in upper-class marriages. And while the novel describes what *really* goes on in upper-class homes, it takes issue, subtly, with some of the central ideas of that class, the ideas by which they justify the class hierarchy to themselves.

Both the Murrays and the Bloomfields make clear that, like other members of their class, they believe their social rank to be natural: they consider those of lower rank to be innately inferior to them, to be, in fact, like animals. The Murray daughters believe the cottagers whom they insult to their faces to be incapable of understanding their humiliation because they are "stupid and brutish," and indeed Rosalie Murray's favorite epithet for those without money is the term "vulgar brute" (154). Mr. Bloomfield describes Agnes's hygienic standards as bestial: he condemns Agnes for the mess his children have made, exclaiming, "No wonder your room is not fit for a pigsty—no wonder your pupils are worse than a litter of pigs!" (99). Little Tom Bloomfield shows that he has assimilated this idea that his social inferiors are to be treated like animals when he sees his uncle kicking a dog, and vows that he will make him kick Agnes instead. It seems that to be treated like an animal by the ruling classes is to be treated as insentient, to be treated as an expendable commodity. Mrs. Bloomfield voices this attitude when she defends Tom's practice of torturing fledgling birds to death in various diabolical ways by telling Agnes, with an eerie calm, that she seems to have forgotten "that the creatures were all created for our convenience" (105).

But in *Agnes Grey,* Anne Brontë slyly reverses the ruling-class conceit that the lower classes are like beasts whom they may burden at will. She repeatedly compares the young Bloomfields to animals—they behave like "wild, unbroken colt[s]" (84), or quarrel over their food "like a set of tiger's cubs" (98). The Murrays are also animal-like: John Murray is as rough "as a young bear" (124). Even the young ladies are likened to beasts. As Agnes says of Matilda, damning her with faint praise, "As an animal, [she] was all right, full of life, vigour, and activity" (124). Of Rosalie, who prides herself on her delicacy and her ladylike behavior, Agnes comments, bitingly: "Dogs are not the only creatures which, when gorged to the throat, will yet gloat over what they cannot devour, and grudge the slightest morsel to a starving brother" (196). Unable to reason with her unreasoning charges, Agnes has to resort to the ploys of animal trainers—she deprives the little Bloomfields of their food until they cooperate, and to assert dominance over Tom, she uses what is in fact a technique from dog training, "throw[ing] him on his back, and hold[ing] his hands and feet till the frenzy was somewhat abated" (85). Perhaps the novel's most sarcastic equation of the ruling class with animals comes from Mr. Weston, the curate. Matilda Murray comes "panting" up to him and Agnes, after running with her dog, as he captures a hare out of season, asking them whether it was not a fine chase. "Very!" Mr. Weston replies, "for a young lady after a leveret" (209).

Those of high social rank in *Agnes Grey* also acquire a sense of superiority by envisioning themselves as civilized and Christian in relation to the ignorant "savages" beneath them. This colonial metaphor is conceptually linked to their sense of themselves as human and others as bestial. In the same passage in which Mr. Bloomfield compares Agnes's schoolroom to a pigsty and defends his standards of decency against her low influence, he goes on to tell her that there was never anything like her room "in a Christian house before" (99). And when Mr. Bloomfield complains about the way the servants have cut the meat, he reviles them as "savages" (83).

But the novel is concerned, throughout, to reveal the un-Christian, uncivilized behavior of these professed Christians. The two Murray girls go to church twice on Sundays, not out of devout spirituality, but to flirt with anyone available. When Rosalie describes her husband-to-be, Sir Thomas Ashby, a womanizing, gambling rake whom she imagines marriage will reform, as the "greatest scamp in Christendom" (172), Anne Brontë wryly suggests that those who think like Rosalie have very little idea of in what true Christianity consists—or who lives within a moral space that might truly be termed "Christendom." The elitist, wealthy rector of the church they attend similarly has a self-serving idea of Christianity: he preaches sermons about the duty of the poor to obey the rich with deference. He dismisses a poor, elderly parishioner, who comes to him in spiritual distress, by sneering at her and telling her not to read the Bible on her own but to hobble to church to hear him speak, despite her debilitating rheumatism. In following his advice old Nancy Brown contracts a telling ailment: she catches a cold in her eyes and is no longer able to read the Bible. The self-styled, superior Christianity of the ruling class, the novel indicates, simply serves to support the class structure, and to impede the poor from direct access to the egalitarian Word.

Not only are the rich not civilizing Christians, Brontë suggests, they themselves are the barbarians they imagine the lower classes to be. The novel directly reverses this authorizing metaphor by representing Agnes, in the homes of the wealthy, as a civilized person among colonial savages. It does not seem to occur to Anne Brontë to question British colonialism or to criticize the concept of a racial hierarchy as she does so; she simply uses the supposed racial hierarchy as a metaphor to question the class hierarchy rather than to support it. When Agnes arrives at the Murray household, she compares her feelings to those of a colonist who awakes one morning to find himself "at Port Nelson, in New Zealand, with a world of waters between himself and all that knew him" (118). Indeed, in her various positions, Agnes finds an uncle of the Bloomfields who engages in and encourages the children in "barbarities," while Matilda Murray is "barbarously ignorant" (103, 124). In the course of her civilizing mission among the barbarous upper class, Agnes begins to fear at one point, as British colonists sometimes feared, that she will "degenerate" until she is like those around her, that she will, as it were, "go native." "Those whose actions are ever before our eyes," she comments:

> whose words are ever in our ears, will naturally lead us, albeit against our will—slowly—gradually—imperceptibly, perhaps, to act and speak as they do. I will not presume to say how far this irresistible power of assimilation extends; but if one civilized man were doomed to pass a dozen years amid a race of intractable savages, unless he had power to improve them, I greatly question whether, at the close of that period, he would not have become, at least, a barbarian himself. And I, as I could not make my young companions better, feared exceedingly that they would make me worse. (155)

In an article on Victorian images of Africa, Patrick Brantlinger describes the pervasive anxiety, on the part of the nineteenth-century British in the colonies, that they would "degenerate" or "go native"; he points out that missionaries were particularly subject to the fear that they would regress to the state of the "heathens" around them. He quotes one, J. S. Moffat, who writes that a missionary must be "deeply imbued with God's spirit in order to have strength to stand against the deadening and corrupting influence around him. . . . I am like a man looking forward to getting back to sweet air and bright sunshine after being in a coal-mine" (Brantlinger 194). In an absolute reversal of the self-authorizing metaphors of the upper class, Anne Brontë has Agnes imagine herself, among them, as one living, as it were, on a "dark continent" among "savages." Only the presence of Mr. Weston appears like the "morning star in my horizon," Agnes writes, "to save me from the fear of utter darkness" (155).[3]

In an attempt to escape the darkness created by the upper class, and to keep their words *out* of our ears, Anne Brontë's novel calls into question not only their metaphors, but also their more direct wielding of the power of language, their mode of assigning names to things. Agnes's first encounter with the father of the Bloomfield children is one in which he uses the power of naming to put her in her social place. The little Bloomfield children are disobeying Agnes's fruitless commands and dabbling in the water when Mr. Bloomfield rides up and rebukes her, never introducing himself, but simply exclaiming, "Don't you see how Miss Bloomfield has soiled her frock?—and that Master Bloomfield's socks are quite wet?" (82). Agnes is surprised that "he should nominate his children [at the ages of seven and five] Master and Miss Bloomfield, and still more so, that he should speak so uncivilly to me—their governess, and a perfect stranger to himself" (82). Agnes continues to feel that the formal naming of children is "chilling and unnatural," but she finds, while with the Bloomfields, that if she calls the children by their simple names, it is regarded as "an offensive liberty" (118). Having learned this lesson, she determines, when she arrives at the Murrays, to begin "with as much form and ceremony as any member of the family would be likely to require . . . though the little words Miss and Master seemed to have a surprising effect in repressing all familiar, open-hearted kindness, and extinguishing every gleam of cordiality that might arise between us" (118).

The terms "Miss" and "Master" repress cordiality, of course, because they emphasize the children's superior rank, and in her own writing about them Agnes resists this convention, using the terms only ironically, to emphasize the children's offensive training in the behavior of dominance. She describes one of her pupils, for example, as "John, *alias* Master Murray" (124), and she notes at one point that seven-year-old "Master Tom, not content with refusing to be ruled, must needs set up as a ruler" (84). The novel also brings to our attention the way in which class rank is imposed through the dehumanizing naming of servants: Agnes notes that on her arrival at the

Murrays, Matilda Murray says that she will "tell 'Brown'" that Agnes is in need of a cup of tea (116). As we later meet a poor woman with the same surname, the cottager Nancy Brown, and are given a more full and humanizing portrait of her, the novel suggests what it is that the elite are preventing themselves from seeing about other human beings by their system of appellation.

Agnes Grey's narrative was compiled, she notes, from the diary she kept during her years as a governess. The diary and subsequent narrative are her quiet act of resistance to the words of those around her, her resistance to the way that they dominate through language and metaphor, to the way that they silence those of lesser means. At one point in the novel, Agnes is reading an eagerly awaited letter from her sister at home, when Rosalie Murray interrupts her, and tells her she should bid her friends to write "on proper note-paper, and not on those great vulgar sheets!" Her own mother, she tells Agnes, writes "charming little lady-like notes" (130). Although Agnes does reluctantly fold up her letter at Rosalie's command, she also quietly tells her that she would be very disappointed to receive a "charming little lady-like note" from her family. Rosalie may be surprised and disconcerted by this, but Agnes is happy only when she is able to write, speak, and communicate at length with those like herself. In *Agnes Grey*, Brontë enables her protagonist to respond to the verbal suppression that she and others experience by answering it in her own words, the words of her own class, indited on the "great vulgar sheets" of the novel itself.

The novel comes to an end with Agnes's marriage to Mr. Weston: she notes, after recounting his proposal, that the diary, "from which [she has] compiled these pages, goes but little further" (250). By this point, it would seem, she has made her critique of the oppressive forces to which she has been subject, pointed out the moral failings of the upper class, and thus come to the end of the need for resistant speech. The end of the novel holds up as an alternative the middle-class domestic sanctity of the marriage between Agnes and Mr. Weston, one in which a mother educates the children herself, and in which the family is able to subsist happily on their modest income.

The novel's ending, which is, like those of many novels, more conservative than the rest of the novel, does not fully resolve the problems of social class it has brought to the reader's attention. By returning Agnes to a modest middle-class home, the novel does restore her to a more secure status, and continues its critique of the misplaced values of the wealthy. And it is also true that, unlike many nineteenth-century novels, *Agnes Grey* does not hint that class status is innate by returning all protagonists to the class position from which their families have fallen: although Agnes's mother was the daughter of a squire, who disinherited her when she chose to marry a man beneath her in rank, the novel ends with Agnes and her sister happily married to modest clergymen, and their mother presiding over a school for girls. The novel even evokes the possibility of such a restoration of originary class status and has the protagonists reject it. On the death of her father, Agnes's maternal grandfather writes to Agnes's mother and the girls offering to make her a "lady" again "if that be possible after [her] long degradation" as long as she is willing to repent of her "unfortunate marriage" (214). The novel has both mother and daughters refuse this proposal with scorn. The money they decline on such terms goes, at the grandfather's death, to some already wealthy, remote cousins.

But, nonetheless, when it comes to its close, the novel does not reject the system of inherited wealth, nor does it evoke a vision of significant changes in the class structure. The Nancy Browns of the world, to whom the solution of a middle-class marriage is not available, are left largely outside the space of the reader's vision in the novel's last pages. Through strenuous exertions, we are told, Edward Weston has worked "surprising reforms" in his parish, though we are not told in what exactly those reforms consist. The novel's attention turns at the last to Agnes and Edward Weston themselves, who, by practicing "the economy . . . learnt in harder times," manage each year to have, Agnes reports in the novel's penultimate sentence, "something to lay by for our children, and something to give to those who need it" (251). A system of inherited wealth, tempered by a true Christian charity, is the only solution the novel finally poses to the problems of class inequality detailed in its pages.

The novel ends with the sentence "And now I think I have said sufficient," as if to imply that now that the novel has come to something of a solution to the problem of the unjust class hierarchy, there is no need for further resistant speech. But the cessation of speech has been shown in the novel to be ambiguous. We have learned, as readers, to be wary about what the absence of words signifies. And if the novel seems to have come to a solution, satisfactory in middle-class terms, to the problem of class, the problem of gender remains, at the novel's close, more submerged and unresolved.

Immediately after the account of Mr. Weston's proposal to her, Agnes's narrative comes to a pause, and she notes: "My diary, from which I have compiled these pages, goes but little further" (250). Only one page of the novel remains, in which Agnes sums up the events of the subsequent years. But it is disconcerting for the reader to see Agnes once again falling silent, and at such a crucial moment: the period of Agnes's resistant use of language comes to a close with the proposal of marriage. What is more, the title given the novel, this space of free expression, is Agnes's name in her maidenhood, not her married name, as if, with her marriage, her capacity for resistant speech comes to an end.

These two disquieting facts might be explained away as common conventions in nineteenth-century fiction were it not that other subtleties in the novel's conclusion draw our attention to the way Agnes's marriage has a silencing effect. During Weston's preliminary visits to her and her mother, Agnes regresses into the state of near speechlessness she has seemed to be coming out of—so much so that even her mother asks her, after one visit, "But why did you sit back there, Agnes, . . . and talk so little?" (247). When Weston does propose, her assent is almost wordless, monosyllabic. Weston explains that, knowing what Agnes would like, he has already asked her mother to live with them, and continues:

> "And so now I have overruled your objections on her account. Have you any other?"

> "No—none."

> "You love me then?" said he, fervently pressing my hand.

> "Yes." (250)

With this monosyllable of assent, Agnes moves back into a period of virtual wordlessness.

It is disconcerting also to notice that the animal/human metaphor, through which the novel has expressed and resisted an oppressive class hierarchy, comes back at the end of *Agnes Grey*. As the next to last chapter of the novel comes to a close, Mr. Weston and Agnes have a conversation about his dog, Snap, whom he has rescued from the rat-catcher because he once belonged to Agnes. "Now that he has a good master, I'm quite satisfied," Agnes says. "You take it for granted that I *am* a good one, then?" Mr. Weston rejoins (245). The question remains resonant and unanswered, but it prepares us for the next chapter, in which Weston will ask Agnes to be his wife—and in which she will, implicitly, answer the question with which the previous chapter ends. "Master Tom" will no longer be around to assert dominance over Agnes, the novel very discreetly suggests in this exchange, but Agnes may have found herself another, far more subtle "master."

If there is a problem even with Agnes's marriage to the good and gentle Mr. Weston, the novel quietly suggests, it is because the relationship between men and women unfortunately mimics the relationship between the wealthy and the poor. The novel has taught us to attend carefully to the system of names, to the way they establish hierarchies and set up barriers. It can hardly be accidental, then, that the novel, in its final pages, draws our attention also to the change in the system of appellation that takes place between Agnes and Weston during his courtship of her. Up until this point in the novel, he has, in accordance with the conventions of politeness, addressed her as "Miss Grey," precisely as she has addressed him as "Mr. Weston." But during his series of visits to Agnes and her mother, he begins to use her Christian name. Agnes records that she is glad of the change, and, given her earlier comments on the way little words like "Miss" and "Master" repress cordiality, the change would seem to be a sign of their growing intimacy and equality, were it not that she continues to address him as "Mr. Weston." Trained by the novel to attend to such nuances, we can hardly be completely easy with the inequality thus established.

The return of the subtle cues of a problematic hierarchy in the marriage with which *Agnes Grey* draws to a close suggests Anne Brontë's consciousness that, while she may have brought the issue of an unjust class hierarchy to a solution satisfactory to herself, she has not yet done so with the problem of gender inequality. It remains an issue that she will continue to pursue in her next novel, *The Tenant of Wildfell Hall*. And so when Agnes Grey ends her narrative with the sentence "And now I think I have said sufficient," it remains ambiguous what degree of completion or satisfaction her cessation of speech indicates. Has Agnes now "said sufficient" because Anne Brontë has made her critique of the British upper class in the words indited on the "great vulgar sheets" of the novel? Or has Agnes "said sufficient" because the solution to the problem of hierarchy, insidiously entering the relationship between loving men and women, remains, for now, inconceivable, for now beyond the scope of Anne Brontë's resistant words?

*Notes*

1. Janet Freeman discusses the issues of speech and silence in *Agnes Grey*, but in her reading the novel disqualifies all words as worldly, and turns instead to a silence that Brontë expects few to understand, and in which the highly moral commune. Terry Eagleton briefly describes the novel as a critique of the moral failings of the aristocracy in favor of values with "petty-bourgeois roots"; Priscilla Costello similarly sees the novel as a critique of a materialism located particularly in the upper class. My argument builds on these readings by attending to the patterns of imagery through which this critique is made, and by discussing the way this imagery links the issues of class and gender in the novel. See Langland for another reading of the novel attentive

to issues of gender: she argues that the novel emphasizes the acquisition of female independence. I agree that this is quite true, until the novel comes to its close.

2. See for example George Saintsbury, who dismisses Anne Brontë as "a pale reflection of her elders" (243). Eagleton agrees that "the orthodox critical judgement that Anne Brontë's work is slighter than her sisters' is just" (134).

3. The presence of these metaphors in Anne Brontë's fiction shows the influence of the childhood games with which she and her brother and sisters invented themselves as writers. All four children collaborated in creating an intricate imaginary world set in a fictitious British colony in Africa. See my "'Black' Rage and White Women: Ideological Self-Formation in Charlotte Brontë's African Tales."

## Works Cited

Brantlinger, Patrick. "Victorians and Africans: The Genealogy of the Myth of the Dark Continent." *Critical Inquiry* 12 (1985): 166–203.

Brontë, Anne. *Agnes Grey*. Edited by Angeline Goreau. New York: Penguin, 1988.

Costello, Priscilla. "A New Reading of Anne Brontë's *Agnes Grey*." *Brontë Society Transactions* 19 (1986): 113–18.

Eagleton, Terry. *Myths of Power: A Marxist Study of the Brontës*. New York: Harper & Row, 1975. 123–38.

Freeman, Janet H. "Telling over *Agnes Grey*." *Cahiers Victoriens et Edouardiens* 34 (1991): 109–26.

Langland, Elizabeth. *Anne Brontë: The Other One*. London: Macmillan, 1989.

Meyer, Susan. "'Black' Rage and White Women: Ideological Self-Formation in Charlotte Brontë's African Tales." *South Central Review* 8.4 (1991): 28–40.

Saintsbury, George. *The English Novel*. London: J.M. Dent, 1913.

## Selected Secondary Sources

Priscilla Costello, "A New Reading of Anne Brontë's *Agnes Grey*," *Brontë Society Transactions* 19 (1986): 113–18; Terry Eagleton, *Myths of Power: A Marxist Study of the Brontës* (New York: Harper & Row, 1975. 123–38); Janet H Freeman, "Telling over *Agnes Grey*," *Cahiers Victoriens et Edouardiens* 34 (1991): 109–26; Winifred Gérin, *Anne Brontë* (New York: Thomas Nelson & Sons, 1959); Elizabeth Langland, *Anne Brontë: The Other One* (London: Macmillan, 1989); George Moore, *Conversations in Ebury Street* (New York: Boni and Liveright, 1924).

# At Home upon a Stage

## Domesticity and Genius in Geraldine Jewsbury's *The Half Sisters* (1848)

*Judith Rosen*

Though known today mainly for her long correspondence with Jane Welsh Carlyle, Geraldine Endsor Jewsbury (1812–1880) was one of her era's most versatile women of letters. As a novelist, she was ranked with the gifted, socially conscious and controversial: "How many of us can write novels like Currer Bell, Mrs. Gaskell [or] Geraldine Jewsbury . . .?" asked G.H. Lewes in 1850. Her first three novels—*Zoe* (Chapman and Hall, 1845), *The Half Sisters* (1848), and *Marian Withers* (1851)—engaged "the woman question" with particular if conflicted passion. In 1859 she gave up novel writing for the steadier earnings of reviewing, and her long career as a fiction reviewer for the *Athenaeum* and as a reader for Richard Bentley's publishing house exerted an important influence on middle-class tastes of her day. The AMS Press has issued rather costly reproductions of *The Half Sisters* and *Marian Withers*; a paperback edition of *The Half Sisters* is now available in Oxford's World's Classics series.

Most "respectable" Victorians considered acting to be a dangerous and degrading profession for women. Unlike a writer, who might at least claim the modest shields of a nom de plume and the page, an actress placed herself physically on display, rejecting the protective privacy of the domestic realm. Furthermore, her profitable commerce in the passions called another public woman to mind, one whose existence "good women" blushed to admit. Yet actresses appear frequently as heroines in fiction of the mid and late nineteenth century, a prominence that seems at odds with their marginalized place in society.[1] As characters whose desires and talents did not fit dominant, middle-class norms of female behavior, however, they often proved strategically useful, allowing authors to present possibilities not found in women's usual plots. By dwelling on actresses' lives, at a time when resistance to domestic restrictions was growing, writers explored pressing questions about middle-class women in general: whether women could or should step outside the bounds of their accepted role to act a more public and self-centered part; whether female identity might form itself through work as well as through love.

Part of the interest of the actress's appearance in Victorian texts lies in her potentially double position, a doubleness that critics have thus far neglected. Authors of domestic conduct books, for example, were surprisingly dependent on the figure of the female performer in constructing an ideal model of female duty and selfhood, however vehemently these same writers denigrated acting as a profession. "How admirably . . . are the character and constitution of woman adapted to the part which it becomes her duty and her privilege to act," marvels Sarah Stickney Ellis in her influential *Daughters of England* (269); she and other domestic writers describe femininity as a carefully disciplined performance, one that sets "self" aside to represent, in the protected realm of the home, those communal values and truths endangered by the selfish competition of the marketplace.[2] Drawing on these conventions of domestic theatricality, Geraldine Jewsbury was able to present the actress's work as an extension of domestic duty into the public sphere, even as her heroine's appearance on stage violated the division between public and private on which domestic ideology depended.

Insisting that women never really "leave home" when in public, of course, restricts the forms their goals and desires can take. In examining the complex, often contradictory position of the actress in *The Half Sisters*, Jewsbury's attempt to redefine how and why middle-class women's lives signify, I will attend to the ways that her ongoing attachment to the forms of femininity she challenges at once enables and undercuts her critique.

Geraldine Jewsbury was a single and a singular woman; she smoked cigars, swore with relish, and offered her hand in marriage to at least three men, "not one of whom could quite overcome the shock of being asked" (Clarke 39). Her productivity as a writer was striking; in addition to publishing six novels and two children's tales, she kept up a steady stream of articles and book reviews (including, most notably, some sixteen hundred reviews for the *Athenaeum* alone). She was also vehement in her belief that middle-class women needed a wider sphere of action than the domestic and dependent one then allowed them. Jewsbury scorned the selfless "Mrs. Ellis woman" idealized in conduct books (*Letters* 349); an 1841 letter urges Jane Carlyle to "patronize the pronoun 'I' as much as I do myself!" (12), while a later missive longs for "better days, when women will have a genuine, normal life of their own to lead." Only when women are allowed an existence outside the relational terms of the love plot, Jewsbury argues, will they be able to "make themselves women, as men are allowed to make themselves men" (347): not as the absence of what man is and has, but in their own image and on their own terms.

Yet the women Jewsbury could admire as a future ideal confounded her in the present. As she wrote to Carlyle in 1850:

> It is a problem that bothers me—viz., that when women get to be energetic, strong characters, with literary reputations of their own, and live in the world, with business to attend to, they all do get in the habit of making use of people, and taking care of themselves in a way that is startling! . . . . In short, whenever a woman gets to be a personage in any shape, it makes her hard and unwomanly in some point or other. (367–68)

Here the language of literary construction highlights a link between authoring and self-authorization; these unidentified writers develop their own "characters" through creating those of their fictions. They would seem to fulfill Jewsbury's best hopes for female self-making, and yet she finds their achievements unnerving. By creating themselves as public and autonomous beings, the women abandon the selflessness that Jewsbury at once dismisses and clings to. Despite her earlier bravado, she cannot quite comprehend a female existence outside the absolutes that define and divide the two genders; to defy the rules of one group is to align one's self with its opposite. In this context, her assignment of literary terms acquires a far less favorable resonance. Instead of substantiating themselves through their efforts, the women become in one sense fictitious, having written themselves out of the cultural plot that determines "reality's" shape.

"I am bothered to explain how [this] is, or why it is, or how it should be otherwise," Jewsbury's letter continues, "because, if women chance to have genius, they . . . must do something with it . . . . I cannot at all reconcile the contradictions." Her 1848 novel, *The Half Sisters,* had been one attempt at reconciliation. The novel's gifted heroine, Bianca, is the child of an English iron master and his abandoned Italian mistress, who journeys in vain to England with her young daughter to find him. Stranded there after her mother's death, Bianca finds employment in the seedy world of the traveling circus. Though ashamed at first of her "conspicuous position" as a performer, her talents and growing devotion to her work convince her that acting is her vocation. She resolves to attain the highest ranks of her profession, and by the novel's end, through a combination of hard labor and luck, she has risen from pantomime parts to fame on the legitimate stage.

However mild the story may sound to modern ears, it is worth remembering that Jane Carlyle found it "perfectly disgusting for a young Englishwoman to write" and "quite unfit for circulation in families" (letter to John Forster, in Clarke 186). Carlyle located her objections to the novel tartly and succinctly: "*actresses*! . . . 'hysteric seizures' . . . 'all that sort of thing!'" (in Clarke, 186). The association of actresses with shrieks and twitching limbs rehearses familiar Victorian categories of abhorrence: uncontrolled and uncontrollable physicality, the accompanying suggestion of sexual appetite, and indecorous self-display. Given Jewsbury's pains to separate Bianca from the very vices Carlyle invokes—*The Athenaeum's* reviewer complained of Bianca's "preternatural grace, sobriety and intellectual development" (18 March 1848, 289)—Carlyle's condemnation points up the tenacity of the connection between actresses and shameful female excess. Bianca herself states repeatedly that her life on the stage is one few women should follow: "I do not set myself up as an example of what women in general should be . . . . I would not, I tell you again, wish the generality of women to resemble me" (249). As in Jewsbury's letter, the "chance" grant of genius and its public expression to an aberrant few would not seem to challenge directly the norms of female behavior and "place."

But the discomforts that Jewsbury's novel occasioned did not arise solely from its use of a female performer as its heroine. Carlyle's linkage of "actress" and "hysterical seizures" points up the way that the text enforces a blurring of the very distinctions Carlyle would keep clear by excluding the novel and its excesses from proper homes; the hysteric Jewsbury equates with the actress is not Bianca, but her properly domestic half-sister, Alice. Alice is an outwardly docile, middle-class girl who lacks Bianca's talents but is miserable with her domestic lot. She marries well in the hope of finding fulfillment, fails, and dies in the agonies Carlyle protests, having repented of her decision to elope with Bianca's fickle ex-lover. As its title suggests, then, *The Half Sisters* tells the story of two women who are both set apart *and* related: naturally related by birth and yet divided socially by the manner of it; linked and split too, as we shall discover, by their relationship to the theatrical metaphors that define female duty and selfhood. It is the novel's focus on what the two women share—a common father, for example, which suggests their related condition under patriarchy—as well as on the differences that divide them, that proves a potent source of the novel's social critique.

*The Half Sisters* pays particular attention in this respect to the narrative and social conventions that direct most heroines' destinies. As the narrator describes a journey through Derbyshire—at whose conclusion the traveler, Alice, will marry—she mourns the prevalence of guidebooks that "[teach] us all the walks, and drives, and 'points of view,'" for with predetermined goals and expectations, individual agency comes to an end: "We know, beforehand, all we are going to see and . . . cannot help wishing it were possible to set out like the heroes of old to seek our fortune, and walk to the end of the world" (58). The narrator's "we" forges community from what it claims is a common impulse towards natural liberty (an impulse that has been approved, more commonly, only in heroes). Now deviance describes the freedom to wander "without meeting on every hand straight narrow paths, hedged in by sharply asserted limits," and "to indulge in our own hopes and fears without dictation" (110). Since a heroine's longing to stray from strictly defined paths has itself been conventionally figured as deviant, the passage slips a subversive revision of the female plot into its nostalgia for the "natural." Jewsbury's narrative will enact a similar pattern, first linking and then reversing categories of the natural and the transgressive, the private ("female") sphere and the public one. By doing so, she will attempt to redefine the sources of authorized female identity, even as she claims her authority from them.

"Whether [Alice] or her poor unknown half-sister Bianca were in the worse position for all that regards real help and training for the lifetime opening before each, it would be hard to say," intones the narrator after introducing the women (23). Even this tentative alignment of spheres and situations might have surprised readers schooled in the "natural" superiority of the domestic realm. But as the story progresses, the comparisons grow more direct—and the advantages of "position" are shown to lie increasingly with Bianca. Jewsbury's preference, as well as her accompanying uneasiness, are evident in the book's opening structure. Bianca, not Alice, receives the narrator's initial attention, an ordering that subtly challenges the usually privileged powers of the domestic realm. However unusual the pattern of Bianca's life might appear (a question I will return to), its narrative priority gives it a certain normative status. Bianca's story forms the context in which the domestic plot will be introduced and evaluated; female domesticity, as a result, must answer the concerns of a sphere outside its own.

Yet Jewsbury modifies the effects of this structuring, for her unconventional frame-tale is itself framed. The Half Sisters eases its way into unorthodoxy, opening with a scene that would put the most fervent domestic writer at ease:

On a bed, scantily hung with faded print, lay a woman apparently in extreme suffering. A girl [Bianca] about sixteen stood over the fire, carefully watching the contents of a small pan; at length it seemed sufficiently prepared, and she poured it into a tea-cup, and, approaching the bed where the sick woman lay moaning and restless, she addressed her in Italian, and endeavoured to raise her up . . . .

"Come, Mamma mia," said the girl, "I have made you something delicious . . . ." (3)

Despite Jewsbury's declared antipathy to "the Mrs. Ellis code" of domestic femininity, this scene dramatizes, to cite Ellis herself, all "the self-sacrifice, the patience, the cheerful submission to duty" that made women (particularly "high-minded and intellectual" women) "truly great" when "performing kind offices for the sick" (*Women* 42). Bianca steps center stage only in response to her mother's suffering, and the few actions that signal her presence direct attention away from her. Furthermore, the only physical description of Bianca that Jewsbury provides, in a chapter filled with concrete detail, is contained in the terse phrase "a girl about sixteen." As a result, Bianca appears an oddly transparent character in her realistic surroundings, as if selflessness could indeed comprise her sole substance. Even her name underscores that impression. "Bianca," or whiteness, defines one whose purity resides in a lack of distinguishing color. In this context, Bianca's transparency "makes sense"; she not only stands for the untroubled relation between an appearance and the (selfless) essence it represents, but she also embodies perfectly the domestic woman's primary function as symbol, her status in representation *as* representation. As the transparent transmitters of moral and cultural norms, women are nothing in and of themselves; they are, in the words of Sarah Ellis, "a total blank" (*Daughters* 133), and Ellis describes women who are "striking and distinguished in themselves" but "without the faculty of instrumentality" as "dead letters in the volume of human life, filling what would be a blank space, but doing nothing more" (*Women* 155).

Bianca's description suggests that even unconventional heroines must find legitimacy through conventional definition. Certainly Jewsbury draws on domestic patterns to absorb or translate aspects of Bianca's life that the reader might find unusual. Bianca's tender nursing, for example, closes much of the distance her foreignness introduces, and even the Italian words that might set her apart from the reader are clearly terms of familial affection. Jewsbury's invocation of accepted patterns can prove strategically useful, as we shall see; having established Bianca's "goodness" in conventional terms, Jewsbury can then introduce elements into the equation that subtly question rules of female significance, virtue and "place." And yet she seems intent on highlighting differences in her heroine that domesticity cannot comprehend. If Bianca clearly represents the domestic ideal, she also stands as its opposite, for she occupies, as we have noted, the simultaneous positions of foreigner, bastard, and actress.

Bianca's language proves an easily surmountable otherness—she learns English with truly fictional speed—but more substantial barriers remain. Making an actress foreign or half-foreign, usually on the mother's side, was a common strategy in novels and stories of the period; it allowed authors a safety valve of sorts, for it could excuse or diffuse their characters' passionate and expressive "natures" by placing them outside the bounds of "true" womanhood.[3] The most far-reaching otherness, however, is Bianca's illegitimacy. The "bar sinister" places her, in the broadest sense, outside social definition, for the unregulated passion that produced her has violated the related rules of marriage and economic exchange—and thus of social connectedness and communication itself.[4] The breakdown of valuations Bianca embodies renders her at once void of meaning and excessively replete. Unclaimed and unnamed, she embraces all possibilities.

Acting and illegitimacy bear some relation in this respect, for each can signal a similar, simultaneous structure of excessive and absent meaning, an unsanctioned separation of self and role and name. But Jewsbury does not use acting to reinforce the conjunction of foreignness and illegitimacy, as other authors often do. In Bianca's case, theatricality does not stand as the sign of false or nonexistent correspondences or of proliferating identities. Instead, it expresses a coherence outside of—and supposedly prior to—social definition. "She is from foreign parts, and it was as much as I could do to make out what she said," explains the innkeeper who first aids Bianca; "I thought at first she might have been a play-actor, for she made me understand by her looks and actions I don't know how" (7,8).

The narrator will step in to assure us a few pages later that "Bianca, little as she knew it, had been intended by nature for an actress" (29). Whether the reference is to Bianca's own character or to the unconstructed Nature Jewsbury values is not entirely obvious, but then the correspondence between the terms is precisely Jewsbury's point; Bianca, Nature and representation are unproblematically linked.[5] "Something in [Bianca's] voice and manner announces *reality,*" asserts her future husband, Lord Melton, after watching her perform (180). Domesticity gives Bianca's actions clear meaning in the novel's beginning; now acting performs the same function. As *The Half Sisters* progresses, public performance will come to usurp that function entirely, borrowing legitimacy from its association with the domestic ideal but denying, at the same time, the possibility of the ideal's achievement within the bounds of home.

The life of Bianca's sister, Alice, provides the main grounds of Jewsbury's critique. Alice shares Bianca's aspirations, but not her opportunities. As a child Alice was "haunted by a sense of hidden meaning in all she saw":

> When she was at play, her doll-bonnets of leaves, her chains of rushes, dust gardens, and pebble houses, were really clumsy compared with those of her companions; but there was a feeling, a striving after some meaning she could not express, which made a difference between her work and theirs. (22)

Alice tries to express her perceptions through a natural medium of leaves and pebbles and dust. But the patterns in which she attempts to make meaning visible prove unyielding to her purpose. Domestic ideology constructs the home as a place of moral and spiritual revelation, opposing it to the public sphere, where a preoccupation with material values overwhelms higher concerns; here, however, the domestic realm blocks matter's transformation to metaphor, for its main concern, Jewsbury shows, is also for the surface world of appearances. And women, as the "natural" medium of domestic representation, are reduced to mere matter as well, for their aspirations are permitted only the most restricted forms of expression.[6] "What have you to expect all your life?" questions Alice's mother, worried that her daughter's "devotion to books and accomplishments" will "unfit" her for her duties; "Your life will be domestic" (14). "But why must I marry at all?" Alice will ask. "For what else do women come into the world," replies her mother, "but to be good wives?" (47).[7]

So "typed" and regimented is domestic existence that "a love of singularity . . . is the only impropriety a well-brought up young woman has it in her power to commit," as Alice's mother insists (63); she then cautions her daughter that "a young woman must never let her real sentiments appear" before men. A woman's life becomes "a sort of fictitious existence," a lesson Alice's sister-in-law reinforces as she tutors her in wifehood: "A woman . . . may *seem* to do as much as she likes, but woe to her! the instant she really lets [her husband] see or know any thing about her" (76).

The only power a domestic woman can exercise over her meaning is the limited resistance of the mask; she preserves some sense of internal self-possession by turning herself into a blank surface upon which men project their own desires and visions.[8] Modesty, that most prized of female virtues, depends on women's maintaining a gap between their inner "self" and its external manifestation; this metaphorical impenetrability, in turn, is constructed as a clear sign of women's moral (and physical) integrity. The stakes of this convoluted formulation of femininity are made evident in the behavior of Conrad Percy, Bianca's feckless first love, who abandons her because he becomes "thoroughly disgusted with all that was theatrical, or had a tinge of display in women" (178). Conrad envisions the womanly ideal as "some white-robed vestal whom he should only have been allowed to see at a distance, and who would have had the grace to shrink back with alarmed modesty, had he attempted a nearer approach" (179). As this ideal woman is appropriated and constructed as sign—in this case, as the sign of absolute chastity—her potential for clear signification dissolves. She cannot stand for any absolute value, let alone for her "self"; her relative status means that anyone can reinterpret and claim her. This combined with what Jewsbury terms the "good" woman's "helpless negativity" is doubly fatal to female integrity, for such women have no internal sense of autonomy to define themselves to themselves. Alice, whose selfless modesty attracts Conrad to her, will be persuaded to leave her husband for him; the domestic pattern of female virtue, ironically, permits no resistance to promiscuous possession.

Conrad had earlier complained that Bianca's position as a "public character" prevented one from "having her all to one's self" (212). But Jewsbury places her faith in female self-possession as the vital source of constancy. Bianca's life, despite its exposure, contains what domestic lives lack: "They [domestic women] want a strong purpose. . . . I have had a clear definite channel in which all my energies might flow." Despite "daily contact with the most undesirable environments," she continues, "I was kept clear of ENNUI, which eats like a leprosy into the life of women" (249). Bianca's pronouncement does not disturb familiar associations of the public sphere with moral danger. Her words do reconfigure the spatial dimensions assigned to female virtue. Though protected from the world's coarseness, domestic women have their energies blocked and turned back upon them. Leprosy's unspoken symptoms evoke a gruesome portrait of their lives' progressive mutilation, for their disease is a self-consuming one; penned within the walls of home, they are more threat to themselves than any external danger, for corruption arises from desire's frustration, not from its active fulfillment. Domestic life, as we have seen, thus leads to self-abandon. But acting serves as a kind of moral prophylactic for lives lived in the public sphere; Bianca's channel of action keeps her pure in polluted terrain.[9]

Yet the clear and definite pathway Jewsbury speaks of seems tellingly ambiguous about the nature of Bianca's fulfillment. "Clear," after all, brings us back to the idea of transparency and the question of what women's lives signify. Does Bianca's "strong purpose" enable the production of her "self" as individual rather than type, or does she stand once again for Woman's selfless role in representation, a role simply extended into the public realm? As domestic conduct manuals commonly linked female sexuality to egotistical excess, the image of Bianca's "clear definite channel" can suggest the well-regulated direction of ego *away* from the self, the purification of what would otherwise be unhealthfully self-oriented. Both possibilities are held in tension as Jewsbury attempts to negotiate the attractions of a substantial, independent female identity earned through a profession and the "legitimate" but more selfless vocation of making the self into a medium for other people's enlightenment.

Jewsbury's difficulties are particularly evident at her work's close, where, as Blau DuPlessis and others have noted, dominant ideologies often assert their patterns with particular strength. For despite Bianca's assertion that "it is my destiny to be an actress, and I must work it out" (115), she will marry and step off the stage into wifehood. Many reviewers, shocked by the challenges *The Half Sisters* posed to accepted beliefs, declared the novel immoral. But at least one commentator, despite his conviction that the novel ought to "clothe" itself more carefully in the "respectabilities . . . it has been too much the habit to satirize," found Jewsbury's final message reassuringly conventional. Henry Chorley opens his unsigned review in *The Athenaeum* (18 March 1848) by using the heroine's final position to define the rest of her plot; Bianca, he says, "works her way up by her brilliant talents and remarkable worth to a high marriage." Such a domestic trajectory to genius is "a familiar invention," he claims (he is not above citing his own works, *Conti* and *Pomfret,* along with George Sand's *Consuelo* and de Staël's *Corinne* as examples), for "in most of these . . . the career of the Artist comes to its close" as soon as she marries. In Chorley's opinion, this familiar pattern bears faithful, if unwitting, witness to truth:

> What a light on the peculiarity of Woman's position is shown in this unconscious coincidence! It is not introduced merely because novels usually cease with the marriage ceremony,—but because the wife or the mother on the stage is imagined, by retaining her position, to be rendered more or less unfaithful to love, duty, or delicacy,—because it has never been admitted that Art can be the main business of her life, as of Man's. This, indeed, is emphatically marked out by the provisions of Nature. . . . She moves under the shadow of impending sacrifice (supposing her love of art genuine) from the moment that she allows herself to indulge in Woman's most impassioned and purest hopes.

*The Half Sisters'* narrator declares that Bianca is meant "by Nature" for an actress; for Chorley, nature asserts itself most strongly at the moment she falls in love. Love of art is an artificial and even adulterous passion. By indulging it Bianca strays from the destiny to which she is pledged, placing her moral and sexual character in doubt. Chorley's description also renders the actress nearly invisible, her independent presence blotted into shadow by the impending domestic self-sacrifice that, he believes, forms her legitimate substance. If Bianca ends the novel on a path as predictable as those the narrator initially claims to resist, then the extent and effect of her transgression need questioning.

As we saw earlier, Bianca first appears in the book as a figure of conventional female virtue; her entrance into the theatrical world is figured similarly as an extension of domestic self-sacrifice and devotion. "Her sole idea of the circus was, that it was the means of earning a certain number of shillings, on which she might support her mother," the narrator assures us as Bianca gratefully seizes her first opportunity of employment; "it never occurred to her whether it was a mode of life she would like or dislike" (31). Acting permits the practice of disinterested moral activity, and economic need merely certifies Bianca's spiritual richness; work that denies her middle-class status renders her all the more exemplary.

As Bianca moves up in her profession, however, and necessity no longer drives her, more self-centered motives appear. "A sense of her own powers gradually made itself felt, and there was a pleasure in the exercise of it. . . . Accident had thrown Bianca into this line of life; but we are obliged to confess she continued in it from choice" (33). The sentence describes Bianca's movement from acquiescence to self-assertion; it also initiates a plot line foreign to the heroine's usual text, for it locates the possibility of female desire and fulfillment within an erotics of public achievement, not of romance. "The stage to me is a *passion,* as well as a profession," Bianca later claims; "you cannot change my nature, I must be what I am" (134).

Despite this appeal to a nature outside femininity's artificial restrictions, the redirection of Bianca's domestic plot is highly conflicted. In the quote that traces the movement from "accident" to "choice," for example, the passives that separate Bianca from both power and pleasure even as they describe them and the reluctance of the narrator's "confession" both signal the narrator's discomfort. It is almost immediately after this moment of Bianca's admitted self-interest that the erotic plot begins its loud counterpoint: "as [Bianca's] consciousness of power in her profession increased, her only idea was, that it would be something to display to [Conrad]. It was with reference to him that she valued it" (36). The power of self-production turns its main purpose outward; here we have the familiar scenario of a woman creating herself as an object of display, with the reference-point of self constituted in the gaze and judgement of a man. Bianca no longer performs as an artist, but as Woman. Now her work reinforces the constructions (and constrictions) of the love plot, and Conrad becomes "the ideal hero to whom she acted" all her parts (36).

This "consecrat[ion] to a purpose outside herself" keeps Bianca from becoming "too self-reliant, too much self-concentrated," notes the narrator approvingly (165). And yet Bianca's total dedication to the man she loves also puts her at risk. Her mother's passion for her father had led to the mother's sexual fall; interestingly, Jewsbury describes the mother as having "los[t] sight of herself altogether." Sexuality is not equated with the assertion of selfish desire in this instance, but with being overly "womanly," with the mistaken erasure of all sense of private selfhood, the full but mistaken bestowal of self on another. Bianca's mother loses her mind, the final stage of self-abandon; and as Bianca dreams of Conrad, her mother's vacant presence "warn[s] her against the perilous adventure towards which she was turning." But, the narrator warns, Bianca "had no longer the power to guide herself" (91).

The old actor, her mentor, urges her to an alternative self-consecration; not to a lover through art, but to Art as an Ideal. She must raise the stage from its degenerate state. "It needs to be purified from the sensualism that has defaced it before it can assume its legitimate rank," he asserts. Instead of acknowledging her self-creative powers, the actor directs her efforts entirely outward; he assigns her the domestic woman's responsibility for creating and maintaining the moral tone of the world she inhabits, for bringing to the stage the ideals of Home. And that "purifying" task requires her absolute purity in turn. "You are consecrated to act a certain part, and must give yourself with your whole soul to the work appointed you," he tells her (162). The metaphor of sanctification turns "profession" to holy "vocation," a call that requires an abdication of self just as complete as the love that Conrad called forth. (Bianca will reinforce the connection of self-sacrifice and holy calling when she states that she was born "with as clear a vocation for being an ACTRESS, as any of the saints of old had for being martyrs" [253].) Even the personal, if personally destructive, pleasures of love are denied her; the actor considers Conrad a selfish distraction, just as another admirer chides her for her devotion to a motive "too low, too entirely personal to be worthy of you" (227).

When Bianca discovers that Conrad is indeed unworthy of her and rededicates herself to the stage, she becomes even more clearly a transparent vessel, appropriating domestic ideology's central metaphor for womanly selflessness, the maternal, to describe art's bringing forth:

> Oh! . . . to enter into that world, which as it were lies unseen around
> us, and bring out thence the thoughts and conceptions that are hid-
> den there, and force them into a visible shape, a bodily expression, I
> would consent to dwell in darkness my whole life. Let *me* be noth-
> ing for ever, if I may only once give shape to those unutterable
> mysteries . . . striving to become manifest. (163)

Bianca's nothingness is not her sister's helpless negativity; even as she condemns herself to nonexistence she asserts her force and her power "to shape."
Yet her pleasure in her own artistry and her power over others through art
is constantly tempered by acting's construction as a form of self-control, so
that "self-expression" becomes a kind of self-limitation. The maternal metaphor does not wipe out completely the sense of "intoxication" in a successful performance" (254). But she insists she cannot rely on mere personal
motive to take her "out" of herself.

Interestingly, Bianca's return to a more moderate passion for a man
(Lord Melton) as the source of inspiration for her acting reasserts a limited
personal need and desire. Thus Bianca's final decision to marry at once "nor-
malizes" her by returning her story to the central conventions of female
development and manages to present her embrace of domesticity as an exercise of individual will, not a surrender to prescriptive plots. Yet the limitations the narrative imposes are also strikingly clear. Bianca has married a
man who approves of women's independence, but Jewsbury does not permit her the double passions of wifehood and art. Bianca "now . . . belongs
to us," in her mother-in-law's phrase, and must choose to appear no longer
on stage; the rigid distinctions between public and private spheres, independent and relative femininity, assert themselves once again (389). Genius, finally, gains its legitimacy by renouncing the qualities that made it unique,
thus muting Jewsbury's urgent plea to permit women new plots. The narrator praises Bianca for her "well ordered" household and assures us that genius is not shown "in one special mode of manifestation alone" but "inspires
its possessor, and enables him [*sic*] to feel equal to all situations" (391).

The only glimpse of an alternative outcome takes place in a brief subplot as the novel draws to a close. Bianca's young protegee (named "Clara,"
significantly) marries and remains on the stage; she and her husband then
journey to Italy, Bianca's native land, to continue her training. "Clara's voice
kept its promise," the narrator assures us, "and, there was every reason to
expect that she would take the lead amongst English singers on her return"

(396).[10] The novel leaves the reader with hope; desire for an independent and public identity, one that does not necessarily terminate with romance, is not completely effaced.[11] And yet the novel can only gesture outside its own limits, towards a place and a time that are literally and figuratively distant, to suggest its promise fulfilled. The further story of female self-making must be left to the next generation.

## Notes

1. A highly selective list of these works would include: Mrs. Edwin James, *Social Fetters* (London, 1867); George Eliot, "Armgart" (1871) and *Daniel Deronda* (London, 1876); Mrs. Riddell, *Home, Sweet Home* (London, 1873); B.H. Buxton, *Jennie of "The Prince's"* (London, 1876), *Nell—On Stage and Off* (London, 1879) and *From the Wings* (London, 1880); Florence Marryat, *My Sister the Actress* (London, 1881) and *Facing the Footlights* (London, 1883); Mabel Collins, *In the Flower of Her Youth* (London, 1883); Harriet Jay, *Through the Stage Door* (London, 1883); Mrs. Humphry Ward, *Miss Bretherton* (London, 1884); and Henry James, *The Tragic Muse* (1890).

2. See Rosen, "The Theatricality of Domestic Duty."

3. Brontë's Vashti, modeled on the French actress Rachel, and Eliot's Armgart and the Alcharisi are just three of the most familiar examples.

4. See Tony Tanner for a helpful summary of the theoretical underpinnings of this connection. Society's various rules are all intimately related to a system of communication based on the exchange of women, Tanner asserts, and thus "rules of marriage, economic rules and linguistic rules are in some way systematically interdependent," and "the breakdown of one" imperils "all three" (85).

5. Jewsbury's careful phrase, "little as she knew it," not only divorces Bianca from the egotism so commonly associated with the stage, it also underscores the artlessness of that link.

6. Early in *The Half Sisters* the narrator contrasts two paintings in Alice's home. The first, which Alice has hung in her room, depicts a remote Spanish cloister and provides "an opening through which she escaped from the contact of the dull, harsh, common details by which she was hemmed in on all sides." "Her whole soul was athirst after the ideal," the narrator adds, "and there was that in the picture which it soothed her to look upon" (41). The picture used to hang in the dining-room, but Alice's mother replaced it with a portrait of herself, "taken in the most stylish turban and best-fitting gown that Miss Higgins, chief milliner and dress-maker to the town of——, could invent for the occasion." Mrs. Helmsby's portrait reveals nothing but the surface of its subject; its creation occasions and then represents nothing more than a manufacture of millinery. The cloister, by contrast, points beyond itself to the (female) spirituality it literally and metaphorically stands for. The site of communal self-renunciation becomes a space of self-development where women are set free from the demands of the domestic sphere, a space notably foreign to British society. The connection with the language of vocation that describes Bianca's public career is telling, though Bianca will reject the self-sacrificial extremes such a formulation imposes.

7. In a particularly pointed contrast of the narrative possibilities open to each sister, an early scene depicts Alice's absorption in the story of an actress and singer that had transfixed Englishwomen since Austen's day, Madame de Staël's *Corinne*. "The first reading of 'Corinne' is an epoch a woman never forgets," Jewsbury's narrator declares, suggesting both the opening of a new era of imagined possibilities and the inevitability of its closure as readers' lives move in more conventional directions (60). Alice's life demonstrates how brief that epoch can be. As she finishes *Corinne* amid the solitary splendor of the "Romantic Rocks," the manufacturer, Bryant, ar-

rives to propose. Alice had been drawn to Bryant by his tales of his journey to a part of Hungary "which has never yet figured in any hand-book for travelers" (51). She attempts to unite herself with adventure in the only way she knows, but her dreams of Romantic independence find no fulfillment along the preordained path of romance.

8. Jewsbury's allusion to the mask suggests that there is an authentic being prior to and unrepresented by the masquerade, which enforces the production of a culturally sanctioned and falsifying "femininity." For a contemporary account of gender as an effect of performance, as something that has "no ontological status apart from the various acts which constitute its reality," see Butler, especially chapter 3 (136).

9. Her varying roles, furthermore, allow her "full control over [her] own faculties" and "a sense of freedom, of enjoyment of [her] existence" (249)—terms that echo the narrator's earlier description of the self-creative quest—and enable her to "go freely and fearlessly abroad into the wide region of human nature" (224).

10. Authors sometimes draw a moral distinction between the actress and the singer, as the voice can be more easily spiritualized and disassociated from the body's display in the singer's case. Jewsbury does not seem to draw that distinction here. Her most unflattering portrait of a female artist is of the Italian singer, the Fornasari, whose resemblance to Bianca "almost shook [Lord Melton's] faith" in his beloved, as the Fornasari's genius is "marred by the constant intrusion of *herself*" and her self-love into her performances (340). The moment of Lord Melton's near blurring of the two women underscores the text's recurring discomfort with "public women" and with female self-representation, as does the novel's need to bring in a stereotypically "bad" theatrical woman to clarify Bianca's character further through their contrast.

11. Clara's spouse is pleased to think that "the sanction and protection of a husband" will shield her on the stage, but Jewsbury makes it obvious that Clara's desires and ambitions do not follow from his approval.

## WORKS CITED

Butler, Judith. *Gender Trouble: Feminism and the Subversion of Identity*. New York: Routledge, 1990.

Clarke, Norma. *Ambitious Heights: Writing, Friendship, Love—The Jewsbury Sisters, Felicia Hemans and Jane Carlyle*. New York: Routledge, 1990.

DuPlessis, Rachel Blau. *Writing beyond the Ending: Narrative Strategies of Twentieth-Century Women Writers*. Bloomington: Indiana UP, 1985.

Ellis, Sarah Stickney. *The Daughters of England*. London: Fisher, Son and Co., 1845.

———. *The Women of England: Their Social Duties and Domestic Habits*. London: Fisher, Son and Co., 1838.

Jewsbury, Geraldine. *The Half Sisters*. Edited by Joanne Wilkes. 1848; rpt. Oxford: Oxford UP, 1994.

———. *Selections from the Letters of Geraldine E. Jewsbury to Jane Welsh Carlyle*. Edited by Mrs. Alexander Ireland. London: Longmans, Green and Co., 1892.

Miller, Nancy K. *Subject to Change: Reading Feminist Writing*. New York: Columbia UP, 1988.

Rosen, Judith. "The Theatricality of Domestic Duty," *Victorian Studies,* forthcoming.

Tanner, Tony. *Adultery in the Novel: Contract and Transgression*. Baltimore: Johns Hopkins UP, 1979.

## SELECTED SECONDARY SOURCES

Norma Clarke, *Ambitious Heights: Writing, Friendship, Love—The Jewsbury Sisters, Felicia Hemans and Jane Carlyle* (New York: Routledge, 1990); J.R. Fahnestock, "Geraldine Jewsbury: The Power of the Publisher's Reader," *Nineteenth-Century Fiction* 28 (1973); Monica Correa Fryckstedt, "Geraldine Jewsbury and *Douglas Jerrold's Shilling Magazine*," *English Studies* 4 (1985), and "New Sources on

Geraldine Jewsbury and the Woman Question," *Research Studies* 51 (2) (1983); J.M. Hartley, "Geraldine Jewsbury and the Problems of the Woman Novelist," *Women's Studies International Quarterly* 2 (1979); Virginia Woolf, "Geraldine and Jane," *The Common Reader* (second series, 1959).

# Rewriting the Male Plot in Wilkie Collins's No Name (1862)

## Captain Wragge Orders an Omelette and Mrs. Wragge Goes into Custody

*Deirdre David*

(William) Wilkie Collins (1824–1889) was the son of a well-known land-scape painter and was educated at several London private schools. After a two-year trip to Italy with his family in 1836–1838, he published a biography of his father; it was followed by many pieces of popular journalism written for Dickens's periodicals, as well as other magazines. His first novel, *Antonina* (1850), is about the fall of Rome and is heavily influenced by Gibbon and Bulwer-Lytton. Collins made his major contribution to Victorian literature and also his lasting reputation, however, within the genre of mystery and suspense novels. He is regarded as a pioneer of the form. *Basil* (1852) is his first such "novel of sensation," followed by *The Woman in White* (1860), *No Name* (1862), *Armadale* (1866), and *The Moonstone* (1868). (Many of Collins's novels are now available in Oxford's World's Classics Series; some are available in Penguin editions.) Both formally and thematically, his novels are notable for their consistent preoccupation with the act of narration; they are also significant for their representations of women confined by Victorian codes of sexual and gender conduct. Collins never married, preferring instead to establish long-lasting relationships with at least two women with whom he had several children. For most of his adult life, he was known to be addicted to opium.

Whether Wilkie Collins was a feminist, deployed popular literature for feminist ideology, or even liked women, is not the subject of this essay. My interest is in something less explicit, perhaps not fully intentional, to be discovered in his fiction: an informing link between restlessness with dominant modes of literary form and fictional critique of dominant modes of gender politics. In what follows, I aim to show how the narrative shape of one of Collins's most baroquely plotted, narratively complex novels is inextricably enmeshed with its thematic material. I refer to *No Name,* a novel whose

33

subversion of fictional omniscience suggests Collins's radical literary practice and whose sympathy for a rebellious heroine in search of subjectivity suggests his liberal sexual politics.[1] To be sure, there are other Collins novels as narratively self-reflexive as *No Name—The Moonstone,* for one; and *Man and Wife,* for example, mounts a strong attack on misogynistic subjection of women (particularly when exercised by heroes of the Muscular Christian variety). But no Collins novel, in my view, so interestingly conflates resistance to dominant aesthetic and sexual ideologies as *No Name,* even as it ultimately displays its appropriation by the authority that both enables its existence and fuels its resistance.

Challenging authoritarian, patriarchal-sited power in his interrogation of form and theme, Collins collapses a binary opposition between the two, a separation assumed in Victorian criticism of the novel and still, perhaps, possessing a lingering appeal in these deconstructive times. The intense dialogism, the insistent relativism, of *No Name* makes it impossible to align in one column what is represented and in another the *ways* in which representation takes place. Neither is it possible to construct a neat alignment of fictionality and representation, to say that at this moment the novel performs self-reflexive cartwheels and that at another we are in the realm of strict mimesis. Mimesis, one might say, is always simultaneous with semiosis in *No Name,* so much so, in fact, that representation, say, of a character obsessed with the record-keeping which is the means of his social survival, becomes a field for self-reflexive fictionality; and, to a lesser extent, fictionality is sometimes the ground on which Collins maps his persuasively realistic narrative.[2] Collapsing the neat polarities of literary analysis, upsetting the conventions of omniscient narrative, showing a woman's struggle for survival as she is both exiled from and enclosed within patriarchal structures— all this is the business of *No Name,* in my view an exemplary novel for "naming" Collins's disruptive place in the tradition of Victorian fiction.

The original publication of Collins's novels covers some forty years, from *Antonina* in 1850 to *Blind Love,* left unfinished at his death in 1889, and his career encompasses two distinct periods in the history of Victorian fiction: at the beginning we are in the age of Dickens and Thackeray; at the end we enter a new generation composed of Hardy, Stevenson, Moore, Gissing, and Kipling (Page, i–xvi). With *Antonina,* a historical romance set in fifth-century Rome and owing much to Gibbon and Bulwer-Lytton, Collins established himself as a powerful storyteller with a commendable eye for detail, and by the time of his fifth novel, *The Woman in White,* he emerged as a master of diegesis with a narrative something for everyone: omniscience, free indirect discourse, autobiography, diary, letter, newspaper story, ledger book, memoranda. *No Name* appeared during the 1860s (Collins's stellar decade of literary production) between his two best-known novels, *The Woman in White* and *The Moonstone*, and was first published in Dickens's weekly magazine *All the Year Round* from March 1862 to January 1863 and published in three volumes at the end of 1862. Divided into eight dramatic "scenes," punctuated by groups of letters which are, in turn, interpolated with newspaper stories and journal entries, *No Name* was phenomenally successful. Collins received three thousand pounds for the first edition, sold nearly four thousand copies on the day of publication, netted fifteen hundred pounds for American serial rights, and obtained five thousand guineas from Smith Elder for his next novel before having written a word (Page 169).

Unlike most Collins novels, however, *No Name* discloses no secrets, rattles no nerves with sensational excitement; rather, as he observes in his brief preface, "all the main events of the story are purposely foreshadowed, before they take place—my present design being to rouse the reader's interest in following the train of circumstances by which these foreseen events are brought about." For some critics, the absence of suspense seriously impairs *No Name*'s success. Jerome Meckier, in particular, finds "the biggest mistake" to be "procedural" and believes Collins "sadly misjudges his own strengths" in forgoing surprise. From another perspective, however, one can argue that even before it begins, *No Name*, a story about an unconventional female response to legal disinheritance, seeks to demystify the power of conventional, one might say inherited, Victorian narrative discourse. Rather than demanding from the reader acquiescence in a controlled revelation of plot, the narrator collaboratively offers a chance to see how plot comes into being, an opportunity to experience plot-in-process, so to speak, rather than plot-as-product. What's more, as several contemporary critics perceived, in forgoing narrative suspense for readerly collaboration, Collins situates his narrative practice in contention with the sort of instructive discourse perfected by George Eliot, whose *Adam Bede* and *The Mill on the Floss*, with their exemplary narrative discursions into questions of social responsibility, artistic representation, and cultural change, preceded *No Name* by several years.[3]

As it is difficult to discuss any Collins novel without summarizing what happens, I shall do that briefly before showing how *No Name* disrupts conventional narrative discourse in the process of interrogating Victorian gender politics. On the death of their father, Andrew Vanstone, eighteen-year-old Magdalen and her older sister, Norah, are unable to inherit his considerable fortune. As a young officer in Canada, he married impetuously, repented quickly, and returned to England, where he met the mother-to-be of Magdalen and Norah, a woman courageous enough to live with him without benefit of marriage. In the opening chapter, Vanstone and his forty-four-year-old, pregnant again, not-wife learn of the death of his legal wife and quickly go off to London to marry. But a few days later Vanstone is killed in a railway accident, and the now legal second wife rapidly declines into death after childbirth, leaving her newly orphaned daughters to discover that, although now legitimate, they are disinherited because Vanstone, who made his will before marrying their mother, did not make it over again after marrying her. They are named "Nobody's children," and their inheritance goes to a mean-spirited uncle who quickly departs the novel—leaving his puny son Noel immensely rich and vulnerable to Magdalen's considerable attractions. A born actress, she undertakes numerous disguises with the assistance of one Captain Horatio Wragge (a scoundrel who achieves respectability by the end of the novel), marries Noel under an assumed name, is unmasked by her husband's craftily intelligent housekeeper, falls desperately ill after the death of Noel, and is dramatically rescued by the son of a friend of her father, a Captain Kirke—whom she marries in a symbolic reconciliation with the father figure who left her legitimate yet disinherited at the beginning of the novel. Exiled from patriarchal protection in the opening chapters, she is enfolded within patriarchy's embrace by the end. And to complete this story of return to one's heritage, her sister marries the man who inherits the estate from Noel Vanstone.

No Name is notable for Collins's bold delineation of a heroine who sells her sexuality to regain her rightful fortune. An outraged Mrs. Oliphant (always good for a scandalized response) declared in 1863 that Magdalen engages in "a career of vulgar and aimless trickery and wickedness, with which it is impossible to have a shadow of sympathy," that she is tainted by "the pollutions of . . . endless deceptions and horrible marriage" (Page 143). The "horrible marriage" part distressed almost all reviewers, and even now, in our far less prudish time, it is difficult not to be troubled, even embarrassed, by Collins's sexual frankness. He describes a young woman bursting with "exuberant vitality," possessed of "a figure instinct with such a seductive, serpentine suppleness, so lightly and playfully graceful, that its movements suggested, not unnaturally, the movements of a young cat . . . so perfectly developed already that no one who saw her could have supposed that she was only eighteen," undergoing "the revolting ordeal of marriage" to a frail little man with a miserable moustache, the complexion of a delicate girl, an appalling habit of screwing up his pale eyes, and a forehead that is always crumpling "into a nest of wicked little wrinkles" (6, 357, 205). But the chilling picture of sexual bargain between vibrant young woman and sickly older man, undisguised as it is by the cosmetic of Victorian piety, serves its political purpose: Collins makes us see that disinherited middle-class women, deprived of paternal protection, assume an identity that is both inscribed and concealed by the gender politics of their social class—that of sexual object. We also see how the literal incarceration of women to be found in Collins's earlier novel, *The Woman in White,* becomes, in *No Name,* an incarceration formed of rigid laws, of patriarchal injunctions.

In his focus upon the "sensational" aspects of *The Woman in White,* the ways that this novel (like others in the "sensation" genre) elaborates "a fantasmatics of sensation," D.A. Miller observes that Laura Fairlie "follows a common itinerary of the liberal subject in nineteenth-century fiction: she takes a nightmarish detour through the carceral ghetto on her way *home,* to the domestic haven where she is always felt to belong" (172). In *No Name,* Magdalen Vanstone also makes that journey. But whereas Laura is essentially passive, the quintessentially pale and quivering victim, Magdalen is aggressive, robustly in rebellion against the law that confines her to impecunious humiliation. What's more, Magdalen's awesomely vibrant performances (first in legitimate roles as Julia and Lucy in an amateur production of *The Rivals* at the beginning of the novel, then in illegitimate impersonations of her former governess and a parlormaid) constitute energetic difference from the passivity of women in *The Woman in White* (excluding, needless to say, that fascinating pioneer woman detective, Marian Halcolme).

Magdalen possesses a frightening ability to lose her own self in the assumption of other identities,[4] and her first strategy for survival when she finds herself "Nobody's" daughter is to leave home and seek out the manager of the amateur theatricals, who, amazed by her talent for mimicry, had given her his card and declared her a "born actress." Unable to find him, she is befriended (or, rather, appropriated) by Captain Wragge: He will turn her into a professional and will be compensated when Magdalen recovers her rightful fortune. Wragge's recounting (in one of his numerous Chronicles, which I shall discuss in a moment) of her first appearance in an "At Home" (a performance featuring one actor assuming a series of extraordinarily different characters) indicates some of the larger meanings of gender politics in the novel. Wragge devises "the Entertainment," manages "all the business," writes two anonymous letters to the lawyer authorized to find Magdalen, fortifies her with sal volatile as antidote to unhappy memories of her family, and sends her on stage:

> We strung her up in no time, to concert pitch; set her eyes in a blaze; and made her out-blush her own rouge. The curtain rose when we had got her at red heat. She dashed at it . . . rushed full gallop through

her changes of character, her songs, and her dialogue; making mistakes by the dozen, and never stopping to set them right; carrying the people along with her in a perfect whirlwind, and never waiting for the applause. (175)

Endowed with a natural vitality which is "managed," disciplined, and shaped by Wragge, Magdalen, during the actual performance, reasserts her naturally vital, rebellious female self in "out-blushing" her own rouge, thereby suggesting how the novel, in general, addresses the way women's "natural" talent is shaped by patriarchal culture, society, and the law. If Wragge, then, as stage manager, operates as an omnipotent string puller, let us see how his other activities strongly suggest the omnipotence associated with narrative omniscience. Wragge may be seen as parodic emblem, as Collins's embodied and symbolic critique of prevailing literary form in the Victorian period.

Omniscience, according to J. Hillis Miller, finds its authority and its origin in the unsettling of established religious beliefs: "The development of Victorian fiction is a movement from the assumption that society and the self are founded on some superhuman power outside them, to a putting in question of this assumption, to a discovery that society now appears to be self-creating and self-supporting, resting on nothing outside itself" (30). As remedy for the profound unease occasioned by such a discovery, society authorizes the fictionally omniscient/omnipotent narrator to fill the void, retard slippage from belief to skepticism. Through his unrelenting insistence on diegetic relativism, which is expressed in the multiple narrative perspectives we encounter in almost all his fiction, Collins refuses to perform the consolatory functions Miller identifies. Very much like Thackeray in *Vanity Fair,* who interrogates all forms of authority and wants us to examine the unthinking ways we accept fictions of various sorts, how, especially, we believe in a novelist's total knowledge of the world, Collins insists that we see the subjective, arbitrary nature of fictional representation, the hubristic nature of novelistic omnipotence.

Defining himself as a "moral agriculturalist; a man who cultivates the field of human sympathy," Wragge scoffs at being labeled a "Swindler": "What of that? The same low tone of mind assails men in other professions in a similar manner—calls great writers, scribblers—great generals, butchers—and so on" (153). Identifying himself with "great writers" who cultivate "the field of human sympathy," he becomes, of course, both like and unlike Wilkie Collins, the Victorian inheritor and reviser of conventional narrative discourse. But this is not all; Wragge's deft talent for inventing characters and identities also associates him with the creation of fiction. For example, one of the books in his "commercial library" (a repository of reference works in roguery and deception) is entitled "Skins to Jump Into." Concocting plausible identities for himself, Mrs. Wragge, and Magdalen in the plot to attract and snare Noel Vanstone, he selects the "skins" of a Mr. Bygrave, Mrs. Bygrave, and niece Susan and instructs Magdalen as follows:

> My worthy brother was established twenty years ago, in the mahogany and logwood trade at Belize, Honduras. He died in that place; and is buried on the south-west side of the local cemetery, with a neat monument of native wood carved by a self-taught negro artist. Nineteen months afterwards, his widow died of apoplexy at a boarding-house in Cheltenham. She was supposed to be the most corpulent woman in England; and was accommodated on the ground floor of the house in consequence of the difficulty of getting her up and down stairs. You are her only child; you have been under my care since the sad event at Cheltenham; you are twenty-one years old on the second of August next; and, corpulence excepted, you are the living image of your mother. (235–36)

His imperative omniscience, his persuasive attention to detail, his energetic keeping up of numerous journals and ledgers that record assumable identities, characteristics of different "districts," narratives of successful and unsuccessful swindles—all affirm his status in *No Name* as parodic narrator, as emblem of convention, order, and legitimacy (despite and because of his vagabond status).

Insisting "he must have everything down in black and white," announcing that "all untidiness, all want of system and regularity, causes me the acutest irritation," in a manner worthy of Conrad's accountant in *Heart of Darkness,* he writes his narratives of deception in precise pages of neat handwriting, obsessively aligns rows of figures, and permits no blots, stains, or erasures (147). To complete this empire of fiction making, of fabrication of identity, he has, quite literally, authorized himself; everything, he proudly declares, is verified by "my testimonials to my own worth and integrity." In sum, Wragge performs a kind of burlesque of Victorian narrative discourse, of the sovereign omniscience that dominates the period—and this, of course, is the mode of arbitrary narrative from which Wilkie Collins implicitly disinherited himself in his persistent interpolation of omniscience with the relativism of diary, letter, journalistic fragment, and so on. Bakhtin's observation that the novel form "is the expression of a Galilean perception of language, one that denies the absolutism of single and unitary language," is richly borne out by the dialogism of *No Name* (Bakhtin 366).

If Captain Horatio Wragge serves as vehicle for Collins's restlessness with dominant modes of literary form, then it is his wife, Matilda Wragge, who, absolutely unconsciously, expresses Collins's critique of dominant modes of gender politics. *No Name,* thick with the inherited themes of Victorian fiction—marriage, family, money, wills, female desire, male governance—contains an irregular, disruptive episode that functions as an important signifier for Collins's indictment of patriarchal law. Mrs. Wragge is the alarming center of this episode, an illegitimate, irregular, symbolically political action that molests the attempts at omnipotence practiced by her husband. She is affiliated more with modes of signification, with interrogations of fictionality, than with the events of the signified, with what is being represented. I'm going to name this episode "Captain Wragge Orders an Omelette." And to explain what I mean by this, let me take you to the scene where Magdalen meets Matilda for the first time.

Characterized by her husband as "constitutionally torpid" and declared by Lewis Carroll to be an uncanny anticipation of his White Queen (Page 245), Mrs. Wragge is a physical marvel. A gigantic six feet, three inches, she has an enormous, smooth, moonlike face, "dimly irradiated by eyes of mild and faded blue, which looked straightforward into vacancy" (146), and complains constantly of a "Buzzing" in her head. This buzzing is not helped by her husband's compulsion to bark orders like a sergeant major: confiding to Magdalen that he is a "martyr" to his own sense of order, Wragge shouts, "Sit straight at the table. More to the left, more still—that will do" (151), and "Pull it up at heel, Mrs. Wragge—pull it up at heel!"—this occasioned by the sight of her worn slippers. The buzzing, she explains, began before she married the Captain and was working as a waitress in Darch's Dining Rooms in London: "The gentlemen all came together; the gentlemen were all hungry together; the gentlemen all gave their orders together" (148). Years later she is still trying to get the gentlemen's orders sorted out; becoming "violently excited" by Magdalen's sympathetic questioning, she begins to repeat the orders retained in her muddled mind:

> Boiled pork and greens and peas-pudding for Number One. Stewed beef and carrots and gooseberry tart, for Number Two. Cut of mutton, and quick about it, well done, and plenty of fat, for Number Three. Codfish and parsnips, two chops to follow, hot-and-hot, or I'll be the death of you, for Number Four. Five, six, seven, eight, nine, ten. Carrots and gooseberry tart—peas pudding and plenty of fat—pork and beef and mutton, and cut 'em all, and quick about it—stout

for one, and ale for t'other—and stale bread here, and new bread
there—and this gentleman likes cheese, and that gentleman doesn't—
Matilda, Tilda, Tilda, Tilda, fifty times over, till I don't know my own
name. (148)

In this City chophouse, eerily suggestive of Harold Pinter's *The Dumb Waiter*
where two hit men attempt to fill orders for steak and chips, jam tarts, and
so on, Matilda, disoriented by the barrage of gentlemen's orders, does not
know her own name, feels herself deprived of identity by the incessant discipline of male directions; she becomes, in a sense, somewhat like Magdalen,
a woman deprived of her identity as inheriting daughter and disciplined by
laws that legislate legitimacy and correct irregularity.

It is at Darch's Dining Rooms that Mrs. Wragge meets the Captain,
"the hungriest and the loudest" of the lot. Once married, her servant duties
are transferred from a multitude of hungry and demanding gentlemen to one:
She shaves him, does his hair, cuts his nails, presses his trousers, and, misery of miseries, cooks his meals. This latter duty requires constant recourse
to a "tattered" cookery book, and when Magdalen meets her, she is attempting to master the directions for making an omelette (ordered by the Captain for breakfast the next day). As I'm going to suggest, this is an omelette
with many fillings.

Here's how she interprets the recipe to Magdalen:

"Omelette with Herbs. Beat up two eggs with a little water or milk,
salt, pepper, chives, and parsley. Mince small." There! mince small!
How am I to mince small when it's all mixed up and running? "Put
a piece of butter the size of your thumb into the frying pan."—Look
at my thumb, and look at yours! whose size does she mean? "Boil,
but not brown."—If it mustn't be brown, what colour must it
be? . . . "Allow it to set, raise it round the edge; when done, turn it
over to double it . . . Keep it soft; put the dish on the frying-pan, and
turn it over." Which am I to turn over . . . the dish or the frying-
pan? . . . It sounds like poetry, don't it? (150)

Probably not, I think, is our response, but Mrs. Wragge's innocent
deconstruction of a recipe generates a kind of narrative poetics and gender
politics for *No Name*.

On the level of narrative, her contention with the cookery book implies female subversion of male-authorized texts or laws (the cookery book
written by a woman for the instruction of other women in filling male or-

ders); on the level of story, her resistance to accepted interpretation intimates the larger battle in this novel between legitimacy and illegitimacy, between male governance and female revenge. And she doesn't let up. Grandiosely introducing Magdalen to the Wragge way of life, the Captain offers "A pauper's meal, my dear girl—seasoned with a gentleman's welcome"; his wife begins to mutter, "Seasoned with salt, pepper, chives, and parsley." Negotiating terms with Magdalen for her dramatic training, the Captain begs her "not to mince the matter on your side—and depend on me not to mince it on mine"; his wife (of course) mutters that one should always try to "mince small." Her "torpid" yet disruptive presence not only prefigures Lewis Carroll's White Queen but also anticipates the interrogation of arbitrary systems of signification that we find in *Alice in Wonderland*. If her husband's attitudes, despite his raffish demeanor and picaresque career, represent conformity and conservatism, then Mrs. Wragge's attitudes represent resistance and interrogation.

And what of Mrs. Wragge's omelette? Well, she makes it, but, as she says, "It isn't nice. We had some accidents with it. It's been under the grate. It's been spilt on the stairs. It's scalded the landlady's youngest boy—he went and sat on it" (161). Her interpretation of male orders results in something not "nice," and certainly illegitimate as an omelette. And what of Captain Wragge? Abandoning "moral agriculture" for "medical agriculture," he goes in for the manufacture and sale of medicinal cures. Turning his talent for narrative to production of stories about "The Pill," and his skill in creating identities to the fabrication of testimonials about its dramatic effects, he becomes very rich. Meeting Magdalen at the end of the novel, "the copious flow of language pouring smoothly from his lips," he declares, "I merely understand the age I live in" (529). It seems as if his attitudes no longer *represent* conformity and acceptance (as I suggested earlier); speaking the dominant sociolect of "the age," which will never be understood by his wife, he ceases to function as parody or burlesque and becomes the thing itself. In other words, he goes legit. And instead of shouting at his wife, he appropriates her astonishing physical presence for the narrative that makes him rich: She is, he says, "the celebrated woman whom I have cured of indescribable agonies from every complaint under the sun. Her portrait is engraved on all the wrappers, with the following inscription beneath it:—'Before she took the Pill, you might have blown this patient away with a feather. Look at her now!!!'" (526). Just as Magdalen's story of return to legitimate social identity in marriage assumes conventional narrative form, so Mrs. Wragge's story of respectable celebrity puts an end to her disruption of parodic omnipotence. No longer the resisting reader of a recipe, like the Captain she becomes the thing itself and is read by others, engraved and inscribed as she is on all the wrappers for "The Pill." Mrs. Wragge is in custody, just as, one might venture, Collins's interrogations of narrative form, patriarchal law, misogynistic sexual politics are (must be) eventually placed in the demanding custody of his serialized novel. They are disciplined by the contingent demands of his career, by the male-dominated directives of his culture. In sum, the subversiveness of *No Name* must ultimately be contained by the structure that enables its existence. Shall we say real life as opposed to fiction? But perhaps we should remember Noel Vanstone's astonished response to the revelation of Magdalen's plot for revenge: "It's like a scene in a novel— it's like nothing in real life" (403). In deconstructing Collins's literary practice and gender politics in *No Name,* we should not try to break the dialectical bond between theme and form, life and novel.

## Notes

1. Comparing *No Name* with *Great Expectations* (which it followed in Dickens's periodical *All the Year Round*), Jerome Meckier finds Collins's novel inferior. Meckier's interest is in the way these two novels address barriers to "social progress," their meaning as "serious philosophical critique of shortcomings traceable to the very nature of things" (129). Meckier's tendency to focus exclusively on informing connections between the private plight of Pip and public disorder blinds him, I think, to the very real social difficulties experienced by women in Collins's novel.

2. For stimulating discussion of relationships between mimesis and semiosis, I am indebted to Michael Riffaterre's lecture series at the University of Pennsylvania, February 1988.

3. An unsigned review in *Dublin University Magazine* in February 1861 observes that "a writer like George Eliot may look down from a very far height on such a dweller in plains as he who wrote *The Woman in White*." For this critic, Collins's novel is infected by "the spirit of modern realism." In 1863, Alexander Smith in the *North British Review* more neutrally noted that Collins was "a writer of quite a different stamp from George Eliot." See *Wilkie Collins: The Critical Heritage,* 104, 140.

4. Jonathan Loesberg makes the interesting point that "sensation novels evoke their most typical moments of sensation response from images of a loss of class identity. And this common image links up with a fear of a general loss of social identity as a result of the merging of the classes—a fear that was commonly expressed in the debate over social and parliamentary reform in the late 1850s and 1860s" (117). Part of the implicit threat to established gender and class politics posed by Magdalen's protean ability to switch roles may be ascribed to such a fear.

## WORKS CITED

Bakhtin, Mikhail. *The Dialogic Imagination: Four Essays by Mikhail Bakhtin.* Translated by Caryl Emerson and Michael Holquist. Austin: U of Texas P, 1981.

Collins, Wilkie. *No Name* (1864). Oxford: Oxford UP, 1986.

Loesberg, Jonathan. "The Ideology of Narrative Form in Sensation Fiction." *Representations* 13 (Winter 1986): 115–38.

Meckier, Jerome. *Hidden Rivalries in Victorian Fiction: Dickens, Realism, and Reevaluation.* Lexington: UP of Kentucky, 1987.

Miller, D.A. *The Novel and the Police.* Berkeley and Los Angeles: U of California P, 1988.

Miller, J. Hillis. *The Form of Victorian Fiction: Thackeray, Dickens, Trollope, George Eliot, Meredith and Hardy*. Notre Dame, Ind.: U of Notre Dame P, 1968.

Page, Norman, ed. *Wilkie Collins: The Critical Heritage*. London: Routledge and Kegan Paul, 1974.

## SELECTED SECONDARY SOURCES

Thomas Boyle, *Black Swine in the Sewers of Hampstead: Beneath the Surface of Victorian Sensationalism* (New York: Viking, 1989); Patrick Brantlinger, "What Is 'Sensational' about the Sensation Novel?" *Nineteenth Century Fiction* (June 1989): 1–28; Tamar Heller, *Dead Secrets: Wilkie Collins and the Female Gothic* (New Haven: Yale UP, 1992); Jonathan Loesberg, "The Ideology of Narrative Form in Sensation Fiction," *Representations* 13 (Winter 1986): 115–38; Sue Lonoff, *Wilkie Collins and His Victorian Readers* (New York: AMS Press, 1982); Margaret Oliphant, "Sensation Novels," *Blackwood's Edinburgh Magazine* 91 (May 1862): 564–84; Norman Page, ed. *Wilkie Collins: The Critical Heritage* (London: Routledge and Kegan Paul, 1974); Jenny Bourne Taylor, *In the Secret Theatre of Home: Wilkie Collins, Sensation Narrative, and Nineteenth-Century Psychology* (London and New York: Routledge, 1988).

# SILENT WOMAN, SPEAKING FICTION

## CHARLES READE'S *GRIFFITH GAUNT* (1866) AT THE ADULTERY TRIAL OF HENRY WARD BEECHER

*Laura Hanft Korobkin*

Melodramatic, socially conscious, and erotically charged, the sensationalist novels of Charles Reade (1814–1884), including *It Is Never Too Late to Mend* (1853), *Hard Cash* (1863), *Griffith Gaunt* (1866) and *The Cloister and the Hearth* (1861), were hugely successful. Reade used notebooks of newspaper clippings to fashion his "matter of fact romances," which also protested oppressive conditions in prisons, mental asylums, and merchant ships. In his best works, Reade's intelligent, realistically sexual heroines negotiate wildly improbable plots involving murder, bigamy, and torture, yet triumph over all. Frustrated by the perennial bachelorhood imposed by his lifetime fellowship at Magdalen College, Oxford, Reade poured his eccentric energies into litigation, vituperation against critics, and all things theatrical. Though little known today, Reade enjoyed a contemporary reputation equal to that of Wilkie Collins and just behind those of Dickens and Eliot, well deserving Henry James's praise for "those great sympathetic guesses with which a real master attacks the truth." While no paperback editions of his best novels are available, readers can find *Peg Woffington* and *Christie Johnstone* (BCLI), a seventeen-volume reprint of the 1898 edition of his works (AMS), and a volume of his plays (Cambridge UP).

In a series of recent articles, feminist critics have argued that reading sensationalist novels of the 1860s and 1870s stimulated women toward a new assertiveness, encouraging them to see "new possibilities for themselves" that included, ultimately, "new fantasies, new expectations, and even female insurrection."[1] This essay examines one woman's epistolary account of how Charles Reade's sensationalist bestseller *Griffith Gaunt* (1866) triggered, not insurrection, but an apparently conservative moral reevaluation of her own unconventional behavior, and how that account became, amazingly, the evidentiary crux of the most scandalous American trial of the nineteenth

45

century. Because Elizabeth Tilton's letter accorded Reade's novel the power to interpret the text of her own life, the novel itself became central to the trial's project of determining whether or not she had committed adultery with the nation's foremost preacher, Henry Ward Beecher. In the relations of silenced woman to empowered heroine, sentimental reader to sensationalist text, fictional evidence to legal inference, we can begin to unpack the complex role that novels like Reade's played in the lives of the women who read them, and, not at all coincidentally, the ways that legal process in nineteenth-century America erased the self-creating female voice.

On 20 August 1874, New York editor and author Theodore Tilton sued Henry Ward Beecher for adultery, claiming that the minister had seduced Tilton's wife, Elizabeth, and seeking one hundred thousand dollars damages (Tr. I 3).[2] The six-month civil trial on charges of criminal conversation received daily coverage in every major newspaper in the country, "pushing politics off the front pages for months at a time" (Wendt 248). Spectators waited all night outside the courthouse for a ticket to one of the limited seats inside. Immense bouquets of flowers were delivered to Beecher and Tilton as they sat with counsel, until the competition by each party's supporters to produce ever more magnificent bouquets upstaged the ongoing interrogation of witnesses (Rugoff 207–8, Shaplen 216–19). On the 112th trial day, after eight days of deliberation and fifty-two ballots, the jury announced that they were deadlocked. Judge Neilson reluctantly dismissed them and the case ended without a verdict.[3]

Criminal conversation, the classically homosocial tort in which a cuckolded husband sues his wife's lover for the damages to him caused by her adultery, has traditionally reduced the wife to a species of "damaged goods."[4] The claim is one of commercial injury, for deprivation of the husband's property interest in the exclusive use of his wife's body and services. Neither plaintiff, defendant, judge, nor juryman, and crucially excluded even from the role of witness by the procedural ban on interspousal testimony, the wife functions in the case is as its contested object.[5] In narrative terms, she is the plot's silent fulcrum, the blank but pivotal space into which male litigants and their attorneys write the character their self-justifying stories require.

The oppositional storytelling drive that powers all litigation makes the testimonial construction of character and behavior a process dominated by each party's need to characterize the facts in the way most likely to win the case. In most litigation, the structural tendency toward fictionalization that this need produces is counteracted by the narrative subject's ability to enter the testimonial arena herself. But in criminal conversation cases a wife cannot take the stand; her reputation, privacy, and future life may therefore be wholly destroyed by a lawsuit she is powerless either to enter or to defend.

So, at the Beecher–Tilton trial, Elizabeth Tilton was a silent, spectral, constant presence among the boisterous courtroom spectators. Even Beecher's attorneys called her "the true defendant in this cause—she whose lips are sealed and whose hands are tied, while the battle is waging over her body" (Tr. II 5). Precluded from testifying, she was peremptorily silenced by the judge when she rose "like an apparition" on the seventy-seventh day and attempted to read a written statement (Tr. III 323, 325). But while the criminal conversation "story" thus dramatically suppressed the live voice of its only potential heroine, the project of discursively constructing her remained central to the trial. Interestingly, it was carried on largely through a literary analysis of *Griffith Gaunt*.

The forensic manipulation of Elizabeth Tilton's private record of a life-changing reading experience recast it as evidence from which the jury might legitimately infer the fact of her adultery. My analysis of this episode makes two main points. First, Elizabeth's sentimental response to Reade's wildly sensational novel suggests that the idiosyncrasy of the individual reading experience determines its impact, rather than the genre-related attributes of the text. Second, a legal or cultural order that erases the vocal authority of women and excludes them from the adversarial process reduces them, ultimately, to textual constructs indistinguishable from the explicitly "fictional" characters in novels.

At the Beecher–Tilton trial, Theodore Tilton testified that in July 1870, his wife Elizabeth tearfully confessed to him that, after long resistance, she had given in to Beecher's passionate importunities and had carried on an affair with him for close to eighteen months (Tr. I 396–400). Her confession, and Beecher's alleged admission of the affair to Tilton and others, were evidenced to the jury only through the second-hand recitals of Tilton and his witnesses. Not surprisingly, Beecher denied every word (Tr. II 755, 758–74). Part of Theodore's claim was based on Elizabeth's own words, however. He alleged that reading *Griffith Gaunt* had convinced Elizabeth for the first time to reject Beecher's claim that their adultery was so "pure" that it did not violate her marriage vows (Tr. III 919–20). As proof, Tilton introduced a letter Elizabeth had written to him about a year after her initial confession. This key document merits full quotation:

June 29, 1871

My Dear Theodore: To-day, through the ministry of Catherine Gaunt, a character of fiction, my eyes have been opened, for the first time in my experience, so that I see clearly my sin. It was when I knew that I was loved, to suffer it to grow to a passion. A virtuous woman should check instantly an absorbing love. But it appeared to me in such false light. That the love I felt and received could harm no one, not even you, I have believed unfalteringly until 4 o'clock this afternoon, when the heavenly vision dawned on me. I see now, as never before, the wrong I have done you, and hasten immediately to ask your pardon, with a penitence so sincere that henceforth (if reason remains) you may trust me implicitly. Oh! my dear Theo., though your opinions are not restful or congenial to my soul, yet my own integrity and purity are a sacred and holy thing to me. Bless God, with me, for Catherine Gaunt, and for all the sure leadings of an all-wise and loving Providence. Yes; now I feel quite prepared to renew my marriage vow with you, to keep it as the Savior requireth, who looketh at the eye and the heart. Never before could I say this. I know not that you are yet able, or ever will be, to say this to *me*. Still, with what profound thankfulness that I am come to this sure foundation, and that my feet are planted on the rock of this great truth you cannot at all realize.

When you yearn toward me with any true feeling, be assured of the tried, purified and restored love of ELIZABETH. (Tr. III 741)

Responding to Elizabeth's epistolary assertion that Reade's novel had triggered a profound moral reevaluation of her past life, lawyers for both sides described and interpreted the novel at length to the jury. In a three-link chain of interactive analysis, arguments about the novel's meaning were used to interpret the letter, and the letter as interpreted was then used to fill the crucially empty place where "Elizabeth Tilton" belonged in the parties' litigation narratives. Complex acts of literary interpretation were thus offered to the jury as legitimate components in the juridical process of evidentiary evaluation. The seemingly clear boundary lines between fact and fiction, letter and testimony, literary heroine and "true defendant" were inevitably eroded, and eroded in ways that had very real adverse consequences for the silenced woman who was the trial's most important narrative subject. To understand how this process worked, we need to look more closely at both novel and reader.

Serialized simultaneously in English and American periodicals and published in book form in 1866, *Griffith Gaunt* was a scandalous bestseller on both sides of the Atlantic. It tells of Catherine Peyton, beautiful, rich, and headstrong, whose marriage to the weak-willed but handsome Griffith Gaunt leads from happiness through disaster to an almost parodically domestic resolution. A devout Catholic, Catherine's deepest passions are aroused for the first time in her life by the fiery sermons of her newly arrived priest, Father Leonard, whose words leave her "thrilled, enraptured, melted," and send her home to her husband of seven years all "hot and undiluted" (71). Through long hours of intimate religious conversation and a willingness to deceive themselves about the nature of their mutual attraction, Catherine and her priest fall deeply in love. Griffith, a hard-drinking but good-natured Protestant country squire, is incited from annoyance at his wife's apparently spiritual preoccupation to fits of uncontrollable jealousy by Catherine's maid, Ryder, who is playing a complex game of her own to win Griffith's love. The priest requires "all the self-possession he had been years acquiring not to throw himself at her knees and declare his passion to her," as he spends hours of "strange intoxication" confessing "his idol, directing and advising his idol, and all in the soft murmurs of a lover" (101). When, "literally unable to contain his bursting heart any longer, he uttered a cry of jealous agony and then, in a torrent of burning, melting words, appealed to her pity," Kate is "in a whirl" (102). She asks him to leave, but when he procrastinates she meets him in the woods with money to help his journey. Griffith, who has seen but misunderstood, bursts in, convinced that the worst has occurred. In a jealous rage, "he literally trample[s] the poor priest with both feet" and rides off (109).

After returning briefly, Griffith again disappears, just after his voice is heard shouting for help. When his unexplained absence is linked to the discovery of an unidentifiable body, Kate is tried for her husband's murder. Deprived of defense counsel by the setting of the novel in the mid eighteenth century, she defends herself, brilliantly.[6] Eloquent and intelligent, she cross-examines the witnesses against her, destroys the credibility of the malevolent Ryder by revealing the purportedly single maid to be both married and a mother, and ultimately obtains her acquittal, clears her name, and achieves a reunion with her husband. Griffith, meanwhile, has bigamously married Mercy Vint, an innkeeper's daughter who nursed him through a long illness. While he cowers drunkenly during the trial, Mercy bravely seeks out Kate, becoming her closest ally and most able defender. "[C]omprehending at last that to have been both of them wronged by one man was a bond of sympathy, not hate, the two wives of Griffith Gaunt laid his child [by Mercy] across their two laps and wept over him together" (197). Mercy testifies that Griffith is alive, thus winning Kate's acquittal. After the trial, Kate arranges Mercy's marriage to a former suitor of her own, and, minimally subdued by adversity (and by a childbed transfusion which sends "some of Griffith Gaunt's bright red blood smoking hot" into her veins [209]), lives in peace with her now permanently submissive husband.

At first glance, Elizabeth Tilton seems a good candidate for status as a sensational heroine herself. Sensational best-sellers were often based on scandalous trials, and this one not only placed her at the center of a bitter rivalry between two well-known men, but revealed precisely the kind of secretly immoral passion beneath a surface of familiar respectability that has been called the very heart of the genre.[7] But whereas sensationalist heroines like Kate Gaunt tend toward a convention-defying assertiveness, Elizabeth Tilton seems to have been the essence of pliability itself. In one twenty-four-hour period, she wrote a "confession" of adultery which her husband showed to Beecher, a "revocation" of those accusations when Beecher visited her where she lay in bed recovering from a miscarriage, and a "retraction" of the revocation when her husband came home and found out about the letter she had given Beecher (Waller 125–26, Shaplen 86–98). Her correspondence, read at length at the trial, records a constant struggle to assume the shapes required both by her husband and by the mid-Victorian cult of sentimental Christian domesticity: to be pure, spiritual, submissive. A great reader of fiction and a much-appreciated listener, Elizabeth developed an intimacy with Beecher as he read to her from drafts of his own best-selling novel, Norwood (Tr. I 455, II 742).

Elizabeth Tilton thus approached the burning passions and bigamous illegitimacies of Griffith Gaunt with a set of skills and expectations developed through her participation in mid-Victorian sentimental and religious culture. Significantly, the most striking aspect of her "Catherine Gaunt" letter is its spirituality, a response that presumes an overpoweringly moral stimulus. Had Reade's novel disappeared, we might reconstruct it on the basis of this letter as a work of sentimental Christianity in the genre of Maria Cummins's The Lamplighter or Susan Warner's The Wide, Wide World, never suspecting that an influential review in the New York Round Table could have condemned it as "an indecent publication" so "immoral," "so compact with crime, so replete with insidious allusions" that it was what "no modest woman can read without a blush, and what no man should think of placing before his wife or sister or daughter, whose perusal modesty cannot survive untainted"("An Indecent Publication," 3). Asked by Wilkie Collins to testify in Reade's libel suit against the London Review, which had reprinted the Round Table article, Charles Dickens admitted that while he admired the work greatly, he would not have published it in his own magazine because many incidents "might be impurely suggestive to inferior minds (of which there must necessarily be many among a large mass of readers)."[8] Wayne Burns, Reade's modern biographer, goes even further, declaring that "[t]he passages in question are not 'impurely suggestive to inferior minds,' they are purely (or merely) 'suggestive' (or pornographic) to all perceptive minds" (262). Reade's righteous indignation against those who dared to suggest that his novel made sin attractive was vented in an open letter to the American press in which he railed against those "prurient prudes" who "take my text and read it, not by its own light, but by the light of their own foul imaginations; and having so defiled it by mixing their own filthy minds with it, they sit in judgment on the compound" (Reade 1883, 316).[9] Yet Burns, expressing an opinion typical of those few modern critics who have considered *Griffith Gaunt*, confidently asserts that "despite his published denials" Reade "most certainly . . . intended Kate's experiences and feelings to be titillating" (240).[10]

In short, modern and Victorian critics identify the novel's steaminess as its most salient characteristic. And while they may disagree heartily about the advisability of encouraging female readers toward a more assertive sexuality, both sets of critics agree that, like other sensational bestsellers, *Griffith Gaunt* did just that. But if many readers found the work more salacious than seemly, Elizabeth Tilton was not among them. Her letter suggests that, for one reader at least, the novel's signifying center was precisely its capacity not just to render but to judge sexuality. The moral framework that Winifred Hughes dismisses as an example of "the cautious hedging and . . . inevitable disavowal of his meaning" that colored all of Reade's novels, one of the "variety of ingenious solutions to the problem of Victorian censorship" employed by sensation novelists was, for Elizabeth Tilton, the novel's heart (103, 30). And, where Hughes, Garrison, and Showalter all see novels like Reade's as triggering "a demand for greater individual autonomy" which would include "a liberalization of controls over sexual and familial norms" (Garrison 158), Elizabeth's letter declares that reading *Griffith Gaunt* led her to an acute consciousness of sin and a highly respectable resolution to "renew my marriage vow with you and to keep it as the Savior requireth."

For Elizabeth Tilton, Reade's novel fulfilled a function we associate with explicitly religious works, and prototypically with the Bible: it provided a redemptive morality to be applied to her own behavior, and a set of spiritual goals toward which to strive. Her descriptive vocabulary is wholly religious; she refers to Catherine Gaunt as performing a "ministry," and to herself as having experienced a "heavenly vision," which is one of "the sure leadings of an all-wise and loving Providence." Religious inducement to submit to the secular authorities that controlled a woman's life has persuasively been identified as the central goal of sentimental fiction by such recent critics as Jane Tompkins, who argues that "learning to renounce her own desire is the sentimental heroine's vocation," a "vocation" which is understood to mean "the achievement of Christian salvation" (176). Indeed, perhaps the most striking difference between sentimental and sensationalist fiction is that, while the dominating heroines of the latter genre frequently triumph over law, convention, and the weak men in their lives, sentimental heroines remain, as Cathy Davidson has observed, powerless, dominated, and exploited by men (Garrison 145, Davidson 117).[11] Such heroines find empowerment, not through acts of worldly mastery like Catherine Gaunt's courtroom performance, but through such self-willed conquest of their own unruly impulses as Susan Warner's Ellen Montgomery achieves in *The Wide, Wide World,* guided and supported by the moral authority of Christian teachings.

That Elizabeth Tilton could achieve a successfully sentimental and religious reading of a scandalously sensationalist text like *Griffith Gaunt* suggests that reader–text interactions may be a great deal less predictable than genre critics would have us believe.[12] Reade himself seems to have understood this; in accusing his readers of "mixing" their minds and imaginations with his novel to produce a "compound," he implicitly recognizes the reading process as an interactive negotiation in which reader and text interpret each other.

This process of mutual interpretation is the key to Elizabeth Tilton's "heavenly vision." Reading *Griffith Gaunt,* she seems to have experienced both a conflation of herself with Catherine, a collapse of distance between the real and the fictional, and, simultaneously, the opening of a space or vantage point from which her own experience became recognizable as a parallel, perhaps interchangeable narrative version of Catherine's life. By absorbing Catherine's assertiveness and virtuous integrity, by permitting their "ministry" to work, Elizabeth suggests that she may find a way to become the triumphant heroine of the story of her own life. The possibility of such a transformation recognizes not only that both women's lives are "stories," but that they are equally open to the process of interpretation, to new readings that reformulate the moral valence of events. So the "story" of Elizabeth Tilton's relationship to Henry Ward Beecher is recast in the transformative text of her letter from a spiritually pure romance to a parable of sin and false understanding, and the sexual activity at its center comes to signify, not the pure consummation of love but its sinful betrayal. At the same time, however, Elizabeth herself becomes a newly purified and spiritually superior heroine who is (at least for the moment) in control of her own story. Reading thus empowers her because it engenders narratives of interpretation that clarify the ambiguous set of experiences described by the text, infusing them with meaning. For Elizabeth Tilton, reading *Griffith Gaunt* produced an awareness of not one but two life stories, interrelated and mutually informing. That awareness helped her make sense of both of her own illicit passion and Catherine Gaunt's. If she used her knowledge and experience to interpret the text, she also entered into a negotiation with it that stimulated a reinterpretation of her own life.

The semiotic slippage reflected in Elizabeth's letter, its circulation of signification between heroine and reader, fictional and factual life story, was of course exactly what made it useful for Beecher's and Tilton's attorneys at the trial. Elizabeth's absence from the testimonial stage had produced a narrative gap, which the letter's confessional tone seemed at first glance to fill. On closer inspection however, the letter's text was clearly ambiguous, admitting only the "sin" of loving and being loved, while never mentioning sex at all.[13] In their search for a narrative of events about Elizabeth Tilton's life that would not dissolve into ambiguity, absence, and gap whenever pressure was applied, Beecher's attorneys turned quite naturally and unironically to fiction, to the novel that Elizabeth had identified as stimulating a "heavenly vision" of her own sin and redemption.

William Maxwell Evarts, Beecher's lead counsel, treated *Griffith Gaunt* as a black-letter narrative of the relations between Elizabeth, her husband, and Beecher. For him, the correspondence between fictional heroine and actual woman was absolute: Elizabeth was sexually faithful to her husband because Catherine Gaunt did not commit adultery with her priest. Indeed, argued Evarts, the novel, the letter, and the reader's life all can have "but one meaning, and it is an absolute refutation of all pretenses of carnal intercourse or bodily impurity of any kind on the part of this woman" (Tr. III 741). In one sense, the forensic conflation of woman and reader is appallingly appropriate: "Elizabeth Tilton" was already a wholly fictional character, "present" at the Beecher–Tilton trial only through the testimony and arguments of others. To interpret one fictional character in terms of another seems almost reasonable, and, while Elizabeth's letter stops short of claiming to have lived every event of Catherine's life, it does invite an equation of fictional heroine with responding reader. Evarts's argument thus recast the interactive negotiation between Elizabeth Tilton and Catherine Gaunt as an unambiguous, essentially static correlation between Elizabeth's entire life and the novel's entire plot. "You see now," he assured the jury, "as in a mirror, the heart of this woman, the life of this woman . . ." (Tr. III 743). Evarts's interpretive narrative of the novel thus became a typological instrument deployed to interpret the ambiguous text of her letter, which was then used to produce what he had been after all along, an unambiguous narrative of the letter-writer's life. In his hands, all three "Elizabeths" became freely interchangeable objects, verbal signifiers unconnected to any speaking subject and therefore able to be substituted for each other at will. Elizabeth's admissible written statements were ambiguous and inconsistent, and her exclusion from the trial's litigative discourse reduced her to a manipulable verbal construct. In contrast, the novel's seemingly straightforward narrative offered a relationship that, however intense, unambiguously evaded sexual consummation.

Evarts was an adversarial advocate for his client. He used Reade's novel to rid Elizabeth Tilton of all "bodily impurity" because his task of persuading the jury that Beecher had not committed adultery necessitated exculpating her from the charge as well. But if he acquitted her of adultery, Evarts based Beecher's defense on the wholesale sacrifice of Elizabeth Tilton's honor, and here his interpretation of *Griffith Gaunt* was of particular assistance. Not only did Beecher's attorneys deny that he had seduced Elizabeth, they suggested that whatever improprieties did occur were caused by her overwhelming passion for him, a passion he had neither encouraged nor reciprocated. To prove Beecher's innocence from Reade's novel, Evarts did not hestitate to make unequivocal, though unsupportable assertions about its content. His argument rewrote the novel's story to conform more closely with the exculpatory narrative of "real-life" events that constituted Beecher's defense, a narrative that was, in all historical likelihood, also a fiction. Evarts erased Reade's explicit revelation of Father Leonard's sexual passion for his "idol" Kate, describing the "entangled affections" at issue as having been solely hers, and he ignored what Burns has called Reade's "frantic efforts to maintain Kate's innocence and purity . . . by shifting the burden of moral responsibility wholly onto Leonard" (256). In Evarts's version of the text, the only sexuality that exists is Catherine Gaunt's. This instrumental distortion of Reade's *fictional* text was thus preferred to the jury as substantive evidence from which an exculpatory inference about Beecher's *actual* behavior could legitimately be drawn.

In his effort to eliminate all traces of ambiguity and impropriety from the book, Evarts naturally omitted the transatlantic scandal that had surrounded its publication, assuring the jury that *Griffith Gaunt* "is and *is known to everyone to be*, an exposition of how there may come to be unsuitable disturbances of domestic peace, unsuitable exaggerations of grounds of religious discord between husband and wife, by the entirely innocent, the entirely pure, and religious relation between a clergyman and a penitent or a devotee" (Tr. III 741, emphasis added). Accusing Tilton's attorneys of not being able to "tell a story about a crime or an iniquity, without missing the whole point of its guilt or its wickedness," Evarts declared that Beecher's only sin was to have "heedlessly and blindly allowed an intimacy that began and proceeded on the footing of pastor and parishioner to come to a point where it led to the wrong that is portrayed in this 'Griffith Gaunt,'" a wrong wholly attributable to "the wife's affections" and in which the minister can "thank God I have not fallen except by errors of a course of respectful attention and affection, and not under any pursuit of carnal sin or under the impulse of any carnal passion" (Tr. III 746–47).

Evarts's reading of *Griffith Gaunt*, like Elizabeth Tilton's, exploits the essential openness of both fictional and factual life stories. Both readings were produced with redemptive aims, but where Evarts sought the legal exoneration of his client, Elizabeth recorded her private search for moral salvation. Elizabeth's letter was not written as evidence, of course, nor as an item of gossip for a nation of newspaper readers, though it eventually became both. Rather, it was part of the intimate marital correspondence in which she struggled to win her husband's love and her own self-definition. If her letter seems to blur the distinction between a real and a fictionally identified self, we should remember that the circulation of identity between heroine and reader forms part of a wholly private, self-referential experience.

Evarts's forensic deployment of the novel is more disquieting, because it suggests that in the narrativizing process by which the events giving rise to a lawsuit are transformed into testimonial and argumentative narratives for the jury, fact and fiction can be not just easily but appropriately interchanged. This is a disturbing thought indeed, even to those who, like most of us, assume that courtroom rhetoric generally includes a certain amount of exaggeration and "fictionalizing." Evarts's argument dissolves the boundaries between literary text and historical events, and it rewrites both fictional and factual narratives. This suggests that, for him, the verbal surface of evidence and argument through which trials are conducted is itself always and only a fictional text, wholly severed from the "real world" and accountable only to its instrumental goal of winning the case.[14]

But perhaps the ultimate irony in Elizabeth Tilton's relationship to Catherine Gaunt is that while both women's life stories climax in dramatic trials in which they are implicitly or explicitly accused of serious, reputation-destroying crimes, Catherine is empowered in precisely the ways that Elizabeth is silenced. Where Elizabeth sits mute among the courtroom spectators, Catherine is both party defendant (and therefore direct and explicit subject of the litigation) and lawyer (and therefore able to examine witnesses and argue to the jury). While Catherine's lack of in-court defense counsel initially intensifies her "feminine" helplessness, it soon becomes the direct means to her unmediated victory. Authorized by the legal system to speak *for herself*, she becomes author and interpreter as well as subject of the "story" of the events leading up to the trial and the trial itself. When witnesses testify that she received a peddler in her bedroom on the night of the supposed murder, she forces them to admit that the interview took place in an anteroom outside her boudoir which in turn was outside her bedroom, eliminating any impropriety. When the dead body is identified as Griffith's by means of a mole on its forehead, she demonstrates that an identical mole was known to be on the forehead of the peddler, Griffith's illegitimate half-brother, who has also disappeared. In each instance, Catherine destroys the credibility of the inculpatory narratives introduced against her. Unlike Elizabeth Tilton, she is legally authorized to contradict, to oppose false narratives with true ones, or, more precisely, to counter condemnatory stories with exculpatory ones in which she casts herself as a virtuous, wise, and womanly heroine. Then, in a lengthy and eloquent summation, she presents a new, whole, credible story which exonerates herself and reduces the opposition's narratives to fragmentary falsehoods.

Catherine's summation mentions neither Father Leonard nor any explanation of Griffith's volcanic jealousy. But these gaps in what a reader might call "the whole truth" provide important evidence of her self-creation as an author: authorial power creates truth by creating persuasive narratives. As William Maxwell Evarts did in discussing the text that created her, but acting on her own behalf, Kate Gaunt understands how to exploit the power of interpretive storytelling. For her, the relation of voice to personhood to power is absolute. In the shift from discursive object to authoring subject, a transition constituted through the receipt of *legal* authority to speak in court, she gains control not only over the story of her past, but, at least as important, over the unfolding story of the rest of her life.

Catherine's reversal of the "traditional" exclusion of women from power-creating legal discourse is enhanced by her bond with Griffith's second wife, Mercy Vint. Mercy too has her moment of adversarial triumph in court, coolly facing down the prosecutor, and it is her evidence that wins Catherine's acquittal. Kate and Mercy represent a striking inversion of Eve Sedgwick's paradigm of homosocial interaction: their heroic intimacy—created through their having shared a male sexual object both have desired though neither much respects—enables them together to prevail over the masculine legal and social order. Indeed, Catherine's finest moment comes in attacking the prosecutor who has been aspersing Mercy: "For shame! This is one of those rare women that adorn our whole sex, and embellish human nature; and, so long as you have the privilege of exchanging words with her, I shall stand here on the watch, to see that you treat her with due reverence: ay, sir, with reverence; for I have measured you both, and she is as much your superior as she is mine" (202).

In sharp contrast to the way that Kate Gaunt's authoritative voice marks her self-creating narrative control, the suppression of Elizabeth Tilton's legal voice indicates her complete exclusion. Powerless to contradict or to explain the accusations against her, she could only listen mutely while Beecher, having seduced her with the lure of a pure and spiritual love, unhesitatingly grounded his defense on insinuations that she was both over-sexed and mentally unbalanced. The jury's inability to agree did not prevent the media from pronouncing its verdict. In a pamphlet titled "The Beecher Trial: A Review of the Evidence," The *New York Times* concluded that Beecher, though guilty, might be dismissed with a mild reprimand, while "as for the woman who has been the immediate cause of these darkened homes and blighted reputations, she may be dismissed to the general contempt of mankind. A city full of such women would not be worth the trouble and misery which this one has occasioned" (34).

If this seems a rather extreme example of blaming the victim, it should remind us that the project of suppressing Elizabeth Tilton's voice began long before the litigation was initiated and far from the Brooklyn courtroom in which it was played out. While it was the legal order that excluded her testimony from the trial, a decision permitting her to speak would not have been likely to produce any truly authentic self-expression. Elizabeth Tilton's correspondence and her out-of-court statements are a stunning record of inconsistency, registering throughout an urgent desire to be and to say what the men in her life wanted to have and to hear. Indeed, her various confessions and retractions must ultimately be read as the ventriloquized statements of whichever men happened to be dictating at the time. Beecher and Tilton recognized this, and each eagerly accused the other of dictating Elizabeth's written words while defending as spontaneous and sincere any statements that supported his own position. These two forms of silencing are of course connected. A legal cause of action that structurally refuses to recognize women as speaking subjects is but a particularly dramatic instance of a more generalized devaluation of women's voices within the surrounding culture. Criminal conversation litigation, like Victorian culture in general, anxiously attempted to control the circumstances under which women could speak and, directly or indirectly, the content of their speech.[15]

Elizabeth Tilton's attempt to intervene in the Beecher–Tilton trial can also be read as a gesture toward Kate Gaunt, in which she "became" Kate by trying to reenact Kate's victory-winning forensic self-assertion. The statement Elizabeth Tilton was prevented from reading in court was printed in the published transcript of the trial. In it she declared "solemnly before you, without fear of man and by faith in God, that I am innocent of the crimes charged against me. I would like to tell my *whole* sad story *truthfully*—to acknowledge the frequent falsehoods wrung from me by compulsion—though at the same time unwilling to reveal the secrets of my married life, which only the vital importance of my position makes necessary" (Tr. III 355, emphasis in original). Three years later, in 1878, Elizabeth Tilton reversed herself yet again, publishing an unequivocal admission of the affair (Shaplen 266; Waller 145). By then however, few were interested. Separated from her husband and publicly vilified, Elizabeth Tilton was, in Victorian terms, "ruined"; she lived out the remainder of her life in lonely isolation.

But before we consign her to silence and submission, or reduce her to a merely pitiable victim, let us return briefly to Elizabeth Tilton's letter. It is not, entirely, a register of unremitting submission. Along with her admissions of sin and petitions for pardon, Elizabeth included the uncharacteristically independent comment that Theodore's "opinions are not restful or congenial to my soul." And, after asserting her own readiness to renew her marriage vows, she rather haughtily challenges her husband's promises of future chastity by observing: "I know not that you are yet able, or ever will be, to say this to *me*." Finally, her assurance of unending devotion is apparently to become available only "when you yearn towards me with any true feeling." Surely some of Catherine Gaunt's proud sense of superiority to her weak-willed and adulterous husband has crept into Elizabeth Tilton's verbal self-representation. And, while these glimmers of self-assertion may be examples only of her imitative receptivity to the nearest strong personality, the "ministry" of a character of fiction may also be more salutary than the oppressive dictation of a self-interested husband or lover. Reading *Griffith Gaunt* she became, at least for a time, a headstrong, articulate, judgmental heroine. If Elizabeth Tilton could not receive a permanent infusion of Kate Gaunt's assertive personality by reading, as Kate receives a permanently effective transfusion of her husband's submissive blood, still, she could keep reading even in the isolation of her posttrial life, and, one hopes, she did.

As a final point, I want to acknowledge that this article may be read as merely the latest in a long line of textualizations of Elizabeth Tilton. The real woman who lived through these events is, of course, as elusive and unknowable as ever. Once again, she has been subjected to analysis, her intimate relationships made the stuff of public discourse, the ambiguities of her life (or more accurately, of the texts that "evidence" her life) used to produce conclusions that she could neither influence nor control. Yet, if Elizabeth Tilton's posthumous reputation can thus be actively reformulated, a twentieth-century revival of interest in the Beecher–Tilton case can no longer affect a living woman's life, feelings, or thoughts. This essay has tried to affirm Elizabeth Tilton's devalued voice. While investigations like this one are clearly necessary to the work of feminist historians and cultural critics, it is also important to recognize that they cannot be carried out without, to some extent, "fictionalizing" their subjects.

## Notes

1. Sicherman 214 and Showalter 115. The same point is made, in varying ways, by Garrison, Pykett, Tillotson, and Hughes.

2. Trial transcripts were printed daily in New York newspapers, and the entire transcript appeared in two three-volume editions shortly after the trial. All transcript references are from the McDivitt edition and are indicated parenthetically in the text by transcript volume and page number.

3. Critical accounts of the Beecher–Tilton scandal include Altina Waller's *Reverend Beecher and Mrs. Tilton* and Robert Shaplen's *Free Love and Heavenly Sinners*, as well as useful studies by Rugoff (192–212), Clark (197–232) and Fox (103–32).

4. For discussions of criminal conversation, see Stone 231–300, Staves, and Weinstein. In using the term "homosocial," I intend to invoke Eve Sedgwick's triangulation model, in which two men attain intimacy through their complex sharing of a woman who, as the object of their exchange, is denied subjectivity.

5. The wife is doubly excluded from criminal conversation. First, because the action is a civil suit for damages by the injured party (husband) against the injurer (lover), the wife is neither plaintiff nor defendant. Second, the long-standing ban on spouses testifying for or against each other in any kind of litigation, based on the public interest in preserving domestic peace and marital unity, disqualified the wife as a witness. See Best 154–56.

6. In felony cases in the mid eighteenth century in England, the prosecution was permitted to have counsel while the defense was not. There was no privilege against self-incrimination. The accused might consult with a lawyer outside the courtroom, as Catherine Gaunt did, but the in-court examination of witnesses and address to the jury were performed by the defendant on his or her own behalf (Langbein 307–14). This rule was gradually relaxed beginning with isolated cases in the 1740s and 1750s, but it was not until the Prisoners Counsel Act of 1836 that felony defendants were at last given the right "to make full answer and defense thereto by counsel learned in the law" (Baker 418).

7. See Hughes 7–8. Hughes and Burns note that Reade kept enormous notebooks of newspaper clippings of criminal trials and other scandals to use as the basis for plots (Hughes 74–75, Burns 182–99). The Beecher–Tilton trial featured not only the probable adultery of a national symbol of morality and family values, but also allegations of Tilton's adulteries, and of domestic abuse, apostasy, and blackmail. *Frank Leslie's Illustrated Newspaper* declared: "we are reading the most marvelous of human dramas, greater in plot, development and effect than Hawthorne's 'The Scarlet Letter,' Charles Reade's 'Griffith Gaunt,' George Eliot's 'Romola,' or Shakespeare's 'Othello.' It has its only counterpart in 'Faust.'"

8. Letter from Dickens to Collins, 20 February, 1867 (Paroissien, ed. 358–59).

9. Reade, who delighted in litigation, sued both the *Round Table* and the *London Review*. The novel was read to the jury in the *Round Table* suit by a well-known elocutionist (Mott 92). Reade had the unsatisfactory pleasure of winning the case but

obtaining a verdict for only six cents in damages, though the trial publicity caused the novel to sell "like hot cakes" (Mott 92).

10. Modern reviewers include Burns, Elwin, and Hughes.

11. My characterization of sensational heroines is not meant to deny that they are also frequently evil, amoral, or insane, or, like the heroine of M.E. Braddon's *Lady Audley's Secret*, all three at once. Their triumphs are often short-lived. Nevertheless, it is fair to say that the heroines of the sensationalist novels of the 1860s, taken as a group, are more assertive, unconventional, sexual, and dominant than their sentimental sisters in the novels of Warner, Cummins, and Stowe.

12. If she was an atypical reader, Elizabeth Tilton's sexual sophistication may have been as much the cause as her sentimental religiosity. Where most readers probably found Catherine Gaunt's erotic temptation quite outside their experience, Elizabeth well knew the dizzying combination of spiritual and sexual that characterized Catherine's not-quite-criminal conversations with her priest. Henry Ward Beecher's famous "Gospel of Love," which stressed the spiritual affinity of like-minded souls, had prepared the way for him to express more earthly desires. For Elizabeth, *Griffith Gaunt*'s center of impact was not its vivid rendering of female sexuality, something she would have found more familiar than shocking, but its explicitly moral grappling with the consequences of sexual attraction, a problem that was, for her, both current and overwhelming.

13. My analysis of the letter has of course assumed what the letter never asserts: that the "sin" referred to is the sin of adultery. While that assumption seems to me justified by my own study of the transcripts and related historical materials, we should not forget that it was the central fact at issue in the case. I believe, and write on the assumption that Elizabeth Tilton did in fact have a sexual affair with Beecher. The adultery was never proved in court, nor did Beecher admit it. Biographers and historians are split. While my arguments about reading would still be valid in the absence of an affair, I do not take the position that whether or not the relationship was consummated is irrelevant.

14. One might expect that Evarts's forays into fiction would be effectively countered by his opponent, Theodore Tilton. In most litigation, the trial's adversarial structure ensures that a party who strays too far from the facts does so at his peril. With Elizabeth excluded from the legal arena, only her husband could provide an equalizing counter-pressure. But Tilton's legal interests were at odds with his wife's: winning his case required him to prove her an adulteress. Tilton's chief counsel, William Beach, insisted that no woman writes a letter like Elizabeth's "without a consciousness that there has been a grievous fault" (Tr. III 919). In dealing with the novel, Beach attempted to avoid the "problem" of Catherine's sexual guiltlessness by rejecting flat-footed parallelisms of reader and text, arguing that "it was not necessary, for the purpose of awakening any such reflection . . . that the particular crime or sin of which she had been guilty was portrayed in this work" (Tr. III 919). Rather, it is "the slight and inconsiderable circumstances," "a single sentence casually read" that will touch the reader's conscience, producing a profound change of heart and character.

15. If Elizabeth Tilton's smothered selfhood can be read as typically Victorian, we should also note that both she and her husband were involved in the Women's Suffrage Movement (Theodore was president of the Union Suffrage Association), and that both were friends of such strong and reformist women as Susan B. Anthony and Laura Curtis Bullard. The proximity of Elizabeth to women like Anthony and Bullard is one more piece of evidence that the unique convergence of each person's circumstances, rather than cultural generalities, determine her character and behavior.

WORKS CITED

Baker, J.H. *An Introduction to English Legal History*. 2d ed. London: Butterworths, 1979.

*The Beecher Trial: A Review of the Evidence*. Reprinted with additions from the *New York Times*, July 3, 1875. New York: 1875.

Best, William Bowdesley. *Principles of the Law of Evidence*. Albany: 1875.

Burns, Wayne. *Charles Reade: A Study in Victorian Authorship*. New York: Bookman Assoc., 1961.

Clark, Clifford. *Henry Ward Beecher: Spokesman for Middle-Class America*. Illinois: U of Illinois P, 1978.

Davidson, Cathy N. *Revolution and the Word: The Rise of the Novel in America*. New York: Oxford UP, 1986.

Dickens, Charles. *Selected Letters of Charles Dickens*. Edited by David Paroissien. London: Macmillan, 1985.

Elwin, Malcom. *Charles Reade: A Biography*. London: Jonathan Cape, 1931.

Fox, Richard Wightman. "Looking for and Looking at the Beecher–Tilton Affair." *The Power of Culture: Critical Essays in American History*. Edited by R.W. Fox. Chicago: U of Chicago P, 1993. 103–32.

Garrison, Dee. "Immoral Fiction in the Late Victorian Library." *Victorian America*. Edited by Daniel Walker Howe. Philadelphia: U of Penn P, 1976. 141–59.

Hughes, Winifred. *The Maniac in the Cellar: Sensation Novels of the 1860's*. Princeton: Princeton UP, 1980.

"An Indecent Publication." Unsigned. *The Round Table* July 28, 1866.

Langbein, John H. "The Criminal Trial before the Lawyers." *University of Chicago Law Review* 45 (1978): 263–316.

McLoughlin, William G. *The Meaning of Henry Ward Beecher: An Essay in the Shifting Values of Mid-Victorian America*. New York: Alfred A. Knopf, 1970.

Mott, Frank Luther. *Golden Multitudes: The Story of Best Sellers in the United States*. New York: Macmillan, 1947.

Pykett, Lyn. *The "Improper" Feminine: The Women's Sensation Novel and the New Woman Writing*. London and New York: Routledge, 1992.

Reade, Charles. *Griffith Gaunt; or Jealousy*. Boston: Ticknor and Fields, 1866.

———. *Readiana: Comments on Current Events*. London: Chatto and Windus, 1883.

Rugoff, Milton. *America's Gilded Age: Intimate Portraits from an Era of Extravagance and Change 1850–1890*. New York: Henry Holt, 1989.

Sedgwick, Eve Kosofsky. *Between Men: English Literature and Male Homosocial Desire*. New York: Columbia UP, 1985.

Shaplen, Robert. *Free Love and Heavenly Sinners*. New York: Alfred A. Knopf, 1954.

Showalter, Elaine. "Family Secrets and Domestic Subversion: Rebellion in the Novels of the 1860s." *The Victorian Family: Structure and Stresses*. Edited by Anthony S. Wohl. London: Croom Helm, 1978. 101–16.

Sicherman, Barbara. "Sense and Sensibility: A Case Study of Women's Reading in Late-Victorian America." *Reading in America: Literature and Social History*. Edited by Cathy N. Davidson. Baltimore: Johns Hopkins UP, 1989. 201–25.

Staves, Susan. "Money for Honor: Damages for Criminal Conversation." *Studies in Eighteenth Century Culture* 11 (1982): 279–97.

Stone, Lawrence. *Road to Divorce: England 1530–1987*. Oxford: Oxford UP, 1990.

Tillotson, Kathleen. "The Lighter Reading of the Eighteen-Sixties." Introduction to Wilkie Collins, *The Woman in White*. Boston: Houghton Mifflin, 1969. i–xxviii

*Tilton versus Beecher, Action for Crim. Con.* 3 vols. New York: McDivitt, 1875.

Tompkins, Jane. *Sensational Designs: The Cultural Work of American Fiction, 1790–1860*. Oxford: Oxford UP, 1985.

Waller, Altina. *Reverend Beecher and Mrs. Tilton: Sex and Class in Victorian America*. Amherst: U Mass. P, 1982.

Weinstein, Jeremy D. "Adultery, Law and the State: A History." *Hastings Law Journal* 38 (1986): 195–238.

Wendt, Lloyd. *Chicago Tribune: The Rise of a Great American Newspaper*. Chicago: Rand McNally, 1979.

SELECTED SECONDARY SOURCES

Winifred Hughes, "Charles Reade and the Breakdown of Melodrama," in *The Maniac in the Cellar* (Princeton: Princeton UP, 1980); Elton Edward Smith, *Charles Reade* (Boston: Twayne, 1976); Arthur Pollard, "Griffith Gaunt: Paradox of Victorian Melodrama," *Critical Quarterly* 17 (1975); Wayne Burns, *Charles Reade: A Study in Victorian Authorship* (New York: Bookman, 1961); Malcom Elwin, *Charles Reade: A Biography* (London: J. Cape, 1931); Walter Clarke Phillips, *Dickens, Reade and Collins* (New York: Columbia UP, 1919).

# Mrs. Oliphant, *Miss Marjoribanks* (1866), and the Victorian Canon

*Joseph H. O'Mealy*

Margaret Oliphant Wilson Oliphant (1828–1897) was an astonishingly pro-lific writer. She wrote ninety-two novels, more than two dozen biographies and histories, and scores of essays. For more than thirty years she was an important contributor to *Blackwood's,* publishing not only much of her early fiction in its pages, but also virtually all of her voluminous literary criticism. Popular in her day (she is reputed to have been Queen Victoria's favorite novelist), she achieved her greatest success with *The Chronicles of Carlingford* ("The Rector" 1861; "The Doctor's Family" 1861–1862; *Salem Chapel* 1862–1863; *The Perpetual Curate* 1863–1864; *Miss Marjoribanks* 1865–1866; *Phoebe Junior* 1876). Set in a quiet town not far from London, the Carlingford series examined with wit and sympathy the lives of the professional, religious, and trading classes during the mid-Victorian years. Sometimes seen as a Dissenter's version of Trollope's Barset, the Carlingford stories were early mistaken for the work of George Eliot, an iden-tification neither woman liked. Among Oliphant's notable later works are the novels *Hester* (1883), *The Ladies Lindores* (1883), and *Kirsteen* (1890); her supernatural tales *Stories of the Seen and Unseen,* including the celebrated "A Beleaguered City" (1885); her history of the Blackwood firm *Annals of a Pub-lishing House* (1897); and her posthumous *Autobiography* (1899). After a brief revival in the 1980s, when many of her best novels were reprinted by Virago, nearly all of Mrs. Oliphant's novels are once again out of print. The sole ex-ceptions are two editions of the first two stories in the *Carlingford* series— "The Rector" and "The Doctor's Family" (World's Classics and Viking Pen-guin)—and four editions of her supernatural tales (the most reasonably priced being the World's Classics' *A Beleaguered City and Other Stories).* Several of her nonfiction works are in print, including her history of the Blackwoods' publishing house, her *Autobiography,* and her *Literary History of England in the End of the Eighteenth Century and the Beginning of the Nineteenth.*

John Sutherland's magisterial *Companion to Victorian Fiction* (which synopsizes 554 novels and gives brief notes on 878 novelists) warns against accepting the "Lilliputian dimensions" of our current sense of the Victorian novel.[1] It is a monument to his belief that the dozen or so novelists who regularly dominate bibliographies of Victorian fiction need some fresh companions, lest late-twentieth-century readers never learn "what the Victorian novel actually meant to the Victorians" (Sutherland 1). Since Sutherland does not put forth any particular candidate for an expanded canon, the task of partisan promotion falls to others. In the spirit of what I hope is enlightened partisanship, I would like to advance the claims of Mrs. Margaret Oliphant, who as the so-called Queen of Popular Fiction (Terry Ch. 4), has as great a historical claim as any to reconsideration, revaluation, and, I would argue, ultimate recovery as an important Victorian novelist.

Consider her curious case. During Margaret Oliphant's life one critic called her "the most remarkable woman of her time" (Skelton 80); at her death William Blackwood the publisher wrote, "Mrs. Oliphant has been to the England of letters what the Queen has been to society as a whole. She, too, was crowned with age and honour in her own empire" (Terry 68). But today, when many women's literary reputations are being recovered and their works are finding a place in either the traditional canon or an all-female counter-canon, this prolific and once-admired Victorian novelist is still largely overlooked. Lillian Robinson's question "Is the canon . . . to be regarded as the compendium of excellence or the record of cultural history?" (112), instead of laying out the possible strategies for Oliphant's achievement of canonical status, points out the precise nature of the dilemma. In either direction Oliphant's progress to canonical status is thwarted since she pleases neither the old guardians of the canon nor the new revisionists. To some traditionalists, the quality of Oliphant's work is questionable; to some feminists her political conservatism is an insuperable barrier. However, a close look at *Miss Marjoribanks* (1866)—arguably her best novel—reveals qualities that should please both camps. Its ambivalent ironies, beautifully controlled and surprisingly directed, demonstrate a high degree of literary sophistication, while its subtly crafted feminism points out Oliphant's sympathetic understanding of the limitations placed on the talented Victorian woman. In recovering the best of Oliphant it is possible to recover not only a fine and satisfying novel but also, more importantly, a truer sense of the immense range of high-quality Victorian fiction.

As the author of ninety-two novels, scores of essays, and over two dozen nonfiction works, Oliphant could once lay claim to a degree of productivity unrivaled by any serious contemporary. She could also measure her success in the distinction of being Queen Victoria's favorite novelist (Colby xiii, Sutherland 477), as well as in the large audiences many of her books attracted: "Just think of the millions she has made happy" (Skelton 76). Yet, even during her lifetime, Oliphant's future oblivion seemed inevitable. This same critic, John Skelton, introduced a caveat about Oliphant's abilities that has hung over her reputation ever since—she wrote too much, too fast. Comparing her output of two or three novels a year to Charlotte Brontë's and George Eliot's more modest production levels, Skelton admitted their greater "imaginative force," and asked, "Had Mrs. Oliphant concentrated her powers, what might she not have done? We might have had another Charlotte Brontë or another George Eliot" (80). Laying aside the question of whether a facsimile of a literary genius is ever desirable, Skelton's point about overproduction carries even more weight with a modern audience. Steeped as we are in the late-twentieth-century belief that less is more, and conditioned by the modernist examples of lapidary and/or slowly gestated novels, the knowledge that the Oliphant canon contains nearly one hundred novels not only discourages the modern reader but probably gives rise to a mild contempt for the author of such excess. Even Robert and Vineta Colby, whose 1966 study of Oliphant was the first serious attempt at a revaluation, temper their advocacy with disapproval of the sheer quantity of her output. "Mrs. Oliphant predicted that she would be forgotten by the next generation, and perhaps her eclipse is a Dantean justice for one who wrote too fast and too much" (xiv).

Henry James's 1897 obituary notice of Oliphant shares a similar tone of apparent praise that, under further examination, sounds like damning.

> Her success had been in its day as great as her activity, yet it was always present to me that her singular gift was less recognised, or at any rate less reflected, less reported upon, than it deserved: unless indeed she may have been one of those difficult cases for criticism, an energy of which the spirit and the form, straggling apart, never join hands with that effect of union which in literature more than anywhere else is strength. (1411)

Again there is the reference to her great activity (he earlier refers to her "copious tribute" to the "great contemporary flood" of literature). More damaging is the orotund suggestion that perhaps Oliphant falls short of the Jamesian ideal of literary artistry; "the spirit and the form," the subject and the technique, are not in harmony. James hints at what Oliphant would never have denied. She was not an "artist" in the Jamesian sense. In her *Autobi-*

*ography,* published posthumously, she refused to analyze her work, claiming that she wrote "because it gave me pleasure, because it came natural to me, because it was like talking or breathing, besides the big fact that it was necessary for me to work for my children" (4). Trollope's *Autobiography,* which Jamesians found distressingly nonchalant about the novelist's elevated calling, astonished Oliphant with its analytical comments on fictional creations: "I am totally incapable of talking about anything I have done in that way" (4), she averred.

Her male contemporaries did little to keep the memory of her novels alive, and early-twentieth-century literary historians like Ernest Baker followed their lead. In his ten volume *History of the English Novel* (1924–1939) Baker found room for only a few sentences about Oliphant, dismissing her as a "domestic novelist" (8 : 111), that hoary euphemism for "damned scribbling woman." Once the novels fell out of print (for the longest time only *Salem Chapel,* 1863, not her finest work, was available in the Everyman's Library series), Oliphant's reputation rested increasingly on her literary criticism. As recently as 1977, Elaine Showalter, in a pioneering study of the female tradition in the novel—*A Literature of Their Own*—based most of her discussion of Oliphant, not on her novels, but on quotations from her literary criticism (*passim*). Not surprisingly, it proved a somewhat unsteady prop. For more than thirty years the virtual house critic of *Blackwood's,* Oliphant had conservative taste. She preferred the traditional English novel of Scott and Trollope, "not so much perhaps for what critics would call the highest development of art, as for a certain sanity, wholesomeness, and cleanness unknown to other literature of the same class" (102 : 257). She was no stranger to skepticism, but she didn't like to see it in other people's books. *Vanity Fair,* for example, offended her sense of fairness in its satire against Amelia and Dobbin (77 : 89); Chadband in *Bleak House* she regarded as a cynical and unrepresentative portrait of an evangelical clergyman (77 : 463). She hated the "nasty sentiments and equivocal heroines" of sensation novels with their often glamorous depictions of female villainy (102 : 280), and, even though she admired the revolutionary passions and vitality of *Jane Eyre,* she thought Charlotte Brontë skirted too close to indelicacy in her subject matter, and she worried that Brontë's legions of imitators, lacking her skills, would only debase the novel (77 : 557–59).

The review that has made her appear most out of touch with modern sensibilities (Stubbs 141–42) was written the year before her death when she locked horns with Hardy over *Jude the Obscure.* She decried the novel's depiction of marriage as "shameful," reviled the creation of the openly sexual Arabella ("a human pig"), and characterized the whole enterprise as a product of "grossness, indecency, and horror" (159 : 138). Finally, she accused Hardy of hypocrisy for profiting twice from the novel, once in a "clean" version for serial publication, and again in the unexpurgated book edition. Her heavy-handed indignation did not sit easily with Hardy. His contemptuous dismissal of her as "propriety and primness incarnate" (Page 24) summed up the way many modernists saw her: an Eminent Victorian relic whose very name—MRS. Oliphant—reeked of the respectability of antimacassars, horsehair sofas, and whale-bone corsets.

For many feminists interested in recovering lost women's voices, Oliphant has been, to use James's phrase, "one of those difficult cases for criticism." Virginia Woolf, in *Three Guineas*, established one approach to her, which is to regard her as a cautionary example. She asks whether a look at Oliphant's *Autobiography* does not lead the reader "to deplore the fact that Mrs. Oliphant sold her brain, her very admirable brain, prostituted her culture and enslaved her intellectual liberty in order that she might earn her living and educate her children" (91–92). It's not that Oliphant couldn't do better, Woolf implies; it's just that she was not allowed to. Oliphant, to Woolf, is an exemplary victim of a patriarchal system that forces women to worry first about the bare mechanics of scraping a living together and then, much later and further down the line, the claims of "disinterested culture and intellectual liberty." Woolf is quick to admire Oliphant's courage and her compassion in putting her family first, but she is even quicker to emphasize the short circuiting of her literary abilities. Like Skelton, Woolf prefers to think more of what Oliphant might have been than look closely at what she was.

Later feminists have not been even so equivocally generous. Sandra Gilbert and Susan Gubar's twenty-five-hundred-page *Norton Anthology of Literature by Women* (1985), for example, does not mention Oliphant at all. Novelists admittedly are not allowed much space in traditional anthologies, but Gilbert and Gubar, realizing the centrality of the novel to women's writing, have broken with tradition and included three complete novels: *Jane Eyre, The Awakening,* and *The Bluest Eye.* Excerpts from Maria Edgeworth, Jane Austen, Mary Shelley, Elizabeth Gaskell, Emily Brontë, and George Eliot, and summary references to Rhoda Broughton and Mary Elizabeth Braddon constitute their canon of nineteenth-century fiction. To exclude Oliphant from a survey of women's literature, "designed to serve as a core curriculum text" (xxvii), crammed with works whose "historical, intellectual, or aesthetic significance seems clearly to merit inclusion" (xxx) is to make her doubly marginal—neither part of the woman's tradition nor the man's.

Perhaps Gilbert and Gubar do not place Oliphant in their "great tra-dition" of women's writing because her novels do not question or challenge the prevailing patriarchy, nor does she treat her women characters as the repressed "other." (Oliphant does not privilege alterity.) In a similar way other feminists have faulted Oliphant for her political timidity: her "super-ficially emancipated heroines . . . remain well within the limits of moral and social convention" and are "in no way a serious challenge to patriarchal ste-reotypes of feminine character or behaviour" (Stubbs 39). Perhaps it is dif-ficult for some critics to forgive Oliphant's opposition to what she once called "the mad notion of the franchise for women" (*Autobiography* 211). Yet, as Merryn Williams reminds us in her recent biography, Oliphant made that remark in 1866, and during the remaining thirty years of her life she altered her views considerably. "She believed in a Married Women's Property Act, a mother's right to the custody of her children, women doctors, and Uni-versity education for girls. . . . By 1880 she was prepared to say in public, 'I think it is highly absurd that I should not have a vote, if I want one'" (108). Oliphant apparently did not want the vote herself, but then neither did George Eliot, Christina Rossetti, or Elizabeth Barrett Browning.

Nevertheless, Oliphant has her modern advocates. They admit with-out hesitation that not all her work is first-rate, but, rather than dismiss her because of it, they single out those works that represent her best efforts. They look beyond the limitations imposed on her by the need to write fast and publish frequently and emphasize their belief that "what remains remark-able is what she did achieve within those limitations" (Terry 101).

The greatest amount of positive critical attention so far has been given to Oliphant's five-volume *Chronicles of Carlingford: The Rector and The Doctor's Family* (1863); *Salem Chapel* (1863); *The Perpetual Curate* (1864); *Miss Marjoribanks* (1866); and *Phoebe Junior: A Last Chronicle of Carlingford* (1876). Among them the most consistent praise has been directed at *Miss Marjoribanks*. Q.D. Leavis, who wrote an introduction to a 1969 reprint of the novel, deserves credit for beginning the modern recovery of *Miss Marjoribanks*. She places Oliphant in the same company as Jane Austen and George Eliot as novelists of manners, and assigns Lucilla Marjoribanks, the title character, a prominent position in the pantheon of strong women characters, somewhere between Emma Woodhouse and Dorothea Brooke, judging Lucilla "more entertaining, more impressive, and more likable than either" (1). She concludes with the hope that "perhaps our age will at last do justice to this wise and witty novel in which every sentence is exactly right and every word apt and adroitly placed" (23). While more temperate minds might balk at claims of perfection, a few other critics of the novel do share

Mrs. Leavis's enthusiasm. Merryn Williams has asserted that "it is hardly possible to overpraise *Miss Marjoribanks,* which grows more impressive every time it is read" (84), and R.C. Terry has called it "a novel that can stand comparison with the best contemporary novels of its kind" (89).

*Miss Marjoribanks* is an ironic comedy about power, the story of a young unmarried woman's efforts to achieve power within the narrow confines allowed to daughters of the genteel classes. Lucilla Marjoribanks returns home from school at the beginning of the novel to her widowed father, a prosperous physician in the quiet Tory town of Carlingford, and to a traditional patriarchal society. It's a man's world, where the major social event is Dr. Marjoribanks's weekly all-male dinner, "to which naturally, as there was no lady in the house, ladies could not be invited" (42). To make matters worse for the wives left at home, Dr. Marjoribanks's cook is so skillful at creating exquisite sauces that she spoils the men for their wives' plainer fare. For the unmarried young woman, like Lucilla, the only respectable option is to become the socially unimportant wife of such a spoiled man.

Lucilla, however, has decided during her years of exile at the Mt. Pleasant girls' school that her mission upon return will go beyond looking on at her father's festive table. Her real ambition is "the reorganization of society in Carlingford" (40). She plans to create a coherent social life for all members of the genteel classes, male and female, and to make herself the central point around which their activities revolve. The other women of the town are not up to the task, disqualified as they are by virtue of age, circumstance, or disposition from doing "anything in the way of knitting people together, and making a harmonious whole out of the scraps and fragments of society" (43). Lucilla deems herself perfect for the job: she has a passion for organization, she is unattached, and she has her father's large house and not inconsiderable income at her disposal. The first thing she does to build public confidence in her resolve to reshape Carlingford is to dispel rumors that she might marry at any time. She makes it clear to her father, to her cousin Tom, who loves her, and to anyone who asks, that she intends to devote herself to Carlingford for at least ten years. Lucilla hangs out her shingle, so to speak, and commences her "career" when she establishes her "Thursday nights." When her cousin Tom tries to impress her by declaring "I am called to the bar, and I have begun my Career" (96), Lucilla solemnly ignores him. She knows that her own "Career" as the social doyenne of Carlingford, which is as close to a public career that a Victorian young lady could hope for, is so much more real and active than a fledgling barrister's.

Lucilla is much smarter and abler than any of the men in her world.

She becomes thereby Oliphant's emblem of the unfair limitations placed on Victorian women. In a world where female imagination has no real outlet, and female ability can gain no real power, Lucilla makes impressive use of the meager resources at her disposal. She takes the Victorian home, which was supposed to be the realm of the private, and turns it into the public, subverting the Victorian "ideology of home and family [which] was consistently employed to oppose emergent feminism" (Stubbs 7). Her Thursday nights create a community where once there was alienation and separation. The genteel classes of Carlingford gather each week for dinner, gossip, and light entertainment. And a woman's hand guides it all. Lucilla of course performs the time-honored feminine tasks of harmonizing and unifying that Virginia Woolf recognized as Mrs. Ramsay's greatest gift and limitation. It's an ambivalence that Oliphant shares. When Oliphant refers ironically to Lucilla's Thursdays as her "great work" (122), the double-edge of that phrase is unmistakable: ordinarily a genteel Victorian woman's "work" meant her needlework or embroidery, symbols of the limits placed on female productivity. Even her father recognizes the waste inherent in Lucilla's "Thursdays." He had often complained that his sister-in-law had the son, Tom, that he had wanted, yet he has to admit "how great a loss it was to society and to herself that Lucilla was not 'the boy'" (400).

Despite gender restrictions, Lucilla's brilliance cannot be completely dimmed, only somewhat contained. Her ability to exploit convention, even to subvert it when necessary, is revealed clearly in three masterful scenes. In each of them, Lucilla demonstrates her will to power, and her skill at controlling circumstances so that a weak strategic position is converted into a commanding triumph.

When she first arrives in Carlingford the initial obstacles to Lucilla's empire building are her father and his housekeeper, Nancy. Only nineteen, Lucilla has to establish early on her determination to run the house. Since she's a rank outsider, having been away a decade at school, and since the current inhabitants of the house are content doing things their own way, Lucilla must begin swiftly but subtly. She amuses her father with stories about her grand tour of the Continent, and while he compounds his good mood with a glass of claret, she, "as she herself expressed it, harmonised the rooms, by the simple method of rearranging half the chairs and covering the tables with trifles of her own" (50). When her father sees her handiwork he is restrained by his usual Scottish phlegm from saying anything. The next morning, however, Lucilla "unfolded her standard" (50). She arises before he does and when he enters the breakfast room discovers her seated in his usual place blithely offering him a cup of coffee. "Dr. Marjoribanks hesitated for one momentous instant, stricken dumb by this unparalleled audacity; but so great was the effect of his daughter's courage and steadiness, that after that moment of fate he accepted the seat by the side where everything was arranged for him and to which Lucilla invited him sweetly" (50). Lucilla acts not without trepidation, but her firm belief in the wisdom of seizing opportunity by the forelock sustains her. She apologizes for taking her father's place and explains that otherwise she "should have had to move the urn, and all the things, and I thought you would not mind" (50). Her father grumbles quietly and then submits, aware that "the reins of state had been smilingly withdrawn from his unconscious hands" (50).

Oliphant pointedly concedes that "it is no great credit to a woman of nineteen to make a man of any age throw down his arms; but to conquer a woman is a different matter" (52). To win over Nancy is the real challenge. And Lucilla does it through a confident sweetness that encourages Nancy to consider Lucilla her ally in upholding the great tradition of Marjoribanks dinners: "I have heard of papa's dinners . . . and I don't mean to let down your reputation. Now we are two women to manage everything, we ought to do still better" (52). Nancy, who had been prepared to resist any high-handed attempts to wrest control from her, is completely disarmed by Lucilla's conciliatory tactics, and "gave in like her master"(52).

Lucilla's home triumph is not yet secure, however. Her free hand at home raises the eyebrows of at least one townsperson, the evangelical rector, Mr. Bury. He considers it irregular, if not improper, for Lucilla to mix in male society without an older woman as her chaperone. Since her mother is dead, he decides to provide her with a live-in companion. Lucilla plays a little fast and loose, but all is fair, as she sees it, in her war for an independent dominion. She reads Bury's candidate, Mrs. Mortimer, quickly—"a deprecating woman, with a faint sort of pleading smile on her face" (85)— and parries Bury's pious declaration that he has found someone to take her mother's place with the disingenuous question "Do you mean you have found some one for him [her father] to marry?" (86). The introduction of a sexual perspective completely unnerves Mrs. Mortimer, as Lucilla knew it would, and she collapses in a faint. Lucilla takes control by nearly carrying her to the sofa, and ministers to her. So much for Mrs. Mortimer as her protector. After the disgusted Bury washes his hands of Mrs. Mortimer, Lucilla candidly apologizes to her, "I knew it would hurt your feelings . . . but I could not do anything else" (89).

In these two scenes Lucilla has appropriated the conventional image of the innocent young woman whose blundering intrusions and indelicacies are well-meaning but unconscious errors at worst. Because no one can imagine her real motives (except her father, who is soon amused by them), she can subvert convention and have things her own way by appearing to personify conventionality itself. As she admits: "I always make it a point to give in to the prejudices of society. That is how I have always been so successful" (72). She serves up revolution with a smile, founded as it is on a paradoxical adherence to the hoariest Victorian standards of decorum.

Lucilla most brilliantly manipulates the conventional code of conduct when she must save the integrity of her Thursday evenings. She learns that Mr. Cavendish, who has long been a prized jewel in her social crown, is about to be denounced as an impostor by a visiting prelate, Archdeacon Beverley. Lucilla knows that the exposure of Cavendish, who is not a member of that illustrious family but merely a Kavan, would rend the fabric of her carefully created society, throwing everything in doubt. If Cavendish is Kavan, then who is Cavendish's sister, Mrs. Woodburn? And what status can Mr. Woodburn claim now that he is no longer married to a Cavendish? And so on. For the elite of Carlingford to discover that they have nourished an upstart in their bosoms would mean admitting that they cannot distinguish between a gentleman and a pretender. To save the status quo, Lucilla is willing to lie and risk embarrassment. At the moment the archdeacon recognizes Cavendish at the table, Lucilla silences him by coyly confessing that "he is one of my—very particular friends" (308), in other words, that she's engaged to him, and that "he has no secrets from me" (308). The archdeacon is confounded: "What was he to do? He could not publicly expose the man who had just received this mark of confidence from his young hostess, who knew everything" (309). Lucilla has counted on the conventional code of decorum to prevail; no one would embarrass a young lady in her own house about a suitor and expect to be considered a gentleman. Archdeacon Beverley is no cad, so Lucilla is safe. Once again, her utter confidence in her own peculiar genius and her profound understanding of the conventional minds surrounding her have turned a near disaster into a personal triumph.

No reader can fail to detect the irony in Oliphant's treatment of Lucilla's aspirations. She is fond of referring to Lucilla as "the young sovereign" (49) or as a "distinguished revolutionary" (41), eager to begin "her campaign" (98) to bring Carlingford under her sway and establish "her throne" (65) where "her subjects" (266) can pay homage to her. Some critics have worried about this irony, judging the tone "bitter" and "cold": "The portrait of Miss Marjoribanks has wit, freshness, and originality, but it lacks humanity" (Colby 63, 67). Another agrees that there is "a hardness of tone," but adds that "the wit and irony never falter; from the first page to the last it is extremely funny" (Williams 81). Oliphant's mock heroic language, laced with imperial and military tropes, can be withering, but its consistent use forces the reader to see the other side of the deflationary mock-heroic. Even as it supposedly diminishes, the comparison of Lucilla's domestic battles with the Napoleonic campaigns paradoxically elevates. We soon see that in Lucilla's milieu her ambitions do set her above the conventionality of her peers. She is both deluded to think of herself as Queen Lucilla and yet perfectly right in assuming that she is a superior being.

Perhaps it is true, as Chesterton said of Dickens's creation of Pickwick—he came to scoff but stayed to pray (70)—that Oliphant's attitude toward Lucilla changes in the course of the novel. Certainly the irony softens in the last third. And perhaps it is also fair to say that Oliphant feels some affection for her own creation, although certainly not to the uncritical degree that Stubbs suggests: "she . . . approves of both Lucilla and her activities" (41). Part of Oliphant is horrified by Lucilla's shallowness, part of her admires her spunk, and the rest admits that Lucilla is the inevitable product of a world that circumscribes talented and ambitious women so narrowly.

At the end of the novel, for example, Lucilla is ten years older, a little stouter, a little less satisfied with the regular round of Thursday evenings, and conscious of her precarious position as a woman reaching thirty without a husband. Mrs. Oliphant reminds her readers of the paradoxical Victorian usage of the word "independent" to denote both the freedom from being encumbered and the status of a married woman, no longer dependent on her parents or family.

> She was very comfortable, no doubt in every way, and met with little opposition to speak of, and had things a great deal more in her own hands than she might have had, had there been a husband in the case to satisfy; but notwithstanding, she had come to an age when most people have husbands, and when an independent position in the world becomes necessary to self-respect. To be sure Lucilla *was* independent; but then—there is a difference, as everybody knows. (342)

Like Oliphant, Lucilla is a realist and has not ignored the social advantages of marriage. She has always kept her eye out for the appropriate fellow, preferably someone, like an M.P., with access to power. Since "she had come to an age at which she might have gone into Parliament herself had there been no disqualification of sex" (394), and since "when a woman has an active mind, and still does not care for parish work, it is a little hard for her to find a sphere" (395), Lucilla faces a life crisis. Simply put, "her capabilities were greater than her work" (395). When she does marry, Lucilla chooses her cousin Tom, who has no professional standing in England, having been a barrister in India for ten years, and who cannot offer her a conventional position in society. This only gives Lucilla the chance to create a fresh mission: "the thing we both want is something to do" (483). To all Tom's protests that he hopes eventually to take care of her so she can remain idle, Lucilla turns a deaf and mildly contemptuous ear: "What was to be done with a man who had so little understanding of her, and of himself, and of the eternal fitness of things?" (484). Lucilla's view of the "eternal fitness of things" is certainly not that of the typical Victorian male. She finds a country estate for sale, fittingly named Marchbank (her name is pronounced the same), which needs a great deal of work. The tenants lead wretched, disorderly lives, much in need of a strong organizing hand. Tom, she decides, can "improve" the land, while she "improves" the people. Perhaps in a few years Tom, who has "a perfect genius for carrying out a suggestion" (496), will stand for Parliament. "Then there rose up before her a vision of a parish saved, a village reformed, a county reorganised, and a triumphant election at the end, the recompense and crown of all, which should put the government of the country itself, to a certain extent, into competent hands" (497).

Lucilla's horizons grow absurdly large at the end, her Carlingford fiefdom gladly exchanged for the prospect of a national domain. Yet underneath our amusement at her grandiose ambitions lies our realization, thanks to Oliphant, that the irony is not directed only at Lucilla. It's directed also at the world that has made Lucilla. Six years before *Middlemarch* we meet in Lucilla a comic Dorothea, also "foundress of nothing," but one who is too bustling, too bourgeois, and too bullheaded to care that her life "spent itself in channels which had no great name on earth" (Eliot 4, 613).

Perhaps our unsentimental age has finally caught up with Lucilla and with Oliphant's ironic genius. *Miss Marjoribanks* is permeated with a sense that underneath Lucilla's grand schemes and ambitions lies compromise. Since she cannot partake in the imperial public life open to young men like her cousin Tom, who goes to India, she will create her own private empire in Carlingford; since she cannot stand for Parliament herself, she will look for a mate whom she can maneuver into a seat. Since she cannot remain single forever, and share in the world's power, she will marry someone she can control. In Oliphant's world everyone has to settle for the best she can get. Men and women do not necessarily understand one another, nor do they expect to. Romance and sexual attractiveness do not last long; only the foolish think so. Religion, which might be expected to answer the big questions, doesn't, nor does anyone ask them of it. Marriage does not by some immutable law bestow eternal happiness; women are not always content to be only wives and mothers, and so on. We see our disillusioned selves in the mirror that Oliphant holds up. As Q.D. Leavis pointed out, *Miss Marjoribanks* lacks the "infusion of warm feeling" that Victorian readers had come to expect: "it is not simple-minded or self-indulgent . . . [Lucilla] had neither the Victorian sentimentality nor even the necessary reticence and sense of propriety" (23) to achieve mass popularity. We who do not demand warm feelings or propriety in our favorite characters do not miss their absence in Lucilla. In fact we delight in the wit and hard good sense that leaves them out.

Yet this is not a bitter or cynical novel. Oliphant's ironic narrative voice keeps reminding the reader of the folly in all human endeavor, yet accepts the absolute fitness, in a disappointing world, of striking the best bargain you can for yourself. Lucilla maintains a cheerful determination throughout her campaigns, occasionally disappointed but never discouraged. She doesn't analyze the unfairness of her disabilities, sometimes isn't even aware of them, but Oliphant recognizes them and prepares the reader to do likewise. The sustained artistry of Oliphant's ironic technique, poised delicately between scorn and sympathy, recognizing that Lucilla's personal shortcomings are directly related to Victorian society's narrow definition of what was an appropriate ambition for a woman, may be the greatest strength of *Miss Marjoribanks*.

If it's true, as I believe and as Margarete Holubetz asserts in her excellent but little-known essay, that "there is [not] another novel of the period which dissects the Victorian conventions of feeling and behavior with such subversive irony"(42), then it is also appropriately ironic that a novel so subversive should remind us that the "Queen of Popular Fiction" can offer as complex a response to society and literature as her more canonical fellows.

WORKS CITED

Baker, Ernest. *History of the English Novel* (1924–1939). New York: Barnes and Noble, 1957.

Chesterton, Gilbert Keith. *Charles Dickens* (1906). New York: Press of the Readers Club, 1942.

Colby, Vineta and Robert A. *The Equivocal Virtue: Mrs. Oliphant and the Victorian Literary Market Place*. Archon Books, 1966.

Eliot, George. *Middlemarch* (1871–1872). Boston: Houghton Mifflin, 1956.

Gilbert, Sandra M., and Susan Gubar. *The Norton Anthology of Literature by Women*. New York: Norton, 1985.

Holubetz, Margarete. "The Triumph of the Gifted Woman: The Comic Manipulation of Cliché in Mrs. Oliphant's *Miss Marjoribanks*." *Proceedings of the Second*

*April Conference of University Teachers of English, Cracow 1981* (Warsaw/Krakow, 1984), 41–56.

James, Henry. "London Notes" (1897). *Henry James: Literary Criticism*. Edited by Leon Edel and Mark Wilson. *The Library of America*, 1984.

Leavis, Q.D. Introduction. *Miss Marjoribanks* by Margaret Oliphant. London: Zodiac Press, 1969.

Oliphant, Margaret. "The Anti-Marriage League." *Blackwood's* 159 (1896): 135–149.

———. *Autobiography and Letters of Mrs. Margaret Oliphant* (1899). Leicester: Leicester UP, 1974.

———. "Charles Dickens." *Blackwood's* 77 (1855): 451–66.

———. *Miss Marjoribanks* (1866). London: Virago, 1988.

———. "Mr. Thackeray and His Novels." *Blackwood's* 77 (1855): 86–96.

———. "Modern Novelists—Great and Small." *Blackwood's* 77 (1855): 554–68.

———. "Novels." *Blackwood's* 102 (1867): 257–80.

Page, Norman. "Hardy, Mrs. Oliphant, and *Jude The Obscure*." *Victorian Newsletter* 46 (Fall 1974): 22–24.

Robinson, Lillian. "Treason Our Text: Feminist Challenges to the Literary Canon." *The New Feminist Criticism*. Edited by Elaine Showalter. New York: Pantheon, 1985.

Showalter, Elaine. *A Literature of Their Own*. London: Virago, 1978.

Skelton, John. "A Little Chat about Mrs. Oliphant." *Blackwood's* 133 (1883): 73–91.

Stubbs, Patricia. *Women and Fiction*. Sussex: Harvester Press, 1979.

Sutherland, John. *The Stanford Companion to Victorian Fiction*. Stanford: Stanford UP, 1989.

Terry, R.C. *Victorian Popular Fiction, 1860–1880*. Atlantic Highlands, N.J.: Humanities Press, 1983.

Williams, Merryn. *Margaret Oliphant: A Critical Biography*. London: Macmillan, 1986.

Woolf, Virginia. *Three Guineas* (1938). San Diego: Harcourt Brace Jovanovich, 1966.

SELECTED SECONDARY SOURCES

John Stock Clarke, "Mrs. Oliphant: A Case for Reconsideration," *English* 28 (1979); Vineta and Robert A. Colby, *The Equivocal Virtue: Mrs. Oliphant and the Victorian Literary Market Place* (Archon Books, 1966); Valentine Cunningham, *Everywhere Spoken Against: Dissent in the Victorian Novel* (Oxford, 1975); Elisabeth Jay, *Mrs. Oliphant: A Fiction to Herself* (Oxford, 1995). Q.D. Leavis, Introduction to *Miss Marjoribanks* (London: Zodiac Press, 1969); Joseph H. O'Mealy, "Scenes of Professional Life: Mrs. Oliphant and the New Victorian Clergyman," *Studies in the Novel* 23 (1991); Margarete Rubik, *The Novels of Mrs. Oliphant* (Peter Lang, 1994); D.J. Trela, ed., *Margaret Oliphant: Critical Essays on a Gentle Subversive* (Susquehanna, 1995); Kathleen Watson, "George Eliot and Mrs. Oliphant: A Comparison in Social Attitudes," *Essays in Criticism* 19 (1969); Merryn Williams, *Margaret Oliphant: A Critical Biography* (London: Macmillam, 1986); Robert Lee Wolff, *Gains and Losses: Novels of Faith and Doubt in Victorian England* (New York: Garland, 1977).

# The Vampire in the House

## Hysteria, Female Sexuality, and Female Knowledge in Le Fanu's "Carmilla" (1872)

*Tamar Heller*

A journalist, editor, and author of historical novels, the Irish writer Joseph Sheridan Le Fanu (1814–1873) is best known today for his ghost stories and memorably eerie narratives of mystery and suspense, which include his most famous novel, *Uncle Silas* (1864). In works like *Uncle Silas* and the short story collection *In a Glass Darkly,* which contains such brilliant tales as "Green Tea" and "Carmilla," Le Fanu takes his place beside noted Victorian Gothicists like Wilkie Collins while also proving that he deserves critical attention in his own right. Of particular interest to the feminist critic is Le Fanu's use of the genres of mystery and supernatural fiction to explore the family romance of Victorian domesticity, an institution refracted in his tales, to borrow the title of his short story collection, "in a glass darkly." Le Fanu's works are published in their entirety in an expensive edition from Ayer Publishing Company; more readily accessible is *Uncle Silas,* available both from Dover and Oxford University presses, *In a Glass Darkly* (Oxford University Press), *Wylder's Hand* (Dover), and a selection of the supernatural fiction from Dover entitled *Best Ghost Stories.*

In 1877 the American physician Weir Mitchell, best known to literary scholars as the man who almost drove Charlotte Perkins Gilman insane, wrote a book on the treatment of neurasthenic and hysterical female patients entitled *Fat and Blood: And How to Make Them.* Since, as Mitchell claims, nervous women "as a rule are thin, and lack blood," the male physician must fatten up his patients, and, in the process, manufacture his own ideal woman: cheerful, plump, and contented (7). Despite this benevolent paternalism, however, Mitchell also betrays the distrust of female patients that historians have argued was typical of doctors who treated hysterical women.[1] Characterizing the nervous woman as greedy and selfish, Mitchell uses a metaphor that implies women who lack blood are in fact blood suckers: "A hysterical girl is, as Wendell Holmes has said in his decisive phrase, a vampire who sucks the blood of the healthy people about her; and I may add that pretty surely where there is one hysterical girl there will be soon or late two sick women" (Mitchell 35). This narrative of the female vampire who makes another woman sick resembles the plot of Joseph Sheridan Le Fanu's vampire story "Carmilla," published in the collection *In A Glass Darkly* in 1872, five years before Mitchell's *Fat and Blood*. In Le Fanu's tale, Laura, the narrator, who lives with her widowed English father in a lonely eastern European castle, befriends a mysterious and beautiful guest, Carmilla, whose strange habits include not eating, and sleeping much of the day. Yet Carmilla is not the story's only "nervous" invalid (286, 303), for Laura gradually and yet alarmingly loses her own health and energy. Only the revelation that Carmilla is a vampire—a discovery made by men—saves Laura from becoming a victim of the woman who had busily been draining the fat and blood of her (in more ways than one) bosom friend. The parallel between this story and Mitchell's image of the self-reproducing hysteric suggests an interdisciplinary cultural dialogue: not only, for doctors, is the hysterical woman like a vampire but, in tales like Le Fanu's, the vampire can be read as a figure for the hysterical woman.[2] Moreover, as all this male nervousness about voracious women suggests, both the female hysteric and the female vampire embody a relation to desire that nineteenth-century culture finds highly problematic.

In order to understand the ideological charge of Le Fanu's influential representation of the female vampire, in fact, I would argue that it is necessary to examine attitudes about female appetite implicit in Victorian definitions of the hysterical woman. Attempts during this period to taxonomize hysteria were the more strenuous, one suspects, because the hysterical woman represented an interpretive problem: in particular, the question of whether her malady expressed appetite or desire was a troubling one for nineteenth-century physicians both before and after Freud. Some doctors (Weir Mitchell included) shied away from explicitly linking hysteria and female sexuality and instead ascribed the illness to the peculiar sensitivity of the female nervous system. A series of metonymic associations in Victorian physiological theory, however, linked the female reproductive system not only to nervousness and hysteria but also to women's capacity for sexual arousal, suggesting that nerves were, as Cynthia Eagle Russett says in *Sexual Science*, "apparently synonymous with female sexuality" (Russett 118; see also Poovey 142–43, 146–47). Moreover, a tradition of ascribing hysteria to sexual frustration persisted into the nineteenth century and underlies the theory of Freud. Thus, given the anxiety about female sexuality in Victorian gender ideology, in medical discourses about hysteria the disordered—one might say *errant*—womb that was the synecdoche for Woman shifted from signifying passionless motherhood to suggesting instead intense, even potentially insatiable, sexual desire.[3] Hence, the thematics of appetite in "Carmilla"—which I will link to medical discourses about the related female maladies of hysteria, anorexia, and chlorosis—encode this fear of the devouring, sexually voracious woman lurking beneath the docile surface of the devoured woman, her apparent victim. Such anxieties about "uncontrollable female hungers," as Susan Bordo claims, are particularly marked "during periods when women are becoming independent and are asserting themselves politically and socially" (161). As Bordo says, echoing critics and historians such as Bram Dijkstra and Peter Gay, the second half of the nineteenth century witnessed not only the growth of feminism but "a virtual flood of artistic and literary images of . . . 'biting, tearing, murderous women'" (161)—a context in which we can situate the influential portrayal of the female vampire in "Carmilla."[4]

In this climate of contested definitions of the nature of woman, the theme of female knowledge is as important and vexed as that of female appetite. Since the assumption of female passionlessness undergirded domestic ideology, female sexuality was a central concern in the debates about women's social position known as the Woman Question. Yet, if the question of whether women were sexually responsive was important, so, implicitly, was the question of whether they acknowledged their sexuality—for female sexual knowingness considerably complicates the innocence, or sexual ignorance, that defines "Woman" in domestic ideology. In "Carmilla," sexual knowledge is an important aspect of the story of hysterical contagion whereby one hysterical girl infects, and creates, another. For, while critics have read Carmilla's murderous designs on Laura as sexual advances (i.e., McCormack 190–91; Veeder 197–98; Melada 99–101), it is equally important that the would-be victim's narrative reveals an ambivalent, but still pronounced, awareness of her attraction to the woman who tries to kill her. That Laura does not fit the most obvious role available to her, and which she tries to write for herself—that of innocent or ignorant victim—transforms the angel in the house into yet another "vampire," or knowing accomplice in sexual crime. Moreover, since female homoeroticism excludes men and eludes male control, to figure female sexuality as lesbianism underscores the threat that women's desire poses to male authority—a threat that would become increasingly pronounced in the decades to follow Le Fanu's story, as feminist agitation further politicized bonds between women. Indeed, "Carmilla," which Sue-Ellen Case has called the "first lesbian vampire story" (7), is an important example of how late-nineteenth-century texts begin to demonize the domestic friendships that Carroll Smith-Rosenberg has famously called the "female world of love and ritual," making Le Fanu's story a precursor of fin-de-siècle and early-twentieth-century antifeminist narratives like *The Bostonians,* in which lesbians "vamp" young girls. In Le Fanu's early version of this ideologeme, both the body of the lesbian and the mind of the victim she brainwashes are the site of a battle over who gets to define, and hence to control, femininity and its desires: women or the fathers, priests, and doctors who are the story's male "knowers."

The narrative structure of "Carmilla" reproduces the epistemological structure of the tale, in which male knowledge subjects female experience to scrutiny. Before we hear the words of Laura, the female narrator, we hear the voice-over of male science. The tale's prologue is written by a friend of Doctor Hesselius, the physician interested in psychology who appears in the other narratives of *In a Glass Darkly,* and who has presumably used Laura's manuscript as data in his own essay on vampirism, which will "form but one volume of the series of that extraordinary man's collected papers" (274). Helen Stoddart has commented that Hesselius functions as a "prototype psychoanalyst," a collector of Freudian case studies of hysteria and paranoia (Stoddart 20); in this light, it is significant that the doctor's friend refers to vampirism in the prologue with teasing indirectness as "this mysterious subject," a resonant phrase since not just vampirism but femininity will be the "mysterious subject" male detectives try to decode. This image of femininity recalls Weir Mitchell's reference to hysteria as "mysteria," an emblematic illness for women who have traditionally been the great enigma (Showalter 130).[5]

The language used by nineteenth-century medicine to diagnose the female patient echoes throughout "Carmilla," particularly in describing the female vampire. Carmilla is introduced through the language of diagnosis: when she conveniently has a carriage accident outside the gates of Laura's home—thus ensuring that Laura's father will take her in while she recuperates—the woman who leaves her there, and who poses as her mother, claims that her daughter "was in delicate health, and nervous, but not subject to any kind of seizure . . . nor to any illusions, being, in fact, perfectly sane" (266). Similarly, the physician who examines Carmilla after the accident says that "the little shock to her nerves had passed away quite harmlessly" (287). Still, despite these attempts to give her a clean bill of health, Carmilla epitomizes the nineteenth-century female invalid. "*[V]ery* languid" in her movements (290), she sleeps late, does not eat, and can scarcely walk several steps before becoming completely exhausted. In not eating, the "slender" (290) Carmilla is like the "fasting girls" whom Joan Brumberg has discussed in her study of the history of anorexia, a condition which resembled hysteria and which was identified as a distinctive syndrome in 1873, the year after "Carmilla" was published. Yet some nineteenth-century physicians read anorexia as evidence, not of the denial of desire, but of its pathological expression; Philippe Pinel, head of the Salpêtrière, claimed that in his anorexic female patients periods of starvation alternated with "nymphomania" and the "impulse toward frantic desires" (Bell 5).

Feminine modesty, in other words, is most threatened when women appear almost parodically subservient to its rules.[6] Power-hungry and sex-starved, Carmilla, as Carol Senf notes, acts the role of anorexic invalid to get what she wants in a charade of female self-effacement (30).[7] Not only does she pretend to waste away elegantly by day while gorging herself at night on dangerously stimulating fare, but Carmilla is a master of disguise. Her vampire modus operandi is to appear in new incarnations in each family she enters, with the letters of her real name—Mircalla—rescrambled in new combinations (Carmilla, Millarca), a fluidity of identity that suggests how impossible it is to define the enigma of woman.[8] Like other melodramatic villainesses in nineteenth-century literature such as Braddon's Lady Audley or Dumas's diabolical Lady de Winter, Carmilla is a masquerader, an actress, an image linked in medical discourses with the hysteric, whom doctors distrust because her illness may be a cover for and indeed may be caused by her sexual immorality. As the French physician Falret said of hysterics, in a comment that resembles Pinel's on anorexics: "These patients are veritable actresses; they do not know of a greater pleasure than to deceive . . . the life of the hysteric is nothing but one perpetual falsehood; they affect the airs of piety and devotion . . . while at the same time secretly abandoning themselves to the most shameful actions" (Veith 211).

If Carmilla's languor and apparent lack of appetite make her a figure for both the hysteric and the anorexic (the latter a relatively new type of invalid), her symptoms would also call to mind a female malady particularly familiar to a Victorian audience: chlorosis, or "green sickness," the lack of energy and appetite caused by menstruation to which doctors frequently referred in discussions of female adolescence (Brumberg 172–74). Of course, Carmilla has found an unusual remedy for the anemia characteristic of the ailment, since her "brilliant" complexion [290] is presumably the result of human iron supplements. Yet, as in the images of the duplicitous hysteric and anorexic, this paradoxical image of the female vampire, drained of blood and yet hungry for it, rests on a similarly contradictory reading of the physiological process that causes chlorosis—menstruation—and which in Victorian medicine becomes a trope for femininity. Many Victorian medical texts imply that menstruation was symbolic not so much of feminine lack—the loss or wounding of blood-letting—but of the violent sexual appetite its onset could precipitate. One of the story's more chillingly demonized menstrual images is of Laura's awaking one night to find Carmilla standing at the foot of her bed in a "white nightdress bathed, from her chin to her feet, in one great stain of blood" (308). Such violent images of vampirism literalize the violent narrative implicit in medical descriptions of menarche as a dangerous time for young girls, in which they are susceptible not only to nervous disorders but to the awakening of a potentially uncontrollable sexuality (Smith-Rosenberg, "Puberty to Menopause," esp. 184–91, and also Brumberg 174–76).

Since Victorian culture associated menstruation with the incursion of unruly desires, we can read Carmilla's advent in the story—the entry of the woman who drains blood—as symbolizing the menarche of the adolescent narrator. The carriage accident that deposits Carmilla on Laura's doorstep occurs on a night whose full moon, evoking the female menstrual cycle, also signifies an inevitable tide of female nervousness and hysteria (as Laura's governess describes the moon in this scene, "it acted on dreams; it acted on lunacy; it acted on nervous people" [281]). Explaining her own obsessiveness as mimicry of her friend's elaborate precautions to lock out burglars, Laura remarks that "the precautions of nervous people are infectious" (303)—but then her upbringing makes her an ideal candidate for the cluster of female appetitive disorders—chlorosis, anorexia, and hysteria—embodied by Carmilla. The French physician Pinel, who believed that hysteria was caused by sexual repression, claimed that one circumstance that predisposed women to the illness was "severe restraint and secluded life" (Veith 179), and Laura, describing her motherless childhood with an aging father in a melodramatically Gothic "schloss," admits that "My life was rather a solitary one, I can assure you" (276). Moreoever, Laura appears already to have met her murderous guest, and her description of this scene from her childhood emphasizes how sexuality is indeed the cause of female nervousness. When she was little, Laura tells us, she was visited one night in bed by a "young lady," whom she will later recognize as her mysterious guest, and who "caressed me with her hands, and lay down beside me on the bed, and drew me towards her, smiling. . . . I was awakened by a sensation as if two needles ran into my breast" (277). Laura tells us that she was "very nervous" for a long time after this incident (277), and no wonder, given what nineteenth-century medicine had to say about young girls and nighttime caresses. For, while Carmilla's caresses of Laura can be read as homoerotic, they are also autoerotic, if we see Carmilla not just as the demonic outsider but, as

Bram Dijkstra says, a "mirror image" of Laura and thus an externalization of her own sexuality (341).

Le Fanu implies this feminine doubling through the plot, familiar from Victorian narratives such as *Aurora Leigh,* of the mother as Other; though Laura's father is English, her mother was a foreigner, a Styrian and member of the Karnstein family to which Carmilla also belongs.[9] That this foreign family is renowned for its "atrocious lusts" (327) is not surprising given the nineteenth-century association between racial Otherness and transgressive sexuality. While one of the "atrocious lusts" so portentously invoked appears to be homosexuality, another could be masturbation, since both types of sexual activity show that young girls can be prematurely and illicitly knowing about sexuality. First associated solely with boys, but then, from the 1860s onward, increasingly linked with girls, masturbation was the target of a vehement and well-organized nineteenth-century medical campaign arguing that autoeroticism caused hysteria in girls and was encouraged by such practices as eating red meat.[10] (In other words, what cures chlorotic young girls can also make them nymphomaniacs.) Carmilla's nighttime excursions to drink her friend's blood—her way of eating flesh, or red meat—cause Laura to display classic symptoms of the masturbator according to nineteenth-century medicine: she is pale and her eyes are "dilated and darkened underneath" (308).[11] Revealingly, one popular nineteenth-century treatise described masturbation in girls as a "vampire feeding on the lifeblood of its victims" (Shuttleworth, "Demonic Mothers" 50), an image in which vampire and victim are twin faces of an all-consuming feminine desire; referring, in 1851, to the "vicious habits" of masturbation in girls as "lesbian pleasures," an article in a medical journal similarly conflated the homo- and autoerotic (Shuttleworth, "Female Circulation" 67 n. 45).

While the episode from Laura's childhood thus suggests she knows too much too soon about sexuality, the behavior of the adults to whom she relates her experience reveals their anxiety about this knowledge. The nervous reaction of Laura's nurses and father, though ostensibly to a supernatural menace, recalls the reaction of Victorian doctors to the notion that young girls might have sexual feelings: they deny that anything could have happened while, at the same time, betraying a fear that the very worst has. "Pale with an unwonted look of anxiety" (277), they call in both a priest and a doctor to see the girl, a suggestive pairing given that Weir Mitchell claimed that one duty of physicians to their female patients was "moral medication" (Mitchell 43). Yet, like Laura's aging father, who prides himself on being "something of a physician" (282), these male professionals are desiccated and elderly, too impotent to stave off a powerful and predatory female sexuality.

This feminine invasion is figured in terms of imperialist anxiety, for Carmilla rides into Styria—already, because of its orientalism, an only tenuously domesticated zone—like the return of the repressed colonized Other. As she swoons delicately in the foreground after her carriage accident, the reader is given a backstage glimpse, through a virulently racist image, of what lurks beneath the surface of conventional femininity: "a hideous black woman, with a sort of coloured turban on her head, who was gazing all the time from the carriage window, nodding and grinning derisively towards the ladies, with gleaming eyes and large white eye-balls, and her teeth set as if in fury" (286). The threatening gestures of the black woman recall the nineteenth-century photographs of hysterical women clenching their fists and grimacing, the pose that Charcot, teacher of Freud, labeled in one example "passionate attitude: menace" (Didi-Huberman 136).[12] In a later scene the languidly pretty Carmilla assumes the same menacing attitude as the black woman. In the story's most explicit reference to hysteria, the vampire goes into a fit as she and Laura hear the singing of a hymn that heralds the funeral procession of one of Carmilla's peasant victims:

> Her face underwent a change that alarmed and even terrified me for a moment. It darkened, and became horribly livid; her teeth and hands were clenched, and she frowned and compressed her lips, while . . . she trembled all over with a continued shudder as irrepressible as ague. All her energies seemed strained to suppress a fit, with which she was then breathlessly tugging; and at length a low convulsive cry of suffering broke from her, and gradually the hysteria subsided. (294)

As Carmilla's face darkens, she becomes what figures like the black woman in the carriage symbolize in nineteenth-century racist and sexist iconography: the woman as angry, demonic, and animalistically sexual Other,[13] for the "irrepressible" shuddering of *globus hystericus* in this scene suggests both menace and orgasm.

Yet the theme of knowledge is as important as that of appetite in descriptions of the vampire. That Carmilla, whom Laura calls pagan in her indifference to prayer (303), ascribes her hysteria to Christianity ("that comes of strangling people with hymns," [294]) emphasizes her preference for an alternative system of knowledge. In one exchange, Carmilla, discussing with Laura's father the alarming epidemic of dying peasant girls in the neighborhood, answers his pious claim that "We are all in God's hands. . . . He is our faithful creator" with scorn: "Creator! *Nature!* . . . And this disease that invades the country is natural. Nature. All things proceed from Nature—don't they?" (297). After dismissing male medical authority ("doctors never did me any good" [297]), Carmilla then proceeds, in a conversation with Laura, to sound like a student of natural history, referring to the French naturalist Buffon's book to draw a parallel between young girls and caterpillars. The purpose of this analogy is to suggest to Laura that girls should not be afraid to die, if they "die, as lovers may" (297)—one of Carmilla's numerous puns on death and orgasm. Significantly, Carmilla draws on her feminine experience and her own knowledge of science to redefine what is natural behavior for women. Nineteenth-century literature is filled with images of sexual women as perverted and unnatural, yet Carmilla, in her erotically charged dialogues with Laura, tries to convince her friend that female sexuality and homoeroticism are natural, using a Darwinian language of biological determinism to describe her passion for her friend: "I obey the irresistible law of my strength and weakness" (291).

As critics have noted, Laura's response to these seductive arguments is fraught with an ambivalent complicity (Veeder 207; Waller 54). In reacting to what she sternly calls Carmilla's "crazy talk and looks" (301), Laura experiences "a strange tumultuous excitement that was pleasurable, ever and anon, mingled with a vague sense of fear and disgust" (292). The orgasmic overtones of this language of tumultous sensation resonate in the dreams Laura has once Carmilla starts to suck her blood, dreams in which it seems as if "warm lips kissed me" as she feels the classic hysterical symptoms of "strangulation" and "convulsion" (307). In her descriptions of these "feverish sensations" (308), we hear the voice of the older, presumably wiser, Laura commenting from the vantage point of greater knowledge: "Had I been capable of comprehending my condition, I would have invoked aid and advice on my knees. The narcotic of an unsuspected influence was acting upon me, and my perceptions were benumbed" (308).

What Laura is saying, in other words, is that she did not know what was happening to her while it was happening: Carmilla's influence, like a clandestinely administered cup of opium, is "unsuspected." Of course, it is a convention in female Gothic narratives for the heroine to be painfully naive, but here, with Carmilla muttering such lines as "No sacrifice without blood" while her friend becomes anemic (303), Laura appears more than ordinarily obtuse. The extent of Laura's vacuousness, indeed, constitutes the most ideologically charged and contested terrain in the narrative. William Veeder has claimed that Laura is so repressed that she "cannot" know fully what Carmilla means (Veeder 198, 201); yet it is useful to think that Laura's desires, and her knowledge, exist on the level not only of the unconscious but of a conscious self-censorship. Her claim that Carmilla's advances were "unintelligible" (292) may well reflect the pressure that young women of the Victorian period felt to deny they had any knowledge of sexuality, particularly of such illicit forms as auto- and homoeroticism.

The daughter's need to hide her sexuality is determined by the way her role is defined in the Victorian household. As Paula Marantz Cohen argues, the mother is absent in much Victorian literature (as she is in "Carmilla") because a daughter "physically, emotionally, and intellectually embodies the nineteenth-century ideal of femininity" more than does the mature woman: reassuringly asexual, a childlike and dependent daughter is also more malleable to the father's control (Cohen 22).[14] That the "stable dyadic relationship" (Cohen 22) in nineteenth-century representations of domesticity is that of father and daughter, not husband and wife, explains both the father–daughter pairings in "Carmilla" and the well-nigh jealous horror with which father figures react to the possibility that their daughters may be sexually knowledgeable. In a letter that Laura and her father read on the night when Carmilla arrives, General Spielsdorf, a family friend whose niece and ward, Bertha, was Carmilla's target before Laura, fulminates against the houseguest who he claims killed his niece—charges vague enough not to identify Carmilla which nonetheless hint that Bertha's illness was a contagious sexual disease. Yet the general is unutterably relieved that Bertha escaped this contagion by knowing nothing about what happened to her: "She died in the peace of innocence and in the glorious hope of a blessed futurity. . . . She is gone without so much as conjecturing the nature of her illness, and the accursed passion of the agent of all this misery" (280). That Bertha can inspire but still does not recognize Carmilla's "accursed passion" for what it is presumably makes her an angelic rather than a fallen woman. The illustrator for *In a Glass Darkly* appeared to recognize the fine line dividing these two states, however: in his drawing, the sleeping Bertha lies in a pose at once unconsciously and voluptuously inviting, while Carmilla stretches her arm as if to grab her friend's exposed breast and General Spielsdorf springs out of hiding brandishing his phallic sword.[15] In the context of such rampant male paranoia about female sexual knowledge, Laura evidently seeks to prove that she, like Bertha, is far from "conjecturing the nature of her illness"; in a sensuous passage where she describes how she loved to play with Carmilla's luxuriant hair, she breaks off with the melodramatic frisson: "Heavens! Had I but known all!" (290).

Still, what is intriguing about such a comment, in light of the general's definition of female innocence as utter ignorance, is the tantalizing and perhaps purposeful vagueness of "all": Laura's "Had I but known all" suggests that she very well may have known *some*. And, indeed, Laura cannot keep herself from conjecturing what is going on; noticing that Carmilla's passionate attraction to her is "like the ardor of a lover," Laura questions if her guest is in fact a boy in drag: "What if a boyish lover had found his way into the house, and sought to prosecute his suit in masquerade?" (293). While such a theory shows that Laura cannot yet imagine a same-sex love plot, she still has come a long way toward identifying what "embarrassed" her (301), as she puts it, about Carmilla's embraces.

One may ask, of course, whether a genteel young Victorian girl could have recognized homoeroticism if she had seen it. (Queen Victoria, after all, reportedly refused to believe that such a thing existed.) "Carmilla" still predates the emergence of a clearly defined category of lesbianism by several decades. Nonetheless, it is worth remembering, as Sara Putzell-Korab reminds us, that, even in the presumed heyday of the "female world of love and ritual," there was some anxiety about close friendships between young women. This anxiety sprang from a fear, even if as yet only partially articulated, of the sexual implications of such friendships, while also belying a wariness about the formation of emotional bonds that might hinder a girl's entry into the world of heterosexuality (Putzell-Korab 180–85). Putzell-Korab reminds us that Diderot's *La Religieuse,* which describes a mother superior's lesbian advances toward one of her nuns, went through twenty English editions between 1800 and 1870 (Putzell-Korab 181). The lesbian chapters of Diderot's novel strikingly resemble the situation in Le Fanu's tale: like Laura, Diderot's Suzanne claims she has no idea what is going on, even when her superior is having an orgasm that Suzanne describes with clinical precision.

In discussing what she calls the "privilege of unknowing" in *La Religieuse,* Eve Sedgwick refers to Suzanne's "labor-intensive ignorance" (Sedgwick 114), a formulation useful when assessing Laura's continued denials of knowledge. Yet what differentiates Le Fanu's female narrator from Diderot's is that Laura, despite her nervousness in describing moments where she may be aware of her friend's sexual overtures, is nonetheless trying to figure out what is happening. Such an attempt to be a detective—as the apparently passive heroines of female Gothic try to do—threatens to decenter the authority of male medical detectives. Laura's attempt at detection is most visible in the comment where she wonders whether Carmilla is a boyish lover, but an even more revealing moment where her desire to know wars with her desire to cover up is a perplexed comment on her "trembling" response to Carmilla's "hot kisses": "Are we related? What do you mean by all this? I remind you perhaps of some one whom you love; but you must not, I hate it; I don't know you—I don't know myself when you look and talk so" (292). While Laura's "you must not; I hate it" sounds as if she is protesting too much, her line "I don't know myself when you look and talk so" suggests that she is aware of her own sexual responsiveness to Carmilla's advances, even if that knowledge only brings with it fear, bewilderment, and self-disgust.

Before Laura, however, can identify herself as a sexual being, the story's male authorities, in marked contrast to their previous lack of energy, dramatically intervene to appropriate the power of knowledge for themselves. Finally noticing his daughter's illness, Laura's father calls in a doctor who persuades him that the ancient superstition of the vampire, at which he had previously scoffed, is empirical fact. This revelation that superstition is science is intriguing in light of the story's self-consciously archaic misogyny, which draws an analogy between women and libidinous vampires. Such a "superstition" may be likened to the belief in the inherent depravity of women that predates the mythology of the angel in the house, and which that Victorian ideology rewrote. In "Carmilla," this older view of women as lustful is the true *revenant*, returning to unsettle bourgeois domesticity.

As Helen Stoddart claims in her reading of "Carmilla," this type of misogyny implies a class allegory in which decadent aristocrats are pitted against the virtuous ascendent bourgeoisie. Drawing on Eve Sedgwick's discussion of how Victorians figure homosexuality as aristocratic decadence, Stoddart argues that Carmilla, the decadent lesbian, represents an outmoded feudalism that must be destroyed because its nonprocreative nature threatens the bourgeois family (Stoddart 30–32). Such a reading sheds a valuable light on the ideological agenda of Le Fanu's text, which like many Victorian narratives attempts to normalize the authority of the bourgeois family. Yet Le Fanu's misogynistic portrayal of female sexuality is not just nostalgic, an originary fable about bourgeois domesticity. Rather, his misogyny is also forward-looking, anticipating a trend in representations of female friendship. That lesbianism is a form of nonprocreative sexuality would render it obnoxious to proponents of domestic ideology, and yet, in "Carmilla," female homoeroticism *does* represent one type of propagation. Mimicking the process of hysterical contagion, lesbianism in Le Fanu's tale sets in motion a kind of mental or intellectual parthenogenesis whereby one woman's knowledge spawns another's. That one can make such a link in "Carmilla" between female mind and female body—between sexuality and knowledge—is revealing in a historical moment in which lesbianism and women's education were starting to be metonymically linked. Citing American examples, Nancy Sahli claims that the mid-1870s mark a watershed moment when close women's friendships start to be viewed, not as innocent, but as the possible source of a contaminating homoeroticism—an anxiety that coincides with the beginning of an era when women are forming associations through higher learning (Sahli 17–27).[16] While the exact date of the "morbidification" of female friendship is controversial,[17] it is suggestive that "Carmilla," with its demonization of the bonding between women, was written in the early 1870s. Thus, although Le Fanu's story is not yet *The Bostonians* (1886), which more explicitly links lesbianism and feminist intellectual community, his vampire tale makes a similar metonymic association between female homoeroticism and female knowing, both processes that make women independent of male control.

Indeed, as male authorities in "Carmilla" begin to recognize that the female friendships they previously thought were innocent are in fact dangerous, the process of the reproduction of female knowledge—the transmission of sexual knowingness from one woman to another—is interrupted. The doctor called in to examine Laura looks for something that he had been expecting to see, but which evidently comes as a shock to Laura's father: the mark on the girl's neck that is evidence for vampirism, and, in terms of the narrative's allegory of female desire, of sexual contact between her and Carmilla. The transmission of knowledge between men in this scene proceeds, as it were, over Laura's nearly dead body; when she asks, terrified, what the mark they have been discussing means, she is told that she must wait until later to find out (315).

Yet, although her father promises that she will soon know what is going on, Laura's relation to knowledge becomes increasingly mediated by male authority. The most spectacular scene from which Laura is barred, and which she can only summarize from an "official paper" (336), is also the one most populated by hordes of male authorities: the scene of Carmilla's "expulsion," or ritual execution. The "Imperial Commission," no less, is called in to hold the "Inquisition . . . according to law (336)." In what Laura describes as a "shocking scene" (336), these authorities perform a rape-like surgery on Carmilla: "The body, therefore, in accordance with ancient practice, was raised, and a sharp stake driven through the heart of the vampire, who uttered a piercing shriek. . . . Then the head was struck off, and a torrent of blood flowed from the severed neck" (336). If, as Hélène Cixous says, the hysterical woman is the "woman who disturbs and is nothing but disturbance" (Cixous 49), we can see what happens to such disorderly women. One can, indeed, borrow the title of Cixous's essay about hysteria—"Castration or Decapitation?"—to decode the meaning of the punishment meted out to Carmilla. With its echoes of the kinds of sexual mutilation, such as clitoridectomy, performed by some Victorian surgeons on troublesomely libidinous female patients,[18] Carmilla's execution suggests a feminized version of castration; moreover, the stake driven through the body of the lesbian vampire whose biting had mimicked the act of penetration is a raw assertion of phallic power. Yet, in light of the tale's thematics of female knowledge, it is also telling that Carmilla is decapitated, and that her head, site of knowledge and of voice, is struck off.

But is Laura also lobotomized? What can readers make of her silence at the execution of her best friend—an act of extraordinary violence, even granted that it is presumably done for her own good? As is so often the case with Laura's narrative, she does not say precisely what she is feeling, but at one point the careful emotional distancing in her description of Carmilla's death gives way to an uncontrollable fit of feminine nervousness: "I write all this you suppose with composure. But far from it; I cannot think of it without agitation. Nothing but your earnest desire so repeatedly expressed, could have induced me to sit down to a task that has unstrung my nerves for months to come" (336). Although Laura's "agitation" could be precipitated by the reminder of how close she came to death, her emotion could also be caused by her memory of her conflicted feelings for Carmilla. "Hysterics suffer mainly from reminiscences," wrote Freud's collaborator Breuer (Breuer and Freud 2:7), and, in this sense, the writing that unstrings Laura's nerves is the hysterical text that traces, albeit in a muted and strangled way, the narrative of her dangerous desire.[19]

Yet this hysterical text in one sense eludes the control of the male analysts like Hesselius who attempt to fill in the gaps of the hysteric's knowledge with their own narratives. Laura's words "your earnest desire," addressed to the person who urged her to record her experiences, remind the reader that she is writing not to a male doctor or scientist, as the prologue would have us believe, but to a female friend she calls at one point a "town lady" (293). Even if the doctors eventually commandeer this letter, it presumably reached its destination first. Could this narrative about sexual desire exchanged between women itself be a source of hysterical contagion, particularly if the lady who so earnestly wishes to hear the story has (like the readers of the tale) to reproduce in a kind of literary voyeurism Laura's process of figuring out the meaning of Carmilla's advances? According to one of the story's male vampire-hunters, the victims of vampires develop into vampires themselves "in the grave" (338). If this is the case, then Laura, who we hear in the prologue has died since writing her story—were her nerves too unstrung?—may well be on her way to becoming another Carmilla; as Carmilla says to Laura at one point, "As I draw near to you, you, in your turn, will draw near to others" (291). In this sense, Carmilla is what Terry Castle has called the "apparitional lesbian," the "much-ghosted yet none-theless vital lesbian subject" who cannot be exorcized (Castle 8). For, de-spite the strenuously brutal efforts of male authority to erase women's sexual knowledge, this desire continues to haunt their writing, just as Laura ends her narrative imagining that Carmilla, her image shifting from innocent an-gel to knowing demon with "ambiguous alternations" (339), is at her cham-ber door.

## Notes

I am indebted to my student Eva Berkes, whose research on "Carmilla" influ-enced the development of my argument, and also to Charles Hatten, Teresa Mangum, Susan Griffin, and those who responded to this essay when it was delivered as a talk at the Center for Literary and Cultural Studies, Harvard University, December 16, 1992.

1. For a classic and concise analysis of doctors' ambivalent attitudes toward their hysterical female patients, see Smith-Rosenberg, "The Hysterical Woman." An-other useful source (and one that specifically addresses the British context) is Oppenheim 210–15, 230–32. See also Poovey 153, where she cites some of the com-ments by doctors that I look at in this essay.

2. In making this argument, I am expanding on the work of those critics who have noticed the representation of hysteria in "Carmilla"; see Veeder 214 and Stoddart 29–30.

3. There is a wealth of information on Victorian medicine and hysteria; sev-eral particularly helpful sources are Chapter 6, "Neurotic Women," in Oppenheim, esp. 188–91, and Showalter 129–32. For more on Victorian science and its theories about the link between women's nervous and reproductive systems, see Russett 116–18 and Helsinger, Sheets, and Veeder 2:75–84. Poovey's essay on chloroform discusses how troubled some Victorian physicians were by the idea that childbirth—presum-ably one of the holiest moments in a woman's career of motherhood—could cause sexual arousal; see esp. 146–147.

4. Compare also Carol A. Senf's claim that "the growing awareness of women's power and influence" as "feminists began to petition for additional rights" explains the popularity of the femme fatale characters in the late nineteenth century (*The Vam-pire in Nineteenth-Century Literature* 154). See also Dijkstra 333–51 and Gay 197–213.

5. Silas Weir Mitchell called hysteria the "nosological limbo of all unnamed female maladies" (Showalter 130).

6. See Yeazell for a perceptive discussion of ideological tensions in the very definition of modesty; women's strenuous attempts to maintain innocence suggest they might not naturally have it. Yeazell's chapter on women's consciousness of sexuality (51–64) is relevant to my discussion of "Carmilla," particularly her formulation that "the young woman's unknowing . . . was always engaged in undoing itself" (57). I am indebted to Susan Griffin for pointing out the usefulness of Yeazell's reading for my own.

7. Senf argues that in her role as delicately drooping invalid Carmilla shows how fashionable Victorian ladies are "languid and ornamental parasites," economi-cally dependent "bloodsucker[s]" who use their apparent passivity to "manipulate others" (29–31). This reading is similar to Nina Auerbach's argument in *Private The-atricals* that Victorian women used illness as performance art to gain some degree of power in their families.

8. For more on women's mutability and cultural anxieties about their transformative powers, see Auerbach, *Woman and the Demon,* and also her *Private Theatricals* 80–83. Interestingly, in *Private Theatricals,* Auerbach speaks of the affinity between actors and *male* vampires, but not female ones; the female vampire is a particularly disturbing image for the Victorian angel's potential ontological shiftiness.

9. A full examination of the role of the mother in "Carmilla" is beyond the scope of this essay. Nonetheless, it is suggestive that Carmilla's homoerotic attentions (while indubitably phallic) make Laura into a figure for the mother by simulating lactation, or sucking at the breast. Laura's own mother enters the story in a peculiarly disembodied away, apparently as the voice that exclaims, in the midst of one of Laura's tumultuous dreams, "Your mother bids you beware of the assassin" (308). Perhaps, however, this portrayal of the mother as guardian angel is meant to offset the implication, particularly threatening to domestic ideology, that she is in fact the transmitter of the demonic female sexuality associated with the Karnstein line.

10. See for instance Brumberg 175–76. In his chapter on vampirism, Bram Dijkstra discusses the late-nineteenth-century treatment of encouraging anemic young women to drink the blood of animals (337–38). Given, however, the medical paranoia about women's ingesting red meat, which was associated with the dangerous stimulation of their carnal desire, it is easy to see how such a cure could also be viewed as a source of disease.

11. As Deborah Gorham says, "If a Victorian adolescent girl exhibited pronounced 'chlorotic' or 'hysterical' symptoms, her family or the medical practitioner attending her might decide in the absence of other evident causes that masturbation was the cause" (89). For a discussion of Victorian young women and the symptomatology of masturbation, see Chapter 3 of Hartman, esp. 93.

12. I am indebted to Eva Berkes for drawing my attention to this photograph.

13. As Bram Dijkstra says, the black woman is the "veritable personification of woman's animal nature emanating from the evil East" (341). I am indebted to Sue Lonoff for pointing out to me that the illustrator of the 1886 edition of *In a Glass Darkly* emphasizes the Orientalized otherness of Carmilla by depicting her, during one of her nighttime visits to Laura, wearing a turbanlike headress; see the illustration in Le Fanu facing 304.

14. Cohen is influenced by Gorham, who claims that "unlike an adult woman, a girl could be perceived as a wholly unambiguous model of feminine dependence, childlike simplicity and sexual purity" (7). I would argue that in "Carmilla" we can see that this feminine ideal is far from "wholly unambiguous," as the text is permeated by a paranoid fear that the daughter may be a sexual woman after all.

15. This illustration, taken from the 1886 edition of *In a Glass Darkly,* may be found in Le Fanu, facing 332.

16. For more on women's communities and associations in this period, see Vicinus *Independent Women.*

17. See, for instance, Faderman. There has been much debate among feminist historians and literary scholars about when and how to read the presence of female homoeroticism in nineteenth-century sources. For instance, Martha Vicinus questions Sahli's dating of the morbidification of female friendship in her "Distance and Desire," 522 n. 4. Yet Vicinus also acknowledges, in a more recent essay, that, not only is "lesbian history . . . in its initial stages," but "I think we may have exaggerated the acceptability of romantic friendships" in the nineteenth century ("'They Wonder to What Sex I Belong'" 467, 483). One refreshing response to what she wittily describes as to the "no sex before 1900" school of lesbian history is Terry Castle's *The Apparitional Lesbian,* which sees lesbianism as the ghostly presence and locus of anxiety in texts written well before Ellis and Krafft-Ebing. Certainly, a text like "Carmilla" is a fascinating, relatively early example of the morbidification of female friendship and its links to homoeroticism and female sexual knowledge.

18. For more on this type of sexual mutilation as an extreme way of control-

ling feminine sexuality, see Dally 146–64, and Showalter 75–78.

19. In *Reading Woman,* Mary Jacobus, taking Breuer's comment about hysterics and reminiscence as a touchstone, characterizes the Gothic as a version of the hysterical text in a reading that is relevant to this discussion of "Carmilla" (249–74).

## WORKS CITED

Auerbach, Nina. *Private Theatricals: Lives of the Victorians.* Cambridge: Harvard UP, 1990.

———. *Woman and the Demon: The Life of a Victorian Myth.* Cambridge: Harvard UP, 1982.

Bell, Rudolph M. *Holy Anorexia.* Chicago: U of Chicago P, 1985.

Bordo, Susan. "Anorexia Nervosa: Psychopathology as the Crystallization of Culture." *Unbearable Weight: Feminism, Western Culture, and the Body.* Berkeley: U of California P, 1993. 139–64.

Breuer, Josef, and Sigmund Freud. *Studies on Hysteria.* Translated and edited by James Strachey. Vol. 2 of *The Standard Edition of the Psychological Works of Sigmund Freud.* 24 vols. London: Hogarth Press, 1953–1974.

Brumberg, Joan Jacobs. *Fasting Girls: The Emergence of Anorexia Nervosa as a Modern Disease.* Cambridge: Harvard UP, 1988.

Case, Sue-Ellen. "Tracking the Vampire." *differences* 3 (1991): 1–20.

Castle, Terry. *The Apparitional Lesbian: Female Homosexuality and Modern Culture.* New York: Columbia UP, 1993.

Cixous, Hélène. "Castration or Decapitation?" (Translated by Annette Kuhn) *Signs* 7 (1981): 41–55.

Cohen, Paula Marantz. *The Daughter's Dilemma: Family Process and the Nineteenth-Century Domestic Novel.* Ann Arbor: U of Michigan P, 1991.

Dally, Ann. *Women under the Knife: A History of Surgery.* New York: Routledge, 1992.

Didi-Huberman, Georges. *Invention de l'hystérie: Charcot et l'iconographie photographique de la Salpêtrière.* Paris: Macula, 1982.

Dijkstra, Bram. *Idols of Perversity: Fantasies of Feminine Evil in Fin-de-Siècle Culture.* New York: Oxford UP, 1986.

Faderman, Lillian. "The Morbidification of Love between Women by Nineteenth-Century Sexologists." *Journal of Homosexuality* 4, 1 (1978): 73–90.

Gay, Peter. *Education of the Senses.* Vol. 2 of *The Bourgeois Experience: Victoria to Freud.* New York: Oxford UP, 1984.

Gorham, Deborah. *The Victorian Girl and the Feminine Ideal.* Bloomington: Indiana UP, 1982.

Hartman, Mary. *Victorian Murderesses: A True History of Thirteen Respectable French and English Women Accused of Unspeakable Crimes.* New York: Schocken, 1977.

Helsinger, Elizabeth K., Robin Lauterbach Sheets, and William Veeder, eds. *The Woman Question: Society and Literature in Britain and America 1837–1883.* 3 vols. Chicago: U of Chicago P, 1983.

Jacobus, Mary. *Reading Woman: Essays in Feminist Criticism.* New York: Columbia UP, 1986.

Le Fanu, Joseph Sheridan. "Carmilla." *Best Ghost Stories.* Edited by E.F. Bleiler. New York: Dover, 1964. 274–339.

McCormack, W.J. *Sheridan Le Fanu and Victorian Ireland.* Oxford: Clarendon Press, 1980.

Melada, Ivan. *Sheridan Le Fanu.* Boston: Twayne, 1987.

Mitchell, Silas Weir. *Fat and Blood: And How to Make Them.* New York: J.B. Lippincott, 1877.

Oppenheim, Janet. *"Shattered Nerves": Doctors, Patients, and Depression in Victo-*

*rian England*. New York: Oxford UP, 1991.

Poovey, Mary. "Scenes of an Indelicate Character: The Medical 'Treatment' of Victorian Women." *Representations* 14 (1986): 137–68.

Putzell-Korab, Sara. "Passion between Women in the Victorian Novel." *Sexuality and Victorian Literature*. Edited by Don Richard Cox. *Tennessee Studies in Literature*, vol. 27. Knoxville: U of Tennessee P, 1984. 180–95.

Russett, Cynthia Eagle. *Sexual Science: The Victorian Construction of Womanhood.* Cambridge: Harvard UP, 1989.

Sahli, Nancy. "Smashing: Women's Relationships before the Fall." *Chrysalis* 8 (Summer 1979): 17–27.

Sedgwick, Eve. "Privilege of Unknowing." *Genders* 1 (Spring 1988): 102–24.

Senf, Carol A. *The Vampire in Nineteenth-Century Literature*. Bowling Green, Ohio: Bowling Green State University Popular Press, 1988.

———. "Women and Power in 'Carmilla.'" *Gothic* 3 (1986): 25–33.

Showalter, Elaine. *The Female Malady: Women, Madness, and English Culture 1830–1980*. New York: Penguin, 1985.

Shuttleworth, Sally. "Demonic Mothers: Ideologies of Bourgeois Motherhood in the Mid-Victorian Era." *Rewriting the Victorians*. Edited by Linda M. Shires. New York: Routledge, 1992. 31–51.

———. "Female Circulation: Medical Discourse and Popular Advertising in the Mid-Victorian Era." *Body/Politics: Women and the Discourses of Science*. Edited by Mary Jacobus, Evelyn Fox Keller, and Sally Shuttleworth. New York: Routledge, 1990. 47–68.

Smith-Rosenberg, Carroll. "The Female World of Love and Ritual: Relations between Women in Nineteenth-Century America." 1975. Reprint. *Disorderly Conduct: Visions of Gender in Nineteenth-Century America*. New York: Knopf, 1985. 53–76.

———. "The Hysterical Woman: Sex Roles and Role Conflict in Nineteenth-Century America." 1972. Reprint. *Disorderly Conduct*. 197–216.

———. "Puberty to Menopause: The Cycle of Femininity in Nineteenth-Century America." 1973. Reprint. *Disorderly Conduct*. 182–96.

Stoddart, Helen. "'The Precautions of Nervous People are Infectious': Sheridan Le Fanu's Symptomatic Gothic." *Modern Language Review* 86 (January 1991): 19–34.

Veeder, William. "'Carmilla': The Arts of Repression." *Texas Studies in Literature and Language* 22, 2 (Summer 1980): 197–223.

Veith, Ilza. *Hysteria: The History of a Disease*. Chicago: U of Chicago P, 1965.

Vicinus, Martha. "Distance and Desire: English Boarding School Friendships 1870–1920." *Hidden from History: Reclaiming the Gay and Lesbian Past*. Edited by Martin Duberman, Martha Vicinus, and George Chauncey, Jr. New York: Penguin-Meridian, 1989. 212–29.

———. *Independent Women: Work and Community for Single Women 1850–1920*. Chicago: U of Chicago P, 1985.

———. "'They Wonder to What Sex I Belong': The Historical Roots of Modern Lesbian Identity." *Feminist Studies* 18, 3 (Fall 1992): 467–97.

Waller, Gregory A. *The Living and the Undead: From Stoker's* Dracula *to Romero's* Dawn of the Dead. Urbana: U of Illinois P, 1986.

Yeazell, Ruth Bernard. *Fictions of Modesty: Women and Courtship in the English Novel*. Chicago: U of Chicago P, 1991.

## SELECTED SECONDARY SOURCES

Marjorie Howes, "Misalliance and Anglo-Irish Tradition in Le Fanu's *Uncle Silas*," *Nineteenth-Century Literature* 47, 2 (September 1992): 164–86; W.J. McCormack, *Sheridan Le Fanu and Victorian Ireland* (Oxford: Clarendon Press,

1980); Ivan Melada, *Sheridan Le Fanu* (Boston: Twayne, 1987); Alison Milbank, *Daughters of the House: Modes of Gothic in Victorian Fiction* (New York: St. Martin's Press, 1992), 158–97; Carol A. Senf, "Women and Power in 'Carmilla,'" *Gothic* 3 (1987): 25–33; Helen Stoddart, "'The Precautions of Nervous People are Infectious': Sheridan Le Fanu's Symptomatic Gothic," *Modern Language Review* 86 (January 1991): 19–34; William Veeder, "'Carmilla': The Arts of Repression," *Texas Studies in Literature and Language* 22, 2 (Summer 1980): 197–223.

# SOLICITORS SOLICITING

## THE DANGEROUS CIRCULATIONS OF PROFESSIONALISM IN DRACULA (1897)

*Jasmine Yong Hall*

Like Jonathan Harker, Bram Stoker (1847–1912) began his professional life as a bureaucrat in a Gothic setting—he worked as a clerk in Dublin Castle. Bored with his work, Stoker volunteered his services as unpaid drama critic to the *Dublin Mail*. It was through this extracurricular activity that Stoker met the actor Henry Irving who was to act as Stoker's mentor, business partner, and model for his best-remembered creation, *Dracula*. Stoker first became interested in vampires after making the acquaintance of Professor Arminus Vamberg, an expert on Eastern European legends, at one of Irving's backstage entertainments. (In the novel, Van Helsing makes mention of his friend "Arminus" as a fellow vampire scholar.) Stoker was also inspired by John Polidori's *The Vampyre* (1819), and Sheridan Le Fanu's more recently published (1872) "Carmilla." The influence of "Carmilla" is evident in the first drafts of the novel, in which Dracula's castle was to have been located in Styria, the setting for Le Fanu's story.

Though *Dracula* was a success, the years following its publication were years of declining health and fortune for Stoker. He became increasingly ill with what was recorded at his death in 1912 as "general paresis," but which his biographer and great-nephew, Daniel Farson, describes as tertiary syphilis. Critics like Robin Tracy have implied that Stoker was infected with the disease through contact with prostitutes after his wife refused sexual contact following the birth of their first and only child. Other critics have suggested that the homoeroticism underlying Stoker's relationship with Henry Irving did not remain, as Farson asserts, unconscious, but was acted upon with the consequence of Stoker's infection. In both cases, the infection of vampirism which Stoker made famous is often said to be a symbolic stand-in for the disease that took his own life.

Other works by Stoker include *Dracula's Guest, and Other Weird Stories* (London: George Routledge, 1914); *The Jewel of Seven Stars* (Scholastic Book Services, 1972); *The Lady of the Shroud* (London: William Heinemann, 1909); *The Lair of the White Worm* (London: Arrow, 1960).

Until recently, *Dracula* was "underread" in academic circles, though it has received much critical attention in the last several years. Even before its circulation among professional readers, however, *Dracula* was very much a focus of popular interest, as the recent retelling of the tale in Francis Ford Coppola's film attests. The curse of vampirism is not eradicated by the closing of Stoker's novel, for the vampire rises in other forms, recirculating in the cultural bloodstream.[1] Perhaps the undead can never be underread.

Blood circulation is the central plot concern of the novel, but circulation is also more generally the novel's central device. Beginning in Transylvania, the "centre of some sort of imaginative whirlpool" (2), a movement begins which carries "the whirlpool of European races" (28) in the person of Count Dracula to "the whirl and rush of humanity" (20) which characterizes the fin-de-siècle London street. While blood-flow is its most sensational circulation, the novel also traces the flow of money, bodies, and land in and out of Transylvania accompanied by a bureaucratic stream of paper and red tape, and accomplished by means of transport ranging from trains to horsemen, from sailing ships to a steam-launch to a gypsy flatboat. Finally, the text itself is presented as the product of many sources of information—diaries in shorthand and phonographic disc, newspaper clippings, letters, telegrams—which circulate among the band of vampire hunters until, transcribed by Mina Harker, they coalesce as the words that pass before the reader.

Critical readings of the text have illuminated various aspects of these whirls of movement. The greatest number focus on sexuality with vampirism as a displaced form of sexual intercourse.[2] With the substitution of blood-sucking for intercourse, the circulation of blood becomes the threat of venereal disease,[3] or miscegenation;[4] gender itself circulates in the apparent bisexual thirst of the vampire, and the vampire's phallically potent mouth which confuses male and female genitalia.[5] Other borderlines are similarly threatened: Franco Moretti sees *Dracula* as representative of the English fear of an invasion of monopoly capital from Europe. Stephen D. Arata also analyzes the text as a story of invasion, a "reverse colonization" (623) in which "Dracula imperils not simply his victims' personal identities, but also their cultural, political, and racial selves. . . . Having yielded to his assault, one literally 'goes native' by becoming a vampire oneself" (630). In all these ways, *Dracula* illustrates a central crisis in the identity of the liberal subject "when the languages of selfhood and otherness . . . become unfixed" (Glover 984).

That crisis is most fully embodied in the novel's ostensible hero, Jonathan Harker. As Christopher Craft explains, Harker is the one man in the text who comes close to being vamped by Dracula—a homoerotic embrace which places Harker's male identity in question. Harker is also the only character to venture into foreign territory alone, and in so doing comes very close to "going native." Harker's journal, which opens the novel, highlights the unknown quality of this strange land: "the East," where trains don't run on time, and there are no Ordnance Survey Maps (1). Here, Harker discovers new gustatory pleasures: "a chicken done up some way with red pepper . . . very good but thirsty" (1), "for breakfast more paprika" (2), "Golden Mediasch" wine "which produces a queer sting on the tongue" (5). But acquiring foreign tastes is dangerous, for, as Nancy Armstrong notes in relation to Rider Haggard's heroes, "food contains possibilities of pollution for Englishmen" (28). As the color, "sting," and effects (thirst and, later, sleepless nights) of this food suggest a vampiric transformation, Harker shows the necessity for the "self restraint" which "makes all the difference . . . in determining whether such moments of . . . quite literal incorporation . . . invigorate or corrupt the European" (Armstrong 28–29).

Harker's self-control is later tested and found wanting when he longs for a kiss from the red lips of Dracula's vampire women. From eating Transylvanian food to becoming a Transylvanian meal, Harker circulates through this section of the novel with an increasingly dissociated identity, an identity which is put under pressure by the female role of subservience which Harker must adopt as a solicitor in relation to his client, Dracula. At last, Harker loses his identity altogether when Dracula leaves the castle in Harker's clothes, with his notes, railway schedules, and letters of credit, and with letters written by Harker as if on return route which Dracula posts along his own way to England.

The alliance with Dracula which threatens Harker's identity is literally a business relationship, and it is in these terms that the novel can be accurately described as "underread" by academic critics. While most analyses have focused on the text's barely suppressed eroticism (if "suppressed" is the right term to describe a novel which touches on so many Victorian "perversions"), I would argue that it is Harker's profession which is central to an understanding of the novel's representation of the threat of sexuality and the blurring of gender roles. Harker eventually comes to the guilty realization that his job has been to facilitate Dracula's penetration of England and its inhabitants: "This was the being I was helping to transfer to London, where, perhaps for centuries to come, he might amongst its teeming millions, satiate his lust for blood, and create a new and ever widening circle of semi-demons to batten on the helpless" (51). As a solicitor he is responsible not only for acquiring Dracula's London property, but for instructing him on the best means to ship his boxes of Transylvanian earth, his tombs away from home, into England where they will be distributed by his fellow solicitors, allowing Dracula freedom of movement within the entire country. These instructions, in turn, allow Dracula to step into Harker's position as the count leaves the castle in the guise of the solicitor. It is Harker's profession, then, which puts him at the center of the whirlpool—the catalyst for all the other circulations of the text, and the male subject whose gender identity is most at risk.

The danger of these circulations, primarily the dangerous vampiric draining of Harker's professional skills, will be circumvented in the second half of the novel as the access to knowledge becomes regulated and controlled in the hierarchy of a different profession—medicine. In this hierarchy, control is returned to the male professional as women's appetites make them the object of knowledge. Finally, the last section of the novel will replace the male professional Harker with his wife Mina as the center of circulation, thus constructing a new ideal version of womanhood—the feminized clerk, the professionalized wife. What I focus on then, in contrast to earlier readings of gender and sexuality in *Dracula,* is the radical reconstitution of gender roles as the emergent ideology of professionalism comes into conflict with the Victorian construction of man as the independent, self-sufficient breadwinner, and woman as the dependent guardian of the hearth.

Harold Perkin's description of *The Rise of Professional Society* helps to explain Harker's centrality as a professional man to plots of circulation and vampirism. The emergent ideology of professionalism opposed earlier means to power/prestige/wealth based on land and bloodties (the aristocracy) or on investment and entrepreneurship (capitalism) with the ideal that society should "reward expert service based on selection by merit and long arduous training" (117). However, the question of how reward and merit are assessed is problematic: the professional is "offering a service that is . . . esoteric, evanescent, . . . beyond the layman's knowledge or judgment, impossible to pin down or fault" (117). The professional man's abilities are immaterial and protean; they cannot be judged by appearance, for they have none. Like that of the vampire, the professional man's true nature will not appear in the mirror.

Barriers which keep each class, gender, race, and culture in its proper place become rules and regulations rather than "natural" and "inherent" definitions. The new ease of entry created by this regulation-governed society is clarified by Dr. Van Helsing when he describes how the vampire hunters will attempt to gain access to Dracula's London house. As he explains to Jonathan: "You go take the lock off a hundred empty houses in this your London, or of any city in the world; and if you do it as such things are rightly done, and at the time such things are rightly done, no one will interfere." To illustrate this point, Van Helsing tells the story of a burglar who broke into a house, pretended to live there, sold all the belongings in an auction, and then had the house itself sold and torn down. "And your police and other authority help him all they can. . . . This was all done *en règle;* and in our work we shall be *en règle* too" (293). As no outward sign distinguishes the burglar from the man in whose proper place the burglar takes up residence, following the rules and regulations only serves to make the invader's position appear legal and respectable. In such a world, the substitution of the foreign, female other for the English male subject becomes more imaginable.

Land and capital, at least at the ideological level, are replaced by human skills and abilities as the means to social progress and prosperity: "Before the end of the century the most important kind of waste had come to be recognized as the waste of *human* resources" (Perkin 155). Such a description accords with Foucault's summary of the change from older mechanisms of power based on sovereignty to new mechanisms of power based on the disciplines (schools, armies, universities, prisons), and on regulatory controls directed against the reproductive body: "It is no longer a matter of bringing death into play in the field of sovereignty, but of distributing the living in the domain of value and utility" (144)—a power, in other words, which looks like that of the vampire, whose "ultimate aim is not to destroy the lives of others according to whim, to waste them, but to *use* them" (Moretti 91).

This vampiric desire to make use of human capital is literally rendered in Dracula's relationship to Harker, for while Dracula's desire later expresses itself as blood-sucking, what he wants from Jonathan is "to pump him for his knowledge of English law, custom, and language" (Craft 219). He sucks Jonathan's mind rather than his heart. Eliciting this desire for one's services is, in fact, the means by which the professional man lives, "by persuasion and propaganda, by claiming that their particular service is indispensable to the client or employer" (Perkin 6). The solicitor survives by soliciting, by placing himself in the female position as object of desire. Like women who solicit, however, the solicitor is not "indispensable" but infinitely replaceable, and he is replaceable not only by others who offer a similar service, but also by the client himself, if that service involves passing on one's training and expertise. Giving Dracula skills in English language and customs,

Harker allows the Transylvanian to acquire an Englishman's tastes, at least to the extent that Dracula can circulate in London and satiate his taste for the English unnoticed.

The eventual substitution of Dracula for Harker highlights the dangerous instability presented by professional society. This danger helps to explain the seemingly odd juxtaposition of Harker's thoughts about his career with his entry into Castle Dracula:

> Was this a customary incident in the life of a solicitor's clerk sent out to explain the purchase of a London estate to a foreigner? Solicitor's clerk! Mina would not like that. Solicitor—for just before leaving London I got word that my examination was successful; and now I am a full-blown solicitor! I began to rub my eyes and pinch myself to see if I were awake. It all seemed like a horrible nightmare to me and I expected that I should suddenly awake, and find myself at home, with the dawn struggling in through the windows, as I had now and again felt in the morning after a day of overwork. (15)

Here the reality of Harker's life—his examination, his promotion to solicitor, his days of overwork—are overlaid with an uncanny, nightmare existence; yet the two are tied together in Harker's notion that such nightmares follow days of overwork. Within the castle, further connections are made wherein each aspect of the professional's life is perversely reflected back to him.

Harker carries with him a letter from his employer, Mr. Hawkins, explaining why Harker, a "sufficient substitute," has been sent in Hawkins's place. The letter goes on to describe Harker and his professional qualifications; he is

> full of energy and talent in his own way, and of a very faithful disposition. He is discreet and silent, and has grown into manhood in my service. He shall be ready to attend on you when you will during his stay, and shall take your instructions in all matters. (17)

The letter first reinforces the idea that the professional man is dispensable— his place can be filled by those that he trains in his service—and then attempts to make that service indispensable through the qualities of loyalty, silence, and complete obedience (putting in question the kind of "manhood" that one grows into in "service"). Like the Victorian wife, the professional is only valuable if he is faithful: the qualities of secrecy and dutifulness protect the client himself from being replaced by a rival employer.

Harker's first act of disobedience against Dracula is to wander into areas of the castle where he has been warned he must never fall asleep. In rebellion, then, Harker also plays the female part, that of Bluebeard's overly curious wife. Falling asleep on "a great couch . . . where of old ladies had sat and sung and lived sweet lives whilst their gentle breasts were sad for their menfolk away in the midst of remorseless wars" (37), he immediately finds himself the prey of the rival vampires—the three women to whom Harker passively submits himself to be feasted on. Like the sleep-walking Lucy Westenra later in the novel, Harker is the fallen woman who, walking out of her assigned boundaries, offers herself to strangers in the middle of the night. Taking notes on Transylvanian culture,[6] Harker displays a dangerous appetite which, in the second half of the novel, will be represented as a desire that only women experience. And just as Lucy's appetites will make her the object of Dracula's hunger, Harker's desire threatens to make him into a vampire meal.

That desire expresses itself passively as a desire to be kissed. The solicitor solicits; as a professional, his desire is to be desired, and his passivity places him in an increasingly effeminized role as his stay in the castle progresses. First he finds his schedule rearranged so that he must work at night and sleep during the day: a solicitor's duty forces him to keep the hours of those who work at night, prostitutes and vampires. "This nocturnal existence" produces hysteria: "It is destroying my nerve. I start at my own shadow, and am full of all sorts of horrible imaginings" (33). Dracula will not let him leave the castle though, for he points out that when Harker was "engaged . . . it was understood that my needs only were to be consulted" (32). Harker's only possible response to this tactfully worded command is dutiful obedience: "What could I do, but bow acceptance? It was Mr. Hawkins' interest, not mine, and I had to think of him, not myself" (32). Harker as solicitor can have no interest of his own; he is not "the man himself" (172) but a stand-in. Lacking this agency, he must obey his "master, employer, what you will" (32) for he, again like the Victorian woman, needs the financial support of the male. In the nightmare version of professionalism that Harker faces in Castle Dracula, the professional's role is always that of subservience. In order to make himself valuable he must promise to honor and obey the client. When he disobeys, he becomes the fallen woman, promiscuously offering himself to others. And once he has serviced the client, he can be abandoned—left without male support and protection—a complete dependence which Harker begins to realize after his encounter with the vampire women: "To [Dracula] alone I can look for safety, even though this be only whilst I can serve his purpose" (36).

Dracula's role in this male relationship is empowered not only by his status as client,[7] but also by his occupancy of any and all male positions of power. He is "noble . . . *boyar* . . . master" (20) with an aristocratic lineage going back to the Vikings, Huns, and other "brave races who fought as the lion fights for lordship" (28). But he is also the model of the capitalist "self-made man." Unlike the idle aristocracy, he is constantly at work—whether he is driving the carriage, making the beds, or teaching himself all that is to be known of England. He has a self-sufficiency which allows him to do without servants, and even, seemingly, without nourishment.

The ability to learn new skills is the key to Dracula's powers here, though later he will be transformed by Van Helsing's classification of him as a creature with a "child-brain" to a being who can only repeat old behaviors (341). Though he can embody various male positions of power, he is not fixed in any one of those positions. His protean nature makes him an uncanny double of the professional—able to acquire skills to meet every new contingency. He drains away human capital from first one source then another, making clear the fears of replaceability that underlie the modern professional's world.

Though Dracula's power is connected to the past through its association with blood, money, and land—symbols of aristocracy and capitalism—these symbols are not tied to that past, but are shown to be unfixed and movable. Dracula's money is literally taken from the land, dug up from where it has long been buried by peasants under siege: "Why there is hardly a foot of soil in all this region that has not been enriched by the blood of men, patriots or invaders" (21). Land becomes money through a circulation of blood which mingles the identity of patriot and invader. All three are then put into circulation in England through the medium of the professional. Money circulates[8] through Dracula's use of gold to buy the services of solicitors in England, and through those solicitors into the pockets of various businessmen engaged to ship the count's crates of earth. The count is a man who carries his estate with him; his native soil dug up and shipped to England puts the very nature of homeland in question. Where does England begin and Transylvania end? Can Dracula truly be an invader when he sleeps on the soil of his own country? And finally these little pieces of Transylvania replanted in England give Dracula safe havens from which to begin his central circulation, the mixing of class, gender, and nationality in his attacks on Lucy Westenra and Mina Harker.

These circulations can all be traced back to the training in professional skills which Dracula receives from Harker. He is given these instructions after informing Harker that he does not want to hire a solicitor in each port since he fears that a resident agent might serve a "local interest" and not make his "labours . . . only to my interest" (30–31). Harker explains that the count can place all his business dealings in the hands of one man since "solicitors [have] a system of agency one for the other, so that local work could be done locally on instruction from any solicitor" (31). Again, what is made apparent is the replaceability of the solicitor. He is not a single agent, but a part of a "system of agency." Picking up on this replaceability, Dracula decides that he will be the one man who directs all the others and asks about "making consignments and the forms to be gone through." Harker, admiring Dracula's progress in these lessons in law, is left with "the impression that he would have made a wonderful solicitor. . . . For a man who was never in the country, and who did not evidently do much in the way of business, his knowledge and acumen were wonderful" (31). Taking his teacher's place, Dracula then becomes the center of circulation through which the English will receive instructions, shipments of land, gold, and eventually blood.

It is the relation of power to knowledge which is crucial to these various circulations. Harker only has power when he retains knowledge which Dracula lacks. The alliance of power/knowledge is earlier described by Dracula in a discussion which makes clear that the modern version of this relationship differs from that which existed under a fixed class system:

> Here I am noble; I am boyar, the common people know me, and I am master. But a stranger in a strange land, he is no one. . . . I am content if I am like the rest, so that no man stops if he sees me, or pause in his speaking if he hear my words, to say, "Ha, ha! a stranger!" I have been so long master that I would be master still— or at least that none other should be master of me. (20)

In Transylvania, Dracula is a nobleman among common people—to be known is to be acknowledged as master. But in England, to be known is to be acknowledged a stranger, one who is laughed at because of his lack of knowledge. To acquire knowledge is then a means to mastery, or at the very least a means to become "like the rest." Dracula's final words here show that in the modern world knowledge does not guarantee power, but only allows one to keep pace in the ever shifting movement of power. To bring an end to the circulations of money, land, blood, and the power associated with all three, knowledge must be re-presented in a much more regulated and hierarchical fashion. Such a representation takes place when the setting shifts to England, and the professional man becomes not a solicitor but a doctor.

In the first section of the novel, knowledge is available to all who seek it. Jonathan has learned all he can in advance about Transylvania from a visit to the British Museum (1). His continued recording of the sights and sounds of the country, as we have seen above, shows the danger this acquisition of knowledge poses: it may turn the student into the thing he studies—he becomes "like the rest" rather than a "stranger in a strange land." And just as the Englishman can become Transylvanian, the Transylvanian can become English—a transformation aided and abetted by the position of female dependence and subservience in which the professional man is placed in relation to his client.

It is just this easy circulation of knowledge which comes to an end in the next section of the novel. In the practice of medicine, knowledge is passed on only through specialized training, and, as represented in the novel, is never given to the client/patient. As Van Helsing explains to his pupil John Seward, any patient must be treated with the same circumspection that Seward reserves for his asylum inmates:

> All men are mad in some way or the other; and inasmuch as you deal discreetly with your madmen, so deal with God's madmen, too—the rest of the world. You tell not your madmen what you do nor why you do it; you tell them not what you think. So you shall keep knowledge in its place, where it may rest—where it may gather its kind around it and breed. (118)

Here knowledge has a fixed place; it does not travel in books or journals, or through the medium of one who carries that knowledge with him to foreign climes. As knowledge stays locked within the brain of the expert, there is no fear of miscegenation: knowledge only breeds with its own kind. Such a representation counters the flow of information in Transylvania, and the fear that knowledge, like vampires, grows by mating exogamously, turning the other—the ignorant, the stranger—into the knowing, native, self.

The hierarchy of expertise and ignorance is facilitated in Van Helsing's description by imagining all patients as madmen. Throughout most of this section of the novel, though, the focus is on the female patient, Lucy Westenra, Dracula's first victim. The female dependence of the professional now becomes the dependence of the female patient on the professional. Thus relations between men become a highly regulated and disciplined means by which one acquires knowledge through training from experts—experts who, unlike Jonathan Harker, only give that knowledge to men like themselves—while the position of complete dependence is filled by those to whom knowledge is never allowed, the madman and the woman.

This hierarchy of male rationality which must control the female as source of foreign infection is directly analogous to the attempt to control syphilis through the containment of infection in the female body of the prostitute and through the containment of that body in Lock Hospitals, instituted by the Contagious Diseases Act at mid-century.[9] As Elaine Showalter explains, this mechanism of power/knowledge directed against the female body is analogous to the violent exploration of women's bodies in *Dracula*: "Women undergo the worst effects, and the men must 'save' them by such violent medical interventions as decapitation and phallic stakes through the heart" (99).

Such measures are justified in *Dracula,* as they were in the culture at large, by a need to control female sexual excess. This excess is epitomized by Lucy's desire to marry all three men who have proposed to her, and by the hunger which is symptomatic of vampirism: "I have an appetite like a cormorant, am full of life. . . . Arthur says I am getting fat" (106). It is Harker's appetite, his consumption of Transylvanian meals both literally, and figuratively through the memoranda of his notebook, that begins the novel. Both in the notebook and in the person of Count Dracula, Harker is responsible for importing foreign tastes. The professional man's appetite is monstrously rendered in the middle section of the novel by the madman Renfield, who, like a good clerk, keeps notes on every fly, spider, and bird he consumes. But for the most part, this section of the novel conveniently forgets the central role played by the professional in the circulation of taste and places the sin of appetite very much in the home, and within the person of the idle woman.

This emphasis on female appetite not only symbolizes sexual excess, it also represents a change in female roles as women took over the management of family finances. As Armstrong notes:

> Suddenly shopping was something that women, rather than men, were supposed to do. Moreover, department stores appeared in England and France to display the goods of empire in a setting that uniquely combined shopping with dining out and entertainment. In this way, the new mode of shopping associated the acquisition of objects with the pleasure of surveying and literally consuming, or eating, them. (17)

The goods of empire, consumed by the Victorian middle class woman, are then put on display in the English home; again national boundaries are put under pressure as the Victorian family sits among artifacts of "primitive" peoples. It is just this type of merchandise, pieces of Transylvania, which

Harker has allowed to enter the country, but in focusing on female appetite, the responsibility for the acquisition of foreignness rests with the female consumer rather than the male importer.

This change in women's roles threatened the Victorian ideal of the separation of spheres as women ventured into the previously male public and economic domain. Middle-class women now seemingly occupied the place of the idle aristocracy:

> The capital accumulation of the nineteenth century made it possible for women of this class (bourgeoisie) to enjoy a certain leisure, leave their interiors, and lead a form of aristocratic life modeled on that of the old nobility. The men worked to assure the women the possibility of conspicuous consumption. (Rémy Saisselin qtd. in Armstrong, note 12)

The Victorian home, presided over by its resident Angel, was no longer a retreat from the rigors of the marketplace—a place in which the man was revitalized to face the work-a-day world; instead, home and wife represented a draining away of male vitality into female consumption and acquisition. This draining of male vitality is realized in *Dracula* as Lucy receives transfusion after transfusion from her male suitors only to have that blood sucked away by Dracula. Lucy takes all the human capital of the Englishmen and spends it on foreign goods.

While the domestic front becomes the setting of horrible transformations and exchanges, the workplace is cleansed of all such associations which dominate Harker's professional life in the opening of the novel. In contrast to the terrors of the home, work becomes a means to cure the draining of vitality inflicted by women. Seward describes work's curative powers in regard to overcoming the grief he feels over Lucy's death: "I was settling down to my work with the enthusiasm which I used to have for it, so that I might fairly have said that the wound which poor Lucy left on me was becoming cicatrized" (190). Over and over Lucy's literal draining of the men's blood is tied to the image of the lover's bleeding heart. In the Victorian ideal of the Angel in the House, man's love for woman is imagined as a civilizing force, one which purified the male worker from the contaminations of the marketplace. But here it is the emotional dependence of the men on the woman which forces them to open their veins so that blood may flow through her to strengthen the invasive and contaminating vampire—a symbolic rendering of male financial support, the opening of their wallets, to feed a female desire for foreign merchandise.

The female taste for the exotic is even more directly rendered when Mina Harker becomes Dracula's next victim, for Mina is not only consumed by Dracula, but is forced, in return, to drink the vampire's blood. Having witnessed this horrific display of female appetite within his own bedroom, Jonathan Harker finds solace in the work of fighting the vampire—a duty which Mina urges him to continue to pursue:

> Poor Mina told me just now, with the tears running down her dear cheeks, . . . that God will aid us up to the end. The end! oh, my God! what end? . . . To work! To work! (289)

Mina seemingly represents a return to the Victorian Angel, the domestic woman who keeps her husband's faith intact so that he can continue his struggles in the outside world. But Mina does not completely fit with this older female ideal, in particular because she has learned the value of duty and service by working herself. In her first letter to Lucy, Mina is introduced as a working woman: a schoolteacher who is also learning shorthand "to be useful to Jonathan" (53). She leads a life of utility and support for the male which is contrasted with Lucy's protected leisure. Mina, then, occupies an ambiguous position in the novel, one which illustrates a growing conflict between the cultural bias against work for women and the increasing power of the work ethic, especially as influenced by a professional idealization of work as service to the community as a whole.[10]

As Jennifer Wicke points out, the "economic isolation" of women in the home created "a captive audience for the vampiric ministrations of commoditized culture" (477). To control the appetites thus created requires a training in the values of control, duty, and service which men were receiving in universities and public schools—that is, a training in the discipline of the professional. Mina upholds this new role of woman as public servant primarily through her skills as typist and stenographer: "She is the rewriter, the transcriber, the secretary who arranges all the documents in chronological order and composes the case (legal and medical) of Dracula" (Wall 16). She holds, then, the position of "Solicitor's Clerk" from which Jonathan has just been promoted when the novel opens. In this position, Mina acts to recontain all the feminine attributes which had threatened to emasculate her husband.

It is her solicitous work as secretary which serves to heal the emotional wounds left by the undisciplined and idle Lucy. She takes Seward's phonographic diary which "in its very tones" shows "the anguish of [his] heart" and transforms them into a typewritten text so that "none other need now hear your heartbeat" (222). Similarly, Jonathan's journal, recorded in shorthand, passes through Mina's typewriter to become a text which Jonathan can reread as a cure for the nervous hysteria which continues to plague him. The self which is drained away by his vampiric client is returned to him through his wife's transcription. The ideal woman's role is not just to oversee the personal and emotional life of the man through her domestic influence, but to transform that personal life—whether kept on phonographic disc or in shorthand journals—into a public text, a text which presents the professional man as the unified liberal subject, both knowledgeable and powerful. As Harker remarks on the effects of this transformation, "It seems to have made a new man of me. . . . I felt impotent, and in the dark, and distrustful. But, now that I *know,* I am not afraid, even of the Count" (187–88).

Mina bridges the gap between inner and outer, between domestic duty and social duty, between the private and public self. As Secretary/Angel she gives private comfort to the men while preparing them for the public duty of vampire-slaying. In so doing, Mina plays a key role in upholding "the professional ideal . . . of justification by service to society" (Perkin 123). This justification helps to solve the problem of dependence and consequent emasculation of the professional man faced by Jonathan in the opening of the novel, for here professionalism is no longer imagined as soliciting and servicing the needs of the male client, but performing a social responsibility on behalf of society.[11]

The beginning of the text constructs the public world of the professional man as a world in which he must play the female part; he must be loyal and obedient to the client on whom he is completely dependent. All his energy, all his manhood, is drained away in this professional service. In the middle of the novel, the blame for this draining of male vitality is shifted to home and the woman. It is the woman's new power as financial manager which threatens to drain English male resources into foreign pockets. Harker's experience with Dracula is reimagined, then, as a problem not of professional relations but emotional ones—the emotional hold that women have over men. Healing Jonathan's wound in the construction of a new public identity flowing out of Mina's typewriter, the text conveniently suppresses the knowledge that that wound originates in man's public, professional life. The text focuses attention instead on the ambiguous role Mina plays as the medium for the exchange of information. Placing a woman in the center of this circulation puts her in a powerful position in a world in which knowledge is a means to mastery. In fact, Mina's pivotal role in "curing" the men seems to threaten the exclusion of women from the medical profession which is established in the doctors' treatment of Lucy. The hierarchy of access to knowledge set up by Van Helsing in the middle of the novel begins to collapse as the novel draws to its conclusion. What the last section of the novel must accomplish, then, is to construct a new model of femininity which recontains the effeminizing aspects of the professional man's position, regulates sexual excess through the discipline of the professional, and still works to maintain a gender hierarchy in which women will not gain access to the power that professional knowledge affords.

The construction of this model is highlighted by the constant reevaluation of Mina's role among the vampire killers at the end of the novel, especially in the reevaluation of how much she should be allowed to know. At first, Mina herself declares that each of the vampire fighters must have access to everything that the others know: "We need have no secrets amongst us; working together and with absolute trust, we can surely be stronger than if some of us were in the dark" (223). Here, Mina presents a view in which "the sharing of information is . . . moralized" (Jann 280) under the banner of public service. Soon after this necessity for public knowledge is asserted, however, Van Helsing points out that Mina's gender must exclude her from any more of the men's "committee" (236) meetings. He instructs her to return to the position of isolated Angel in the House: "you no more question. We shall tell you all in good time. We are men, and are able to bear; but you must be our star and our hope" (242). Mina cannot "bear" knowledge because it will make her incapable of bearing children. She can no longer use her "man's brain" (234) because of the effect it may have on her woman's body. And so she is commanded to act only as inspiration, as "our star and our hope." But it is just this isolation from male knowledge which makes Mina vulnerable to attack: "It is precisely by excluding Mina from the man's work of science that the men condemn her to the enclosed world of phantasy and desire" (Wall 18). By taking her out of the male world of rationality, the men take away Mina's professional discipline. She reverts to the older female type—idly wandering through the house and waiting for the men's return. It is while she is thus confined to the house that she falls prey to Dracula's attack, and, having been infected, becomes the model of the accepting and submissive wife. Jonathan, who fears at first the difficulty of keeping "silence after such confidence as ours" finds "it may not be a hard task after all, she herself has become reticent on the subject, and has not spoken of the Count or his doings ever since we told her of our decision" (262). Female silence and submissiveness, commanded by the men, then becomes a tool that is used against them by Dracula. As Daniel Pick notes, "Denial provides no defence against Dracula" (76). Women must have the same discipline and training as men in order to combat the threat of female appetite.

After discovering that Mina has been infected, the men decide that she "should be in full confidence; that nothing of any sort . . . should be kept from her" (290). But here a new problem arises: Mina's blood exchange with Dracula creates a mental connection in which everything that is known by one is known by the other. Van Helsing can gain access to Dracula's mind through hypnosis, but Dracula also gains access to the men's plan of attack. Mina, then, remains a medium for the exchange of information, but she can perform that function only under the guidance of Van Helsing: "He seems to have power at these particular moments to simply will, and her thoughts obey him" (333). The dangerous female dependency of the professional man which first allows knowledge to be drained away, now becomes the means of controlling knowledge. It is Mina's complete passivity which allows the flow of information to be guided by male hypnotic control.

However, as Wicke notes, "There is no such thing as passive transmission" in this text. "Invariably intelligent knowledge is involved, and Mina goes to the heart of things analytically and structurally" (485). It is Mina who studies the transcript of what she has, herself, uttered under hypnosis and thus discovers the route Dracula is taking back to his castle in Transylvania. Mina does for herself what she has done for Jonathan and for Seward—she takes the inner, emotional world and turns it into a text for the public eye. As Rosemary Jann explains: "Once Mina's sibylline utterances are reduced to text, she can apply her 'great brain that is trained like a man's' to forcing them to tell their secrets" (283).

In Mina, a very different model of femininity is constructed. The older ideal of Victorian Angel is critiqued in Lucy Westenra; because she is not trained like a man, Lucy does not have the control to resist the desires of female appetite. Because Mina contains a woman's heart and a man's professional brain, she both provides emotional support—is solicitous of "all who suffer from the heart" (231)—and offsets the danger of emotion, even the effects of her own vampiric heart wound, by submitting those emotions to the analysis of the well-disciplined brain.

Giving Mina professional ability seemingly threatens gender hierarchy, but Stoker nullifies that threat by both describing her ability as masculine, and by placing that ability in the service of reproducing the men—not only Seward and Harker, but also Dracula. She creates him as a text through her analysis of her own hypnotic transmissions, and more generally in her arrangement and transcription of all the documents that tell his story. What passes before the reader's eyes are not the original documents, but a clerically produced copy. Several critics have considered the role of mechanical reproduction in the text with reference to Walter Benjamin's discussion of "aura" in "The Work of Art in the Age of Mechanical Reproduction."[12] In these terms, Mina's reproduction of the men not only produces male subjectivity by composing a version of unified identity fit for the public eye, it also maintains the sense of "aura" surrounding that identity—any defect, any sense that the male identity is not original but replaceable—is the effect of a secretarial reproduction of the authentic and flawless professional self. Mina's skill does not then gain her access to power, but serves to idealize and empower the male role which initially is placed under great pressure by the changes wrought by professionalization.

Mina also reproduces the men by bearing a child who is given all of their names. Her function as both secretary and wife is the same—she services them by producing copies that bear the male name. In creating this analogy between the two functions, the text recontains the threat of secretarial reproduction in the older biological function. At the same time, the dangerous circulation of identity—the substitution of one professional by another—is replaced by the generational substitution of father by son.

This double function of feminized professional and professionalized wife and mother is summarized in the novel's epilogue. In contrast to Harker's opening statement, which asserts that all the records which the reader is about to receive contain no error, and are "exactly contemporary" with the events themselves, his final assessment of the text is that there is "hardly one authentic document! nothing but a mass of typewriting. . . . We could hardly ask anyone . . . to accept these as proofs of so wild a story." Van Helsing's reply, though it denies the need for proof or belief, then goes on to proclaim that the foundation for both rests on the "sweetness and loving care" which Mina shows her son (378). Harker's opening journal remains problematic only when it seems to be "exactly contemporary," when it appears to the reader unmediated by the secretarial typewriter. Here the potential radical dissociation of identity posed by professional life appears in Jonathan's relationship to Dracula. By the middle of the novel, though, this experience becomes "nothing but a mass of typewriting"—transformed from experience to recorded knowledge it makes "a new man" of Harker, both for his own and the reader's benefit. Finally, the central position which Harker as professional man occupied at the opening of the novel is now occupied by his wife. It is her maternal love which provides for the transmission of both public knowledge and private faith—a love which biologically reproduces a child bearing the name of all the male vampire hunters, and mechanically reproduces the text that bears the name, *Dracula*.

*Notes*

1. Several critics have commented on what Robin Wood refers to as Dracula's "fictional persistence" (173). Wood's "Burying the Undead" discusses the meaning of the text in a comparison of the novel with the Murnau and Badham film versions. Both Martin and Gagnier account for this persistence in terms of Dracula's radical otherness, particularly in Gagnier's article (though also alluded to by Martin) his exclusion from modern modes of production in the "operations of modern science, technology and bureaucracy, or information" (Gagnier 147). Jennifer Wicke's recent article, "Vampiric Typewriting," inverts this argument by stressing the similarity between vampirism and mass cultural means of reproduction and consumption.

2. See, for example, Auerbach, Bentley, Cranny-Francis, Griffin, Hurley, Roth, Tracy, and Weissman, as well as works cited in notes 3, 4, and 5 below.

3. Tracy mentions the analogy between vampirism and syphilis and makes a connection to Stoker's own infection with the disease. Showalter discusses the disease in reference to the Contagious Diseases Act, and the misogynistic medical "treatment" of the women in the text.

4. See Steven.

5. For discussions of shifts in gender identity and vampiric bisexuality see Craft, Demetrakopoulos, and Howes. Craft specifically discusses the vampire's mouth as a frightening confusion of gender categories (218).

6. Both Wicke (472) and Arata (635) discuss Harker's notetaking—Wicke in terms of the consumption of "reality" by various forms of media in the text, and Arata in terms of colonization.

7. Stoker's emphasis on the relations between men in the opening of the novel was facilitated by dropping a first chapter in which Harker is confronted by a female vampire in Munich on his way to Transylvania. This female vampire, "the Countess of Dolingen of Gratz in Styria," is generally acknowledged as Stoker's homage to Sheridan Le Fanu's "Carmilla" (Tracy 41–42). Excising this first chapter, Stoker postponed Harker's involvement with female vampires, and highlighted his confrontation with the male.

8. As mentioned above, Moretti sees this circulation as an invasion of monopoly capitalism. What I would emphasize, though, is that the money is always used to pay for various services; it is not invested as capital, but goes to pay for human capital.

9. The most in-depth study of the treatment of prostitutes under the Contagious Diseases Act can be found in Walkowitz.

10. This conflict is explored in the second volume of Helsinger et al.

11. Gagnier's description of the forces that rally together to combat Dracula shows the extent to which the battle has been reimagined from the opening individual struggle that Harker wages for existence, to a battle "waged on behalf of the existence of everyone" (Foucault 133):

> England casts the net that catches the Count . . . by enlisting an international network of scientists and scholars, reflecting contemporary methods of "research" and the progress of professionalization. . . . Their research is further aided by international networks of law, business and government: the Incorporated Law Society, Lloyd's of London, the British Consulate, MacKenzie and Steinkoff of Galatz, Godalming's "people" (i.e. the aristocracy), the police, and numerous other "connections." (149)

12. Wicke, Gagnier, and Martin all make important use of Benjamin's description of "aura."

WORKS CITED

Arata, Stephen D. "The Occidental Tourist: *Dracula* and the Anxiety of Reverse Colonization." *Victorian Studies* 33 (1990): 621–46.

Armstrong, Nancy. "The Occidental Alice." *differences* 2. 2 (1990): 3–40.

Auerbach, Nina. *Woman and the Demon: The Life of a Victorian Myth*. Cambridge: Harvard UP, 1982. 16–24.

Bentley, C.F. "The Monster in the Bedroom: Sexual Symbolism in Bram Stoker's *Dracula*." *Literature and Psychology* 22 (1972): 27–34.

Craft, Christopher. " 'Kiss Me with Those Red Lips': Gender and Inversion in Bram Stoker's *Dracula*." *Speaking of Gender*. Edited by Elaine Showalter. New York: Routledge, 1989. 216–42.

Cranny-Francis, Anne. "Sexual Politics and Political Repression in Bram Stoker's *Dracula*." *Nineteenth Century Suspense: From Poe to Conan Doyle*. Edited by Clive Bloom, Brian Docherty, Jane Gibb, and Keith Shand. New York: St. Martin's Press, 1988. 64–79.

Demetrakopoulos, Stephanie. "Feminism, Sex Role Exchanges, and Other Subliminal Fantasies in Bram Stoker's *Dracula*." *Frontiers: A Journal of Women's Studies* 2.3 (1977): 104–13

Foucault, Michel. *The History of Sexuality*. Translated by Robert Hurley. London: Penguin, 1978.

Gagnier, Regenia. "Evolution and Information, or Eroticism and Everyday Life in *Dracula* and late Victorian Aestheticism." *Sex and Death in Victorian Literature*. Edited by Regina Barreca. Bloomington: Indiana UP, 1980. 140–57.

Glover, David. "Bram Stoker and the Crisis of the Liberal Subject." *New Literary History* 23 (1992): 983–1002.

Griffin, Gail B. "'Your Girls that You All Love Are Mine': *Dracula* and the Victorian Male Sexual Imagination." *International Journal of Women's Studies* 3.5 (1980): 454–65.

Helsinger, Elizabeth K., Robin Lauterbach Sheets, and William Veeder. *The Woman Question: Social Issues, 1837–1883*. Vol. 2 of *The Woman Question: Society and Literature in Britain and America, 1837–1883*. New York: Garland Publishing, 1983. 109–64. 3 vols.

Howes, Marjorie. "The Mediation of the Feminine: Bisexuality, Homoerotic Desire and Self-Expression in Bram Stoker's *Dracula*." *Texas Studies in Language and Literature* 30 (1988): 4–19.

Hurley, Kelly. "Seduction by Surrogate: Stoker's *Dracula*." *Sequoia* 28.2 (1984): 24–36.

Jann, Rosemary. "Saved by Science? The Mixed Messages of Stoker's *Dracula*." *Texas Studies in Language and Literature* 31 (1989): 273–87.

Le Fanu, Joseph Sheridan. *Carmilla*, reprinted in *Best Ghost Stories of J. S. Le Fanu*. Edited by E.F. Bleiler. New York: Dover, 1964.

Martin, Philip. "The Vampire in the Looking-Glass: Reflection and Projection in Bram Stoker's *Dracula*." *Nineteenth Century Suspense: From Poe to Conan Doyle*. Edited by Clive Bloom, Brian Docherty, Jane Gibb, and Keith Shand. New York: St. Martin's Press, 1988. 80–92.

Moretti, Franco. "Dialectic of Fear." *Signs Taken for Wonders*. London: Verso, 1983. 83–108.

Perkin, Harold. *The Rise of Professional Society: England since 1880*. London: Routledge, 1989.

Pick, Daniel. "Terrors of the Night: *Dracula* and Degeneration." *Critical Quarterly* 30 (1988): 71–87.

Roth, Phyllis A. "Suddenly Sexual Women in Bram Stoker's *Dracula*." *Literature and Psychology* 26 (1977): 113–21.

Showalter, Elaine. "Syphilis, Sexuality and the Fiction of the *Fin de Siècle*." *Sex, Politics, and Science in the Nineteenth-Century Novel*. Edited by Ruth Bernard Yeazell. Baltimore: Johns Hopkins UP, 1986. 88–115.

Steven, John. "A Vampire in the Mirror: The Sexuality of *Dracula*." *PMLA* 103 (1988): 139–49.

Stoker, Bram. *Dracula*. New York: Oxford UP, 1983.

Tracy, Robin. "Loving You All Ways: Vamps, Vampires, Necrophiles and Necrofilles in Nineteenth-Century Fiction." *Sex and Death in Victorian Literature*. Edited by Regina Barreca. Bloomington: Indiana UP, 1980. 32–59.

Walkowitz, Judith R. *Prostitution and Victorian Society: Women, Class, and the State*. Cambridge: Cambridge UP, 1980.

Wall, Geoffrey. "Different from Writing: *Dracula* in 1897." *Literature and History* 10 (1984): 15–23.

Weissman, Judith. "Women and Vampires: *Dracula* as Victorian Novel." *Midwest Quarterly* 18 (1977): 392–405.

Wicke, Jennifer. "Vampiric Typewriting: *Dracula* and its Media." *English Literary History* 59 (1992): 467–94.

Wood, Robin. "Burying the Undead: The Use and Obsolescence of Count Dracula." *Mosaic* 16 (1983): 175–87.

## SELECTED SECONDARY SOURCES

Biographies: Daniel Farson, *The Man Who Wrote Dracula: A Biography of Bram Stoker* (London: Michael Joseph, 1975); Harry Ludlam, *A Biography of Dracula: The Life Story of Bram Stoker* (London: Fireside, 1962). Critical Works: In addition to those listed in "Works Cited," see also: Clive Leatherdale, *Dracula: The Novel and the Legend* (Wellingborough, England: Aquarian Press, 1985); David Seed, "The Narrative Method of Dracula," *Nineteenth Century Fiction* 40 (1985); James B. Twitchell, *The Living Dead: A Study of the Vampire in Romantic Literature*, (Durham: Duke UP, 1981); Richard Wasson, "The Politics of Dracula," *English Literature in Transition* 9 (1966).

# Eliza Lynn Linton

## The Rebel of the Family (1880) and Other Novels

*Nancy Fix Anderson*

Eliza Lynn Linton (1822–1898) made her literary reputation as a polemicist who, in her many novels and periodical articles, tackled controversial social issues. In her sensational 1872 *True History of Joshua Davidson, Christian and Communist,* for example, she sharply attacked both modern Christianity and capitalism. Linton was best known for her criticisms of women's emancipation, even though she herself was an ambitious independent woman who had separated from her husband. In her early writings in the 1840s and 1850s she had been an ardent supporter of women's rights and even free love, and had received particular notoriety with her shocking 1851 novel *Realities.* In her middle years, however, she modified her radical views, and her novels such as *The Rebel of the Family* (1880) reflect her growing conservatism and ambivalence about women's rights. In her later writings, Linton's opposition to what she called "the wild women" and "shrieking sisters" increased, culminating in her stridently antifeminist novels *The One Too Many* (1894) and *In Haste and at Leisure*(1895). Although her popularity ebbed as her polemics intensified, Eliza Lynn Linton remained an eminent Victorian woman of letters, respected and admired even by those who did not share her views. Her works are out of print, although three of her novels were reprinted by Garland Publishing in 1975–1976 as part of their Novels of Faith and Doubt series: *The True History of Joshua Davidson, Christian and Communist, The Autobiography of Christopher Kirkland* (Linton's fictional autobiography), and *Under Which Lord?*

Eliza Lynn Linton determined even as a young girl that she would make her mark in the world as a novelist. Born in 1822 in Keswick in the Lake District, Elizabeth Lynn, as she was christened, was the daughter of an Anglican vicar and the granddaughter of a bishop. The youngest of twelve children, whose mother died shortly after Eliza's birth, Linton experienced as a child a painful sense of motherlessness that was an important factor in shaping her personality. Largely self-educated (she had the free range of her father's library), the young Eliza Lynn began writing in her early teens with the goal of publication. At age fifteen, as a self-styled radical and rebel against her father's conservatism, she wrote to the publisher of *Bentley's Miscellany* to inquire if he would let her write for the journal. Not wanting her family to know what she was doing, she asked Richard Bentley to signal his answer by sending to her house a Whig newspaper if the answer were yes, and a Tory one if no. Probably amused, Bentley signaled yes, and she sent in a story, assuring him that "if ever in after life the name of Eliza Lynn shall be known, if I do not live and die a thing overlooked by all, the world and everyone shall know that to Richard Bentley the true the generous is due the *praise*."[1] He did not accept the story, but later, in her early twenties, she did get some poems published in *Ainsworth's Magazine*.

Encouraged by this success, Linton at age twenty-three made the bold decision to go to London to make her way as a writer. Not following the expected route of marriage, she prided herself on being "one of the vanguard of the independent women."[2] Conducting extensive research in the British Library for a historical novel, a genre popular in the 1840s, she published *Azeth the Egyptian* in 1847. The reviews of this ponderous novel were surprisingly favorable, making her feel, as she later humorously remembered, that "the world must be talking of it, and wondering who was the unknown [Eliza Lynn] who, yesterday obscure, today famous, had so suddenly flashed into the world of letters."[3] The next year she published another historical novel, *Amymone,* set in classical Greece, in which she used the character of Aspasia, the mistress of Pericles, to advocate for women's rights and free love. *Amymone* also received generally favorable reviews, despite the controversial themes, in part because of the influential patronage she received from the esteemed poet Walter Savage Landor, with whom she had a father–daughter relationship. Nevertheless, Linton could not support herself with her novels, and she had to get other work to supplement the modest allowance she received from her father. Securing a position writing for the newspaper the *Morning Chronicle* from 1848 to 1849, she was the first woman in England to have a regular salary as a journalist.

In the next seventeen years, Linton published only one novel, *Realities,* in 1851, and wrote instead for periodical publications. She was a regular contributor during this time to *Household Words,* edited by Charles Dickens, and its successor, *All the Year Round,* as well as to *National Magazine, Fraser's, Temple Bar,* and other journals. Writing mainly on social subjects, she avoided controversial topics, although Dickens did warn his subeditor, W.H. Wills, that Miss Lynn "gets so near the sexual side of things as to be a little dangerous to us at times."[4] He did, however, write next to her name in his list of contributors "good for anything, and thoroughly reliable." Among the periodical articles she wrote in 1851 was a little-noticed piece on Mary Wollstonecraft, for the radical journal *The English Republic*, in which Linton called her *Vindication of the Rights of Woman* "one of the boldest and bravest things ever published."[5]

In 1858, at age thirty-six, Linton made the ill-fated decision to marry the editor of the *English Republic*, the radical artisan William James Linton. Eliza Lynn Linton later explained that she married William James Linton, a widower, to provide guidance for his many motherless children.[6] The marriage was a disaster, with the two quite dissimilar personalities in constant conflict. Much to his wife's frustration, the easy-going William was more concerned with political activism, such as aiding Italian revolutionaries, than with furthering his career as an engraver. Eliza, self-disciplined and tightly controlled (from economic necessity as much as because of her personality) had to support the family with her literary earnings. Styling herself professionally as Mrs. Lynn Linton, she was forced to write pot-boiling periodical pieces rather than follow her true ambition to get "out of periodical literature and to succeed as a writer of good novels."[7]

In 1864, the Lintons separated, a separation which became permanent in 1866, and Eliza Lynn Linton was able to start writing novels again. She first published *Grasp Your Nettle* in 1865, and then wrote an additional twenty-two novels, as well as other nonfiction books and collections of short stories, until her death in 1898. Despite her expressed wish to write only novels, she also remained a prolific contributor to the leading periodicals, including the *Saturday Review, Belgravia, Gentleman's Magazine, Fortnightly Review, Nineteenth Century, New Review,* and many others.

Certainly Linton's most famous—or infamous—periodical contributions were to the *Saturday Review,* in which, eschewing her earlier advocacy of women's rights, she developed her reputation as a critic of women. Known as one of the antifeminist "Saturday Revilers,"[8] she published in the *Saturday Review* a steady stream of articles from 1866 to 1875 castigating a broad range of female behaviors. Her most sensational essay was "The Girl of the Period," published in 1868, in which she compared young ladies who wore makeup to prostitutes. In subsequent articles in the *Saturday Review* and in the other periodicals, and in her novels, she increasingly focused on attacking the women's rights women, with their demands for greater freedom and rights for women.

Although a popular writer for most of her career, Linton's later novels, culminating with *In Haste and at Leisure* (1895), were such exaggerated attacks on the women's movement that, though respected by some, she became an object of ridicule to others. Many of her contemporaries were puzzled that Linton, an independent professional woman, would so passionately defend the traditional, domestic role of women. Her ostensible answer was that she did not want other women to make the same mistake she did,[9] but even at the time that answer seemed weak. She clearly enjoyed her success and self-determination, and had no inclination to follow her own advice and live a domestic life. Rather, she provided the key to her personality in her fictionalized autobiography, *The Autobiography of Christopher Kirkland,* published in 1885, in which she wrote of herself as a man. As did other women who achieved success in a patriarchal society, Linton probably developed an unconscious sense of male identity, and could therefore castigate women seeking independence without a sense of self-contradiction and without seeming to devalue her own capabilities. Even in her most virulently antifeminist novels, however, there is an intriguing ambivalence in the authorial position on the proper role of women, an ambivalence which suggests that Linton could never completely separate her own independent, achieving self from the characters she created.

Although resentful that she was never as popular as George Eliot, nor paid as much as Margaret Oliphant, Eliza Lynn Linton was an important literary personage in Victorian England. Jealous of other established women writers, she was generous in helping younger writers with their careers. As a sign of her status in the Victorian literary world, she had the friendship and admiration of many eminent Victorians. Even those who disagreed with her opinions respected her, and, as the *Academy* said, "A woman whose work won the praise of Dickens, Landor, Swinburne, and a bead-roll of illustrious men and women, numbers of whom respected herself no less than her books, cannot leave a record otherwise than attractive, whether or not we are able to share their sympathy for her character."[10]

One of her early iconoclastic novels, written before her marriage and therefore under the name Eliza Lynn, *Realities* (1851) was Linton's most shocking challenge to Victorian morality. Always one to conform externally to the conventional literary styles, when historical novels declined in popularity by the 1850s she switched to domestic novels, following the advice of the critic George Henry Lewes who suggested that Miss Lynn "quit those remote regions of the antique world in which her thoughts hitherto have wandered too much at large, and, leaving Egypt to its mummies and antiquities, no less than Greece, with its temptations, like Sirens, to the young imagination, resolutely move amidst the thronging forms of modern life, and paint from *them*."[11]

Lewes may have thought she followed his advice too resolutely, for *Realities,* a conventionally three-volumed tale of modern life, was anything but conventional in its content. The novel is the story of two contrasting young women, one good and one bad, a polarity that would characterize many of Linton's subsequent novels (although her attributions of good and bad would change with her changing views on women). The heroine, Clara de Saumarez, a thinly disguised Eliza Lynn, is a passionate and free-spirited young woman who is quite unlike her stiff and conventional mother. In fact, unbeknown to the de Saumarezes, Clara is not their child, but is the illegitimate daughter of the wet nurse, who switched babies to give her own child a better home.

When the real de Saumarez daughter, Alice, is by chance brought to live in the household, she fits in perfectly. Mrs. de Saumarez is immediately drawn to the blue-eyed golden-haired Alice (a character closely based on Linton's own pretty, favored sister, of whom she was always fiercely jealous). Not knowing that Alice is her daughter, Mrs. de Saumarez finds her submissive ladylike behavior much more compatible than that of the boisterous Clara. Feeling rejected, Clara develops inner strength, learning, as Linton did, that "by self-help and self-nurture only, can strength and power come to the soul of man; how the lonely mind in youth must bravely bear its loneliness, and come out in maturity all the grander, all the stronger, for that solitude."[12]

Clara runs away from home, going to London to work as an actress—a profession outside the pale of respectability for women in mid-Victorian England. She falls in love with a stage manager, who she does not know is married and who is a well-known philanderer. Taking her out of town to a hotel, he embraces her but then, moved by her innocence, stops there. (Linton was forced to censor part of the novel. The seduction scene probably did not end as innocently in the original version.) He pays her rent, however, and everyone assumes that Clara is his mistress.

A handsome but rigidly moralistic clergyman falls in love with Clara, but marries Alice because she is submissively obedient, in contrast to the independent-minded Clara. Linton then sarcastically reminds her readers that "the majority of men make submission and virtue their feminine synonyms." To men, "an independent thought unsexes her." Even if she loves passionately, "she must be rejected, reviled, undone, because she cannot intellectually obey" (3: 50, 195–96).

Learning the truth of her birth, the lonely, desolate Clara, longing for her now dead mother, is about to commit suicide, when she is rescued by the manly Perceval Glynn, a socialist and freethinker. When Perceval is wounded in a duel, Clara goes alone to his bedroom to see him. Linton dramatically warns all readers "who are very moral and conventional, turn over this page unread: it is a shocking fact that is about to be related. . . . Blame her, ye who will! Cast stones of censure, ye who measure virtue by social rules and deem that to be vice which is not custom. . . . as pure in the deed was she as an angel who comes down to console the stricken and weary" (2: 171–72). Perceval is a tower of strength to Clara, and becomes for her "what a father would have been—what a brother or a mother" (3: 179). Nevertheless, because of his poverty, she has to keep working as an actress after they marry, a fact which Perceval does not regret, because he believes that even for her as a woman, work is a necessity (3: 262).

Linton used *Realities* as a forum to criticize not only conventional views on women, but also other aspects of Victorian society. She attacked the double standard, and blamed prostitution on the low wages and inhumanity of laissez-faire political economy. She graphically described the misery of the poor, probably drawing on the newspaper reports published from 1847 to 1851 by Henry Mayhew, Linton's co-worker at the *Morning Chronicle,* reports which were later republished as *London Labour and the London Poor.* She also exposed the prurience underlying vigilant Victorian moralism. Mrs. de Saumarez, for example, on a visit to an art exhibit, is disgusted by the paintings of nudes. "How keenly she looked after these tabooed nymphs!—and how bitterly she deprecated their admission at all" (3: 217).

In writing this novel, Linton had confidently hoped, as she expressed to the publisher Richard Bentley, that it would be "a success equal to *Jane Eyre.*"[13] *Realities,* however, although a well-crafted story that is penetrating in its social criticism, does not have the depth or complexity of characterization that makes the works of Charlotte Brontë endure. Although her friend, the poet Algernon Swinburne, later praised Linton's books as "the most heroic in temper since the Brontës', and of so much wider intelligence than theirs,"[14] most critics would not agree. Linton was a good storyteller, but she did not have the skill to transmute her polemical and autobiographical material into a narrative with characters who seem to have a life of their own.

What makes *Realities* so memorable is not its literary merit but its subject matter, though this is probably what kept it from being a success in its own time. Even some freethinking Victorians considered it offensive. In fact, Linton had great difficulty in getting the novel published. In the early stages of writing it, she warned Bentley, who had published her previous novel, that it would be daring: "You will not be afraid of anything *rather* heretical and bold? I must write you know as I feel." Bentley and other publishers turned it down, with one suggesting that "it would be best for her welfare and reputation to throw the manuscript in the fire."[15]

John Chapman finally accepted it, but he also had doubts as he prepared it for publication. His wife and his new boarder Marian Evans (who had not yet established her reputation as George Eliot), both agreed with his objections to its "tone and tendency," and to its love scenes "warmly and vividly depicted." He tried unsuccessfully to get Linton to cut the objectionable passages, which he said were "addressed [to] and excited the sensual nature and were therefore injurious." He argued that, because he published works of free thought, he had to be very careful "of the *moral* tendency" of all he issued. His wife was especially upset by *Realities*. Chapman wrote in his diary that "Miss E[vans] had a long talk on the point, when [his wife] became excited and used language in reference to Miss L. unbecoming and unjust."[16]

Chapman enlisted mutual friends to try to get Linton to expurgate the offensive material, but she refused and instead threatened legal action against him. She finally reached a settlement with Chapman, releasing him for a fee from his contract. She then cut the offending material, and had the expurgated *Realities* published at her own expense. Explaining to her readers in her preface that her colleagues who read the book in manuscript form considered it "a species of literary Caliban . . . a monstrous thing of wickedness and deformity—advocating all that was abhorrent to reason and good morals. . . . . Hard names flew like hail-stones around me when I adhered to my unwelcome social doctrines, and still determined to publish them against all advice to the contrary." Neglecting to mention that she did indeed cave in to pressure to bowdlerize it, she proudly asserted that "few women could have withstood such a battery of condemnations" (iv–v).

Despite the efforts of her fatherly patron, Walter Savage Landor, to protect her from criticism, the reviews of *Realities,* even in its expurgated form, were devastating. The *Athenaeum* said that in her attack on "Pharisaical respectability," she "raves like a Pythoness," and that the world she presents exists "in the chambers of her imagination." The *Spectator* expressed the wish that she had followed the advice of her friends not to publish the novel.[17] George Lewes, who had encouraged her to write about "modern life," also criticized the novel: "There will be no one, we believe, to accept this work as giving shape and substance to the Realities of our life." The next year, in an article on "Lady Novelists" in the *Westminster Review,* he praised such women novelists as Charlotte Brontë and Elizabeth Gaskell, but criticized Eliza Lynn. *Realities,* he said, was a "passionate and exaggerated protest against conventions, which failed of its intended effect because it was too exaggerated, too manifestly unjust."[18]

Linton's fellow novelist Geraldine Jewsbury had a similar reaction. Writing to Jane Carlyle, she asked if Jane had read the book. "Oh good gracious! good gracious! that any woman should have ever been given over to such bad taste! She has published it at her own expense, so that says much for her sincerity, but the book makes one feel 'trailed in the mud.' Nightmares are realities, but hardly real life. Yet the book is clever."[19] As courageous and bold as she claimed to be, these criticisms hurt the young Eliza Lynn deeply, which perhaps explains why she did not write another novel for almost fifteen years.

By the time Linton published what became her most widely circulated, and for many her most admired, novel, *The True History of Joshua Davidson, Christian and Communist* (1872), she had solidly established her reputation as a respected if somewhat controversial woman of letters. Her youthful writings were long forgotten, but recent notoriety clung to her for such articles of social criticism as "The Girl of the Period." The aura of notoriety increased with *The True History of Joshua Davidson, Christian and Communist,* in which she challenged what she saw as the hypocrisy of the Established Church by suggesting that a true Christian would be a communist.

Linton's religious criticism was more acceptable to intellectual Victorian society than her earlier challenge to moral values. Many respectable Victorians in that age of Darwinism had lost their religious faith, but few relinquished their public commitment to moral (i.e., sexual) rectitude. Nevertheless, *The True History of Joshua Davidson, Christian and Communist,* debunking the political and economic as well as the religious values in Victorian England, became one of the more controversial novels of the age.

Linton, who identified herself as an agnostic, a term Thomas Huxley coined in 1869, had lost her faith long before Darwinism shook the foundations of Victorian belief. She first rejected orthodox Christianity as a young girl in the vicarage, in part as an expression of her revolt against her clergyman father. Attributing her loss of the last vestiges of theism to the failure of her marriage, she accepted "the barren little rock of agnosticism—I do not know; and there I cling."[20] She remained a follower of what she called "manly agnosticism" for the rest of her life, although she advocated religion as necessary for "the weaker brethren," by which she meant the lower classes and women of all levels, whom she felt needed the moral controls that the church provided.[21]

*The True History of Joshua Davidson, Christian and Communist* is a fantasy of what would happen if Jesus were born again in the modern world. A motif that would be popular in the late nineteenth century, it was later most notably used by Dostoevski in *The Brothers Karamazov* (1879–1880) and in lesser-known works such as W.T. Stead's *If Christ Came to Chicago!* (1891). In Linton's version, Joshua Davidson (a barely disguised Jesus, son of David), is born in Cornwall, the son of a village carpenter. He is descended from King Arthur, evoking the royal genealogy of the biblical Jesus. As a youth, he causes trouble by asking such provocative questions as why the clergymen do not give all their money to the poor, as, according to the teachings of Christ, they should. He especially evokes the enmity of Vicar Grand, a character closely modeled on Linton's memory of her father. Vicar Grand "had no love for the poor, and no pity; he always called them 'the common people,' and spoke of them disdainfully, as if they were different creatures from the gentry." He is a "man of good family himself, and his wife was the daughter of a bishop."[22]

Bothered by the insensitivity and hypocrisy of the church, Joshua rejects Christianity and becomes a freethinker. He does, however, follow Christian ethics by working to achieve a classless society in England. Helping even the "undeserving" disreputable poor, he befriends a "soiled dove," Mary Princeps, the Mary Magdalen figure in this modern tale of Jesus. Linton uses Mary to criticize not only the hypocrisy of the church but also the very structure of Victorian respectability. Denouncing the double standard of morality, Linton describes prostitutes as martyrs to respectability, "as victims rather than criminals, the scapegoats not the polluters of society." Prostitutes, Linton provocatively suggests, are aware that they "make the virtuous wife, the chaste maiden, possible. . . . In their blind way they are vaguely conscious that the root of this fine flower of western civilization, the rich monogamous Christian home, is planted in the filth of prostitution, and that to them is owning the 'self-restraint' so much admired in gentlemen who do not marry until they can have a family" (104).

Linton also uses this novel to lambaste what she considered the inhumanity of laissez-faire economics. She has Joshua enthusiastically participate in the Paris Commune of 1871, a revolutionary experiment which struck terror in the hearts of Victorian property-holders. The commune leaders, whom Linton inaccurately describes as communists, were following "the pattern of Christ in their faithful endeavour to help the poor and to raise the lowly, to rectify the injustice of conventional distinctions, and to give all men an equal chance of being happy, virtuous, and human" (232–33).

After the commune is crushed, Joshua returns to England to preach his doctrine of Christian communism. Just as "the Communist of Galilee" was crucified for preaching "against all the conventional respectabilities which society had then held in honour," so Joshua is literally kicked to death by "the representatives of law and order in their own minds, the champions of God and religion," led by the archetype of hypocritical respectability, Vicar Grand (275–78, 273).

Linton's idea of communism was hardly based on the Marxist concept of class revolution. She used the term synonymously with socialism, and more in the sense of class harmony than abolition of private property or any other radical reconstruction of society. As she has her communist hero Joshua Davidson argue, "It would be no righteousness to bring the rich, the refined, the well educated down to the level of the poor; but to raise up the masses, and to impose on the upper classes positive duties, this is the only way in which the differences between high and low can be lessened" (219–20). Such ideas sounded much more like traditional noblesse oblige than class revolution.

Linton often identified herself as a socialist, and as a communist, even in her older years, despite her increasing political as well as social conservatism. She did so, however, as she did in *Joshua Davidson,* more for shock value than from political conviction. Nor was she advocating socialism in the novel, but was using it to try to expose the fallacies of Christianity and hypocrisy in the church. As she explained to a friend, she did not think "Joshua or Christ wholly right. . . . The book means simply a plea for sincerity. Let us take our choice—Christ and communism . . . or science, and the scientific arrangement of society and the abolition of all pretence of Christianity."[23]

Despite, or perhaps because of, its shocking thesis, *Joshua Davidson* was immensely popular. The first edition, published anonymously by Alexander Strahan, was soon sold out. Within three months a third edition was issued, this time under Linton's own name. By 1901, the novel had reached its eleventh edition. It was translated into German, and sold widely in the United States. As recently as 1960, Professor E.E. Evans-Prichard quoted from *Joshua Davidson* in a lecture which then was the subject of an editorial in the *Times Literary Supplement.*[24] It was most recently reprinted in the 1975 Garland *Novels of Faith and Doubt* series.

A commercial success, *Joshua Davidson* received mixed critical reviews, most of which were written before its authorship was known. W.R. Greg assumed the anonymous author was a woman, for reasons that must have horrified Linton, who prided herself on her masculine virtues: "The eager and wholesome, if sometimes uncontrolled sympathies, the imperfect knowledge of facts, the superficial acquaintance with political economy, the impulsive haste of what might otherwise be powerful thought, the intellect always at the command and at the mercy of the feelings, the prejudices and the fancy which break out in every page, stamp it unmistakably as the work of a woman." Nevertheless, despite his patronizingly gendered denigrations, and his emphatic refutation of its central thesis, Greg did describe the novel as "full of literary skill. . . . Here and there it almost approaches to a sort of genius in the effective naturalness of the style and the graphic simplicity of the description."[25]

Other reviews were less ambivalent in their praise. The *Graphic,* for example, acclaimed it for its practical as well as literary value, saying it would "set readers thinking" and "perhaps it may set them working for the good of their fellow men." The most enthusiastic critics were fellow agnostics, such as the positivist Frederic Harrison, who said that "it afforded me new and singular matter for reflection," and the freethinking Charles Bradlaugh, who bought a thousand copies for distribution.[26]

*Joshua Davidson* certainly increased Linton's reputation for notoriety. The writer Jane Panton remembered that in her youth Mrs. Lynn Linton "was looked upon by us with suspicion and dislike, first because she had just electrified the world with her odious article 'The Girl of the Period' and secondly, because she had produced 'The True History of Joshua Davidson,' a book I learned to thoroughly enjoy and appreciate, but which we heard most emphatically condemned and were not allowed to read." Bringing on Linton both praise and condemnation, *The True History of Joshua Davidson, Christian and Communist* strengthened her reputation as a woman of influence, and, as the *Athenaeum* commented after her death, "She never lost the position she then attained. It quite altered her standing in the world of letters."[27]

Fifty years old when she wrote *Joshua Davidson,* Eliza Lynn Linton continued writing novels for the next twenty-five years, up to the time of her death. Putting aside political and religious themes, she concentrated in most of her later novels on the Woman Question, with her ostensible antifeminism inadvertently sabotaged by both her exaggerated polemics and her persistent if unacknowledged ambivalence about the role of women. The novel that set the tone for her later, more extreme writings, but which still includes a sympathetic analysis of the attractions of feminism, is *The Rebel of the Family.* Serialized in *Temple Bar, The Rebel of the Family* describes the plight of an unsupported and ambitious middle-class young woman who longs for meaningful work, and then it contradictorily condemns the women's movement, which was founded in the 1850s to work for such goals as better training and employment opportunities for single women.

The "rebel of the family," Perdita Winstanley, is so strongly autobiographical that Linton at first tentatively entitled the novel, "The Bishop's Granddaughter," and then "the Democrat of the Family."[28] From a poor but genteel family, Perdita refuses her mother's demand that she make a lucrative marriage. Treated as an outcast, Perdita longs to escape: "How I wish I were a boy! If I were a boy I would leave home tonight and never come back till I had made a name and my fortune! oh, what a dreadful thing it is to be a girl and a poor lady! neither able to earn money nor live independently . . . if only I could go out into the world and do something with myself!"[29]

Beginning as a seeming forerunner to the New Woman fiction of Olive Schreiner, Sarah Grand, and others, who used their novels as pleas for the emancipation of women, *The Rebel of the Family* soon reveals its antifeminist message with the introduction of the villainous character Bell Blount, a mannish, hard, women's rights woman, a "fugleman of that ungazetted Society of Shrieking Sisterhood" (151)—an alliterative pejorative coined by Linton in one of her *Saturday Review* diatribes.

The Mephistophelian Bell tries to tempt Perdita with the "allurements of emancipation" to join the women's movement. Perdita is attracted to the goals of the movement, but repelled by Bell's denunciation of men as brutal creatures who should be slaves to the naturally superior women. (Linton would typically always caricature women's rights women by ascribing such exaggerated views to them.) Perdita cannot accept this part of Bell's views, for she believes too strongly in man's inherent moral strength and superiority, and woman's natural position of obedient submission.

Perdita is also repelled by what Linton unequivocally describes as Bell's lesbianism. In conventional Victorian fiction, romantic friendships between women were usually assumed to be nonsexual, or, even if the author and the reader knew the homoerotic implications, that fact was ostensibly ignored. Not so in this work of the outspoken if prejudiced Eliza Lynn Linton. Unlike in almost any other mainstream Victorian novel, lesbianism is openly discussed in *The Rebel of the Family,* albeit in a distorted and condemnatory way, as a means of stereotyping and denigrating women's rights women. When Bell, for example, invites Perdita to her home, Perdita thanks her by putting her hand frankly on Bell's arm. "Mrs. Blount's face flushed vividly. She started and nearly scared Perdita by suddenly taking her in her arms and kissing her with strange warmth" (32). On another occasion Bell kisses Perdita fondly, and says "my darling" under her breath. When Perdita involuntarily shrinks from her embrace, Bell angrily calls her a "cold inflexible unimpressionable creature" (159–60). Bell urges Perdita to leave home for a life of self-support and independence and of friendship with her own sex, but Perdita replies that she could not live without love. Bell tenderly puts her arm around the woman she lives with and calls her "little wife," telling Perdita that if she wants love, "you have it here—the best and truest that the world can give—the love between women without the degrading and disturbing interference of man" (35). Such a prospect does not appeal to Perdita, who feels "revolted by something too vague to name yet too real to ignore" (151).

Nevertheless, although rejecting many aspects of Bell's opinions and her lifestyle, Perdita is attracted to the idea of female emancipation. She has to get a job to pay her family's debts, but even without the financial necessity she would want to work, for she deplores the life of frivolity and idleness led by her sisters and mother. Perdita cries out to her disapproving mother that she would have "gone mad outright in the idleness and want of purpose in my life, unless I could have found something real to do." Her mother scornfully says that she could have occupation in the home, such as embroidering or painting—occupation of a "refined and ladylike kind." Perdita replies that "embroidering strips of silks for gowns, and painting little frames for photographs are not real work or art to me. I could not have found my life in either of them, mother. I must have done something more serious" (78).

Presenting a strong defense of employment opportunities for women outside the home, Linton then subverts the argument by having Perdita get a boring, menial job in a post office savings bank. Rather than have Perdita find challenging work such as journalism, as Linton herself did, or arguing that women should be better educated so they could support themselves in a satisfying way, Linton suggests that Perdita's frustrating experience would be shared by all women who seek to leave their natural domestic sphere. As a wise motherly woman in the novel advises Perdita, it is better for a woman to work as a servant dusting and cooking in her own home than get a job outside the home. Even if such work might not save the family much money, "it might save something more precious . . . the love of home and the habit of home-staying" (141).

Linton apparently did not recognize that the advice of this motherly woman, which she authorially endorses, is the same advice which she satirized as trivial when given by Perdita's mother. Dusting could hardly satisfy the passionate Perdita's desire for "something serious" to do any more than embroidering could. The dilemma is resolved by a manly man, Leslie Crawford, who rescues Perdita not only from the lonely and confused circumstances of her life, but also from the women's movement. When Bell

Blount convinces Perdita to attend a women's suffrage meeting, and tries to get her to go up on the lecture platform, Leslie suddenly appears in the hall, and firmly remarks to Perdita that he presumes she will not do such a thing. Perdita then has the courage to say no to Bell. Leslie later praises Perdita for thinking "woman's duties higher than her rights, the quiet restrictions of home more precious than the excitement of liberty, the blare of publicity." Perdita thanks him for saving her: "If I had not loved you I should have gone into the Movement out of mere despair at the aimlessness of my life." Asked if she repents of her choice, she exclaims, "No! I never knew true happiness before" (372–73).

It was commonplace in antifeminist rhetoric in late-Victorian England to suggest that women's rights advocates were redundant women who could not get a man. According to a popular slogan, "women's rights were men's lefts." Holding this assumption Linton's audience would have accepted the resolution in the form of the love of a manly man. What makes *The Rebel of the Family* so extraordinary, however, and what makes it so different from the other antifeminist novels at this time, is the passionate and persuasive argument at the beginning of the novel for women's emancipation. It is not structured as a straw argument which could then easily be refuted. Perdita's anguish with the empty life of Victorian young ladies and with the economic vulnerabilities that life often entailed, was so genuinely and poignantly expressed, coming as it did from Linton's memories of her own experiences, that many readers must have strongly sympathized with Perdita's desire for emancipation, and then been frustrated by the ending.

These ambiguities and inconsistencies were perhaps why the novel was not a success. It pleased neither those who supported nor those who opposed the women's rights movement. It received only weak praise in the reviews, with condemnation especially of the character of Bell Blount, whom the *Academy* said was "too odious, and the scenes in which she appears, too odious even for comment." Several critics pointed out the ambivalence in the author's attitude toward women's emancipation. The *Saturday Review* said the novel arouses

> an ardent desire to find out whether what seems at moments the author's advocacy of strange views is serious or not, whether she means to sympathize with or laugh at her heroine's convictions and inconvenient theories, and whether or not she thinks Perdita's example a desirable one, on the whole, to follow. . . . At one moment the reader will think that Mrs. Linton is disposed to applaud, at another to condemn, the unattractive if conscientious ways of the Rebel of the Family.[30]

It is, however, the ambivalences that make Linton's novels such fascinating reading today. Usually following conventional forms, mostly three-deckers on domestic subjects published first serially in periodicals, the novels are in plot and character often entertaining but not noteworthy. What raises them above the level of the other minor Victorian novels are the insights they often unintentionally give on the complexities of the status of Victorian women and of the women's movement. Although in her nonfiction Linton could frame unambiguous vehement diatribes against the emancipation of women, in her fiction, drawn from her own experiences and feelings, she could not. Along with her heroines' desire for love and protection are their yearning for freedom, growth, achievement. No matter how much Linton tried to stamp out those feelings in her heroines, they persist as part of the novels. As much as she tried to condemn them, her emancipated female characters are always the most interesting ones, and even in her last novels often end up in much better circumstances than do the conforming women. In her 1894 novel, *The One Too Many,* for example, the meek self-sacrificing "true woman" commits suicide, while at least one of the university-educated new women achieves love and happiness. As one critic said, "The plain person can hardly fail to rise from a perusal of the story without an impression that in the view of the writer it is wiser to revolt than to submit."[31]

Eulogizing her after her death, Walter Besant paid poetic tribute to Linton's struggle against women's rights: "She fought for Women; yet with women fought, The sexless tribe, the shrieking sisterhood."[32] The message in her novels, however, suggests that in her fight for women she both attacked and endorsed the goals of women's emancipation, and that the women against whom she fought included her own self.

*Notes*

1. Eliza Lynn to Richard Bentley, December 1837, Bentley Collection, University of Illinois Library.

2. Eliza Lynn Linton, *The Autobiography of Christopher Kirkland* 1: 253.

3. Ibid., I: 258.

4. Dickens to Wills, 9 January 1856, Henry Huntington Library MSS, San Marino, California; Autobiographical sketch of Eliza Lynn Linton, Harry Ransom Humanities Research Center, University of Texas, Austin, Texas.

5. *English Republic* 4: 418–24.

6. Eliza Lynn to Walter Savage Landor, [1857], Forster Collection, Henry Huntington Library MSS.

7. Eliza Lynn Linton to Blackwood, 22 April 1863, National Library of Scotland MSS.

8. R.G. Cox, "The Reviews and Magazines," *Pelican Guide to English Literature,* edited by Boris Ford 6: 197.

9. George Somes Layard, *Mrs. Lynn Linton: Her Life, Letters, and Opinions* 140.

10. *Academy,* 25 May 1901, 440.

11. *Leader,* 21 September 1850, 616.

12. Eliza Lynn, *Realities* 1: 54.

13. Lynn to Bentley, n.d., Bentley Collection MSS.

14. Algernon Swinburne to Linton, 30 January 1881, *The Swinburne Letters,* edited by Cecil Y. Lang 4: 188–89.

15. Lynn to Bentley, 5 September 1848, Bentley Collection; quoted in John Chapman's Diary, 17 [19] 1851, in Gordon Haight, *George Eliot and John Chapman,* 133–34.

16. Chapman's Diary, 11 and 12 January 1851, 130–31.

17. *Athenaeum,* 14 June 1851, 626–27; *Spectator,* 24 May 1851, 499.

18. *Leader,* 31 May 1851, p. 517; *Westminster Review,* July 1852, 77.

19. *Selections from the Letters of Geraldine Endsor Jewsbury to Jane Welsh Carlyle,* edited by Mrs. Alexander Ireland, 405.

20. Linton, *Christopher Kirkland,* 3: 71; quoted in Layard, 256.

21. Linton, *Christopher Kirkland,* 3: 159, 161.

22. [Eliza Lynn Linton], *The True History of Joshua Davidson, Christian and Communist,* 35.

23. Layard, 181–82.

24. Cited in Colby, 45.

25. *Contemporary Review,* April 1873, 680–700.

26. *Graphic ,* 30 November 1872, 510; Layard 180.

27. Jane Ellen Panton, *Leaves from a Life* 136; *Athenaeum,* 23 July 1898, 132.

28. Layard, 220.

29. Eliza Lynn Linton, *The Rebel of the Family,* 13–14.

30. *Academy,* 19 February 1881, 131; *Saturday Review,* 20 November 1889, 650.

31. *Athenaeum,* 17 March 1894, 342.

32. *Queen,* 23 July 1898, 135.

WORKS CITED

Anderson, Nancy Fix. *Woman against Women in Victorian England: A Life of Eliza Lynn Linton.* Bloomington: Indiana UP, 1987.

Colby, Vineta. *The Singular Anomaly: Women Novelists of the Nineteenth Century.* New York: New York UP, 1970.

Ford, Boris, ed. *Pelican Guide to English Literature.* New York: Penguin, 1969.

Haight, Gordon. *George Eliot and John Chapman.* New Haven: Yale UP, 1940.

Helsinger, Elizabeth et al. *The Woman Question: Society and Literature in Britain and America, 1837–1883.* New York: Garland, 1983.

Ireland, Mrs. Alexander. *Selections from the Letters of Geraldine Endsor Jewsbury to Jane Welsh Carlyle.* London, 1982.

Lang, Cecil B., ed. *The Swinburne Letters.* New Haven: Yale UP, 1959.

Layard, George Somes. *Mrs. Lynn Linton: Her Life, Letters, and Opinions.* London: Methuen, 1901.

Linton, E. Lynn. *The True History of Joshua Davidson, Christian and Communist.* London: Strahan, 1872. Reprinted in *Novels of Faith and Doubt.* New York: Garland, 1975.

———. *The Rebel of the Family.* 3 vols. London: Chatto and Windus, 1880.

———. *The Autobiography of Chirtopher Kirkland.* 3 vols. London: Richard Bentley and Son, 1885. Reprinted in *Novels of Faith and Doubt.* New York: Garland, 1976.

Lynn, Eliza. *Realities: A Tale.* 3 vols. London: Saunders and Otley, 1851.

Panton, Jane Ellen. *Leaves from a Life.* London, 1908.

SELECTED SECONDARY SOURCES

Nancy Fix Anderson, *Woman against Women in Victorian England: A Life of Eliza Lynn Linton* (Bloomington: Indiana UP, 1987); Herbert Van Thal, *Eliza Lynn Linton: The Girl of the Period* (London: George Allen and Unwin, 1979); Vineta Colby, "Wild Women, Revolting Daughters, and The Shrieking Sisterhood: Mrs. Eliza Lynn Linton," *The Singular Anomaly: Women Novelists of the Nineteenth Century* (New York: New York UP, 1970); Nancy F. Anderson, "Autobiographical Fantasies of a Female Anti-Feminist: Eliza Lynn Linton as Christopher Kirkland and Theodora Desanges," *Dickens Studies Annual* 14 (1985); Elizabeth K. Helsinger, Robin Lauterback Sheets, and William Veeder, "Eliza Lynn Linton and 'The Girls of the Period,'" *The Woman Question: Society and Literature in Britain and America, 1837–1883*, Vol. 1 (New York: Garland, 1983); J.M. Rignall, "Between Chartism and the 1880s: J.W. Overton and E. Lynn Linton," *The Socialist Novel in Britain*, edited by H. Gustav Klaus (New York: St. Martin's, 1982).

# Problems of a "Democratic Text"

## Walter Besant's Impossible Story in *All Sorts and Conditions of Men* (1882)

*Wim Neetens*

Walter Besant (1836–1901) was educated at King's College, London, and Christ's College, Cambridge. From 1861 to 1867 he taught at the Royal College in Mauritius. Back in England, he became secretary to the Palestine Exploration Fund and established himself as a writer. He is chiefly remembered today as the Society of Authors' first president, whose journal, *The Author*, he edited until his death, and as the philanthropist whose efforts helped to establish the People's Palace in London's Mile End Road, an arts center for the local working-class community, whose educational facilities were later incorporated into the University of London. In his own day, however, Besant was tremendously popular as the author of dozens of romantic novels, historical studies, and critical essays. His collaboration with James Rice, editor of *Once a Week*, resulted in fourteen novels in the years from 1871 to Rice's death in 1881. On his own, Besant wrote thirty-two novels, including his greatest success, *All Sorts and Conditions of Men* (1882), published the same year as his antifeminist extravaganza, *The Revolt of Man*. His work also includes literary criticism (*Studies in Early French Poetry*, 1868), *The Art of the Novel* (1884), biographies (among them *Rabelais*, 1879), and historical studies of London. His ambitious *Survey of London* was left unfinished when he died. Besant was knighted in 1895. His work remains available only from antiquarian and second-hand bookshops.

Few novels have had the impact of Walter Besant's *All Sorts and Conditions of Men* (1882); few have come so close to realizing Oscar Wilde's adage that "nature imitates art." Within years of the novel's publication, Besant saw his utopian scheme for a popular "Palace of Delight," with which the story culminates, realized first in the East End of London and later in other big cities.

Walter Besant was a practical man, the first president of the Society of Authors and active in their struggle for fairer contracts and copyright regulations. A professional man in the newly commercialized world of letters, he opposed the romantic cliché of the author as a seer. Yet Besant himself seemed peculiarly in touch with the subliminal anxieties of his audience: he obviously struck a resounding note with this, his first independent venture after a long partnership with James Rice, and his most successful novel.

Besant himself was, of course, closely engaged in the public discussion that accompanied the construction and inauguration of the People's Palace in London. In an article written for *Contemporary Review* in 1887, he applauds its near completion and implores his fellows in polite society to trust the working man to make good use of it. His democratic sentiments are outspoken: "Let us remember, and constantly bear in mind, that the Palace is to be *governed by the people for themselves*. If it is not, better for East London that it had never been erected" (233). Besant's confidence in the workers of East London was based on his fundamental confidence in the power of culture to educate to obedience:

> The People's Palace offers recreation to all who wish to fit themselves
> for its practice and enjoyment. But it is recreation of a kind which
> demands skill, patience, discipline, drill, and obedience to law. Those
> who master any one of the Arts, the practice of which constitutes true
> recreation, have left once and for ever the ranks of disorder: they be-
> long, by virtue of their aptitude and their education—say, by virtue
> of their Election—to the army of Law and Order. (229)

Art versus Anarchy: a practical and optimistic Matthew Arnold seems to be addressing us here, in a period of recurring workers' and unemployed agitation and increasing political organisation within the working class. Written only a year after the *grande peur* of the 1886 riots (which, as Gareth Stedman Jones has noted, William Morris was not alone in interpreting as "the first skirmish of the Revolution," 294), these were uplifting words that must have sounded like music to the ears of a demoralized middle class since the "condition of England question" had reemerged in the distress of the early 1880s and swelled to the level of an urgent national debate. Besant indeed had a sweeter way of putting things than some of his contemporaries, who insisted, like Samuel Smith, that "[t]he proletariat may strangle us unless we teach it the same virtues which have elevated the other classes of society" (Jones 291).

It certainly seemed as if much teaching and elevating would be necessary to prevent a revolution but Besant was undaunted. He was a liberal reformist, an optimistic humanist whose novels celebrated the possibility of social change and progress. His fiction in the 1880s was structured around the hope that nonconfrontational modes of democratic social transformation were possible—to leave things exactly as they were, only better. He was a successful novelist: productive, accessible, and popular. These were no self-evident virtues in the age of laborious naturalist experiment.

Yet literary history does not remember Besant for his novels, if it remembers him at all. What we do find about him usually refers to the literary quarrel he sparked off in 1884. Besant's lecture on "The Art of Fiction," in which he expounded his aesthetic theory, caused a number of comments and reactions from other critics and writers: most notably, of course, from Henry James. In criticism we find Besant produced as a philistine but amiable populist, a deluded and outdated optimist—the better to set off James's "mature" and "definitive" contribution to the English novel (Spilka, Dean; for an altogether more nuanced approach, which also goes into the political implications of the debate, see Goode).

With reference to this crucial point in English literature when the division between popular, "commercial" fiction and more select, "literary" forms of writing began to manifest itself and to be debated in precisely these terms, it is clear which fundamental choices the academy has made. These choices—I am not the first to argue—have profound political implications, if only with respect to the accessibility of the texts which English studies has canonized as the core of "the great tradition." The canonization of an author like James works, amongst other things, to suppress precisely the dialogic context in which he was writing. If we work to recover this context we will not only "understand James better" (though not in the essentialist sense these words are usually given); we shall also understand how this particular choice has helped to release English studies from grappling with a set of profoundly political questions and contradictions about its own history and constitution.

Novels like Walter Besant's should be interesting to us precisely because they are less "literary"—less sophisticated about their strategic displacements, silences, and suppressions, more open about their propaganda content, not so conversant with the art of abstraction. Uncovering this suppressed and embarrassing underside of the literary canon should perhaps, as Peter Widdowson might put it, be part of our exercise in "re-reading English." Walter Besant's work, though far from revolutionary, throws a revealing light on the democratic pretensions of a system that thrives on inequality: in a novel like *All Sorts and Conditions of Men,* "culture" is made to stare its own social and political use value in the face and laugh at its own show of disinterestedness.

"An Impossible Story"

> All Sorts and Conditions of Men is not a very complicated novel. In spite of
> a number of unexpected Dickensian developments in this "bizarre slum pas-
> toral" (Keating 101), the basic story line is quickly summarized.

> Although subtitled "an impossible story" and set in a romantic and
> semiutopian mood and tone, All Sorts and Conditions of Men opens on a
> scene of great topical weight: on a Cambridge lawn, in June 1881, two New
> Women, recent graduates from Newnham College, discuss their future. Like
> her friend, the brilliant mathematician Constance Woodcote (stereotyped
> with glasses and a frown), Angela Marsden Messenger scoffs at marriage
> and traditional feminine aspirations.

> Unlike her friend, however, Angela will not devote her life to science
> and the furthering of women's education. A student of political economy,
> she has latterly been disappointed with this "so-called science": "it treated
> of men and women as skittles, it ignored the principal motives of action"
> (4). Heiress to the biggest brewery in the East End, considerable East End
> property, and "an unconscionable sum of money in the Funds" (5), she is
> resolved to take her responsibilities in the world. "I belong to the People—
> with a great, big P, my dear—I cannot bear to go on living by their toil and
> giving nothing in return." She will leave society life for what it is and "van-
> ish," "disappear": to the East End. She will live as a dressmaker and become
> "one of the people" (7).

> Part two of the double prologue introduces Harry Goslett, who, on
> his twenty-third birthday in a tasteful West End flat, is told the truth about
> his birth. His guardian, Lord Jocelyn Le Breton, picked the boy up when he
> was an orphaned baby in the custody of one Uncle Bunker. The boy was of
> humble origin and the Liberal Le Breton thought "that it would be an in-
> structive and humorous thing to take a boy of the multitude and bring him
> up in all the culture, the tastes, the ideas of ourselves" and to send him back
> to "his own people" when he was grown up, so that he might become a
> prophet to tell them "of the paradise he had seen" (13). Harry is welcome
> to stay in "society" but decides on the spot that he will go and find "his
> own people": "I must compare myself with them—I must prove the broth-
> erhood of humanity" (14).

> The prologue sets the tone for the rest of the novel. The "laws" of
> political economy are criticized from a humanist point of view which rec-
> ognizes the basic exploitative nature of a capitalist economy and centers on
> the "responsibility" of the rich. Darwinist theories on which the supremacy
> of the bourgeoisie and nobility were popularly founded are disproved by the
> "success" of Harry's aristocratic education. A tradition of sensational writ-

ing about the working class and the East End as a foreign and exotic zone—
"the dreadful region" in the mathematician's words (7)—is debunked as
based on ignorance and irrational fear. Women's social responsibility is un-
derlined, but the "unfeminine" female scholar is ridiculed in conventional
and easy stereotype. Woman's true vocation—and liberation—we are made
to understand, lies elsewhere.

Angela and Harry, unaware of each other's schemes, both take rooms
in a Whitechapel boarding house, near the Messenger Brewery. They live with
an odd assortment of East End characters whose lives are revealed as the
narrative develops.

Angela—now "Miss Kennedy"—sets up a cooperative Dressmakers'
Association with working girls from the neighborhood. Her workshop boasts
enormously improved working conditions: shorter hours, dinner paid for by
the association, lawn tennis and gymnastics for recreation, and singing and
dancing for the girls' cultural elevation. The profits of the enterprise are divided among the workers. Custom is initially guaranteed by Angela's "West
End connection"—she places her own orders in Miss Messenger's name.
Harry Goslett, who poses as a cabinetmaker, is offered a well-paid job at
the Brewery. Angela's political project is to make the workers "discontented."
By offering them the experience of what the rich do for recreation—"culture": singing, dancing, playing music, and reading—and by showing them
the material conditions necessary for these entertainments (by giving her
workers leisure) she hopes to make the workers discontented with current
conditions under laissez faire capitalism and to encourage them to demand
better. It is not shown in detail how this process will work, but she swears
by the principle of "combination" and offers, for example, the idea of a
Women's Union.

The idea for her second big project is given her by Harry, with whom
she becomes good friends as they recognize in each other the mark of genteel culture and education but remain ignorant of each other's backgrounds.
Together they fabricate a vision of a "Palace of Pleasure" (quickly renamed
Palace of Delight: "Pleasure seems to touch a lower note" [51]), where the
working men and women of the East End will be able to train themselves
in the arts and enjoy "the pleasures and graces of life" (50). Through her
West End lawyers, Angela orders a block of her property to be demolished
and a Palace of Delight built in its place. As the building works are in
progress, her influence in Whitechapel spreads. She even mellows the hearts
of Dick the Radical, Harry's cousin, and of "the old Chartist," the chair-
man at the Stepney Advanced Club. Harry, predictably, falls in love with her
and when the Palace of Delight is finished Angela finally accepts his pro-

posal. At the wedding ceremony Harry still does not know he is marrying the Messenger heiress, but all is revealed in the evening of the wedding day, when the Palace of Delight is inaugurated. Harry's dream is realized, and he speaks to the crowd: "It is not by setting poor against rich, or by hardening the heart of rich against poor, that you will succeed: it is by independence and by knowledge. All sorts and conditions of men are alike" (330).

## Class, Politics, and Humanism

Fundamentally a romance of the sentimental, feminine type denounced by realists and naturalists, *All Sorts and Conditions of Men* is nevertheless forced by its association with a practical, reformist project to confront real-world politics and existing developments in the social and political sphere. A form of "realism" is therefore indispensable to the narrative if it is to convince readers of the feasibility—or at least the desirability—of the projects it proposes. If it is to charge its entertainment value with any kind of ideological effect, the novel is required to accommodate a realist, documentary component, albeit a marginal one.

We shall see, however, the power of this peripheral realist presence in the text to upset the balance of its "democratic" arrangement of discourses. The confrontation of the narrative's reformist, utopian project couched in melodramatic narrative on the one hand, with the solidity of its realism, however slight, on the other allows the reader to prise open the contradictions and suppressions that reveal its underlying ideological currents.

All of Angela's reformist undertakings fly in the face of accepted political economy: she incurs unjustifiable overheads, pays wages that are too high, allows herself to be swayed by sympathy and emotion when hiring staff. Refusing to play by the rules of economics, and setting morality above profits, Angela shows herself to be a "bad capitalist": a strong moral positive in this novel and also, it is implied, a feminine quality. It is her exceptional insertion into the capitalist class, as a highly educated woman in charge of a large fortune, that offers precisely the key to her success: not miraculously so, as she is able to get round the mechanisms of supply and demand only by providing her own dressmaking business with custom out of the profits of her brewery—a vestige of political economy if there is one in the book. Besant, however, does not elaborate on this contradiction, other than to point out that it is a great unhappiness and a "dreadful responsibility" to be rich (5).

Angela's and Harry's projects work to illustrate the democratic political program they wish to put forward to the people of Whitechapel and Stepney. This is a far-reaching program indeed, containing some of the most progressive ideas current at the time. In a period of increased trade unionism—a militant New Unionism was organizing an unprecedented number of semiskilled and unskilled workers—it hinges on the principle of "combination":

> "If," [Dick the Radical] said, "there's a hundred women asking for ten places, of course the governor'll give them to the cheapest."

> "That," replied Angela, "is a matter of course as things now are. But there is another way of considering the question. If we have a Woman's Trade Union, as we shall have before long, where there are ten places, only ten women should be allowed to apply, and just wages be demanded!"

> "How is that to be done?"

> "My friend, you have yet a great deal to learn. . . . Governments are nothing: you must help yourselves; you must combine." (241)

"Combination" is the clue, but before combined workers can act they have to "find out what they want." It takes a swell in disguise to tell them. "You want your own Local Government" (198), Harry informs the Radicals at the Advanced Club, and more: unadulterated food, better housing, proper training for the children, proper recreation and enjoyment, paid holidays, regulations on women's labor.

Harry's program for a "League of Working Men for the Promotion and Advancement of their own interests" (323) carefully elides questions of opposed class interests and in this alone compares weakly with contemporaneous programs circulating among Radical and early socialist working-class organizations. Still, Harry's speeches contain some stirring "democratic" rhetoric:

> You have always had the Power. You have always had all the Power there is. It is yours, because you are the people, and what the people want they will have. Your Power is your birthright. You are an irresistible giant who has only to roar in order to get what he wants. (196)

> "You think that Governments can do everything for you. You FOOLS! Has any Government ever done anything for you? Has it raised your wages? Has it shortened your hours? Can it protect you against rogues and adulterators? Will it ever try to better your positions? Never:

never: never. Because it cannot. Does any Government ask what you want, what you ought to want? No. Can it give you what you want? No. (197)

But rhetoric it remains. Besant was able to allow Radical discourse ample space in his texts only if it was sanitized and gentrified into a version less threatening and confrontational than that which circulated on leaflets and in workingmen's clubs. Especially debatable is Harry's point on emigration: "In every family it shall be considered necessary for some to go, and the whole country shall be mapped out into districts, and only a certain number be allowed to remain." Emigration was widely believed by the middle classes to be an ideal strategy for ridding the country of its unemployed "residuum." It also, of course, handsomely fit the requirements of imperial expansion: "Now the world being so small as it is, and Englishmen and Scotchmen being so masterful that they must needs go straight to the front and stay there, it cannot but happen that the world will presently . . . be overrun with the good old English blood" (323)! Such lofty sentiments echo H.M. Hyndman's jingoism in the first years of the Social Democratic Federation: "In America, in Australia, all the world over, the Anglo-Saxon blood is still second to none" (Thompson 295). They do not, however, seem to have been shared by the rank-and-file labor movement of the early 80s, who manifestly opposed imperial expansion under Disraeli and Gladstone. A handbill distributed by the Labour Emancipation League in the East End in these years stated pleasantly that "[t]he only emigration at all necessary or desirable is that of the idle, aristocratic, and capitalist classes" (Thompson 287).

A central point in Harry's and Angela's reformist program is that the people of the East End should not wait for the government to improve their position, but do it for themselves. This is linked with the Victorian liberal self-help ideology. Furthermore, the advocacy of any kind of state intervention in problems such as housing could be construed at this time as a dangerous step toward socialism and collectivism. But there is a further dimension to this. The advocacy of collective self-help, albeit in the form of radical trade unions and local governing bodies, can also be seen as effectively keeping the workers out of government and state affairs. They must not presume that any radical change in the state's most powerful apparatuses is desirable, or even possible:

"You know nothing: you understand nothing: of your own country. You do not know how its institutions have grown up: why it is so prosperous: why changes, when they have to be made, should be made slowly, and not before they are necessary. . . . You do not respect the old institutions, because you don't know them; you desire new things because you don't understand the old. Go—learn—make your orators learn and make them teach you. And then send them to the House of Commons to represent you." (196–97)

But only then, of course. We should remind ourselves here of the moral panic that accompanied every extension of the franchise. Each Reform Act effectively gave rise to initiatives in popular education in order to guarantee the proper subjecthood, the recuperability, indeed the embourgeoisement of every new group admitted to national public and political life (Best 176–77).

This representation of the country's institutions as old, venerable, historically necessary, and not easily accessible allows the novel to set in motion the processes of identification and differentiation which contradict and undercut its democratic rhetoric. There is first of all an opportunity here for the text to reinforce the essential Englishness of the political apparatus. It encourages bourgeois identification with the interests of the state by associating it with the values of culture and tradition to which, as a class, the bourgeoisie was permanently struggling to prove itself adequate.

Furthermore, it allows for a sharp differentiation between "us," who orchestrate and arrange the "democratic" master discourse, and "them," who are subject to it. In the following example linguistic accent is the undercover agent that betrays and differentiates Dick the Radical from the educated and politically mature classes—and this at the point where the narrative manifestly endorses his political ambitions. Easy ridicule does the trick here:

> "You are ambitious, are you not?"
> "Yes," he replied boldly, "I am ambitious. I don't tell them outside," he jerked his thumb over his shoulder to indicate the Advanced Club, "but I mean to get into the 'Ouse—I mean the House." One of his little troubles was the correction of certain peculiarities of speech common to his class. (241)

It is clear how these "little troubles" are strategically, though perhaps unconsciously, mobilized to reinforce a social stratification that surreptitiously invalidates the narrative's manifest democratic program.

In general terms, *All Sorts and Conditions of Men* belittles and derides working-class political activity by presenting it as based on ignorance and irrationality. Its aims are reduced to "the Abolition of the House of

Lords" and its practice to little more than an excuse for some good times, an outlet for both enthusiasm and anger: "They [the people] came to the hall [the Stepney Advanced Club] to get these little emotions, and not for any personal or critical interest in the matter discussed" (237). There is little or no political understanding among even the politically active workers. Hence their need for leaders.

But not just any leaders. *All Sorts and Conditions of Men* sings the praise of the respectable working class, but stops short of entrusting their own political activists with any capacity for responsible leadership. Dick the Radical, as we have seen, has "a great deal to learn":

> He is the reddest of the red-hot Rads, and the most advanced of Republicans. I do not think he would himself go a-murdering of kings and priests, but I fancy he regards these things as accidents naturally arising out of a pardonable enthusiasm. (139)

This enthusiasm, as we have also seen, is based on a lack of knowledge of the institutions of the state and on the "emotional" nature typical of the working class. "The old Chartist," another prominent member of the Advanced Club, has the advantage of being trained in "'48 and the dreams of Chartism" (190): "he understood something of what he wanted and why he wanted it. The proof of which is, that they have got all they wanted [!] and we still survive" (237), as Besant comments with a revealing opposition of first and third persons plural.

The old Chartist, however, has important historical knowledge, and he is allowed to counter Harry's all too undiscerning rejection of the working-class struggle for parliamentary representation. His views of working-class attainments are no doubt somewhat overoptimistic and valid only, if at all, for the "respectable," enfranchised (this is 1882), artisanal East-Enders. But he has some interesting lines, as in a talk with his younger friend, Dick:

> We've got what we wanted—that's true—and we seem to be no better off. That's true, too. But we *are* better off; because we *feel* that every man has his share in the rule of the nation; that's a grand thing; we are not kept out of our vote; we don't see, as we used to see, our money spent for us without having a say; that's a very grand thing which he [Harry] doesn't understand; nor you neither, because you are too young. Everything we get which makes us feel our power more is good for us. The chap was right, but he was wrong as well. Don't give up politics, lad. (238)

It is in this light that "we must be educated" (238) if there is to be any political progress at all—if the working class is to produce its own leaders.

At the same time, however, it is implied that the patronage of "substitute heroes" will remain indispensable (Keating 99). And here we stumble upon an interesting cluster of contradictions which the novel has to suppress if it is to avoid the pitfalls of advocating a downright collectivist transformation of the economy on the one hand, or a blunt and too manifestly undemocratic endorsement of the social relations of capitalism on the other.

If the reformist program carried by the story were couched in a fully fledged working-class political project it would, reformist though it remains, constitute a genuine threat to laissez-faire capitalism and bourgeois hegemony at large. It is therefore recuperated within a less confronting and less oppositional social model, in which classes can be seen as cooperative and sharing the same interests. Commercial interests are suppressed from the society in which the characters move, allowing for a genuine confrontation of opposed interests to be avoided. Indeed the very notion of a class society has to be mystified and rewritten into a scenario of rich and poor. The poor must be seen to seek, and find, allegiance outside their class if their project is not to escalate into a genuine revolutionary politics which would confront and challenge class structures and their economic foundations.

Moreover, it is clear why support will have to be found in a sector of society which can be sufficiently mystified, severed from any apparent economic interests in capitalism, indeed "declassed":

> "Sometimes I think, Dick," the old man went on, "that the working man's best friends would be the swells, if they could be got hold of. They've got nothing to make out of the artisan; they don't run factories nor keep shops; they don't care, bless you, how high his wages are: why should they? They've got their farmers to pay the rent, and their houses, and their money in the funds; what does it matter to them? They're well brought up too, most of them, civil in their manner, and disposed to be friendly if you're neither standoffish nor familiar, but know yourself and talk accordin'." (239)

The rudimentary economic identity which the swells—landed gentry and leisured townfolk—receive in this paragraph is lost in the further development of the narrative, until the rich become a completely mystified group in Harry's inaugural speech at the Palace of Delight:

It is not by setting poor against rich, or by hardening the heart of rich against poor, that you will succeed: it is by independence and by knowledge. All sorts and conditions of men are alike. As are the vices of the rich, so are your own; as are your virtues, so are theirs. But, hitherto, the rich have had things which you could not get. Now all that is altered." (330)

Real economic and social class distinctions and oppositions are blurred and transcended in a humanist reconciliation of interests. But this entails another ideological necessity in the text. The working class has to be shown to be worthy of inclusion in the grand humanist family: its members have to be proved full and mature subjects capable of rational decision making. The novel goes to great lengths to illustrate the respectability of the artisanal working class, and in this it is certainly in dialogue with contemporaneous discourses of journalism and sociology which encouraged a moral panic about a degenerated urban proletariat.

Although it does, necessarily as we have seen, belittle the workers' rationality and insight in political matters, *All Sorts and Conditions of Men* is quite optimistic about their capacity to be educated. Besant's "fundamental faith in education and cultural consciousness had its root . . . in the Christian Socialism of Maurice and Kingsley, and in the social theories of Ruskin" (Keating 107). If working-class characters are generally represented as unenlightened and in need of moral leadership, they are also seen to be responsible, honest, intelligent—and capable of "culture," the ultimate touchstone of mature humanity, as we shall presently see.

This somewhat rosy picture of a population of whom, according to statistics, at least a third was living in destitution and a far greater proportion in plain poverty, was no doubt intended to allay bourgeois fears of the democratic mob and to make the idea of their inclusion in any kind of democratic political process palatable. Besant's optimism can be seen as consciously playing on widespread fears about the separation of the classes in a wealthy and complacent West End geographically distanced from a pauperized East End, left to its own devices without the benefit of the moral influence of "a better class of person." (Besant repeatedly offers his readers page-long, glowing descriptions of East End communities, which read like tourist guide copy—doubtless he was luring the rich into closer contact with "the unknown East End.") This concern stems from an older, but still popular organicist view of society:

Servitude! Why, we are all servants one of the other. Society is like the human body, in which all the limbs belong to each other. There must be rich and poor, idlers and workers; we depend one upon the other; if the rich do not work with and for the poor, retribution falls upon them. The poor must work for the rich, or they will starve; poor or rich, I think it is better to be poor; idler or worker, I know it is better to be worker. (126)

Brave words from "the richest heiress in England" (45)!

But what about Arnold's "vast portion . . . of the working class which, raw and half-developed, has long lain half-hidden amidst its poverty and squalor, and is now issuing from its hiding-place to assert an Englishman's heaven-born privilege of doing as he likes" (143)? Clearly, the humanist embrace could not be stretched so far as to include this "residuum," and indeed it isn't. The novel's commitment to however elementary a form of social realism and verisimilitude forces it to acknowledge its existence (if perhaps only on the level of social anxiety and debate, of discourse), while at the same time it refuses to draw it fully into the narrative.

The "populace," that residuum of pauperized casual workers whom some social critics in the same period would have deported to the colonies or interned in prison camps, emerges in *All Sorts and Conditions of Men* as the other against which the respectable working class is defined. If the artisanat is to be drawn into the undifferentiated humanity of a national public sphere, it has to be all the more sharply differentiated from the unfit, the degraded classes, the great unwashed—to quote only some of the epithets in circulation at the time.

The historical reality of a class irrecuperable by any superficially reformist means, however, cannot be denied, and it is glimpsed once or twice around the corners of Besant's rosy picture:

> The really sad thing about this district is that the residents are not the starving class, or the vicious class, or the drinking class. . . .(133)

> The respectable people were all in church, and it was too cold for the lounging of the more numerous class of those who cannot call themselves respectable. (237)

This differentiation is necessary because the narrative partakes of a much more widespread concern: improved educational facilities for the artisanal workers meant not only that they would possibly transform into an embourgeoisé form of respectability. It meant also that they were given the means for organizing themselves, and the knowledge to see the advantages of doing so. This opens particularly dangerous perspectives on social revolution, especially in a text that already queries the validity of political economy and laissez-faire capitalism, and that advocates, albeit within a cooperative framework, the principle of combination.

If the aristocrats of labor had to be educated, they had at the same time to be wooed away from the classes with whom they lived and with whom they shared a number of political interests—and a culture. They had to be won over from a working-class identity to join the ranks of those who felt—correctly or not—that they had a stake in the established order of things. "In a period when the 'residuum' was becoming increasingly threatening, it was urgent that the 'respectable' working class should be enabled to participate more actively within the political system, and that their 'legitimate' grievances should be met" (Jones 301).

*Culture*

"I will bring him to your drawing-room," Harry tells Angela when first talking about his Radical cousin, Dick:

> "That is, if he will come. He does not know much about drawing-rooms, but he is a great man at the Stepney Advanced Club. He is the reddest of red-hot Rads, and the most advanced of Republicans. . . . His manners are better than you will generally find, because he belongs to my own gentle craft. You shall tame him, Miss Kennedy."
>
> Angela said she would try.
>
> "He shall learn to waltz," Harry went on. "This will convert him from a fierce Republican to a merely enthusiastic Radical. Then he shall learn to sing in parts: this will drop him down into advanced Liberalism. And if you can persuade him to attend your evenings, talk with the girls, or engage him in some Art, say painting, he will become, quite naturally, a mere Conservative." (139)

There is obviously an amount of irony and aphorism here, but not to the degree that the novel would abandon the widespread conviction that "culture" was able to polish the rougher character and soften the more strident political persuasion. Despite its frequent associations with the poetic, the dis-utilitarian (and the feminine), culture here is the gate that opens on to the rational space of balanced and equitable human intercourse. And indeed, when Dick walks away from his first meeting with Angela, "humbled and pensive" (143), his set views are disturbed and his confidence in his politics shaken. He who is "so much accustomed to the vague denunciations and cheap rhetoric of his class" (141) is exposed to the "pleasures" of culture—and converted. The process of his conversion is typically couched in gendered terms: "For the first time in his life, he felt the influence of a woman" (143).

Terry Lovell has written about the identification of femininity and culture, or more specifically literature:

> An identical "civilizing power" is attributed to literature and to women. . . . It is clear in the nineteenth-century social problem novel. The civilizing influence of women and literature was to operate beneficially on masters and men and upon the relationship between them. The influence of women and literature might, it was hoped, temper the militant class antagonism of the one and the unfeeling utilitarianism of the other. (141)

In the sex/gender economy of bourgeois culture the bourgeois male is seen as the "civilized," feminized improvement on the raw masculinity attributed to working-class men on the one hand, and as the more "natural," more manly counterpart to effete aristocratic refinement on the other: "In bourgeois culture the bourgeois male marks the position of human normality" (140).

*All Sorts and Conditions of Men* produces this crude scheme in a more complex and necessarily more mystifying way. "Culture" is the feminized discursive zone where, under the aegis of a heroically philanthropic version of bourgeois womanhood, the novel is able to shift its contradictions of sexual and class politics toward their imaginary, mythical resolutions. Crude social and economic antagonisms are elided so that culture may operate as the crucial term through which reform is realized and articulated.

Though in a naive way a materialist project, Angela's operations in the East End hinge on culture as a progressive and enabling force. Both her Dressmakers' Association and her Palace of Delight are solidly material enterprises involving unheard-of arrangements of labor power, wages, managerial power, and capital. However, her workgirls are not emancipated because they earn higher wages, gain more control over their own lives, or participate in the government of their community. Theirs is primarily an emancipation of the mind or the spirit: it consists in their ability to participate in pleasures hitherto reserved for the rich. They have become cultured, "civilized"—the products of an unlikely embourgeoisement: "What I have attempted is, in short, nothing less than the introduction of a love of what we call culture," Angela writes to her mathematician friend at Cambridge. And what do we call culture?

> I find, already, a great improvement in the girls. They have acquired new interests in life; they are happier: consequently, they chatter like birds in spring and sunshine; and whereas, since I came into these regions, it has been a constant pain to listen to the querulous and angry talk of workgirls in omnibuses and in streets, I rejoice that we have changed all this, and while they are with me my girls can talk without angry snapping of the lips, and without the "sezi" and "sezee" and "sezshee" of the omnibus. This is surely a great gain for them. (104–5)

No irony here. Mastery of the standard language is the first step toward civilized subjecthood: the key to the democracy of common humanity. Once "improved," the girls will "convert"—civilize and feminize—their brothers and spread a general taste for culture. The desire for more will create widespread discontent with the way things are, and power the collective will to change: "discontentment must come before reform" (99).

This is an original and ambitious scheme not without its radical and progressive moments, as we shall presently see. Again, however, the narrative finds itself forced to effect a number of suppressions, which we glimpse in its confrontation of real historical circumstances, in its "realism."

For if the convertible strata of the working class are to be represented as open to genteel culture, and indeed in need of it, what to do with the existing forms of working-class culture available to them in the real world? These were the years when skilled workers and artisans who had benefited from the rise in real wages during the Great Depression had started to organize their lives according to new and identifiable patterns, symbolized by newly available consumer goods—decent clothes, cheap but "respectable" furniture, sewing-machines, bicycles, books, and periodicals—and the institutions still popularly identified with "traditional" working-class culture: pubs, music halls, football games, working men's clubs.

The construction of a working-class culture, based on the experience and celebration of a shared history and place in the social formation and hence easily politicized as antibourgeois and anticapitalist, is an alternative which *All Sorts and Conditions of Men* is, of course, unable to consider. If Angela's culture is universal and the satisfaction of an inherently human need, then it cannot be seen to compete with an alternative: to struggle, assimilate, and recuperate. It must be seen to fill a void, to grow on fallow ground: hence the necessity of rewriting the East End as "waste land": "Mile upon mile of streets with houses—small, mean and monotonous houses; the people living the same mean and monotonous lives, all after the same model" (30).

The particularity and materiality of East End history has to be denied and the area has to be produced as the "uninscribed earth" (Spivak 133) on which the colonizer (the philanthropic missionary) is able to draw her map/geography. The bourgeois reformer must be seen to start history rather than intervene in an already existing one. By the same token, bourgeois involvement in an earlier history is eradicated. (Who built these small, mean and monotonous houses in the first place?) The East-Enders are reborn in the eye of their beholder: not as the subjects of their own history, but as object and other of bourgeois knowledge.

Remarkably like the European in the Orient who establishes himself as sovereign and master by passing through the country bodily, so the philanthropic bourgeois who extends charity to the East End initiates this "worlding" of new territory. As Spivak notes, "The truth value of the stranger is being established as the reference point for the true (insertion into) history of these wild regions" (133). Usurping the working-class voice, the philanthropist articulates proletarian desire as if for the first time:

> "What we want here," [Harry] said, "as it seems to me, is a little more of the pleasures and graces of life. . . . See us on Sundays, we are not a bad-looking lot; healthy, well-dressed, and tolerably rosy. But we have no pleasures." (50)

*All Sorts and Conditions of Men* hardly touches upon existing structures and institutions of working-class life; if at all they are represented as the degraded opposite of a truly humanist culture:

> The first beatific vision [of the Palace] was over, and would come no more; she had now to face the hard fact of an unsympathetic people who perhaps would not desire any pleasure—or if any, then the pleasure of a "spree" with plenty of beer. . . . Oh! The Herculean task, for one woman, with two or three disciples, to revolutionise the City of East London! (136)

But of course she succeeds—the objects of her good intentions are easily won over to the universal appeal of "pleasure"—and it is, perhaps contradictorily, in the success of this unlikely and illusive revolution that the novel's progressive potential is to be found. For, naive and implausible a narrative though it is, in its historical context it flew right in the face of one of the most pervasive and most widespread ideologies of high Victorianism: Social Darwinism.

When Besant was writing, Social Darwinism had acquired considerable intellectual prestige and wide currency in popular debates about the reemerging "condition of England question." It was particularly applied to theories of the degeneration of the urban working class. Urban workers were widely believed to suffer degenerational effects from their environment, and there was considerable anxiety among the middle classes that as a "race" they would eventually wither away and become extinct. Relocation projects for the residuum of unemployed and casual workers were proposed as the most daring and advanced solutions to the problem, as were immigration schemes whereby rural workers would be imported to the great cities in order to feed fresh and healthy blood into new generations of the urban proletariat.

Optimism in itself, then, was a remarkable stance to take, to say the least, and a culturalist approach would shake the scientific presumptions on which bourgeois (and, in the imperial context, white) superiority was founded. In a literature obsessed with characters' physiognomy as proof of innate aristocratic worthiness, Besant introduces the ironic opposite: this is our first view of the changeling Harry:

> This interesting young man was a much more aristocratic person to look upon than his senior [Jocelyn le Breton]. He paraded, so to speak, at every point, the thoroughbred air. His thin and delicate nose, his clear eye, his high though narrow forehead, his well-cut lip, his firm chin, his pale cheek, his oval face, the slim figure, the thin, long fingers, the spring of his walk, the poise of his head—what more could one expect even from the descendant of All the Howards? (9)

In Gissing this would be proof of genuine aristocratic descent; in Besant it ironically demonstrates the supremacy of nurture over nature. With all its suppressions, silences, and displacements, *All Sorts and Conditions of Men* articulated a humanist belief in the perfectibility of "mankind," which opened a space for some of the most advanced ideas which bourgeois thinking about the working class could accommodate.

But, of course, it wasn't innocent of ulterior motive. Besant was writing in a period of hardened class antagonism and conflict, when the organicist, evolutionary model of social progress became increasingly difficult to subscribe to even for bourgeois intellectuals. The self-confidence with which the bourgeoisie had over the decades constructed their own historical identity as a class naturally fit to lead the nation was no longer so easily upheld. Several intellectuals lost faith in the bourgeois utopia altogether and defected to socialism. The ideological dominant itself—that precarious conjunction of liberalism, utilitarianism, and a romantic corporatist myth of the organic society—was forced to lift itself on to higher planes of abstraction if it was to incorporate growing conflict and pressure.

It is a telling anecdote that after the violent Trafalgar Square riots of 1886, a Mansion House Fund for the relief of the unemployed "shot up suddenly" (Cole 407), alongside numerous other spontaneous charitable initiatives, greatly to the dismay of the Charity Organisation Society, who kept strictly to the laws of political economy, in a reflexive attempt to allay working-class discontent through a bourgeois counterattack of philanthropy. Philanthropy had always been very much part of the Victorian way of dealing with the problems of poverty, the general consensus being that "deserving" individuals and families should be encouraged to cope through self-help and the occasional philanthropic gesture from their betters. Faced with the troubles of the 1880s, which the better-off feared were genuinely revolutionary, this philanthropic ideology needed to be tuned to a higher pitch if the lost stability of the Golden Years were to be recovered. The bourgeoisie had to prove to themselves, and to the nation, that their ascendancy was still based on a set of vital and necessary social relations.

As a result, the middle classes turned with renewed vigor to their hegemonic project in what amounted to a wholesale ethical revival of bourgeois values. Walter Besant played an important part in translating the terms of this revival into a theory of artistic production and an aesthetic of fiction. In his novels and his lectures for the newly founded Society of Authors, Besant attempted to salvage the "human interest," the "moral purpose," and above all the direct appeal to the readers' heart which high realism had offered and which seemed, with the arrival of naturalism, to be losing their central function on the literary scene. His philanthropic aesthetic, with its optimism about humanity and progress, was intended to work an ethical revival in its audience. Fidelity to nature (that is, to the readers' expectations in terms of intrigue, romance, excitement) occupied a central place in his aesthetic, as it still does in romance fiction. "That he should place the reader at the centre of his aesthetic is not surprising," John Goode writes,

> but it is significant that it is above all the reader's enthusiasm for humanity that he regards as his chief ally. He was lecturing at a time when the most intelligent members of the middle class were beginning to realise that in their own defence they would need to reaffirm in practice the highest virtues of their own class. The 1880s witnessed a renaissance of charitable activity and the birth of scientific sociological research in this country. They realised as well that mere relief was either ineffective or dangerous. The Charity Organisation Society and the Salvation Army were not merely helping out: they were fighting a war in the defence of middle-class values. Besant's theory of fiction was an attempt to engage the genre in this war partly as a recruiting officer and partly as a strategic adviser. (257)

His strategic advice was double-edged: an advocate of far-reaching measures of reform and working-class self-government, he had to couch his projects in an invigorating appeal for more not less middle-class patronage of the working class lest the dynamics of his own program should carry itself through to its logical conclusion and break through the safety boundaries of bourgeois hegemony. Hence the mystifying romantic, Utopian mode. Where forced to commit itself to a form of realism, the novel invites, as we have seen, an all too dangerous scrutiny of its internal, textual, and ideological contradictions.

The detailed analyses of class positions, transactions, and relations which had characterized realism from Austen to Eliot were at Besant's own tense political moment no longer possible if his fiction was to achieve its mythical closure. Instead, he had to draw upon romantic stereotypes of organically allied "rich" and "poor," and on the notion of a common humanity transcendent of class antagonisms, in order to bowdlerize the laborer/employer relationship out of the narrative and to make a reconciliation of irreconcilable interests possible in the cause of a common good.

The aristocratic swell, whose role had become marginal in mainstream fiction throughout the mid-century period, had therefore to reappear on the stage to play a philanthropic role which the bourgeois entrepreneur could not possibly reconcile so successfully with commercial interest. Capital itself has to be produced in a feminized guise—"cultured" and compassionate—if it is not to be written out of the scenario altogether, and a heroic notion of bourgeois woman as moral saviour and reconciler of classes is mobilized alongside the visionary and revolutionary urban aristocrat.

Besant's fiction was widely popular. Perhaps in a less sophisticated way it translated some of the wish-fulfilling ideological strategies of mid-century realism to an ever-increasing reading public. It had, however, to supersede realism in favor of a more romantic, and certainly a more strongly imaginary poetics (heavily dependent on an idealized humanist version of "aristocratic culture") if it were to succeed. Which it did, at least in its own terms: *All Sorts and Conditions of Men* established "a very popular formula for working-class romance" with a wide following in the 90s (Keating 123), accompanying the ongoing wave of missionary work in the East End.

Besant's philanthropic aesthetic was grafted on to a conception and practice of writing which welcomed the proper and definitive commercialization of literature that characterized the late Victorian era. "More than at any time since the invention of printing and the beginnings of the first commodified literary genre, the novel, printed matter in general was becoming just another 'novelty' to be devoured or consumed as fashions changed" (Bowlby 8). Although his work was deeply imbued with high moral ideals, Besant had neither illusions nor reservations about its place in the market of commercialized, commodified fiction. On his view, the progress of the publishing industry toward greater markets, faster cycles of production and consumption, and higher turnover were all part of that *démocratisation du luxe* through which the boons of Victorian industry—and the effects of an ideological revival—became accessible to an ever-increasing (but still predominantly middle-class) public.

Besant and the Society of Authors went to great lengths to dismiss the romantic aura that still clung to writing. Their new public image had to be one of "democratic," professional producers and purveyors of commodities neither superfluously luxurious nor intellectually inaccessible to the great mass of readers. Besant proudly attributed the popularity of fiction to the fact that it required of its audience "no culture, no education and no natural genius" and was thus able to plant the seeds of morality even in the least cultivated of hearts (Goode 249).

His fiction represents the starting point for a bourgeois-populistic tradition in the novel which, with ever-increasing popularity and ever-decreasing support from critical and intellectual establishments, has survived to our own day. Barbara Cartland would be a good example of how "moral purpose" in popular fiction has adapted itself in the twentieth century to the demands of the fiction industry (Brunt 125–57). What has been lost, however, is the will to change which is so notable in Besant's fiction. Despite its patronizing, recuperative movements, there is in *All Sorts and Conditions of Men* a genuine attempt, however confused and contradictory, to engage positively with the historical forces of democracy, and this within an open and accessible narrative mode with wide popular appeal. English studies, however, has chosen to consecrate an altogether different sort of literary discourse. Contemporaneously with Besant, the "literary" novel was producing a number of exercises far less interested in exploring viable modes of democratic writing and living.

## WORKS CITED

Arnold, Matthew. "Culture and Anarchy: An Essay in Political and Social Criticism." *The Complete Prose Works*, vol. 5. Edited by R.H. Super. Ann Arbor: U of Michigan P, 1972.

Besant, Walter. *All Sorts and Conditions of Men* (1882). London: Chatto and Windus, 1887.

———. "The People's Palace." *Contemporary Review* 51 (1887): 226–33.

Best, Geoffrey. *Mid-Victorian Britain, 1851–70*. London: Fontana, 1979.

Bowlby, Rachel. *Just Looking: Consumer Culture in Dreiser, Gissing and Zola*. New York, London: Methuen, 1985.

Brunt, Rosalind. "A Career in Love: The Romantic World of Barbara Cartland." *Popular Fiction and Social Change*. Edited by Christopher Pawling. London: Macmillan, 1984.

Cole, G.D.H. *Socialist Thought: Marxism and Anarchism 1850–1890*. London: Macmillan, 1957.

Dean, Michael P. "Henry James, Walter Besant and 'The Art of Fiction.'" *Publications of the Arkansas Philological Association* 10 (1984): 13–24.

Goode, John. "The Art of Fiction: Walter Besant and Henry James." *Tradition and Tolerance in Nineteenth-Century Fiction*. Edited by David Howard, John Lucas, and John Goode. London: Routledge and Kegan Paul, 1966.

Jones, Gareth Stedman. *Outcast London: A Study in the Relationship between Classes in Victorian Society*. Oxford: Clarendon Press, 1971.

Keating, P.J. *The Working-Classes in Victorian Fiction*. London: Routledge and Kegan Paul, 1971.

Lovell, Terry. *Consuming Fiction*. London: Verso, 1978.

Spilka, Mark. "Henry James and Walter Besant: 'The Art of Fiction' Controversy." *Novel* 6 (1973): 101–19.

Spivak, Gayatri Chakravorty. "The Rani of Sirmur." *Europe and Its Others: Proceedings of the Essex Conference on the Sociology of Literature*. July 1984, vol. 1. Edited by Francis Barker et al. Colchester: Essex U, 1985.

Thompson, E.P. *William Morris: Romantic to Revolutionary*. London: Merlin Press, 1977.

Widdowson, Peter, ed. *Re-Reading English*. London: Methuen, 1982.

## SELECTED SECONDARY SOURCES

The only book-length source on Besant's life and work remains the *Autobiography,* published posthumously in 1902. Frederick Boege's "Sir Walter Besant: Novelist" was published in two parts in *Nineteenth-Century Fiction* (10: March 1956, and 11: June 1956). Critical work tends to concentrate on the Walter Besant vs. Henry James controversy, and on Besant's significance for the history of publishing and the Society of Authors [Simon Eliot, "'His Generation Read His Stories': Walter Besant,

Chatto & Windus, and *All Sorts and Conditions of Men*," *Publishing History* 21 (1987), and "Unequal Partnerships: Besant, Rice, and Chatto 1876–82," *Publishing History* 26 (1989)]. A sympathetic but balanced entry by Clinton Machann in *The Dictionary of Literary Biography* appears in vol. 135.

# NATURALISM IN GEORGE MOORE'S
# *A MUMMER'S WIFE* (1885)

*Judith Mitchell*

Best known for his novel *Esther Waters,* Anglo-Irish writer George Moore (1852–1933) was a focal point for the various aesthetic cross-currents influencing the course of English art and literature at the end of the nineteenth century. Over the course of his long and prolific career, Moore's work was influenced by naturalism, symbolism, decadence, Impressionism, Russian literature, the Irish revival, and Wagnerian opera (to cite a partial list). He experimented with a variety of genres, including poetry, drama, fictional autobiography, and criticism, in addition to novels and short stories. Moore is a quintessentially "transitional" figure; at a time when the course of English fiction was undergoing a radical transformation, Moore's prose experiments anticipated Joyce and the stream-of-consciousness novel, for example. He is undervalued today partly because of the unevenness of his career, which included many failed experiments in addition to his strong realist novels, his hauntingly beautiful short stories, and his unique "melodic line." Several of Moore's works are in print, including affordable editions of *Esther Waters* (Dent/Everyman and Oxford) and *A Drama in Muslin* (Colin Smyth). Arizona State University's Hayden Library houses an extensive collection of original Moore documents assembled by Edwin Gilcher.

*I invented adultery, which didn't exist in the English novel till I began writing.*
—George Moore, qtd. in Hone 373

When *A Mummer's Wife* appeared in 1884 (official publication date 1885), any critical acclaim it received was largely in the form of backhanded compliments. The *Athenaeum* somewhat acidly remarked that "it is on the whole remarkably free from the element of uncleanness" ("*A Mummer's Wife*" 767); the *Saturday Review* commented that "in *A Mummer's Wife* [Moore] attempts to be as offensive as the master [Zola] himself.... But ... Mr.

Moore is only curious and disgusting" ("*A Mummer's Wife*" 214); and George Bernard Shaw, when told that Moore had written a wonderful new naturalistic novel, is reported to have said, "Nonsense! But I *know* George Moore. He couldn't possibly write a real book" (qtd. in Morgan 16).

Moore's second novel remains largely unnoticed and unappreciated. Most readers who are familiar with it will probably have heard of it in connection with the demise of the Victorian three-volume novel, a literary event of some importance in the late nineteenth century.[1] *A Mummer's Wife* was important for more than the part it played in this controversy, however. In his foreword to the 1966 Liveright edition of the novel, Walter Miller asserts that "just as 1492 connotes the opening of the New World, so 1885 signifies the beginning of modern English literature. One of the main reasons is that *A Mummer's Wife* was published in that year. With this experimental novel, George Moore introduced French naturalist techniques into English fiction, dealt a telling blow to Victorian aesthetics, got up momentum for other experiments that helped shape today's art, and secured for himself a permanent place among our leading novelists" (v). While these claims for the novel's importance may be slightly extravagant (it was *Esther Waters,* if any novel, which secured Moore his "place" among English novelists), other critics have agreed that in some sense *A Mummer's Wife* is the first, and possibly the only, naturalistic novel ever written in English.[2]

Certainly in 1884, despite his enthusiastic review of Huysmans's symbolist *A Rebours* in the same year, Moore was still an avowed disciple of Zola, to whom he had been introduced by Manet at a *L'Assommoir* ball (to which Moore went dressed as Coupeau) in 1879. His laudatory preface to the English edition of *Pot-Bouille* also appeared in the same year as *A Mummer's Wife,* and when he was writing his own novel, according to Hone, he wrote to Zola with high expectations: "If I succeed, as I expect, in digging a dagger into the heart of the sentimental school, I shall have hopes of bringing about a change in the literature of my country—of being in fact Zola's offshoot in England (*d'être enfin un ricocher de Zola en Angleterre*)" (qtd. in Hone 101). Moore did not quite succeed in these ambitious aims, or at least not immediately—not even the considerably modified "English" version of naturalism became popular in England until the 1890s—but he certainly helped to lay the groundwork for new freedom of expression in the English novel.

The question of influence is particularly instructive in regard to *A Mummer's Wife*. Nineteenth- as well as twentieth-century critics have tended to see it as a "French" rather than an "English" novel; Henry James said that it seemed to be "thought in French and inadequately translated" (qtd. in Moore, *Avowals* 185), and Stuart Sherman called it "a kind of English 'transposition' of *Madame Bovary*, flavored with a handful of something of Zola's" (134). Milton Chaikin (who reduces it to "very many bits culled from . . . Zola's novels") calls *A Mummer's Wife* "a book written according to a formula" (30), and Douglas Hughes likewise sees Moore "loosely following Zola's fictional formula" (xi) in his second novel. In fact, Moore's method in the composition of his theatrical novel bore a striking resemblance to Zola's hypothetical case in "Du roman":

> Suppose that one of our naturalistic novelists wishes to write a novel on theatrical life. He sets out with this general idea, without having as yet a single fact or a single character. His first care is to gather together in his notes all that he knows of this world which he wishes to depict. He has known such and such an actor, he has witnessed such and such a play. Here are data already, the best, for they have ripened within himself. Then he will set about the business, he will get the men who are the best informed on the subject talking, he will collect their expressions, their stories, and their portraits. That is not all; he then turns to written documents, reading up all that he thinks will be of the slightest service to him. Finally he visits the places, lives a few days in the theater. (211)

This account parallels almost exactly Moore's description in *A Communication to My Friends* of his research for *A Mummer's Wife*. After Vizetelly advised him to document an ugly town, "the uglier the better," for the setting of his next novel, Moore set out to gather information. He chose Hanley (later adopted by Arnold Bennett as the setting for his novels of the Five Towns), in addition to a theatrical milieu. Notebook in hand, in true Zolaesque fashion, Moore went touring with the second company of *Les Cloches de Corneville*, visiting Hanley as well as other factory towns.

The naturalism of *A Mummer's Wife*—undoubtedly one of its most interesting and significant qualities—will be the focus of my discussion in this essay. I shall argue that *A Mummer's Wife* is no mere French copy; that Moore modified the naturalistic formula in this novel in ways that are more subtle and complex than has generally been supposed; and that he wrote an amazingly strong novel in the process, a novel which even more than *A Drama in Muslin* and *Esther Waters* has been overlooked by literary historians. In fact, Moore's modifications of the naturalistic formula constituted improvements on it, resulting in a kind of enhanced realism. Walter Miller speaks of Moore "surpass[ing] the requirements of naturalism, without in any way violating them" (vii), and William Newton asserts that "it is quite possible to find in his novels up through *Esther Waters* almost every trait of naturalism, frequently in purer form than in the pages of the master [Zola] himself" (165). I shall attempt to show in what sense such assertions are true of *A Mummer's Wife,* and how in this supposed "copy" of French naturalistic novels Moore added something immensely vital to the English novel of the time.

The two novels generally acknowledged as the French sources for *A Mummer's Wife* provide a good starting point for my study. Douglas Hughes speaks confidently of "its obvious debt to Zola's *L'Assommoir* and Flaubert's *Madame Bovary*" (xii), and I shall deal with the latter influence first, as it is the more significant. In an article entitled "Flaubert, Miss Braddon, and George Moore," C. Heywood in 1960 argued that Mary Elizabeth Braddon's *The Doctor's Wife* (1864) was not only "the earliest borrowing from Flaubert in English literature" but also "a major source of *A Mummer's Wife*" (151). "Though Moore was . . . familiar with Flaubert's novel by this date," says Heywood, "several aspects of his own novel which have till now been taken as borrowings from Flaubert derive in fact from Miss Braddon" (157). This article is extremely interesting, not so much because of the accuracy of Heywood's claims, but because it points to a novel which is in fact what Sherman accused *A Mummer's Wife* of being: an English "transposition" of *Madame Bovary*. As such, *The Doctor's Wife* provides an excellent point of reference for a study of the naturalism of *A Mummer's Wife*: if Isabel Sleaford (Braddon's heroine) is an English Emma Bovary, what is Moore's Kate Ede? The distance between Flaubert's novel and Braddon's is a convenient gauge for measuring the extent to which *A Mummer's Wife* achieves a complex transference of the principles of one conception of the novel into the traditions of another.

To begin with, it is certain that Moore read *The Doctor's Wife,* to which he refers in *Avowals* as "a derivative *Madame Bovary*" (128). In addition, as Heywood points out, Kate's favorite novel, the "one story that . . . caused her deeper emotions than perhaps even the others had done,"[3] bears a much closer resemblance to *The Doctor's Wife* than to Flaubert's novel:

> It concerned a beautiful young woman with a lovely oval face, who was married to a very tiresome country doctor. This lady was in the habit of reading Byron and Shelley in a rich, sweet-scented meadow, down by the river which flowed dreamily through smiling pasturelands adorned by spreading trees. But this meadow belonged to a young squire, a superb man with grand, broad shoulders, who day

after day used to watch these readings by the river, without, however, venturing to address a word to the fair trespasser. One day, however, he was startled by a shriek; in her poetical dreamings the lady had slipped into the water. A moment sufficed to tear off his coat, and as he swam like a water-dog, he had no difficulty in rescuing her. After this adventure he had, of course, to call and inquire, and from henceforth his visits grew more and more frequent, and by a strange coincidence, he used generally to come riding up to the hall-door when the husband was away curing the ills of the country folk. Hours never to be forgotten were passed under the trees by the river, he pleading his cause, and she refusing to leave poor Arthur—he was too good a fellow. Heart-broken, at last the squire gave up the pursuit, and went to foreign parts, where he waited thirty years until he heard Arthur was dead. Then he came back with a light heart to his first and only love, who had never ceased to think of him, and lived with her happily forever afterwards. (38–39)

This—more or less—outlines the plot of *The Doctor's Wife,* with the exception of Moore's fanciful additions of the heroine's fall into the water and the happily-ever-after ending.

The plot of the real *Doctor's Wife,* however, is just as melodramatic as Moore's version. It begins, like *Madame Bovary,* with a rather foolish young heroine who satisfies her vague romantic yearnings by reading novels. Like Emma, Isabel Sleaford marries a kind but dull young country doctor, with whom she is increasingly bored and dissatisfied. Also like Emma, Isabel is attracted to someone outside the marriage (the young neighboring squire returned from abroad, Roland Lansdell)—but there the similarity ends. As soon as Roland proposes to Isabel that they run away together, the novel turns into a conventional and predictable Victorian melodrama: Isabel renounces him and resolves to be "good"; he pines miserably for her; her blackguard father haunts the neighborhood asking for money and threatening to kill Roland, who once testified against him; Isabel's husband catches a fever from his country patients, Roland is fatally assaulted (by Isabel's father), and both men die nobly within a few days of each other; and Isabel is left in the end sadder but wiser, doing good works for the poor with Roland's fortune, which he bequeaths to her on his deathbed.

From Flaubert's initial situation, then, Mary Elizabeth Braddon deviates widely, in ways that are characteristically Victorian. Her heroine is "not a wicked woman; she was only very foolish" (2: 226). More specifically, Isabel's romantic inclinations lead her away from, rather than toward, a sexual liaison; the biggest disappointment in her life is the shattering of her ideals when Roland asks her to elope. She says,

> I never thought that you would ask me to be more to you than I am now: I never thought that it was wicked to come here and meet you. I have read of people, who by some fatality could never marry, loving each other, and being true to others for years and years—till death, sometimes; and I fancied that you loved me like that; and the thought of your love made me so happy; and it was such happiness to see you sometimes, and to think of you afterwards, remembering every word you had said, and seeing your face as plainly as I see it now. I thought, till yesterday, that this might go on for ever, and never, never believed that you would think me like those wicked women who run away from their husbands. (2: 98)

After this bitter lesson, "Isabel Gilbert was a woman all at once" (2: 104) and develops in maturity and understanding from this point until the end of the novel.

In essence, *The Doctor's Wife* is a tract against the evils of excessive romanticism. The narrator, omniscient and very much in evidence, points out that Isabel in reading so many novels lived "as much alone as if she had resided in a balloon, for ever suspended in mid air, and never coming down in serious earnest to the common joys and sorrows of the vulgar life about her" (1: 38). Such personal moral lessons, of course, derived from the experience of the main character and enunciated by an omniscient narrator, were a salient characteristic of the Victorian novel.

In addition, Braddon's narrator in *The Doctor's Wife* has a wide moral sympathy for her characters. Isabel's conduct is excused because "she only wanted the vague poetry of life, the mystic beauty of romance infused somehow into her existence; and she was as yet too young to understand that latent element of poetry which underlies the commonest life" (2: 227). Even Roland, who initially appears to be a villain, is categorized by the narrator as "a benevolently-disposed young man, desirous of doing as little mischief in the world as might be compatible with his being tolerably happy himself; and fully believing that no great or irreparable harm need result from his appropriation of another man's wife" (2: 105).

Finally, *The Doctor's Wife* displays none of the pessimism of *Madame Bovary*. Indeed, part of the novel's point about novel-reading is made through the narrator "poking fun" at Isabel in an exceedingly good-humored way. Early in the novel we are told:

She wanted her life to be like her books; she wanted to be a hero-ine,—unhappy perhaps, and dying early. She had an especial desire to die early, by consumption, with a hectic flush and unnatural lustre in her eyes. She fancied every time she had a little cough that the consumption was coming, and she began to pose herself, and was gently melancholy to her half-brothers, and told them one by one, in confidence, that she did not think she should be with them long. They were slow to understand the drift of her remarks, and would ask her if she was going out as a governess; and, if she took the trouble to explain her dismal meaning, were apt to destroy the sentiment of the situation by saying, "Oh, come now, Hookee Walker. . . . Who eat a plum-dumpling yesterday for dinner, and asked for more? That's the only sort of consumption *you've* got, Izzie; two helps of pudding at dinner, and no end of bread-and-butter for breakfast." (1: 36–37)

This sounds more like Dickens than Flaubert, and it is obvious that *The Doctor's Wife* has undergone so many Victorian transformations that it bears very little resemblance at all to its French predecessor.

It is germane to the purposes of my inquiry that the novel Braddon chose to "Anglicize" in this way was the novel in which the very roots of naturalism had their being. In Flaubert's letters may be found all of the key principles of naturalism—the impersonality of the author, the adoption of the methods of the natural sciences, the absence of "morality," the depiction of unexceptional characters—and in *Madame Bovary* we have the prototype for two other novels which are acknowledged to be the first naturalistic novels: the Goncourts' *Germinie Lacerteux* (1865) and Zola's *Thérèse Raquin* (1867). Matthew Josephson remarked of *Germinie,* "The whole thesis of Bovary was here, dominant, as it was forever afterward in the realistic masterpieces: *a given personality, conceived as a unit in a mass, pitted against its environment, the milieu into which it is born*" (92). Zola reviewed this "clinique de l'Amour" (preface, *Germinie*) with enthusiasm, pointing out in particular its air of scientific experiment and its freedom from moral constraints in expressing "reality" so frankly. Zola was undoubtedly influenced by both *Madame Bovary* and *Germinie Lacerteux*; as Erich Auerbach points out, he "is twenty years younger than the generation of Flaubert and the Goncourts. There are connections between him and them; he stands on their shoulders" (447). Zola's own *Thérèse Raquin* is also a "clinic of Love" and the official beginning of naturalism. These three novels—*Madame Bovary, Germinie Lacerteux,* and *Thérèse Raquin*—comprise a matrix of naturalist characteristics at the opposite end of the scale from *The Doctor's*

*Wife,* and it is against this scale that I shall set Moore's *A Mummer's Wife.*

The portrayal of sexuality, which marks the widest division between *The Doctor's Wife* and its French counterparts (and, indeed, between the naturalist and Victorian conceptions of the novel), constituted one of the main reasons for the banning of *A Mummer's Wife* by Smith's and Mudie's. Of Moore's boast that he had "invented adultery" in the English novel, Granville Hicks remarked, "He was not . . . far wrong. Gissing's women . . . are incapable of passion. Moore, whether or not he has the profound insight into feminine psychology of which he boasted, at least was courageous enough to record certain elementary observations. There is not only adultery in *A Modern Lover;* there is sufficient passion to make the adultery plausible" (205). I would like to qualify Hicks's (and Moore's) views slightly by adding that although Moore may have in some sense "invented adultery," it was only in the Victorian novel (the English novel in the eighteenth century contained plenty of adultery), and that this "invention" occurred in *A Mummer's Wife* rather than in *A Modern Lover* (1883). There is passion in the latter novel, as Hicks suggests, but *only* on the part of the women, the minor characters; Lewis Seymour, the hero, remains cheerfully self-indulgent rather than passionate.

Kate Ede, the Hanley dressmaker who is the heroine of *A Mummer's Wife,* is at the beginning of Moore's novel in precisely the same situation as Isabel Sleaford, Emma Bovary, and Thérèse Raquin. She is married to an unattractive husband, the asthmatic Ralph, and dominated by her religious mother-in-law. She is romantically inclined, and becomes attracted to her boarder Dick Lennox, the manager of Morton and Cox's Theatrical Company. At this point, however, the turn of events in *A Mummer's Wife* differs widely—and significantly—from that in Braddon's novel as well as from those in the French naturalistic novels.

Isabel, as I have pointed out, renounces her "lover," having learned her lesson. It is noteworthy (and slightly implausible) that there is no physical sexuality at all in *The Doctor's Wife.* Although Isabel is excessively romantic, and deeply in love with Roland, her fantasies all have to do with goodness, in the form of heroic renunciations, noble deaths, and unrequited love. In fact, she is a "pure" Victorian heroine who, when confronted with the option of leaving her husband for her lover, is properly aghast ("Not for one moment did the Doctor's Wife contemplate the possibility of taking the step which Roland Lansdell had proposed to her. . . . The possibility of deliberately leaving her husband to follow the footsteps of this other man, was as far beyond her power of comprehension as the possibility that she might steal a handful of arsenic out of one of the earthenware jars in the surgery and mix it with the sugar that sweetened George Gilbert's matutinal coffee" 2: 102–3). This, complete with the allusion to the handful of arsenic, is obviously what Braddon feels to be a necessary corrective to *Madame Bovary*. In any case, there is no question of adultery in *The Doctor's Wife;* Isabel is simply too pure to sully her hands or even her mind with such an activity.

All three French novels, on the other hand, contain an abundance of adultery. Emma takes two lovers, first Rodolphe and then Léon, and Thérèse takes Laurent. What is noteworthy is that in all three heroines sex is a passion amounting to an illness or obsession, an animal need unadorned by "love" except in an inflamed, unhealthy sense. All three degrade themselves sexually: Germinie has a secret life of excesses with strangers, Thérèse is talked into murdering her husband, and Emma, as Henry James pointed out, "remains absorbed in romantic intention and vision while fairly rolling in the dust" (347).

Between these extremes of the complete absence of sexual desire and sexual desire bordering on mania, is Moore's Kate Ede. Her romanticism, evident from the very first scene of the novel in which she sees Ralph's suffering as "noble," is described in the following way:

> She accepted Ralph as unsuspectingly as she had before accepted the tawdry poetry of her favourite fiction. Her nature not being a passionate one, she was able to do this without an apparent transition of sentiment. . . . She accepted her husband's kisses as she did the toil he imposed on her—meekly, unaffectedly, as a matter of course. Apparently she had known all through that the romances which used so strongly to fascinate her were merely idle dreams, having no bearing upon the daily life of human beings—things fit to amuse a young girl's fancies, and to be thrown aside when the real cares of life were entered upon. (40)

Kate's nature is "not a passionate one," unlike either Isabel's or Emma's; Moore avoids both the extreme idealism of the former and the extreme sensualism of the latter. Also, Kate does not have either Isabel's condescension or Emma's active dislike for her husband. In fact, we are told, "Had he been a little kinder he would have satisfied her. Her dreams did not fly high, and now as she sat by him, holding his clammy hand, she thought she would have felt happy were she sure of even so much affection. A little love would have made her life so much pleasanter. It did not matter who gave it; she sighed for a little, ever so little" (20).

As Richard Cave remarks, "Unlike Emma Bovary, Kate seeks no By-

ronic tempests of the emotions but only tenderness, comfort and security"
(41). It is mainly Dick's kindness and humanity, for instance, which draw
Kate to him: "The man was coarse, large, sensual, even as is a mutton chop.
But each movement of his fat hands was protective, every word he uttered
was kind, the very intonation of his voice was comforting. He was, in a word,
human, and this attracted all that was human in you. The intelligence
counted for nothing; his charm lay in his humanity" (67). This is not to say
that there is no sexual attraction between Kate and Dick, however. When
she takes his breakfast to him, we are told that "Kate could not choose but
like him, and it made her wish all the more that he would cover up his big,
bare neck. . . . There was something very human in this big man, and Kate
did not know whether his animalism irritated or pleased her" (42–43). Dick's
"big, bare neck" and his healthy "animalism" are obviously attractive to
Kate, especially in contrast with Ralph, who, even when he is well, is seen
"picking . . . a bad tooth with a hairpin taken from the drawers" (80).

The love-episode between Kate and Dick that was objected to most
strongly by the libraries seems relatively innocuous by modern standards.
Kate has gone downstairs to open the door for Dick, who is still her boarder
at this point. After a short conversation, the following occurs:

> They could not see each other. After a long silence she said, "We must
> not stop talking here. Mrs. Ede sleeps, you know, in the room at the
> back of the work-room, and she might hear us."

> "Then come into the sitting-room," said Dick, taking her hands
> and drawing her towards him.

> "Oh, I cannot!"

> "I love you better than anyone in the world."

> "No, no; why should you love me?"

> Although she could not see his face, she felt his breath on her
> neck. Strong arms were wound about her, she was carried forward,
> and the door was shut behind her.

> Only the faintest gleam of starlight touched the wall next to the
> window; the darkness slept profoundly on the landing and staircase;
> and when the silence was again broken, a voice was heard saying,

"Oh, you shouldn't have done this! What shall I tell my husband if he asks me where I've been?"

"Say you have been talking to me about my bill, dear. I'll see you in the morning." (qtd in Moore, *Literature at Nurse* 6–7; final three paragraphs omitted from the 1893 text)

This is definitely adultery; however muted and suppressed, there is no doubt that a sexual encounter between a married woman and a man who is not her husband is going on behind the closed door. However tame and conventional it may seem in comparison to the lingering image of the coach crazily whirling with the insatiable Emma and Léon inside, the fact remains that the Doctor's Wife would never have considered any such thing, even for a moment.

Kate and Dick have passion, then, but not in excess. Without this scene their lovemaking consists of a couple of stolen kisses and the following curious description, which occurs just after they have eloped:

The morning hours were especially delightful. Immediately on getting out of bed she went into the sitting-room to see after Dick's breakfast. It was laid out on a round table, the one white tint in the rose twilight of the half-drawn blinds. Masses of Virginia creeper, now weary of the summer and ready to fall with the first October winds, grew into the room, and the two armchairs drawn up by the quietly burning fire seemed, like all the rest, to inspire indolence. Kate lingered settling and dusting little rickety ornaments, tempted at once by the freshness of her dressing-gown and the soothing warmth of the room. It penetrated her with sensations of happiness too acute to be durable, and as they mounted to her head in a sort of effervescent reverie, she would walk forwards to the folding doors to talk to Dick of—it did not matter what—it was for the mere sound of his voice that she came; and, in default of anything better to say, she would upbraid him for his laziness. The room, full of the intimacy of their life, enchanted her, and half in shame, half in delight, she would affect to arrange the pillows while he buttoned his collar. When this was accomplished she led him triumphantly to the breakfast table, and with one arm resting on his knees, watched the white shapes of the eggs seen through the bubbling water. (158)

The thing that is curious about this scene is that its atmosphere is domestic rather than erotic. The quietly burning fire, the freshness of Kate's dressing gown, the sweet delight of the lovers, the homeliness of the boiling eggs, all create the ambience of a typical "young newlyweds" scene in a Victorian novel. In fact, even though Kate and Dick have only recently run away together, they seem married. This is an important point for two reasons. First of all, the narrator through such scenes appears to condone the elopement, a highly unusual attitude in the Victorian novel at this time. Most of the "New Woman" novels which sanctioned love outside marriage were not written until the eighteen-nineties, and *Jude the Obscure* was not published until ten years after the publication of *A Mummer's Wife*. In this respect, at least, Moore succeeded in "digging a dagger into the heart of the sentimental school," and it is in this tacit approval (or lack of disapproval) of Kate's elopement that he can really be said, I think, to have "invented adultery" in the English novel of the time.

The other reason that Kate's and Dick's instant domesticity is interesting is that, given the conventions of the Victorian novel, this was the only way in which Moore *could* indicate the narrator's approval of their liaison. Any other approach (such as the frank portrayal of their sexual enjoyment of each other) would have been regarded as outright pornography. Ian Watt's observation about the nature of courtly love in French and English fiction is pertinent in this regard:

> Gradually, however, the code of romantic love began to accommodate itself to religious, social, and psychological reality, notably to marriage and the family. This process seems to have occurred particularly early in England, and the new ideology which eventually came into being there does much to explain . . . the distinctive difference between the English and French traditions in fiction. Denis de Rougemont . . . writes of the French novel that "to judge by its literature, adultery would seem to be one of the most characteristic occupations of Western man." Not so in England, where the break with the originally adulterous character of courtly love was so complete that George Moore was almost justified in claiming to have "invented adultery, which didn't exist in the English novel till I began writing." (154)

Moore was "almost" justified indeed; the fact that Kate and Dick are actually married shortly after she is divorced further ensures that the amount of "adultery" in the novel is kept to a minimum.

In playing down Kate's passion and yet allowing her to run away with her lover, Moore creates a scenario that is considerably less sensational, we may note, than either Braddon's or Flaubert's. Kate herself is similarly pedestrian, as I have pointed out. Flaubert himself called Emma a "naturally corrupt woman" (qtd. in Becker 94), and Isabel is a sort of purified Emma—purified, however, beyond the point of credibility. Kate is neither excessively good nor excessively bad, but merely weak, as the narrator tells us:

> She was not strong nor great, nor was she conscious of any deep feeling that if she acted otherwise than she did she would be living an unworthy life. She was merely good because she was a kindhearted woman, without bad impulses, and admirably suited to the life she was leading. (38)

And, just as Kate's nature does not run to extremes, neither do the characters of the men she is involved with. Isabel's husband and lover are both finally portrayed as heroes, as I have noted, while the male characters in the French novels are an extraordinary group: Emma's husband is a clown, Thérèse's is a sickly, despicable weakling, and Germinie's fiancé will not even marry her; and the lovers of all three women are brutal cads. "Extraordinary" is not a word that could be applied either to Kate's husband or to her lover. Ralph is harmless, if he is not entirely likable, and Dick is kind and jolly but certainly neither a hero nor a villain. Their ordinariness, in fact, makes Moore's characters seem closer to everyday reality than either the French or the English versions, and in this instance Moore's "slice of life" seems more authentic than that served up by Zola himself.

Apart from its alleged sexual explicitness, the other reason *A Mummer's Wife* was banned by the libraries was because of its "foulness": "It is, we know," said the critic for the *Saturday Review,* "a foolish thing to wash one's foul linen in public. How much more foolish it is to spread out and sort one's foul linen in public, not to wash it, but merely to demonstrate how foul it is" ("*A Mummer's Wife*" 214). The details surrounding Kate's alcoholism, in particular, are highly unpleasant. Moore's source for this part of the novel (the final third) is said to be Zola's *L'Assommoir,* but I think that the drunkenness in that novel is rather more incidental than in *A Mummer's Wife.* Gervaise and Coupeau are victims primarily of indolence, ignorance, and poverty, whereas Kate is a true alcoholic, obsessed, finally, with her need for drink. As Lilian Furst points out, "Both [Kate and Gervaise] indeed die of alcoholism—but surely such thematic parallelism cannot be accepted as proof of influence" (140). (The same point, I would argue, could be made in relation to the influence of *Nana* on the theatrical milieu in *A Mummer's Wife.*)

After Kate runs away with Dick, she becomes a successful actress and a happily married woman. "As the days passed," we are told,

> Kate grew happier, until she began to think she must be the happiest woman living. Her life had now an occupation, and no hour that went pressed upon her heavier than would a butterfly's wing. The mornings had always been delightful; Dick was with her then, and the afternoons had been taken up with her musical studies. It was the long evenings she used to dread; now they had become part and parcel of her daily pleasures. They dined about four, and when dinner was over it was time to talk about what kind of house they were going to have, to fidget about in search of brushes and combs, the curling-tongs, and to consider what little necessaries she had better bring down to the theatre with her. (182)

At this point, no further comparison with either *The Doctor's Wife* or the naturalist "cliniques de l'Amour" seems possible. A simple plot reversal has seemingly occurred: the adultery between the ordinary seamstress and the jolly mummer, never very tempestuous to start with, settles into a comfortable enough routine. Neither the melodramatic renunciations of *The Doctor's Wife* nor the ruined lives of the three French novels have come to pass as a result of their relationship, and the remainder of the novel is devoted to the progress of Kate's alcoholism. Lloyd Fernando finds this development disconcerting, and Moore's novel disunified as a result:

> A claim on behalf of Moore's originality does not . . . overcome successfully this use of a second major source for a single novel. Moore presents Kate's alcoholism with entire conviction, yet the book does not recover from the resulting shift of emphasis. The woman who has fled to freedom degenerates not really on account of her moral incapacity, but on account of a factor introduced mostly as an "experiment" in the Zola manner, and given patently separate thematic treatment late in the novel. (92)

I would disagree. Kate does degenerate "on account of her moral incapacity," in some sense, at least, and I think that Moore's "'experiment' in the Zola manner" in the final third of the novel is a convincing and natural outcome of the situation he establishes in the first two-thirds. In an article on Moore in 1933 Osbert Burdett claimed that "the cause of Kate's drinking is too vague" (419), but it is difficult to see how this is so. Quite simply, she begins to drink because she is ashamed of being a "loose woman" sexually ("loose," that is, according to the tenets of the religion in which she was raised), and she continues to drink because she becomes unreasonably jealous of Dick. Just as much as *Madame Bovary, Germinie Lacerteux,* or *Thérèse Raquin, A Mummer's Wife* is a clinical study of love; but instead of the main character being destroyed directly as a result of her sexual desires, she is destroyed indirectly (but just as effectively) by them as they are replaced, distorted, and transformed into a desire for alcohol. Although Kate does not have Isabel's passion for purity, neither does she have the amoral, animalistic attitude toward sex which characterizes Emma, Germinie, and Thérèse (as well as Nana and Gervaise). Once again, this enhances the realism of Moore's tale; as Peter Ure points out, in choosing sexual mores as Kate's stumbling block, Moore "showed some insight into the pathology of conscience" (93). He also showed some insight into middle-class Victorian moral priorities, it might be added; it is unlikely that a woman of Kate's class in her position would be able to accept her own adultery without qualms. She does not "roll in the dust" like Emma, have a secret shameful life like Germinie, or commit murder like Thérèse, but she feels guilty all the same, and unable to accept her success with equanimity.[4] Kate's use of religion as a vehicle for her romanticism is likewise psychologically astute. This phenomenon, which Moore expands upon in the character of Cecilia in *A Drama in Muslin,* also occurs in *Germinie Lacerteux* ("Dans le prêtre qui l'écoute et dont la voix lui arrive doucement, la femme de travail et de peine voit moins le ministre de Dieu . . . que le confident de ses chagrins et l'ami de ses misères," 44) and in *The Doctor's Wife* ("[Isabel] wanted to find some shrine, some divinity, who would accept her worship. . . . If not Roland Lansdell, why then Christianity," 118–19).

Moore's experiment in *A Mummer's Wife* is thus at least as subtle and complex, both psychologically and artistically, as similar experiments by the naturalists. Interestingly, this third phase of Kate's existence, which springs so convincingly from the first two, constitutes the most typically naturalistic part of the novel in its graphic depiction of sordid physical realities. Kate's drinking progresses inexorably, and the details of it become more and more distasteful until finally she becomes one of the few characters to vomit in English fiction. This scene, presented from Kate's point of view, is rendered literally, unrelieved by the figurative language that occasionally softens the impact of her episodes of drunkennesss up to this point:

Weak and sick she leaned back upon the hard cushions of the clattering cab. Her mouth was full of water, and the shifting angles of the streets produced on her an effect similar to sea-sickness. London rang in her ears; she could hear a piano tinkling; she saw Dick directing the movements of a line of girls. Then her dream was brought to an end by a gulp. Oh! the fearful nausea; and she did not feel better until, flooding her dress and ruining the red velvet seats, all she had drunk came up. The vomit, however, brought her great relief, and had it not been for a little dizziness and weakness, she would have felt quite right when she arrived at the stage-door. She was in a terrible state of dirt and untidiness, but she noticed nothing; her mind was now fully occupied in thinking what she should say, first to the stage-doorkeeper, and then to her husband. (300)

Joseph Hone, who sees A Mummer's Wife as a successful application of the naturalistic method to the English novel, remarks of this scene that "Moore was the first adventurer on this ground; for the other English writers who sought assistance from the methods of the Naturalists shrank from carrying them out to their logical conclusion. Gissing would never have written of Kate Ede vomiting over her dress. . . . Courage was needed for this in the high Victorian period" (106–7). Gissing's own novel dealing with middle-class female alcoholism, The Odd Women (1893), confirms the accuracy of Hone's observation. In it, Gissing surrounds the subject with an air of mysterious discretion, treating it as something too shameful to mention. The Madden sisters speak of Virginia's "wretched state," for example, in the following way: "How can we help her, Monica? Won't you make a sacrifice for the poor girl's sake? . . . She worries so about you, and then tries to forget the trouble—you know how" (1: 246).

Toward the end of A Mummer's Wife, Kate sinks to the lowest depths of alcoholism, and Moore does not spare us in recounting her progressively worsening condition. The latter is no longer described from Kate's point of view; she has become an object, to be described from the outside. Predictably, Kate's final illness and death, with which the novel ends, is depicted as graphically as the deaths of either Emma Bovary or Nana, for example. The description of Ralph's illness with which the novel opens is mild by comparison:

Facing the light, close up against the wall, her stomach enormously distended by dropsy, Kate lay delirious. From time to time her arms, wasted now to mere bones, were waved. . . . She was now a dreadful thing to look upon. Her thin hair hung like a wisp, and she had lost so much that the prominent temples were large with a partial baldness. The rich olive complexion was now changed to a dirty yellow, around the nose and mouth the skin was pinched and puckered. . . . Her eyes were dilated, and she tried to raise herself up in bed. Her withered arms were waved to and fro, and in the red gloom shed from the ill-smelling paraffin lamp the large, dimly-seen folds of the bed-clothes were tossed to and fro by the convulsions that agitated the whole body. Another hour passed away, marked, not by the mechanical ticking of a clock, but by the cavernous breathing of the woman as she crept to the edge of death. At last there came a sigh, deeper and more prolonged, and with it she died. (350–52)

Kate is now indeed "a dreadful thing to look upon." The atmosphere that surrounds her death, however, is subtly different from that which surrounds the deaths of Emma or Nana. Emma's death seems to be a fitting punishment for her foolishness, the culmination of Flaubert's disgust for her, and Nana's corpse becomes a fitting symbol of the corruption of a whole society. In either case, there is an implied judgment by the narrator, a statement about a certain kind of mentality in one case and about a certain way of life in the other. This sense of a pitiless, almost vindictive indifference on the part of the narrator increases the horror of the sordid physical details in each of these episodes. Kate's death scene, while unpleasant, evokes no similar sense of horror or judgment but merely one of pitiable sadness.

The mood of melancholy rather than revulsion which attends this final scene of *A Mummer's Wife* is partly a result of attitudes which have been established or events which have occurred earlier in the novel. For one thing, Moore is able to report his character's death more neutrally than either Flaubert or Zola simply because Kate is a less corrupt and more likable individual than either Emma or Nana. Furthermore, Kate's story has not been one of unrelieved brutality from the beginning, so that her death is invested with a certain amount of pathos, unlike the deaths of Germinie, Gervaise or Thérèse, for example. Germinie and Gervaise have lived like dogs and they die like dogs, a fact which surprises no one, while Thérèse and Laurent's mutual suicide-murder is the logical climax to the grisly tale of their love. Moore's narrator makes no comment about Kate's death, nor does he need to; he merely reports it, and yet his report avoids both the implied contempt and the extreme coldness of the naturalists. It is a nice (and fairly complex) tempering of the naturalistic formula of objectivity to suit the framework of English fiction.

In his second novel, then, Moore followed fairly closely Zola's formula for the creation of a naturalistic novel. He carefully researched and reported the milieux of his novel,[5] including the unpleasant physical details, he adopted a straightforward attitude toward sex, he did not individualize his characters too much, and he recorded, as objectively as he could, the effects of a certain kind of environment on a certain kind of inherited temperament. Although some early reviewers saw the novel as a warning against the evils of alcohol, there is no obvious "moral" to the tale; as Sonja Nejdefors-Frisk remarks, "Kate's behaviour is neither praised nor blamed by the author, and there are no moral conclusions" (83). In his objectivity, in fact, Moore in some respects even outdoes Zola in this book. The straight-laced middle-class world of Hanley and the carefree bohemian world of the mummers are both seen to have desirable and undesirable qualities; neither one is right or wrong; they are simply different. Moore had every reason to be disappointed when Zola refused to write the preface for the French edition of *A Mummer's Wife*.[6]

For all of that, the novel is an individual creation, and not merely a French "copy." Kate Ede is a type rather than an individual; but she is an English type,[7] and *A Mummer's Wife* is a unique creation, an English novel written to French naturalistic specifications. Moore never wrote anything else like *A Mummer's Wife*—his enthusiasm for Zola was speedily supplanted by a host of other influences—but it marked the beginning of a very important strain of realism that runs through all his best work. In the last analysis, naturalism itself was not important for Moore, as he believed that "the great literary battle of our day is not to be fought for either realism or romanticism, but for freedom of speech" (Moore, Preface to *Pot-Bouille*, qtd. in Noël 117); but if the first infusion of naturalism into the English novel could be pinpointed, it could be said to occur here. This is by no means an insignificant event in the history and development of English fiction, and to specialists in transitional literature, *A Mummer's Wife* presents a fascinating study. And, even apart from its historical importance, as I have endeavored to show, *A Mummer's Wife* is on its own merits worthy of critical attention.

## Notes

1. Moore's part in the debate over the censorship of the lending libraries is outlined by W. C. Frierson, Clarence Decker, and Joseph Hone, among others. Briefly, after Smith's and Mudie's banned *A Modern Lover*, Moore persuaded Henry Vizetelly to publish *A Mummer's Wife* in a cheap one-volume edition and to make it available to the public at an affordable price (ten shillings). Other novelists and publishers followed suit, breaking Smith's and Mudie's monopoly.

2. Milton Chaikin refers to *A Mummer's Wife* as "the first naturalistic novel in English fiction," and also as "the first and last naturalistic novel [Moore] wrote" (31, 39); Enid Starkie calls it "the first completely Naturalistic novel in English" (66);

and Walter Allen calls Moore "the only English Naturalist in the French sense" (298).

3. Moore, *A Mummer's Wife*, 38. Citations in the text refer to the 1893 Walter Scott edition, which is a reprint of the 1886 Vizetelly edition (Moore's first revision of the novel). This early version of the novel is the most appropriate for my purposes in this paper because it demonstrates most clearly Moore's connections to both French and English novelistic traditions. Later revised versions of Moore's early novels tend to be more streamlined and "modern" in keeping with the discovery of his "melodic line."

4. Various elements in Kate's downfall are stressed in various versions of the novel. The earlier versions, in true naturalistic fashion, stress the inevitability of the outcome of a certain combination of environment and heredity, as in the narrator's often-quoted analogy between women like Kate and "cheap Tottenham Court Road furniture, equal to an ordinary amount of wear and tear so long as the original atmosphere in which they were glued together is preserved" (311). When Moore revised the novel in 1917, however, he removed virtually all such narratorial commentary, resulting in a much less overtly deterministic novel, a view supported by his own remark in *Salve* (1912): "The Mummer's Wife declines, for she is without sufficient personal conscience to detach herself from the conventions in which she has been brought up" (275). See Richard Cave's discussion of this point, 43 ff.

5. Moore's careful documentation and description of the physical milieux of *A Mummer's Wife*, the factory town and the theater, is an obviously naturalistic feature of the novel. But once again, the naturalistic approach is softened—by touches of humor, by the occasional use of figurative language, by impressionistic "scene-painting," and by the limited inclusion of the characters' points of view—creating a sort of hybrid effect that is at once less pessimistic than that of naturalism and less idealistic than that of English realism (and thereby more thoroughly "neutral" than either). For a discussion of this point, see my "Fictional Worlds."

6. Zola (understandably) refused to write the preface for the novel because of the unkind remarks Moore had made about him in *Confessions of a Young Man* (1888). With characteristic tactlessness, for instance, Moore had described Zola as having "no style" and "seek[ing] immortality in the exact description of a linendraper's shop" (110). For a concise account of Moore's somewhat uneasy relationship with Zola and naturalism, see Susan Dick 241–43, for example.

7. Kate is an interesting creation. She does not display the "complete absence of soul" advocated by Zola in the preface to *Thérèse Raquin*, nor does Moore's narrator maintain Zola's air of unrelieved clinical detachment toward his heroine; yet she never quite becomes an English "character" with whom the reader can identify and sympathize. This effect is achieved through Moore's technique in presenting Kate's consciousness: we are given access to her thoughts and feelings, but these are conveniently obscured by her vagueness and dreaminess, ensuring an objective distancing of both the narrator and the reader from Kate, and of Kate from herself. She thus remains firmly within the typological category of the sentimental middle-class woman, whose story (like that of the naturalists' main characters) partakes of neither tragedy nor character development. (It is likely that Moore "borrowed" this technique from Zola; in his introduction to *Thérèse Raquin*, L.W. Tancock complains of Zola's "astonishing vagueness," 17.) For a fuller discussion of Moore's presentation of Kate's character, see my article "George Moore's Kate Ede."

WORKS CITED

Allen, Walter. *The English Novel*. London: Phoenix, 1954.

"A Mummer's Wife." *Athenaeum* 84 (13 December, 1883): 767.

"A Mummer's Wife." *Saturday Review* 61 (14 February, 1885): 214.

Auerbach, Erich. *Mimesis*. Translated by Willard Trask. Garden City, N.Y.: Doubleday, 1957.

Becker, George J. *Documents of Modern Literary Realism*. Princeton: Princeton UP, 1963.

Braddon, Mary Elizabeth. *The Doctor's Wife*. 3 vols. Leipzig: Bernhard Tauchnitz, 1864.

Burdett, Osbert. "George Moore." *London Mercury* 27 (March 1933): 415–26.

Cave, Richard. *A Study of the Novels of George Moore*. Gerrards Cross: Colin Smythe, 1978.

Chaikin, Milton. "George Moore's Early Fiction." *George Moore's Mind and Art*. Edited by Graham Owens. New York: Barnes and Noble, 1970. 21–44.

Decker, Clarence. *The Victorian Conscience*. New York: Twayne Publishers, 1952.

Dick, Susan, ed. George Moore, *Confessions of a Young Man*. Montreal: McGill-Queen's UP, 1972.

Fernando, Lloyd. *"New Women" in the Late Victorian Novel*. University Park: Pennsylvania State UP, 1977.

Flaubert, Gustave. *Oeuvres Completes*. 28 vols. Paris: Louis Conard, 1926–1933.

Frierson, W.C. *The English Novel in Transition 1885–1940*. Norman: U of Oklahoma P, 1942.

Furst, Lilian R. "George Moore, Zola, and the Question of Influence." *Canadian Review of Comparative Literature* 1 (1974): 138–55.

Gissing, George. *The Odd Women*. 3 vols. London: Lawrence and Bullen, 1893.

Goncourt, Edmond et Jules de. *Germinie Lacerteux*. Paris: Bibliothèque-Charpentier, 1864.

Heywood, C. "Flaubert, Miss Braddon, and George Moore." *Comparative Literature* 12 (1960): 151–58.

Hicks, Granville. *Figures of Transition*. New York: Macmillan, 1939.

Hone, Joseph. *The Life of George Moore*. London: Victor Gollancz, 1936.

Hughes, Douglas A. "Introduction." *The Man of Wax: Critical Essays on George Moore*. Edited by Douglas A. Hughes. New York: New York UP, 1971.

James, Henry. "Gustave Flaubert." *The Art of Fiction and Other Essays*. Edited by Morris Roberts. New York: Oxford UP, 1948.

Josephson, Matthew. *Zola and His Time*. Garden City, N.Y.: Garden City Publishing, 1928.

Miller, Walter. "Foreword." *A Mummer's Wife*. New York: Liveright, 1966.

Mitchell, Judith. "Fictional Worlds in George Moore's *A Mummer's Wife*." *English Studies* 4 (1986): 345–54.

———. "George Moore's Kate Ede." *English Studies in Canada* 12 (1986): 69–78.

Morgan, Charles. *Epitaph on George Moore*. London: Macmillan, 1935.

Moore, George. *Avowals*. New York: Boni and Liveright, 1919.

———. *A Mummer's Wife*. London: Walter Scott, 1893.

———. *Literature at Nurse: Or, Circulating Morals*. London: Vizetelly, 1885.

Nejdefors-Frisk, Sonja. *George Moore's Naturalistic Prose*. Dublin: Hodges, Figgis, 1952.

Newton, William. "Chance as Employed by Hardy and the Naturalists." *Philological Quarterly* 30 (1951): 154–75.

Noël, Jean C. *George Moore: l'homme et l'oeuvre (1852–1933)*. Paris: Marcel Didier, 1966.

Sherman, Stuart P. *On Contemporary Literature*. New York: Henry Holt, 1917.

Starkie, Enid. "George Moore and French Naturalism." Hughes 61–74.

Tancock, L.W. "Introduction." *Thérèse Raquin*. By Emile Zola. Translated by L.W. Tancock. Harmondsworth: Penguin, 1962.

Ure, Peter. "George Moore as Historian of Consciences." Hughes 87–112.

Watt, Ian. *The Rise of the Novel*. Harmondsworth: Penguin Books, 1957.

Zola, Emile. "The Novel." *The Experimental Novel and Other Essays*. Translated by Belle M. Sherman. New York: Haskell House, 1964.

SELECTED SECONDARY SOURCES

Malcolm Brown, *George Moore: A Reconsideration* (Seattle: U of Washington P, 1955); Richard Cave, *A Study of the Novels of George Moore* (Gerrards Cross: Colin Smythe, 1978); Susan Dick, ed., introduction and notes, *Confessions of a Young Man* (Montreal: McGill-Queen's UP, 1972); Janet Egleson Dunleavy, *George Moore: The Artist's Vision, The Storyteller's Art* (Lewisburg: Bucknell UP, 1973) and (ed.) *George Moore in Perspective* (Gerrards Cross: Colin Smythe, 1893); Anthony Farrow, *George Moore* (Boston: Twayne Publishers, 1978); Helmut Gerber, ed., *George Moore in Transition: Letters to T. Fisher Unwin and Lena Milman, 1894–1910* (Detroit: Wayne State UP, 1968); Edwin Gilcher, *A Bibliography of George Moore* (Dekalb: Northern Illinois UP, 1970); Joseph Hone, *The Life of George Moore* (London: Victor Gollancz, 1936); Douglas A. Hughes, ed., *The Man of Wax: Critical Essays on George Moore* (New York: New York UP, 1971); A. Norman Jeffares, *George Moore* (London: F. Mildner and Sons, 1965); Jean C. Noël, *George Moore: l'homme et l'oeuvre (1852–1933)* (Paris: Marcel Didier, 1966); Graham Owens, ed., *George Moore's Mind and Art* (New York: Barnes and Noble, 1970); Frederick W. Seinfelt, *George Moore: Ireland's Unconventional Realist* (Philadelphia: Dorrance, 1975); numerous articles on Moore have appeared in *English Literature in Transition* as well as in other journals.

# Joy behind the Screen

## The Problem of "Presentability" in George Gissing's

## *The Nether World* (1889)

*Barbara Leah Harman*

George Gissing (1857–1903) lived a notoriously troubled life. A gifted student in his boyhood, he became a pupil at Owens College but was caught stealing from the cloakroom to help a young woman prostitute. Gissing was not only expelled, but sentenced to a month's hard labor, and left England for America in shame. The event is generally considered to have been a defining one for Gissing, creating in him the sense of stigma, inevitable exile, and hopeless despair that characterizes so many of his novels. He eventually married the prostitute, Nell Harrison, but the marriage was a catastrophe and the couple separated (Nell died in 1888). Gissing published his first novel, *Workers in the Dawn,* in 1880. The novel attracted the attention of the philosopher Frederic Harrison, who hired Gissing as a tutor for his son, befriended him, and introduced him to editors. Gissing didn't accept help easily, and disliked both tutoring and journalistic work, though he did some of both. His novels of working-class life include *The Unclassed* (1884), *Thyrza* (1887), and *The Nether World* (1889), his last novel in this genre. Gissing's *New Grub Street* (1891) is his finest, and certainly his best known, novel, combining a critique of the world of letters with a meditation on the new situation of women in the late 1880s. After *Born in Exile* (1892) Gissing wrote a group of novels that engage "the woman question": *The Odd Women* (1893), *In the Year of Jubilee* (1894), and *The Whirlpool* (1897). Having remarried in 1891 (again badly) Gissing separated from his wife in 1897. His most successful relationship was with the Frenchwoman Gabrielle Fleury, whom he never married, but with whom he lived happily for the last five years of his short life. He published the fascinating *Charles Dickens, A Study,* in 1898, and in 1903, near the end of his life, the pastoral *Private Papers of Henry Ryecroft,* his most popular, if most uncharacteristic, novel. He died in France at the age of forty-six. Regrettably, most of Gissing's novels (with the exception of *New Grub Street* and *The Odd Women)* go in and out of print. They have been available at different times from Dover, Harvester, The Hogarth Press, Farleigh Dickinson Press, Oxford World's Classics Series, Penguin, Norton, and most recently Dent/Everyman.

When the location of Sidney Kirkwood's home, and later his workshop, are described in one of the early chapters of George Gissing's *The Nether World,* they chart, as Gissing's urban geographies generally do, not only a set of streets, but also a set of social, economic, and personal possibilities. Sidney Kirkwood's lodging house "begins reputably and degenerates in its latter half"—mixing, as his life does when we first meet him, a sense of social possibility with a sense of that same possibility muted, flattened, or lost. Sidney's neighborhood contains "some open space . . . laid out as a garden," though Gissing is quick to point out that children are not permitted to play here, and even adults are allowed to use it only if they are on "good behavior." Like the pleasant, but unusable, park, Sidney's house is also in conflict with itself—neat on the outside, but unable to sustain life within (several pots of flowers struggle to maintain themselves on the balconies). Still, the exterior of the house is described as "promising, with its clean steps and brass plate"—though Gissing quickly asserts that, but a few yards away, the street "falls under the dominion of dry rot" (50).

   Kirkwood's jewelry-making workshop in St. John's Square does not represent promise struggling against the imminence of its own dissolution, but, rather, an already defeated confusion that lodges within it some sustaining memory of a possibility that won't die. The square is described as "irregular in outline," "cut in two by Clerkenwell Road," and composed of "such a number of recesses, of abortive streets, of shadowed alleys, that from no point of the Square can anything like a general view of its totality be obtained" (51). This vision of deformity, emptiness, and absent perspective, contains within it, simultaneously, what Gissing calls "a survival from a buried world" (51)—the old remnant of St. John's Arch, in the rooms above whose gateway Samuel Johnson once labored as a journeyman writer. Gissing's vision of the memory associated with (what is left of) the archway is a moving and, in many ways, a central one to the novel—a vision of art, aspiration, yearning, and even joy, alive, if obscured, in its surroundings. The narrator describes

> the rooms above the gateway [where] dwelt, a hundred and fifty years
> ago, one Edward Cave, publisher of the *Gentleman's Magazine,*
> and . . . a journeyman author of his, by name Samuel Johnson, too
> often *impransus* [i.e. "fasting" or starving]. There it was said Samuel

once had his dinner handed to him behind a screen, because of his unpresentable costume, when Cave was entertaining an aristocratic guest. In the course of the meal, the guest happened to speak with interest of something he had recently read by an obscure Mr. Johnson; whereat there was joy behind the screen, and probably increased appreciation of the unwonted dinner. (51)

In Gissing's presentation of this extraordinary and complex literary moment, aspiration is doubly obscured: once by its own circumstances, and then again (though differently) by history. Gissing describes the hungry journeyman writer concealed "behind a screen" because he is "unpresentable." He eats in solitude, separated from the society of Cave and his guest, whose talk is nonetheless audible to him. Hearing, even if he can neither see nor be seen, and eating alone, while others eat and enjoy themselves in company, the aspiring writer finds that he is somehow alive in the conversation on the other side of the screen, "presentable" after all in his words if not in his person. Gissing is moved by this story because it embodies for him the ambivalent feelings associated with the desire for presentability. The story describes the aspiration of the writer even in the midst of unpromising, indeed obscuring, circumstances, and the triumph of that writer who finds, despite his obscurity, that he exists in the mind and imagination of another. But Gissing is drawn to this account too because of the way the journeyman writer's joy finds its expression "behind the screen." It is real—increasing the "appreciation" of the unusual and unexpected supper—but it has, at least for the moment, no means of finding its way out of hiding, no public manifestation.

Somehow, this is an apt emblem of Sidney Kirkwood's desires, and it casts an intriguing light on Clara Hewett's and Jane Snowdon's complex desires, and on the limits that such desires seem to include in Gissing's imagination of them. Sidney has been told by his father the stories associated with St. John's Arch, and his memory of them represents, in an important sense, his own (muted) aspirations. His hopes are contained, however, not only by the screen that separates the unpresentable from the presentable, but by a larger sense that the interior screen has become a massive social machinery that obscures not only unpresentable persons but also the history of their desires. The arch now carries "a sad, worn, grimy aspect," as if it is "ashamed, tainted by the ignobleness of its surroundings," and of the "sordid struggle for existence" of which Sidney is a part. If Samuel Johnson's joy in the story is both alive and circumscribed, Sidney's memory of it is itself circumscribed—the memory of a contained joy the meager evidence of which has, surprisingly, "not been swept away, in obedience to the great law of traffic and the spirit of the time" (51).

Not yet. For Gissing's presentation of the most central characters in his novel is set on the precarious line along which the aspiration for presentability lives—behind screens or veils, along boundaries, in unstable apartments—struggling for expression, capable of a joy that is often imaginable only in containment, and always on the verge of being "swept away." The characters in whom Gissing's interest resides are those for whom "presentability" is at once a possibility and a problem, something that can be imagined, even if it cannot fully be achieved or sustained. While John Goode is thus right to suggest that "the struggle for success and recognition" in the novel "give[s] way to the struggle for survival" (*Ideology* 26), Gissing's real interest in *The Nether World* is in characters Goode himself identifies as "critical and aspiring" (*Ideology* 24), characters who inhabit the narrow space between total obscurity and partial presentability. This is what John Halperin points to when he describes as "always memorable . . . the collision between the man of intellect . . . and the grinding necessity of his earning an income large enough to satisfy his own yearnings or his family's wants." For transitional characters such as these, "the civilizing effects of education are seen to be in fact pernicious, tantalizing without being able to assuage" (Michaux 68). It is also what Adrian Poole means when he calls Gissing "a connoisseur of the penultimate," a writer for whom "desire continues even at the edge of obliteration" (87). It is in his representation of the "critical and aspiring," that Gissing's most complex characters emerge, though as the cases of Jane Snowdon and Clara Hewett show, both obscurity and, paradoxically, wide recognition, pose a threat to the sort of human knowing that Gissing values most.

*The Nether World* is a novel about the jewelry maker, Sidney Kirkwood, his relationship with the Hewett family (who are living a marginal life in the Peckovers' lodging house when the novel opens) and especially the Hewett's daughter Clara, with whom Sidney is in love but by whom he is not loved in return. Early in the novel, Sidney aids Jane Snowdon, who has earlier been abandoned by her father and transformed into the household drudge at the Peckovers, by helping her to locate the grandfather who has returned to England to find her. Sidney's developing romance with Jane, after Clara Hewett disappears to become an actress, Grandfather Snowdon's emerging plan to use Jane and Sidney in his philanthropic schemes in behalf of the poor, the eventual dissolution of Jane and Sidney's relationship, and the reemergence of Clara Hewett as Sidney's wife, form the substance of the plot.

In the course of the novel, Sidney, Jane, and Clara are depicted in the context of a larger group of the abject poor about whom Gissing seems to feel a mixture of sympathy and outright disgust. John Sloan has suggested that in its description of the working poor Gissing's novel is "completely free of the sentimentalizing strain which we find in the 'industrial novel' of the 1840s and 1850s" (76), but Sloan also points to the "self-exemptions of the narrative voice itself, with its strains of moralism and contempt for 'the people'" (77). Jacob Korg has argued that the prevailing impression created by the poor is one of "barbarity [with which Gissing] did not sympathize" (114); and David Grylls notes that "Gissing's reactions to the lowest classes vacillate between indignant pity and censorious repulsion" (51). In Gissing's view the very poor lack, among other things, the capacity for "presentability" and are frequently described as members of a mob. Bob Hewett's friends, Pennyloaf Candy's family, the crowds at the Crystal Palace—all are unpresentable as individuals because of a poverty they haven't chosen, but also because of their defective capacity to know and represent themselves. The oddly named Pennyloaf Candy, later Bob Hewett's wife, is incapable of self-knowledge and therefore of articulate desire; as Gissing puts it, "her habitual look was one of meaningless surprise" (72). Critics have described her "pathetic, infuriating dolefulness" (Poole 98), and her "stupefied misery" (Goode, *Tradition* 221), in ways which emphasize her inability to make sense of her own condition. Even her husband, Bob Hewett, whose artistic aptitudes and abilities differentiate him both from his compatriots generally and from his mournful wife in particular, is not finally the object of Gissing's sympathy, for, like Pennyloaf, he is only "semi-conscious" (214). While Gissing regularly makes plain that among the poor the "inconvenience of having no foothold on the earth's surface is so manifest" (341; the understatement is almost too obvious to mention), he also suggests that the absence of a foothold makes inevitable the absence of a conscious, articulate, relation to human society and thus the deindividuation which is characteristic of his representation of the very poor. On the other hand, those with a marginal foothold on the earth's surface—the conscious, articulate poor, like Sidney and Clara—live on the margins of presentability, struggling to make themselves known, and finding themselves both distinguished, and endangered, by that struggle.

In many ways it is Clara Hewett who presents the most interesting, and most problematic, example of the operations of this aspiration to live in the minds and imaginations of others. She is endowed with intelligence (79), and the self-knowledge that was denied to her father is not denied to her. She has a "more complex nature" that "gained in subtlety and in power of self-direction" (79). Like her father, Clara is locked in a "feud with fate," but Gissing emphasizes that Clara understands her "defects . . . her vices," and accepts them—though "defiantly" (82).

But what distinguishes Clara both from her father and from Sidney himself is that her ambitions are decidedly public. She is drawn to the theater, watches actresses with "devouring interest [and] burning envy" and asks herself, "Why shouldn't *my* portrait be seen some day in the windows?" (82). The fact that Clara's aspirations take the form of a fierce desire for recognition is not at all surprising in this world of the unrecognized and unpresentable, but the clear statement of this desire on Clara's part—the openness of her passion to be seen and known—differentiates her from the significantly more modest example of the desire for recognition embodied by Samuel Johnson in the narrator's story about his early life. And yet Clara's aspiration is clearly connected to other forms of aspiration in the novel—Sidney's desire to be an artist, for one, and even Johnson's hope, as the anecdote suggests, of imagining a future that is not lived behind the screen. Thus although Gissing stresses the violations of womanliness that Clara's particular rebellion entails (86), the problem is not exclusively (though surely it is partly) a function of her sex:

> Like a creature that is beset by unrelenting forces, she summoned and surveyed all the crafty faculties lurking in the dark places of her nature; theoretically she had now accepted every debasing compact by which a woman can spite herself on the world's injustice. Self-assertion; to be no longer an unregarded atom in the mass of those who are born only to labor for others; to find play for the strength and the passion which, by no choice of her own, distinguished her from the tame slave. (86)

Gissing will suggest that the recognition and distinction Clara seeks are not available to members of her world (those "unregarded atom[s] in the mass"), that they exceed not only the bounds of gender, but of class. The emphasis on Clara's violation of womanliness is central here; and what is "theoretical" in this passage will become actual later, as Clara lives with her "agent" as his mistress, and is unfaithful to her own childhood friend and fellow actress. But the desire for recognition is not exclusively a female desire in this novel, nor in Gissing's work more generally (*New Grub Street* provides, of course, numerous examples of characters for whom obscurity and recognition are the key coordinates of life). As Clara is about to achieve in some form the recognition she so passionately desires, Gissing puts the matter more broadly himself:

You see that she had formulated her philosophy of life. . . . A child of the nether world whom fate had endowed with intellect, she gave articulate utterance to what is seething in the brains of thousands who fight and perish in the obscure depths. The bitter bargain was issuing to her profit at last; she would yet attain that end which had shone through her misery—to be known as a successful actress by those she had abandoned, whose faces were growing dim to her memory but of whom, in truth, she still thought more than of all the multitudinous unknown public. A great success during the remainder of this tour, and she might hope for an engagement in London. Her portraits would at length be in the windows; some would recognize her. (207–8)

Clara's central desire *is* the desire to be known, though her wish to see her portrait in the window is also a desire to be seen and known by those she loves. The oscillation between these two positions suggests that the desire for two kinds of recognition are at work here. Clara needs those she loves to see her portrait and recognize her, but in part that means that she wishes them to see her as someone whose value others have recognized.

In Gissing's view, however, this sort of recognition is simply impossible—unavailable and, one suspects, undesirable. Clara's hopes are destroyed on the eve of her premier appearance, as the friend whose role she has usurped takes revenge by throwing acid in her face, destroying not only the hope of recognition but indeed Clara's very desire ever to be seen again. The desire for recognition will for a time become for Clara its opposite—the desire to live behind a veil or, to put it another way, behind a screen.

I shall return to Clara's predicament momentarily, but it bears noting that Gissing's resistance to publicity is oddly repeated, though in a different form, in the situation of Jane Snowdon. Rescued from virtual slavery in the Peckovers' boarding house, Jane lives with her grandfather in rooms that always impress Sidney with their quietness, their "remoteness from the common conditions of life" (100). Gissing describes this period of Jane's life as one of "fostering": it "enabled features of her character, which no one could have discerned in the helpless child, to expand with singular richness" (135). Sidney will later suggest that what expands is an "instinct of gladness" that was "but one manifestation of a moral force which made itself nobly felt in many another way" (139). Jane's "power for good," which will later move her to forge a relationship with the almost terrifyingly marginal Pennyloaf, is something both Sidney and, we sense, Gissing, admire. But Jane exercises her power for good in individual cases. She has no instinct for generalization, no capacity to theorize, and no wish to move beyond the limits of her protecting world except with respect to individual persons. Indeed, Gissing comments that at this point in her life, Jane is so damaged that she is unable even to acquire book-learning (136), and her development is not in the arena of self-knowledge or self-articulation: "like the weakest child, she craved protection from a dread inspired solely by her imagination, and solace for an anguish of wretchedness to which she could give no form in words" (136). In a later passage, Gissing even says of her that "she knew not self-seeking, knew not self-esteem" (224).

But this is why her grandfather's plan for her is so problematic. He wishes to make her an instrument of his philanthropy, to know that his money would be used "for the good of the poor by a woman who herself belonged to the poor" (178). And yet in Jane's vision, "The world had all at once grown very large, a distress to her imagination; worse still, she had become a person of magnified importance, irrecognizable in her own sight, moving, thinking so unnaturally" (224). As Gissing notes:

> Consecration to a great idea, endowment with the means of wide beneficence—this not only left her cold, but weighed upon her, afflicted her beyond her strength. What was it, in truth, that restored her to herself and made her heart beat joyously? Knit your brows against her; shake your head and raze her name from that catalogue of saints whereon you have inscribed it in anticipation. Jane rejoiced simply because she loved a poor man, and had riches that she could lay at his feet. (226)

Jane has no interest in, no capacity for, this wider beneficence. It is acceptable to her only because it follows "consecration to the warmer love" she feels for Sidney (227). If Clara Hewett's desire for recognition is felt through the desire to be seen and recognized by those at home as her face appears on public placards, Jane's desire works in the opposite direction. For her, public engagement is acceptable only as something that moves outward from, and is in some sense an expression of, personal attachment.

Sidney, however, will find the two don't mix at all, in any order. Jane's "mission" becomes "hateful to him; he could not bear to think of her handing soup over the counter to ragged wretches" (257). Her power for him is connected to her containment, to her ability to generate joy in private places, to rekindle for him childhood memories and desires for self-expression (233). Jane's grandfather's aspirations—his public enthusiasms, his theories—in elaborating and generalizing Jane's power, necessarily dilute and confuse it. In Sidney's view, her instinct for gladness, and her moral power, can only exist as forms of pleasure and happiness when they are guarded or, in Gissing's earlier word, "fostered." Transformed into a theory about and a practice of moral power, cast abroad in the world, they have for Sidney no capacity to produce pleasure. As Sidney sees it, Jane "would fall into miserable perplexity in conflict between love and duty, and her life would be ruined" (234). Instead, as Sidney moves away from Jane, and Jane relinquishes Sidney, accepting her philanthropic role out of a sense of duty to her grandfather, she catches a momentary "gleam of hope in renunciation itself, the kind of strength which idealism is fond of attributing to noble natures"— but even this turns out to be deceptive, and disappears. Poole suggests that "Jane is as near as possible to being a deliberate *exposure* of the 'angel of mercy' image" (99), and this seems exactly right. Gissing has no use for the familiar view that self-renunciation might be for women a meaningful social role. "She had dreamed her dream," Gissing concludes, "and on awaking must be content to take up the day's duties" (318).

Clara's and Jane's desire to emerge out of the thralldom and obscurity of the nether world is something with which Gissing sympathizes. But the thwarting of Clara's aspiration for a wide-ranging publicity also, oddly, resembles the resistance to Grandfather Snowdon's public enthusiasms as he wishes them to be embodied in his granddaughter. Gissing cannot imagine for either woman a "presentability" that moves in this direction—though of course in Clara's case publicity is desired but dramatically and finally denied; in Jane's case it is not desired at all, and its very presence as a possibility undermines her simpler aspirations for a more human mutuality and recognition, what Sidney thinks of as the capacity to be "obscure and happy" (235).

But what sort of space is left between these alternatives? As Gissing undermines the notion that presentability might be achieved through public work—theatricality (for Clara) or philanthropy (for Jane)—he begins to intimate how little the notion of presentability has to do with self-representation in the social world. This notion gains credibility when Clara reemerges, practicing her craft as an actress in new and extraordinary circumstances. To say that Clara's stage has contracted is of course an extreme understatement: no longer on stage, her platform becomes an empty room in the boarding house in which her family lives. Her audience is Sidney Kirkwood himself, and she plays her most important part not only (like Johnson in the anecdote with which I began) behind a curtain, but behind a curtain so foreshortened that it is literally the veil across her (scarred) face. If Jane Snowdon cannot combine her commitment to fulfill her grandfather's political dreams with her own desires for self-fulfillment, Clara Hewett, it seems, has more resources at her command.

Clara's scene is certainly the most remarkable one in the novel. First, Gissing indicates that Clara is "an actress improvising her part . . . [regulating] every tone with perfect skill." But what she will speak of to Sidney is her obscurity and hiddenness: she knows that she must work, but wishes to "be spared going among strangers" (284). Sidney reads this as a sign of her sensitivity about disfigurement, which indeed it probably is, and also as evidence of sympathy between them; but we also note as readers the sudden change, the move toward privacy, which is a reversal of Clara's prior instincts. As she speaks her little speech, Gissing observes too that her voice sinks lower and lower. Shrinking into herself, "she seemed as if she would have hidden her face even under its veil" (284).

The conflict throughout the scene between Gissing's representation to us of Clara's performance on stage, and her representation to Sidney of her own intense and extreme modesty and privacy, is both striking and disturbing. At one point, "Clara rose, as if impelled by mental anguish; she stretched out her hand to the mantel-piece, and so stood between him and the light, her admirable figure designed on a glimmering background"(285). Clara's sense of how to produce a sense of anguish, her capacity to cast her figure in its best light, to make it shimmer, to make herself beautiful even as she darkens her own face, suggest that this is the great stage scene of which, technically, she was deprived by her disfigurement.

In fact one of the most extraordinary aspects of this scene—and one which raises it above any scene Clara might actually have performed on stage—is that her disfigurement actually requires of her far more talent than she was earlier called on to produce. Invoking her own, prior cruelty to Sidney, Clara wants to invite a sympathy she can't claim to deserve:

> "Did I merit it by my words when I last—"
> There came a marvelous change—a change such as it needed either exquisite feeling or the genius of simulation to express by means so simple. Unable to show him by a smile, by a light in her eyes, what mood had come upon her, what subtle shifting in the direction of her thought had checked her words—by her mere movement as she stepped lightly towards him, by the carriage of her head, by her hands half held out and half drawn back again, she prepared him for what she was about to say. No piece of acting was ever more delicately finished. He knew that she smiled, though nothing of her face was visible; he knew that her look was one of diffident, half-blushing pleasure. (287)

Unable to use her eyes, but needing to suggest a change of direction in her thought, Clara uses the tilt of her head, the movement of her hands toward and away from him. Sidney can't see her face at all and yet he can distinguish her subtle shift, can feel her desire to stand forth and at the same time sense her diffidence, can know her "half-blushing pleasure." Clara is thus able to use her remarkable talents as an actress to reawaken Sidney's love for her. Unlike Jane, who is pressed into public service against her will and at the cost of that capacity for quiet love that Sidney so desires, Clara makes use of her theatrical self not to express her love for Sidney ("she had never loved him," 292), but to inspire love in him and thereby win access to the scarce reservoir of human feeling available in her world:

> least of all women could *she* live by bread alone; there was the hunger of her brain, the hunger of her heart . . . that which she feared most of all was the barrenness of a lot into which would enter none of the passionate joys of existence. . . . Hopelessly defeated in the one way of aspiration which promised a large life, her being, rebellious against the martyrdom it had suffered, went forth eagerly towards the only happiness which was any longer attainable. Her beauty was a dead thing; never by that means could she command homage. But there is love, ay, and passionate love, which can be independent of mere charm of face. In one man only could she hope to inspire it; successful in that, she would taste victory, and even in this fallen estate could she make for herself a dominion. (293, 294)

What's fascinating about Gissing's account is its description of the complex, and mixed, operations of Clara's desire. She is talking the language of "passionate love," but it emerges as the language of "dominion" associated with that "large life" whose loss she mourns. Reduced, contained, disfigured, and reconfigured, Clara still conceives a new estate and in it her power over a new "audience." In other words, Gissing makes it clear that Clara's "self deception" in the scene is "complete" (294). She tells herself that this is "kinship" (294), when it is really a "demand for the object of desire" (294)—a demand that exists in direct proportion to the failures and disappointments of her other life, and that manifests itself in the very terms of that other life.

Still, Clara's final scene with her father reveals how much of a sense of loss she feels. Lamenting her disfigurement and its consequent losses, "a great anguish shook her. . . . It was the farewell, even in her fullness of heart and deep sense of consolation, to all she had most vehemently desired" (302). But in this novel of great losses and meager gains, Clara's are complicated by our awareness that she lacks self-knowledge—"gratitude and self-pity being indivisible in her emotions, she knew not whether the ache of regret or the soothing restfulness of deliverance made her tears flow" (302). Gissing comments that "at least there was no conscious duplicity," but this doesn't clarify the question of unconscious duplicity. Sloan's sense that Clara's "survival with dignity depends on a subservience to Kirkwood's own defensive self-sacrifice" thus seems wide of the mark (80). Clara's losses are dramatic and real, but there is little subservience here.

The impossibility of Jane's public role, and the duplicities attached to Clara's, suggest that the problem of presentability is a difficult one to disentangle both for Gissing and his readers. Nor is it made simpler by the fact that, at the end of the novel, Sidney looks rather more like a man who has lost his foothold in the world, whose already minimal access to presentability has been radically reduced:

> As with John Hewett, so with himself; the circle of his interests had shrivelled, until it included nothing but the cares of his family, the cost of house and food and firing. As a younger man, he had believed that he knew what was meant by the struggle for existence in the nether world; it seemed to him now as if such knowledge had been only theoretical. Oh, it was easy to preach a high ideal of existence for the poor, as long as one had a considerable margin over the week's expenses. (374)

And yet Sidney retains, in however reduced a form, the capacity for self-consciousness and articulation—for a minimalist version of human presentability—in his relation to Clara. Attempting to draw her out of inarticulate despair, he pleads with her at the novel's conclusion:

> Only one word—only one promise. . . . We are husband and wife, Clara, and we must be kind to each other. We are not going to be like the poor creatures who let their misery degrade them. We are both too proud for that—what? We can think and express our thoughts; we can speak to each other's minds and hearts. Don't let us be beaten! (379)

Sidney extracts from Clara the promise to keep their relationship alive, and Gissing declares, at the end of the scene, that "the battle was gained once more" (379). Sidney's desire here—to speak to the mind and heart of his wife and be spoken to in turn, to maintain in language his own humanity and hers—reflects Gissing's sense that the capacity for mutuality, for presentability in speech, is also the capacity to keep some meager human joy alive "behind the screen." Goode describes this as "Sidney's momentary victory," which "establishes the minimum conditions on which life can continue" (*Tradition* 222), and Poole more dramatically, and probably more affirmatively, refers to Sidney's as the "voice that survives tenuously on the brink of extinction" as the "'twilight' [that] is all the more precious for its trembling on the edge of darkness" (89). Without wishing to overvalue Sidney's conquest here, it is important to register its significance and to realize how crucial it is that Gissing ends this scene with the insistence that Sidney and Clara express themselves, that they "speak to each other's minds and hearts." Grylls is right to say that, in the absence of any redemptive reformist vision, the novel's only hope resides in "individual acts of human kindness" (53), but it is equally noteworthy that Gissing has in mind a particular vision of how human kindness might operate.

Gissing leaves Jane Snowdon in womanly fellowship, and modest business partnership, with Pennyloaf, refusing a marriage proposal in order to keep her own prior joy alive in her mind, to remain "faithful to the past, and unchanging" (390). What sustains Sidney is language, and language's capacity to keep human feeling alive; what sustains Jane is memory. These versions of presentability, minimal as they are (and Jane's is more minimal than Sidney's), are the only ones Gissing can imagine in the nether world, where Sidney and Jane are "unmarked, unencouraged" by the larger world that does not heed them (390). Their lives, Gissing suggests, offer a protest against total human obscurity on the one hand, and dehumanizing publicity on the other, in the vision of persons presentable to each other in words and memories if in no other way.

WORKS CITED

Collie, Michael. *The Alien Art: A Critical Study of George Gissing's Novels*. Hamden, Conn.: Archon, 1979.

Gissing, George. *The Nether World* (1889). Brighton: Harvester, 1974. Reprint. 1982.

Goode, John. *George Gissing: Ideology and Fiction*. New York: Barnes and Noble, 1978.

———. "George Gissing's *The Nether World*." *Tradition and Tolerance in Nineteenth-Century Fiction*. Edited by David Howard, John Lucas and John Goode. New York: Barnes and Noble, 1967.

Grylls, David. *The Paradox of Gissing*. London: Allen and Unwin, 1986.

Halperin, John. "How to Read Gissing." *George Gissing: Critical Essays*. Edited by Jean-Pierre Michaux. New York: Barnes and Noble, 1981.

Korg, Jacob. *George Gissing: A Critical Biography*. Brighton: Harvester, 1980.

Poole, Adrian. *Gissing in Context*. Totowa, N.J.: Rowman and Littlefield, 1975.

Sloan, John. *George Gissing: The Cultural Challenge*. New York: St. Martin's, 1989.

SELECTED SECONDARY SOURCES

Standard critical texts on Gissing include Adrian Poole's *Gissing in Context* (Rowman and Littlefield, 1975); Michael Collie, *The Alien Art: A Critical Study of George Gissing's Novels* (Archon 1979); John Goode, *George Gissing: Ideology and Fiction* (Barnes and Noble, 1979); John Goode, *George Gissing: A Critical Biography* (Harvester, 1980); *George Gissing: Critical Essays*, edited by Jeanne Pierre Michaux (Barnes and Noble, 1981); David Grylls, *The Paradox of Gissing* (Allen and Unwin, 1986); and John Sloan, *George Gissing: The Cultural Challenge* (St. Martin's, 1989). Gissing's diaries are available as *London and the Life of Literature in Late Victorian England: The Diaries of George Gissing*, edited by Pierre Coustillas (Bucknell, 1978). *The Collected Letters of George Gissing* have been edited by Paul E. Matthiessen, Arthur C. Young, and Pierre Coustillas (Ohio UP, 1990–1995).

# CURIOUS DUALITIES

## THE HEAVENLY TWINS (1893) AND SARAH GRAND'S

## BELATED MODERNIST AESTHETICS

*John Kucich*

Born Frances Elizabeth McFall (1854–1943), the daughter of a naval officer stationed in Ireland, "Sarah Grand" is best known for her blockbuster feminist novel *The Heavenly Twins* (1893). The only work of hers still in print, *The Heavenly Twins* (Ann Arbor: U of Michigan P, 1992) was most notorious for its candid discussion of venereal disease, which focused on the suffering of women who had contracted it from their husbands, although the novel was concerned with a wide range of other feminist issues as well. Grand continued to write novels and short stories until 1916, but the novels in her early trilogy—*Ideala* (1888), *The Heavenly Twins,* and *The Beth Book* (1897)—are her most important literary works. (*The Beth Book* was reissued by Virago but is currently out of print.) Grand also wrote numerous influential essays for literary journals and magazines on women's issues (she is credited with having coined the term "New Woman"), and she was a popular lecturer. Grand separated from her husband, an army surgeon, in 1892, and, after living in London and Tunbridge Wells, she eventually located in Bath, where she served as mayoress from 1923 through 1929.

Sarah Grand's work has suffered from critical neglect for a variety of reasons, but chief among them are two: the aesthetic weaknesses she is supposed to have shared with many New Woman writers, and the seeming middlingness of her feminism. The latter flaw has damaged her reputation even among those who overlook primitive stylistics, crude realism, and literary polemics. While the work of George Egerton or Grant Allen, for example, may also seem sloppy or even defiantly antiaesthetic, at least these writers took up radical positions marking the poles of late-century debates about the status of women—Egerton advocating a chaste verbal expressiveness, and Allen celebrating female sexual excess. New Woman writers were often polarized by the extreme positions they took on questions of sexual morality, motherhood, divorce, work, and cross-gendered conduct (like smoking, or riding bicycles). But Grand seems to have resisted such polarization. Surveying these and other divisions within late-century feminism, one of the foremost experts on Grand's oeuvre, Joan Huddleston, comments that "Grand's novels must be placed midway between all these extremes" (6). Such antiextremism helps explain why a work like Elaine Showalter's *Sexual Anarchy* features extended discussions of novels by Egerton, Allen, Mona Caird, Olive Schreiner, and others, but only cursory references to Grand.[1]

The apparent middlingness of a writer like Grand does typify something fundamental about all New Woman writing: that is, the ways it operated within contradictions that late-century feminism simply could not resolve. More important, however, Grand's evenhandedness helps show how those contradictions resulted in a peculiar aesthetics that resists assimilation to ideals of aesthetic consistency. Her middlingness, in other words, is productive of the very formal characteristics that have troubled critics. Struggling with irresolvable ideological problems, Grand discovered ways of expressing those problems through the calculated discontinuities of her aesthetic logic. Attending to these dynamics, instead of lamenting them, can show us something about the ways New Woman writing anticipated modernist formal experiments, and the ways its apparent intellectual confusions— for which it has been faulted by numerous critics, from Showalter to Joseph Boone—define early attempts to articulate problems that contemporary feminism itself has hardly transcended.[2] Unfortunately, in Grand's case, those problems took shape through her sense of the debilitating belatedness haunting women's literary choices—a sense of belatedness that can, nevertheless, tell us a good deal about the situation of the fin-de-siècle woman writer.

Some of the contradictions embedded in Grand's writing certainly do have an archaic ring to them, and seem to suggest a failure to work through basic feminist issues. In all her novels, for example, Grand struggles with late Victorian conundrums about the roles of candor and secrecy in women's lives, or the centrality of traditional feminine ideals of self-sacrifice within the feminist cause. Other problems, however, may seem more intractable: the tension between women's sexual expression and their autonomy, for example, or between the claims of nature and culture on women's conduct. Far from advocating weak compromises on these and other questions, as she is often supposed to have done, Grand's work foregrounds the dynamism of her characters' impossible choices.[3] Self-contradiction is the psychological state most interesting to her—it is the condition she associates with the greatest moments of self-discovery, and with the greatest powers of critical awareness. In *The Heavenly Twins,* for example, Angelica accounts for the bizarre, liberating experimentalism of her cross-dressing ruse (disguised as her twin brother, Angelica meets with an ecclesiastical singer who is infatuated with the "real" Angelica, while she conceals from him the fact that the real Angelica is already married) by candidly avowing her inconsistencies:

> I see all the contradictions that are involved in what I have said and am saying, and yet I mean it all. In separate sections of my consciousness each separate clause exists at this moment, however contradictory, and there is no reconciling them; but there they are. I can't understand it myself, and I don't want you to try. All I ask you is to believe me—to forgive me. (461)

In *Ideala,* Grand's most straightforward attempt to portray the goals of the New Woman, Ideala herself is characterized by nothing so much as her dynamic paradoxes: "Her own life was set to a tune that admitted of endless variations. Sometimes it was difficult even for those who knew her best to detect the original melody among the clashing chords that concealed it" (9).

Grand's fascination with psychological contradictions, particularly those generated by women's social dilemmas, had aesthetic consequences that cry out to be put in relation to modernist formal innovations. If this has not yet been done, it is partly because of Grand's own philistine affirmations of low-brow aesthetics, which she often expressed through spokespersonlike characters, such as Beth McClure—who aspires in *The Beth Book* to write a "picture" of life so as to "present all sides of it, and not merely one phase— the good and the bad of it, the joys and the sorrows, the moments of strength and of weakness, of wisdom and of folly, of misery and of pure delight" (373). These celebrations of realist writing, however, are part of a histrionic, distorting war with male modernists—a war that is dramatized in the novels themselves—and they seem to entrench Grand in polemical stances not necessarily reflected by her own practice.[4] The strongest evidence for Grand's covert interest in antirealist aesthetics lies in the disjunctive form of the novels themselves. But Grand's more fluid inclinations about literary form are often expressed through indirection as well—sometimes, for example, by the way she confronts her female protagonists with men whose aesthetic dogmatism seems even more vulgar than their own. Responding to a pompous literary authority who quotes De Quincey's dismissal of novels as "the opium of the West" (404), Beth defends them by countering: "I notice in all things a curious duality."

I will focus, briefly, on the curious aesthetic dualities in Grand's most important novel, *The Heavenly Twins,* and the particular ideological dilemmas they express. For in this most popular of all New Woman novels, Grand deliberately exploits the conjunction of realist and antirealist writing. Criticism of the novel has understandably overlooked these formal complexities because of the admittedly spectacular histrionics of the novel's plot. Among its many narrative strands, *The Heavenly Twins* tells the stories of two complementary heroines, Evadne Frayling and Angelica Hamilton-Wells. Having married a man she discovers to have been a rake, Evadne refuses to consummate her marriage, though she continues to live with her husband after promising her parents not to create a scandal. The death of Evadne's husband releases her eventually from this repression, but its effects produce a hysterical depression that her second husband, a psychiatrist, devotes himself to curing. Angelica also marries a man she does not love, though in her case there is mutual respect. More assertive than Evadne, Angelica seeks respectable marriage as a cover for her own radical independence, which her permissive husband indulges. The chief use she makes of this independence is to carry off her aforementioned "romance" with the Tenor. This episode ends in disaster, when the Tenor saves Angelica from drowning, discovers her true sex in the process, cuts off their relationship, and shortly afterwards dies of the pneumonia he contracted from rescuing her. The novel also features a third heroine, Edith Beale, who unknowingly marries a man with syphilis, contracts the disease from him, and dies in terrible suffering that chastens the other two women.

Beneath this wildly sensational plot and its preoccupations with marriage, independence, and sexual pollution, however, *The Heavenly Twins* is also a sustained meditation on the aesthetic strategies of feminist art, which it embodies in its own convoluted formal design. The first half of the novel subscribes largely to the conventions of didactic realism, even though its occasionally exaggerated episodes draw on a more fantastic and improbable narrative vein. The long "Proem" that opens the book, and the theme of wide-eyed secularism it introduces, define Grand as the worshipful heir of George Eliot. But in the fourth book of the novel, titled "The Tenor and the Boy—An Interlude," Grand uses a kind of stylized pastoral mode not uncommon in Yeats, Wilde, and other fin-de-siècle writers—as Linda Dowling has pointed out. This book strikingly breaks the novel's realist frame by creating a shadow world of artificial sexual being. In its bittersweet, symbol-laden, idyllic meetings between Tenor and Boy—set almost entirely in the middle of the night, when the normal world of Morningquest is asleep—the conversation between these two disguised and self-inventing characters revolves around the malleability of sexual difference and sexual relationship. Though this section is succeeded by another book narrated in realist mode, the final book of the novel returns to patterns of decadent aesthetics by introducing one of the favorite conventions of modernist narrative: the unreliable narrator. In this section, Dr. Galbraith's heavily ironized narrative of Evadne's hysteria concludes the novel in an ominously unresolved way, rendering the status of the entire narrative problematic by stressing the dangerous fictive power of even the most scientific discourses. Both of these books bring to the foreground the tangled relations between nature, culture, and literary artifice.

The prominence of these two major narrative disruptions draws attention to other, more nuanced kinds of narrative technique that Grand shares with the "stylists" she often seems to scorn. In *The Heavenly Twins,* as in all of her narratives, Grand uses cyclic repetition, micro-realism, and plot disjunction to frustrate the momentum of linear narrative. Even the more crude antiliterary impulses of the novels—their flaunted lack of literary polish, including the grammatical mistakes Mark Twain complained of—must be seen as part of a desire to violate codes of realistic transparency.[5] In the case of *The Heavenly Twins,* the novel as a whole can be seen to function as the dramatic confrontation of these two modes of narration, both in its disjunctive techniques and in its identification of those techniques with psychologically opposed characters, as I will show in a moment.

It would be easy enough to conclude that these two narrative modes signify a contest between essentialist and antiessentialist feminisms in Grand's work. Recently, we have heard a great deal about the affinities antiessentialist thought has with antirealist literary forms.[6] And, indeed, the history of the essentialist/antiessentialist debate in feminism extends further back into the nineteenth century than contemporary criticism often acknowledges. Grand was one of many New Woman novelists who seem to have entertained both ways of thinking about sexual identity.[7] But critical attention to this debate as a kind of theoretical impasse—always already a destabilizing feature of feminist thought—often distracts from the specific programs of particular writers. In more historically localized terms, Grand's aesthetic doubleness signals her wariness about feminist appropriations of male cultural forms. That is to say, Grand's work simply *assumes* that fin-de-siècle feminists need to reinvent female identity in comprehensive ways. The only question for her is whether that reinvention can involve the appropriation of either performative or mimetic forms of writing, both of which the novel understands to be culturally coded as male.

Grand's complementary heroines, Evadne and Angelica, embody this dilemma—suggesting one of many dimensions to the novel's dominant metaphor of twinship. Evadne is so much a "realist" that, as an adolescent reader, she overtly rejects literature itself in favor of scientific truth. Finding that novels lie, Evadne dismisses them wholesale for knowledge of a more empirical kind. Grand's novel tends to see Evadne's literary attitudes as naive, and Evadne is linked to literary practices despite herself when she is revealed to be an excellent reader of the narratives of other characters. But her rejection of fiction signals a widespread problem, noted in many New Woman novels, with the aesthetic consequences of women's demand for "real" truth. When taken to extremes, feminist realism—as male reviewers never tired of pointing out—could include a contempt for art. "Men entertain each other with intellectual ingenuities and Art and Style," says Beth, "while women are busy with the great problems of life" (376). The larger problem with Evadne's empiricism, however, is that the novel explicitly sees her quest for unmediated knowledge to represent her overidentification with male cultural authority—with her father, with scientific and medical discourses, with John Stuart Mill. Evadne thus becomes a glaringly mis-gendered spokesperson for "real" knowledge, whose promise not to join the women's movement, and whose blindness about her own performative fiction in regard to her marriage seriously damage her. Evadne herself calls attention to the fictive elements she ultimately discovers in scientific procedures, self-consciously revealing herself to be the dupe of male empirical authority. As she tells her manipulative psychiatrist/husband: "knowledge" has "nothing to do" with psychiatric cures; rather, "you alter the attitude of one's mind somehow" (635). Ironically, the woman hungering for realism ends up a character controlled by the realist and psychiatric narratives of a man.

Evadne's degeneration into nervous illness is all the more unsettling because her straightforward style had been provisionally approved, in the early stages of *The Heavenly Twins,* as one means of combating male oppression—that is, through the imitation of masculine strategies of knowledge, education, and brutal candor. In this sense, she represents the manly, scandal-braving realism with which New Woman fiction is often identified. Her ideas about transcending the merely literary in order to arrive at a more accurate and empirical kind of truthtelling are carried forward by Grand's heroine in *The Beth Book,* when Beth turns from imagining private romances to writing feminist nonfiction. However, in Beth's case, too, the inevitable end of feminist "realism" is shown to be an impoverished abandonment of literary possibilities, including realist literature. And in this novel, Beth's choice is clearly shaped by the conviction that such literature is controlled by men. For Beth, the male reviewer of a journal called the *Patriarch,* Alfred

Cayley Pounce (who literally waits to pounce on her book), and her well-meaning but cloying literary advisor, Sir George Galbraith, make some *other* kind of intellectual foray (however nebulously defined) seem crucial to her development as a feminist.

Angelica, on the other hand, represents performative strategies that *The Heavenly Twins* fully identifies with stereotypical female flaws—with age-old saws about feminine caprice and mendacity. It also identifies these strategies, however, with imaginative potentials that are only legitimated when they are employed by men. Angelica is defined over against Evadne in terms of her theatrical inventiveness, which extends from the childish pranks she devises with her brother Diavolo to her elaborate cross-dressing experiment. Her husband's condescending appreciation for her "romances" (479) suggests the harmlessness usually seen in such female foibles. But Angelica's inventiveness becomes deadly when it unleashes the power of female anger. Angelica's performativeness is ultimately portrayed as feverish and misguided, especially in relation to the wise integrity of the novel's male self-inventors.[8] For example, the Tenor, who is Angelica's foil, is, like herself, a character in disguise. Carefully concealing his origins and his connections, the Tenor is content to "bury himself alive" (361) at Morningquest. But the Tenor constructs an openly fictive persona for himself that the entire community treats with grave respect. In fact, his self-embalming role is seen by Angelica herself as Christlike. Similarly, Angelica's brother, Diavolo, continues the pranks and tricks that characterized both twins as children far into his adolescence and beyond, showing such performativeness to be a crucial component of male education. Finally, the stratagems of Dr. Galbraith, used to manipulate his wife for her own good, demonstrate how crucial performance is to male professional skill. Angelica's cross-dressing project thus seems to be the failed, misguided female version of these male privileges in the realm of artifice.

Between them, Evadne and Angelica seem to justify the contradictory charges often leveled at New Woman fiction itself by male critics. On the one hand, such fiction was faulted for being too candid, for lacking masculine discrimination and discretion in handling the truth.[9] On the other hand, it was faulted for its fantastic qualities, for its extravagant sins against the probabilities of realist fiction. Reviewers in England, for instance, were quick to link women's more imaginative literary efforts with hysteria.[10] Diagnosing this double-bind as a condition of belatedness, *The Heavenly Twins* portrays opposed feminine literary potentials distrustfully, as equally imperfect imitations of male models. The debate about women's writing at the end of the century, it goes without saying, was saturated with notions about female redundancy in art, lending greater urgency to Grand's characters' sense of belatedness.[11] What is crucial in Grand's case, however, was her perception that the dawning of new literary possibilities at the fin-de-siècle had already been subjected to an insidious pattern of gendering, in which the very necessity of formal choice was constructed for women as a trap, since both realist and antirealist writing by women could be stigmatized as forms of intellectual imitation and inadequacy. Having to choose between formal strategies, in other words, seemed only to draw attention to female literary dependence.

Grand's disjunctive form thus does more than simply anticipate modernist aesthetics. It also gives her ways to portray the conflicting literary choices facing late-century feminists as a doomed set of options, for such choices have become an occasion for linking together the drawbacks of opposed female mentalities with particular literary forms. In Grand's view, a woman writer's formal choices—either realist or antirealist—will always be invested with a sense of sexual belatedness. *The Heavenly Twins* thus suggests that the bifurcation of narrative modes at the end of the century shifted the focus of literary sexual competition away from questions about which gender owns the novel to questions about which gender owns particular narrative forms. And as Grand's novel shows, this last arena seems to present more complicated problems for women than are usually appreciated by critics of the late-century "battle of the sexes," when such critics assume unproblematically that women anticipated or even preempted antirealist innovations.[12]

By demonstrating the inscription of narrative forms in this double-bind, Grand draws attention to the ways women's writing must confront ideological problems in the guise of insurmountable formal ones. Among other things, her articulation of this dilemma ought to provide us with insight into the reasons for the absence of "great" women writers at the end of the nineteenth century, an absence that has defied explanation, though it seems hardly accidental.[13] For that absence had at least something to do with the perception, voiced by writers like Grand, that a woman's choice of form would always involve a belated selection among possibilities that seemed only to aggravate women's lack of cultural authority. This sense of inevitable belatedness often haunts the late-century woman writer confronting aesthetic choices, who finds that the appearance of choice conceals a dangerous double-bind.

In formal terms as well as thematic ones, *The Heavenly Twins* can only sustain a longstanding tradition of feminist narrative, in which women's opposing choices are shown to present them merely with complementary dilemmas. Evadne and Angelica demonstrate that, in their affinities for different literary forms, one may sing while the other doesn't, but together they will still share a sense of loss. For these reasons, Grand's formal inconsistencies cannot be taken simply at face value. Those inconsistencies, self-consciously meditated upon through theme and characterization, can prove fruitful for studies of the problems faced by the proto-modernist woman writer, especially the hesitation over formal choices from which those writers often suffered.

## Notes

1. Showalter articulated her views of Grand's middlingness more fully in her earlier work. Her attack on Grand in *A Literature of Their Own* centered on what she saw as the fiction's attempt to be "cosmically grandiose" (183) even while it was "the merest extension" of traditional concepts of female virtue, resulting in Grand's "incoherent rebellion" (210), and her "withdrawing from the world" (215).

2. Boone (131) generalizes about contradictory New Woman attitudes toward gender identity and monogamy.

3. On Grand's supposed compromises, see also Caine (253).

4. When speaking in her own voice, Grand was not immune to such distortion. Sounding much like Beth, she remarked in the preface to *Our Manifold Nature* that "[a] novel, it seems to me, should be like life itself—an unfolding, and not a regular structure" (vi).

5. See Rowlette (17).

6. DeKoven's ground-breaking essay usefully charts this relationship. A good summary of recent work on the issue can be found in Scott (esp. 12–14); or in Pykett (esp. 22–29).

7. Ardis traces the presence of antiessentialism in a number of New Woman writers, though she does not include Grand among them.

8. For a more affirmative reading of Angelica's strategies of performance see Gilbert and Gubar (1989, 347–48). Grand's negative judgments against Angelica, however, are teased out convincingly by Dowling (439).

9. A good example is Waugh (esp. 210–12).

10. See Showalter (1990, 40).

11. Tuchman catalogues numerous examples of this charge.

12. I am thinking, in part, of Gilbert and Gubar (1988).

13. Stubbs (120) notoriously claimed that this absence was "quite accidental"—a suggestion that, far from laying matters to rest, has provoked a great deal of speculative critical energy, including my own.

## Works Cited

Ardis, Ann L. *New Women, New Novels: Feminism and Early Modernism*. New Brunswick, N.J.: Rutgers UP, 1990.

Boone, Joseph Allen. *Tradition Counter Tradition: Love and the Form of Fiction*. Chicago: U of Chicago P, 1987.

Caine, Barbara. *Victorian Feminists*. Oxford: Oxford UP, 1992.

DeKoven, Marianne. "Gendered Doubleness and the 'Origins' of Modernist Form." *Tulsa Studies in Women's Literature* 8 (1989): 19–42.

Dowling, Linda. "The Decadent and the New Woman in the 1890's." *Nineteenth-Century Fiction* 33 (1979): 434–53.

Gilbert, Sandra, and Susan Gubar. *No Man's Land: The Place of the Woman Writer in the Twentieth Century, Vol. I: War of the Words*. New Haven: Yale UP, 1988.

———. *No Man's Land: The Place of the Woman Writer in the Twentieth Century, Vol. II: Sexchanges*. New Haven: Yale UP, 1989.

Grand, Sarah. *The Beth Book*. New York: D. Appleton, 1897.

———. *The Heavenly Twins*. New York: Cassell Publishing Co., 1893.

———. *Ideala*. New York: Optimus, 1894.

———. *Our Manifold Nature*. London: Heineman, 1894.

Huddleston, Joan. *Sarah Grand: A Bibliography*. St. Lucia, Australia: U of Queensland, 1979.

Pykett, Lyn. *The Improper Feminine: The Women's Sensation Novel and the New Woman Writing*. London: Routledge, 1992.

Rowlette, Robert. "Mark Twain, Sarah Grand, and *The Heavenly Twins*." *Mark Twain Journal* 16 (1972): 17–18.

Scott, Bonnie Kime. "Introduction." *The Gender of Modernism: A Critical Anthology*. Edited by Bonnie Kime Scott. Bloomington: Indiana UP, 1990.

Showalter, Elaine. *A Literature of Their Own: British Women Novelists from Brontë to Lessing*. Princeton: Princeton UP, 1977.

———. *Sexual Anarchy: Gender and Culture at the Fin de Siècle*. Harmondsworth: Penguin, 1990.

Stubbs, Patricia. *Women and Fiction: Feminism and the Novel, 1880–1920*. New York: Barnes and Noble, 1979.

Tuchman, Gaye. *Edging Women Out: Victorian Novelists, Publishers, and Social Change*. New Haven: Yale UP, 1989.

Waugh, Arthur. "Reticence in Literature." *Yellow Book* 1 (1894): 201–19.

## SELECTED SECONDARY SOURCES

Ann L. Ardis, *New Women, New Novels: Feminism and Early Modernism* (New Brunswick, N.J.: Rutgers UP, 1990); Linda Dowling, "The Decadent and the New Woman in the 1890's," *Nineteenth-Century Fiction* 33 (1979): 434–53; Sandra Gilbert and Susan Gubar, *No Man's Land: The Place of the Woman Writer in the Twentieth Century, Vol. II: Sexchanges* (New Haven: Yale UP, 1989); Lyn Pykett, *The Improper Feminine: The Women's Sensation Novel and the New Woman Writing* (London: Routledge, 1992); Elaine Showalter, *A Literature of Their Own: British Women Novelists from Brontë to Lessing* (Princeton: Princeton UP, 1977).

# MAPPING THE *"TERRA INCOGNITA"* OF WOMAN

## GEORGE EGERTON'S *KEYNOTES* (1893) AND NEW WOMAN FICTION

*Kate McCullough*

An immediate hit in both the United States and Britain, *Keynotes* (1893) marked George Egerton's entry into the scandalous world of British fin-de-siècle literature and established her as one of the leading figures of the period's New Woman writers. So successful that her publisher John Lane later named an entire series after it, *Keynotes* was followed by her other New Woman collections, *Discords* (1894), *Symphonies* (1897), and *Fantasias* (1898), and stands today as an early instance of modernist prose. Egerton's stories radically reshape the genre's form by emphasizing the use of fragments, details, and isolated incidents, and operate at the same time as a critique of woman's position in English and Irish culture. In her own day Egerton's work was frequently read as autobiographical and certainly she had plenty of lived experience of the sorts of "impropriety" for which her writing was criticized. Daughter of an Irish father and a Welsh mother, Egerton was born Mary Chavelita Dunne in Australia in 1859 and raised in Ireland in a large, Catholic, genteelly poor family. After nursing in London and working in New York, she spent two years (1887–1889) living in Norway as the lover of bigamist Henry Higginson, reading the Norwegian writers (such as Ibsen and Strindberg) who would later so greatly influence her writing. Subsequent to Higginson's death, she married George Egerton Clairemont (from whom she took her pseudonym), and began writing in order to support herself. By 1900 she had turned to writing mainly drama, at which she was never very successful, and while her fame as a 'nineties writer had peaked by 1896, Egerton herself lived until 1945. Culturally other in London, she was also, by virtue of her past, foreign to middle-class propriety. Her fiction draws on her Irish, Norwegian, and English experiences, but if inflected by cultural differences her heroines share a common position in being constrained by both their desires and their societies. *Keynotes* and *Discords* were reprinted together by Virago (1983) but are currently out of print.

## I. Desire, Gender, and Narrative Form

By the time that George Egerton published *Keynotes* in 1893 and *Discords* in 1894 to scandalized reviews, she already had over thirty years' experience of standing outside of the British status quo. Both culturally (half-Irish and half-Welsh) and geographically (born in Australia, raised in Ireland, schooled in Germany, employed in New York, and sequestered with a married lover in Norway), Egerton never quite fit the norms of British life or propriety. And certainly she did not identify with the Victorian notion of the "angel of the house." It is thus not surprising that, as Egerton focused on the figure of the woman, she found herself working out a complicated and sometimes contradictory tension between a universalized, essentialized "Woman" and historically and culturally specific "women."

When asked later (in "A Keynote to *Keynotes*") to reflect upon the composition of *Keynotes,* Egerton would write:

> I realized that in literature, everything had been better done by man than woman could hope to emulate. There was only one small plot left for her to tell: the *terra incognita* of herself, as she knew herself to be, not as man liked to imagine her—in a word to give herself away, as man had given himself away in his writings. . . . Unless one is androgynous, one is bound to look at life through the eyes of one's sex, to toe the limitations imposed on one by its individual physiological functions. (58)

Egerton here maps out what she sees as the province of women's writing, staking a claim to a territory for women which is wholly different from an already-mapped male territory. This is a province whose borders are delineated by biology. That is, the source of "womanhood" for Egerton here appears to be biological, an essence of woman grounded in the body, and it is that biological difference which both justifies and forms the subject matter of her writing. But having made this essentializing claim, Egerton goes on to contest, or at least to complicate, it, remarking, "I recognized that in the main, woman was the ever-untamed, unchanging, adapting herself as far as it suited her ends to male expectations, even if repression was altering her subtly"(58). The slide from adaptation to alteration is important here, for it illustrates the contradictions of Egerton's representations. For if Egerton begins by positing a universalized wild woman who only temporarily caters to male whims, she also identifies the cost of such adaptations. The very process of adapting, because it involves reshaping the self according to external cultural standards, alters this allegedly "unchanging" essence. Hence

Egerton reveals that ultimately even "Nature" is constructed by "Culture" and constructed, moreover, to serve the interests of "Culture."

The tension between the essentialized, passionate woman and her cultural constraints suggests the outsider's critique of dominant British gender codes and a concurrent desire to reclaim essentialism as a space from which she (and all women) can speak. Much of the power of Egerton's fiction comes from this tension. Positing inherent erotic and/or maternal desires and a female identity grounded in sexuality ("one is bound to look at life through the eyes of one's sex"), Egerton both essentializes female identity and marks it as responsive to social context, repeatedly examining the impact of "culture" on her women's "nature." Like other New Woman novelists, Egerton engages in a discourse of sexuality in her attempt to figure and refigure female identity. Defining sexuality as the main constituent of female identity, she represents female erotic sexuality as innate and "natural," but also foregrounds maternal desire, representing it as not merely instinctive but dangerous and potentially socially disruptive as well. But her stories go beyond merely essentializing female identity; they also examine the ways in which social systems shape, constrain and, rarely, support female identity. That is, female sexuality in Egerton's work retains its position as a "natural" source of bodily erotic pleasure, but her examination of this culturally bounded female sexuality focuses not only on its displacement into discursive forms, but also on its concrete and daily ramifications—the effect of pregnancy on the life of an unmarried woman, for example. Egerton's use of sexuality as discourse might thus be read as offering a language which thematizes female sexuality. Contextualizing women's sexual and emotional relationships, Egerton's fiction insists upon female solidarity, a position which is echoed in her frequent use of a narrative structured by one woman's telling of her story to another sympathetic woman.[1] By figuring women as sharing an inherent wildness which both produces a sense of sisterhood across class lines and at the same time puts women beyond the comprehension of men, Egerton privileges gender as the prime determinant of identity and social position by eliding all other forms—class, national, racial, religious—of difference.

## II. *"Why a woman will mate with a brute . . . and love him"*

Female desire and social constraints upon it are at issue in nearly every story in both *Keynotes* and *Discords*, particularly as enacted through marriage. As for so many New Woman writers, marriage represented for Egerton the institution which most forcefully repressed and reshaped female desire, the locale where legal, economic, religious, and social forces intersected to determine woman's position. *Keynotes* and *Discords* taken together obsessively play variations on the theme of marriage and its mutilation of female desire: the heroines are prevented from marrying the man they love ("Her Share"); marry the wrong man out of ignorance ("Virgin Soil") or disappointment ("An Empty Frame"); don't want the burden of conventional marriages ("The Regeneration of Two"); invert conventional roles of husband and wife ("The Spell of the White Elf"); suffer the consequences of leaving a marriage ("A Little Grey Glove"); or marry only for the sake of children ("Wedlock"). Egerton maps out this embattled terrain of marriage through a narrative form which eschews linear plots and proceeds instead via a series of vignettes, close-ups which frame the heroines in tight focus, a strategy which foregrounds the individual character's psychological interior. Possibly Egerton's most sophisticated and complex representation of the gendered power relations of marriage and their effect on female identity is *Keynotes'* "A Shadow's Slant," the second part of her "Under Northern Skies" sequence.

In another *Keynotes* story, the heroine warns that men can never understand "why a refined, physically fragile woman will mate with a brute, a mere male animal with primitive passions—and love him" (22): "A Shadow's Slant" might be read as Egerton's attempt to explain that mystery through redefining "love" as several conflicting relationships. More than merely portraying marriage as confinement for women, the story offers a psychological portrait of a marriage, exploring the relation of erotic desire and love to violence and power. As the story is concerned mainly with character study, the action—as in many Egerton stories—is slight, but revolves around the relationship of a brutal, sadistic husband and his wife, in a marriage predicated on domination and control. The story opens by establishing the marriage as based on violent power relations but goes on to rewrite the scenario as one in which the husband is pathetic, not powerful, and the wife resistant, not victimized. Egerton then foregrounds power's relation to class by introducing a band of gypsies. Her heroine identifies with the gypsies, but in the denouement, when forced to choose between the freedom of life with them and the confinement of her married life, she chooses to stay with her husband. Throughout the story Egerton details the ways in which power and violence feed into a certain kind of erotic desire and, further, how that nexus of forces is inflected by and inflects gendered identity.

The opening vignette explicitly grounds the marriage in erotic violence; as a nearby hawk captures its terrified prey, the couple, driving in the woods, stops:

> "Kiss me!" says the man who is driving, his voice is harsh and the eyes that scan her face have a lurid light in them, and as he speaks a smell of spirit mingles with the smell of the pine chips. Her lips tighten still more; she turns to obey. She has to rise up a little, he is very tall. His nose is powerful like a hawk's beak, and his beard is stirred by the breeze, and his eyes peer out from under their fringe of black lashes with a cruel passionate gleam. She almost touches his face but falls back from a rough shove—
>
> "No, keep your kiss and be damned to you!" (141)

He whips the horses and in the process flicks the woman as well: the narrative aligns her both with his horses and with the "little brown bird" preyed on by the hawk (140). His power over her is more than merely that of physical force, however. For while her rising to meet her taller companion serves as a spatial metaphor of their relative physical strengths, this power struggle clearly also operates on the level of will, as signaled by his demand and subsequent rejection of her act of submission. And it is not his will alone which is in play here; if her obedience is silent, the tightening of her lips implies that she is dominating some part of herself even as he dominates her. Further, if this is a battle of wills, it is also a power struggle specifically played out in the arena of the erotic: the "cruel passionate gleam" of the man's eyes codes his domination as erotically charged. And Egerton goes on in the story to emphasize that this power relation also operates in economic terms: the woman's hands are "laden with jeweled bands" (144), and she wears his "heavy gold band" (153), suggesting both wealth and prison fetters.

Yet after establishing the husband's domination of his wife, the third-person omniscient narrative redraws him as somewhat pathetic also, an interpretive transformation effected through a dialogue between the husband and wife, and one which prepares for the later revelation of the wife's sympathy. In one of her most radical narrative moves, Egerton lets the husband speak a monologue which combines need, love, force, power, and supplication and does so explicitly in terms of an erotic bond:

> "I love every inch of you. I'd kiss the ground under your feet. I know every turn of your little body, the slope of your shoulder, I that always liked women to have square shoulders—the swing of your hips when you walk. Hips! ha, ha! you haven't got any you scrap! and yet, by the Lord, I'd *lick* you like a dog" (slower, with emphasis), "and *you* don't care for me. You obey me, no matter what I ask . . . You wait on me, ay, no slave better, and yet—I can't get at you, near you;

that little soul of yours is as free as if I hadn't bought you, as if I didn't own you, as if you were not my chattel, my thing to do what I please with; do you hear" (with fury) "to degrade, to—to treat as *I please?* No you are not afraid, you little white-faced thing, you obey because you are strong enough to endure, not because you fear me . . . You pity me great God! pity *me*—me that could whistle any woman to heel—yes you pity me with all that great heart of yours because I am just a great, weak, helpless, drunken beast, a poor wreck!" (144–45)

The struggle of wills implied in the story's opening is here worked out in considerable detail. A catalogue of power relations, this passage is remarkable for its coterminous yet contradictory relationships: he loves her while she pities him; he owns her yet cannot control her "spirit"; he both abuses and desires her; she capitulates yet resists; both she and he emerge as dominating and dominated. Moreover, while Egerton draws here on the convention of female moral superiority and strength in sacrifice (familiar in domestic ideology manuals of earlier decades) she also recasts it in terms of an explicitly sexual submission. This is at once the most radical moment in the story and the most conventional, the moment which aligns the woman with sacrifice but also posits the woman as an agent who exercises a certain power (if only in resistance), a force of will of her own.

The introduction of a band of gypsies into the narrative and the story's resolution which follows it further complicate this portrait of the woman by aligning her with the gypsies. "Gypsy" is always gendered female in Egerton's work and is a term of praise, connoting for her a naturalness, freedom, and passion which is true to itself and outside of both society's limiting conventions and man's limited understanding.[2] Thus the imaging of her heroines as gypsies, like those heroines' metaphoric transformation into birds, horses, or (in the passage above) dogs to be whistled "to heel," works to essentialize "woman" further, for the gypsy figures an inherent and "natural" wildness in woman, what Egerton calls, in "A Cross Line," "the eternal wildness, the untamed primitive savage temperament that lurks in the mildest, best woman . . . . this primeval trait . . . an untameable quantity that may be concealed but is never eradicated by culture" (22). Both the gypsy and the image of the animal/nature, of course, figure the woman as at best marginalized in relation to culture, at worst (as in the image of the dog brought to heel) inferior to it. If all female identity is defined by an inherent wildness (constituted in part by unmediated passion), then to embrace that identity fully is to accept a marginalized social position. At the same time such a usage of gypsy (as signaled by its structural alignment with animals) replicates the status of gypsy as (inferior) cultural other, even as (and in part because) the story goes on to elide the specific terms of this othering (ethnic, socioeconomic) by conflating it with the othering of women on the basis of gender. Woman's essential wildness cuts across and to some extent erases class lines and so functions as a grounds for community among women. Essentialism thus becomes a politically viable strategy for Egerton, even as it involves material oversimplifications: it is a means by which she can posit solidarity among women and also give women a status different in kind from man's, and so more difficult to appropriate.

Linking the heroine of "A Shadow's Slant" to gypsies thus allows Egerton to image her as simultaneously victim and agent in a way which underscores both the heroine's passion and her consequently marginalized, caged, and relatively powerless social position. The woman is described watching the gypsies dance: "she with a crimson shawl drawn round her spare shoulders, and a splash of colour in her thin cheeks holds one hand tightly pressed over her breast—to still what? What does the music rouse inside that frail frame, what parts her lips and causes her eyes to glisten and the thin nostrils to quiver? Is there aught in common between that slight figure with its jewelled hands and its too heavy silken gown, and those healthy Zingari vagabonds?" (147).

This is obviously a rhetorical question: the woman, even trapped in the silks which bespeak her class and social position, speaks Romany and exchanges sympathetic glances with one of the gypsy girls. Even the old gypsy fortune-teller recognizes their affinity and the unnaturalness of the woman's position, predicting that it will be seven years before "the flag is half-mast, and the cage opens" (148). This scene can be read as an affirmation of commonality among women across class lines (due to their shared female identity/passion) and so a denial of class difference. At the same time, however, it must also be read as confirming the impact of class, which intervenes to differentiate the woman from the gypsies, leaving her isolated in her privileged class position.

But the woman is not merely a trapped bird: the story's denouement shows her as an active agent choosing her fate. Gazing from the sleeping husband to the moonlit gypsy camp, she dresses herself as a gypsy and dreams of freedom, resolving to enact literally her figurative solidarity with the gypsies, saying, "No one would know, no one would dream of it! I would soon get brown!" (151). In the end, however, she chooses not to abandon the lily-white space of the middle-class wife: why she chooses to stay involves several factors, and indicates just how complex a character Egerton has drawn. The woman is motivated in part by the traditional nineteenth-century female notion of redemptive sacrifice: the man needs her and has earlier made her promise never to leave him. The story emphasizes, however, that this is not merely a personal decision but rather one modeled on a culturally enforced and sanctioned female behavior. In the process of making her choice, we are told, the woman

> steps away . . . irresolution is expressed in her face, her head is thrust forward, her fingers spread out unconsciously. . . . She glances across the floor, some shelves are to be nailed up, one of them is leant against the wardrobe door. As she hesitates she notices that the shadow of it and the half-closed door throws a long cross almost to her feet. She folds her hands involuntarily—a whimper from the bed, a frightened call— (152)

The image of the cross, coupled with the childlike vulnerability of the sleeping man, imply a scenario which demands the folded hands of female sacrifice: the script of this cultural play predetermines her part.

Yet the woman is not merely performing a part; she is also motivated by her own conflicting love/hate for her husband. She is irresolute in the passage above because she is studying the sleeping man. And if she "shudders" at the "lewd word" he mutters and steadily examines his "cruel" mouth and "hateful," "ugly" hands (152), she begins by noting, "What a magnificent head it is, and how repellent!" (151), and it is from her point of view that the man is described. "The tossed black locks with their silver streaks lie scattered on the pillow," the description opens, implying venerability as well as the vulnerability of old age. "The ear suggests vigorous animalism," the description continues, "the nose is powerful, the broad forehead shines whitely, and the long lashes curl upward as those of a child." Energy, the natural state of the animal, and strength combine with the reminder of childhood vulnerability to render the man attractive to the woman as well as repulsive, appealing to both an erotic passion and a maternal sense in her. At the same time, this attraction is at least partly grounded in her fascination with (desire for?) his power, and she can only admire him when he is an abstract force, asleep and so no longer dangerous. Her maternal "instincts" function here both to empower her (in her recognition of his vulnerability) and, in conjunction with her erotic desire, to disempower her by keeping her tied to the man. Her conflicting desires shape both her choices and her identity, leading her to deny her "natural" wildness. But unlike the nineteenth-century domestic ideology which would see passion tamed as a lady's moral victory, Egerton represents this decision as something close to,

but not quite, a surrender. Refusing to reduce its heroine to a single motivating element, Egerton's narrative is here a modern one precisely because
it posits a heroine with a split, fragmented identity which is grounded in a
sexuality inflected by violence and power struggles. Egerton posits a female
sexuality strong enough to endure societal pressures but troubled by internal conflict, and uses her narrative to refigure female desire as conflicted and
inherent, staking her own representational claim and dissecting the cultural
contexts which shape her female characters.

### III. *Transgressive Understanding*

In a similar move, Egerton's discussion of the fallen woman, that favorite
literary type, figures her not as metaphor of either female evil or,
contrastingly, female sexual victimization, but rather as a complex individual
woman with a specific history who becomes one half of an instructive friendship. [3] Although *Keynotes* offers a divorced heroine ("I figure as an adultress
in every English-speaking paper," she says [112], in a syntax which suggests
both the force of the cultural shorthand of "adultress" and its inadequacy
as a representation of the woman it describes), it is in *Discords* that Egerton
most fully individuates and interrogates the type and function of the fallen
or kept woman, as well as such an individual's motives, desires, and relation to maternity. While the type appears elsewhere in this collection, this
portrait is drawn in most detail in "Gone Under," where Egerton's sympathetic portrait of the fallen woman as mother was recognized and quickly
deplored by the critics. *The Athenaeum* review of *Discords,* for instance,
announced that "'Gone Under' and 'Wedlock' are simply revolting studies
of drink and lust and murder (there is no use in mincing matters), and should
never have been printed" (*Athenaeum* 23 [1895] 375). Egerton "printed"
her tale for clearly didactic reasons, though its lessons may well have been
part of its shock value. Detailing in "Gone Under" the heroine Edith Grey's
slow descent—her process of going under—Egerton implies that the telling
of the story by Grey to her female listener refigures the trope of the fallen
woman and, potentially, culture's response to it. The fact that a woman enters this discourse in order to tell her own story constitutes for Egerton a
disruption of what might be seen as the regulatory function of sexuality. For
Egerton this is a strategic and liberatory, rather than coercive, deployment
of sexuality: the difference lies in who is doing the speaking.

Like so many Egerton stories, Grey's tale is told to the audience of
another woman, the plain, poor Irish "girl" she meets on the steamer that
both take from New York back to London. This framing of Grey's history
is itself central to "Gone Under," as it signals not only a notion of female

solidarity but also a discursive model for understanding. That the recipient of Grey's tale is characterized as both Irish and a girl (in contrast to Grey, who is always referred to as a woman) is significant. Egerton consistently valorizes the Irish in her fiction, celebrating them in fairly conventional terms as sensitive, poetic, and good-humored, and thus predisposed to a higher level of compassion and empathy than the English. Their cultural identity, however, also marks the Irish as other to British bourgeois culture, and it is this heritage of combined sensitivity and marginality, along with her economic status as a working woman, that enables the girl to sympathize with the outcast Grey. At the same time, the term "girl" signals the Irish woman's lack of experience relative to Grey, a condition of innocence which Egerton sets up in order to stage an education of the girl by means of Grey's story. For the narrative rehearses the woman's "fall" from an innocent sixteen-year-old to the desperate alcoholic she is upon meeting the girl, to her final descent onto the streets of London. It is in certain ways a conventional progression, but the causes of the woman's deterioration are drawn in great detail and the story focuses both on Grey's narrative and on the girl's consequent change in attitude toward the woman, a move from generous sympathy to a more sophisticated understanding of the forces which shape Grey's identity and situation.

Falling into one of the nineteenth century's standard discursive categories of the prostitute, Edith Grey is seduced when she is young and ignorant, and as a result slips into a life which is economically more privileged than was her youth.[4] She tells the unnamed girl, "I am not bad at heart. . . . I was only sixteen when he took me, I was a silly fool of a girl, and I had no one belonging to me. I thought it was a grand thing. Even his relatives didn't know I wasn't married to him" (96). But this play-acting of a comfortable and privileged marriage masks a power differential between seducer and seduced:

> "He petted and spoiled me, and dressed me like a doll, and whenever I wanted to learn anything he laughed at me. There were times when I wanted something better, I used to tire of it all: but I was always a little afraid of him; the set we mixed in was a fast one, and I learnt no good, and the women I met were worse than the men—"
> (96–97)

Like the relationship in "A Shadow's Slant," this is a relationship predicated on a power hierarchy and maintained in part through fear. "He" has the economic control, a control which enables him to infantilize her, keep her uneducated, and so limit her options.

What he cannot control, however, is her "maternal instinct" (100), a desire which operates throughout Egerton's texts as essential and essentially good. By locating this maternal desire in the kept woman Egerton conflates the categories of mother (shaped by the image of the middle-class Angel in the House) and prostitute, and seemingly offers the conventional trope of redemptive maternity. But while Grey is "crazy with delight" at discovering her pregnancy (97), her lover reinforces the mutual exclusivity of the categories of mistress and mother. Grey recalls that he "was as angry as ever he could be. . . . He said it would spoil me; he didn't want it; it would make complications; he had no intention of marrying me; we were quite well as we were—we had a dreadful scene" (97). And while she defies him, he asserts his cultural and economic power by taking her to a midwife, (the predictably French) Madame Rachelle, who kills the newly born infant.

But Egerton's story does not end here: in a disruptive twist it moves beyond merely replaying the image of the fallen woman reformed by maternity. Instead, it makes this maternal instinct the provocation of the real crisis in Edith Grey's life, the crisis which makes her aware, finally, that impersonating a wife is not the same—legally, socially, or economically—as actually having a legal claim to the title. At the death of the child the woman sinks into "every dissipation" (100), as a result both of being denied access to the role of the maternal, and of her realization of the social and economic system which silences her while it allows the man to have the child killed. When the listening girl objects to this part of the woman's story, exclaiming, "I would have had them up for murder. I would never have rested—," Grey corrects her naïveté, explaining, "So you think, but I guess you wouldn't. Money can do everything; the certificate of death said it was still born, and it was signed by a medical man. It was only last year the death of a schoolgirl of good family caused such scandal that the place was closed; but too many big people were implicated to make a fuss, and Madame Rachelle escaped" (100). The legal and medical systems work against women such as Grey, women who have neither the power of the privileged gender identity of men nor the protection of a class identity of the "schoolgirl of good family." Instead, as Grey recognizes, systemic power serves the interests of the already powerful, implicitly condoning the actions of "big people" like her lover. "Culture" imposes itself upon the "nature" of the maternal instinct, deciding which women will be allowed to play that most "natural" of all female roles: the mother.

Once Grey realizes her position and the fact that her lover will allow no crossing of boundaries from mistress to mother, she herself internalizes that split by replicating her "fall," taking lovers other than the father of the child. Her passion and recklessness were awakened after the death of the child, she recalls, and the man was her "only check" (102), so that when he temporarily leaves town she takes a new lover. Her description of this event is fraught with remorse, but suggests both a loss of self-control and a concurrent assertion of erotic control:

> I was lonely and wretched, and I don't know what madness possessed me—you can't understand. One just gets insane, and lets oneself be carried away. I think the devil gets hold of one. I tried to attract him; there was a kind of excitement in it . . . all through there was a kind of fascination in the danger, though we didn't really care a bit for one another. (103)

Egerton implies that once Grey is forced to surrender her potential identity as mother (and the cultural prestige it implies), she purposely steps into the space of the fallen woman, claiming the limited power of erotic appeal as the only kind of power left available to her. Grey later loses "control" over herself again and, possessed by "something," takes another lover, an action she later explains by claiming that "*one stifles the memory of the first with the excitement of the second*" (104, emph. in original). That is, the gain of operating as an agent with (albeit limited) power helps stifle the loss of respectable status and the knowledge that it can never be regained. Further, representing these two men as the first and the second, the woman draws a distinction between them and the father of her child—the two men are not her first and second lovers, but rather the first and second for whom she considers herself morally culpable. In her relationship with the child's father, on the other hand, she had not yet, in her own eyes at least, traded the position of respectable mother for that of fallen woman/temptress. And while the child's father, as the girl points out, "taught" Grey to "be as" she is (104), his pride is wounded by her behavior, and he reestablishes his control by punishing her with isolation and solitude, threatening to abandon her entirely if she disobeys him. But Grey cannot be recuperated as loyal mistress, let alone respectable woman, and the story ends with the girl, three years later, meeting Grey who is nearly dead and living on the street.

While Grey's trajectory through the story is toward a predictably painful end, the girl who tracks this progress moves in quite a different direction and provides a subtle commentary on the social categories which ultimately destroy Grey. Portrayed as initially quite naïve, the girl sympathizes with Edith Grey because she, too, is alone, and because they are both women (94). She observes, however, that the other passengers, at the mention of "Mrs. Grey," "purse their lips, look virtuous, and change the sub-ject" (93). Slowly she realizes that bad reputations are contagious; after help-ing the ill Mrs. Grey, the girl becomes "conscious of a difference in her [own] treatment . . . a shrinking on the part of the women, a touch of insolence in the glance of the men. It hurts her a little" (95). Finally she comes to under-stand that Edith Grey's position is unchangeable partly because of society's policing of its own gender categories. At the end of the voyage she tells the two maiden ladies who have shunned both her and Grey, "She is a lost soul, I tried to do what I could for her. You are old, the others were married, you had nothing to lose, and yet you held back. It is good, untempted women like you, whose virtue makes you selfish, who help to keep women like her as they are" (109). Egerton here stresses that women themselves help to en-force their own oppression by replicating cultural condemnations of their "fallen" sisters.

The girl, however, not only rejects this hypocritical position, but also moves beyond her original, fairly conventional position of Christian pity for the Magdalene to a more complex understanding both of Grey's motives and the girl's own position of privilege. She begins by positing love as the source of Grey's fall, insisting that Grey must have cared for her seducer (96), and asking anxiously, "[b]ut he was really fond of you?" (97). She then aban-dons these romantic assumptions but still posits an escape for Grey through work, only to have Grey tell her, "what could I do? . . . I haven't learnt a single useful thing. I know how to attract men . . . that is all" (101). Next, told of Grey's first affair, the girl "is dumb with pained realisation; it is her first actual contact with a problem of such a nature," and "so little does she grasp it" (103), that she advises Grey with conventional Christian wisdom to confess her sins to the father of the child and to ask his forgiveness. But as the girl begins to understand the reality of Grey's social and economic position she also begins to reflect on their implications for her own life. Re-alizing that the circumstances of her life, however difficult, have left her with more options than Grey, she also comes to recognize the structural similar-ity of their positions: both are locked into a system which narrowly defines and harshly judges women's behavior. Ultimately, then, while horrified at the revelation of the other lovers, the girl finally abandons conventional middle-class propriety as an inappropriate standard in this situation and tells Grey, "I have no right to sit in judgement; I have never been tempted. I sim-ply can't understand it. I am as ready to help you now as before" (105). In the end, the girl acknowledges that she could be put in the same position of "temptation" as Grey was and, by implication, judged by the same system. She concurrently sees the individual history of Edith Grey and the larger

cultural forces which define her and all women's position, a dual vision signaled by her response to finding Grey's tattered shoe in the street:

> to her to whom life had brought a deep understanding of its misery
> and makeshifts, it is a mute epitome of a tragedy of want; and through
> her great agony of distress the narrow practical question forced it-
> self in a comically persistent way: Had the poor weary foot without
> this frail covering even the sorry shelter of a stocking to protect it?
> (113–14)

There is no protection for Edith Grey—"Gone Under" draws a portrait of
a woman hopelessly outmatched by the cultural codes which define her[5]—
but for the girl there is at least a transformative understanding, a growth in
(self-) knowledge for a woman which results from the discursive resistance
of Edith Grey's tale.

IV. *Murderous Maternity*

> I have known many women, and I think the *only divine* fibre in a
> woman is her maternal instinct. Every good quality she has is conse-
> quent or coexistent with that. Suppress it, and it turns to a fibroid,
> sapping all that is healthful and good in her nature, for I have seen
> it. . . . Every woman ought to have a little child, if only as a moral
> educator. I have often thought that a woman who mothers a bastard,
> and endeavours bravely to rear it decently, is more to be commended
> than the society wife who contrives to shirk her motherhood. *She* is
> at heart loyal to the finest fibre of her being, the deep, underlying
> generic instinct, the "mutter-drang," that lifts her above and beyond
> all animalism, and fosters the sublimest qualitites of unselfishness and
> devotion.

> —"Gone Under" (100–1)

While defending the fallen woman's right to be a mother, the "girl"
in "Gone Under" offers the above defense of motherhood, a defense which
constructs maternal love and desire as innate and redemptive, and in so doing constructs an alternate scale of human value. The maternal here is
marked as superior to both the mere animal (which may be free and natural but is also incapable of personal loyalty and devotion) and the society
wife (whose conventional class privilege here becomes not the marker of sta-

tus but rather the cover for maternal neglect). This position is reiterated throughout Egerton's fiction, for she, like many New Woman writers, valorized what seemed like the inevitable link between womanhood and maternity. But while *Keynotes'* "A Cross Line" ends with the heroine's joyful realization that she is pregnant and *Discords'* "Gone Under" mourns the lost opportunity for maternity, there are, strangely, very few *actual* mothers in either *Keynotes* or *Discords*. Egerton's fiction ultimately displays an uneasiness with maternity, so that while seemingly valorizing it, the stories also represent her fears of it fairly directly.

*Keynotes* contains one mother, in "the Spell of The White Elf" a woman who is a writer and the family breadwinner who leaves her housekeeping to her husband, George, who stays at home, and to her housekeeper, Belinda. Thus if the story celebrates maternity and the difference it makes to these adoptive parents' lives, it also depicts a mother who has given over most of the practicalities of the child-rearing to a spouse and servant: "[i]t made such a difference in the evenings," she tells her female listener, "I used to hurry home,—I was on the staff of the *World's Review* just then—and it was so jolly to see the quaint little phiz smile up when I went in" (87). More like a conventional father than mother, she recalls with amusement the housekeeper's and husband's territorial disputes over the child, recalling that "Belinda was quite jealous of George. She said 'Master worrited in an out, an' interfered with everything, she never seen a man as knew so much about babies, not for one as never 'ad none of 'is own'" (87). But while Belinda resents what she views as the husband's interference, she is not, tellingly, jealous of the woman herself. The maternity which Egerton celebrates here thus has a symbolic rather than a literal status: typically it is the *idea* of maternity this heroine and others embrace more than the actuality of it.

Part of this idea involves personal redemption, but Egerton also figures maternity as central to the redemption of humanity. Reflecting contemporary interest in genetics, Egerton views mothers as central to breeding and cultivating improved versions of mankind. The heroine of "The Regeneration of Two," for instance, refutes St. Paul's doctrine of man's superiority to woman by telling her pastor that woman's "maternity lifts her above him [man] every time. Man hasn't kept the race going, the burden of centuries has lain on the women. He has fought, and drunk, and rioted, lusted, and satisfied himself, whilst she has rocked the cradle and ruled the world, borne the sacred burden of her motherhood, carried in trust the future of the races" (207). Maternity, once again disembodied and idealized, thus serves the double purpose of elevating the mother and, through her, the entire race.

Theories of heredity also inform *Discords'* "Wedlock" in a curious way: a bricklayer explains to his co-worker that his own wife drinks because of heredity, stating, "It woz then I came acrorst a book on 'ereditty,' wot comes down from parents to children. . . . At fust I woz real mad, I gave 'er a black eye onst; but then I came acrorst that book . . . an' I found out about 'er folk, an' I see az 'ow she couldn't 'elp it" (121). He amends this genealogical causality, however, by noting that he had six happy years of marriage before his wife began drinking, and explains that she did so only after the death of their son: environment in the shape of maternal loss provokes what heredity enables. Egerton uses this vignette of the bricklayer's wife to frame and implicitly to comment upon the main action of this story: the history of "Mrs. Jones," another mother who drinks. But curiously, for a writer who celebrates maternity, Egerton's only portrait of an actual mother represents the maternal instinct as fueling violence: "Wedlock" is the story of how Mrs. Jones comes to murder her three step-children. It is remarkable as much for the specificity of its detail, the building point by point of the environment which drives Mrs. Jones to murder, as for the intensity of the violent passion springing from the maternal. For if the bricklayer's tale suggests that alcoholism in women is a cross-class problem and is caused by thwarted maternity, Mrs. Jones's narrative locates the sources of both her drinking and her violence in the specific cultural codes defining maternity.

Mrs. Jones, in a familiar narrative strategy, tells her tale to her sympathetic lady-boarder, claiming, "I never knew a woman drink for the love of it like men, there's most always a cause" (130). Like Edith Grey, as a single woman she was seduced and became pregnant. Unlike Grey, however, Mrs. Jones bore a healthy daughter whom she gave to her married step-sister to raise while she, an ex-cook, "went out to service again" (130). Mrs. Jones emphasizes that this move was economically motivated and, in fact, went against her maternal desires for the child, saying, "I used to see 'er onst or twice a week. But she was fonder of 'er nor me, an' I couldn't bear it, it made me mad, I was jealous of every one as touched 'er" (130). It is this fear of being supplanted in her daughter Susie's heart that prompts Mrs. Jones eventually to marry the widower Jones: "'e promised me that I could 'ave 'er if I married 'im. I didn't want to marry, I only wanted 'er, an' I couldn't 'ave 'er with me, an' 'e promised . . . 'e swore as 'ow I could 'ave 'er" (130–31). Maternal love is thus represented as a natural instinct beyond—and indeed here in conflict with—the law, but ironically, Mrs. Jones contradicts her instinctual preference against marriage in an effort to legally fulfill her maternal instinct.

But in a situation analogous to that of Edith Grey and her seducer, social codes as enforced by the husband deny Mrs. Jones her maternal place despite all: he will not let her have her child. Having married her to help his business (she is a cook, he is a barman) and "be a mother to the kids as well" (119), he distinguishes between his three children from his first marriage and her illegitimate child. Mrs. Jones recalls that he "says 'e never meant to keep it. . . . 'E says I would neglect 'is children, an' 'e called 'er names an' says 'e won't 'ave no bastard round with 'is children. That made me 'ate 'em first, nasty yellow things—" (191). Her instinctual desires will not be placated by surrogate motherhood: instead of loving all four children she comes to hate his.[6] When she discovers that her husband has hidden from her news of Susie's impending death and she reaches her step-sister's to find her child already dead, she is left with only a necklace of the child's and her own pain.

In a finely honed conclusion, Egerton then shows how such a pain can turn to violence, and a violence which, like the maternal instinct which prompts it, is powerful but outside of the law and so sparks no remorse. The closing image of the story shows the woman sitting asleep:

> Her hands are crimson as if she has dipped them in dye . . . and she is fast asleep; and she smiles as she sleeps, for Susie is playing in a meadow, a great meadow crimson with poppies, and her blue eyes smile with glee, and her golden curls are poppy-crowned, and her little white feet twinkle as they dance, and her pinked-out grave frock flutters, and her tiny waxen hands scatter poppies, blood-red poppies, in handfuls over three open graves. (144)

The maternal figures here as enormously powerful, but threatening to mother, child, and cultural norms as well; Mrs. Jones smiles at being reunited with her daughter, but the daughter is dead and reunion is only in a dream. If the woman in "A Shadow's Slant" infantilizes her sleeping husband by pitying him, thus rendering him less powerful and terrifying, and Edith Grey's lover infantilizes her in refusing to allow her to accede to maternal power, Mrs. Jones's maternal power is so strong that it cannot merely be rechanneled by cultural norms, and becomes, in fact, explosively violent instead. Egerton's female protagonists' instincts may be boxed and reshaped by culture, but remain as forceful motivating elements of the women's identity, unwittingly furthering society's manipulation of women by self-destructively turning against themselves.

Calling for representations of female erotic and maternal desire instead of displacements of them, Egerton not only defines these desires as constituent of female identity, but also reads them both as coexistent within an individual woman and as potentially both furthering and restraining women's resistance to dominant cultural codes. That is, maternal instinct may lead a woman to resist society's constraints, but may also lead her to destroy herself. Laying claim to certain essentialized notions of femininity, Egerton's texts locate the danger and the power of such essentialism in maternity and pose her heroines both in direct opposition to and ironically complicit with what she views as the dangers of "culture." This contradiction results from Egerton's selective use of dominant cultural ideals of womanhood; her claiming, in a fully conventional way, a valorized and essentialized notion of maternity but at the same time insisting that all women have erotic desires as well as maternal ones. This leads her into a peculiar double bind in which she on the one hand emphasizes the material forces (legal, economic, cultural) which determine women's lives, while on the other hand she elides material differences among women in order to underscore a commonality of gender. As a result her narratives are able to rework female identity, but at a cost. A marginalized speaker in British culture, Egerton launched a critique of its gender norms, and her essentializing of woman provided her with a space from which to speak. But, clearly, resistance has its costs and reworking dominant ideology still leaves one playing by the dominant culture's rules: Egerton's strategic essentialism allowed her to offer a new representation of female identity, but only by erasing the other sorts of differences among women which were so crucial in shaping her own life.

## Notes

1. See, for example, in *Keynotes* "Now Spring Has Come" and "The Spell of the White Elf" and in *Discords* "Her Share," "Gone Under," and, to a lesser extent, "Wedlock" and "Virgin Soil."

2. The image of gypsies as signifiers of freedom is obviously not unique to Egerton—Maggie Tulliver's running away with the gypsies in *The Mill On The Floss* (1860) is only one of many instances of this literary trope. What is more original in Egerton's gypsy, however, is its functioning as signifier not only of female passion but a *consequent* marginalization.

3. At the end of her career as a short story writer, however, Egerton moved away from this narrative technique to a narrative drawing far more heavily on metaphor, archetype, and fairy tale. While her third collection, *Symphonies* (1897), followed the model of *Keynotes* and *Discords,* her final collection, as signaled by its name, *Fantasias* (1898), departs entirely from a detailed and specific rendering of women's lives. That collection's story "The Mandrake Venus," for instance, is an extended conceit in which the title character stands as a symbol for the prostitute. In a typically veiled allusion to prostitution and its structural position and necessity within patriarchal culture, one of the "harlots" says, "it's all in the interests of morality. . . . Nations change, creeds arise and die; the house of the Mandrake Venus is alone invincible . . . we are the great world sore, the serpent coiled round the homestead of men. Your wise men say we are the victims necessary to your perfected system of human relationship. I know not; I only suffer, and sow the flower of revenge, or death, and downfall in the youth of mankind." *Fantasias* (London: John Lane, The Bodley

Head, 1898): 70–71.

4. For more on conventional nineteenth-century discourses on prostitution, see Judith R. Walkowitz. The most prominent and influential texts on prostitution were produced by W. R. Gregg and William Acton in the 1850s.

5. "The Woman," the third part of *Discords'* "A Psychological Moment in Three Periods," offers a more hopeful view of the kept woman's future. Interestingly, this story is told from the kept woman's point of view: she is the agent rather than the object of the narrative.

6. Elaine Showalter quite rightly points out that this hatred works as a displacement of anger from a powerful enemy to a less powerful one. See pages 210–15 for a brief discussion of Egerton.

## Works Cited

Acton, William. *Functions and Disorders of the Reproductive Organs in Childhood, Youth, Adult Age, and Advanced Life: Considered in Their Physiological, Social, and Moral Relations.* London: John Churchill, 1857.

———. *Prostitution Considered in Its Moral, Social, and Sanitary Aspects in London and Other Large Cities.* London: John Churchill, 1857. Reprint of 2nd ed. (1870), MacGibbon and Kee, 1968.

Egerton, George [Mary Chavelita Dunne Bright]. "A Keynote to *Keynotes.*" *Ten Contemporaries: Notes toward Their Definitive Bibliography.* Edited by John Gawsworthy. London: Ernest Benn, 1932.

———. *Keynotes & Discords.* London: John Lane, 1893 and 1894. Reprint. Virago, 1983.

Gregg, W.R. "Prostitution." *Westminster Quarterly Review* 53 (1850): 448–506.

Showalter, Elaine. *A Literature of Their Own: British Women Novelists from Brontë to Lessing.* London: Virago, 1978.

Walkowitz, Judith R. *Prostitution and Victorian Society: Women, Class and the State.* New York: Cambridge UP, 1980.

White, Terence de Vere, ed. *A Leaf from the Yellow Book: The Correspondence of George Egerton.* London: Richards Press, 1958.

## Selected Secondary Sources

Contemporary reviews of Egerton's work include: "Discords," *Athenaeum* 23 (23 March 1895): 305; "Keynotes," *Bookman* (December 1893): 87; "Keynotes," *Review of Reviews* 8 (July-December 1893): 671; and J.A. Noble, "The Fiction of Sexuality," *Contemporary Review* 67 (1895): 490–98. Critical assessments include: Ann Ardis, *New Women, New Novels: Feminism and Early Modernism* (New Brunswick: Rutgers UP, 1990); A.R. Cunningham, "The 'New Woman' Fiction of the 1890s," *Victorian Studies* 17 (1973): 177–86; Gail Cunningham, *The New Woman and the Victorian Novel* (New York: Macmillan, 1978); Lloyd Fernando, "'New Women' in the Late Victorian Novel* (State College: Penn State UP, 1977); Wendell V. Harris, "Egerton: Forgotten Realist," *Victorian Newsletter* 33 (1968): 31–35; Wendell V. Harris, "John Land's *Keynote* Series and the Fiction of the 1890's," *PMLA* 83 (1968): 1407–13; Elaine Showalter, *A Literature of Their Own: British Women Novelists from Brontë to Lessing* (London: Virago Press, 1978).

# "TRANSITION TIME"

## THE POLITICAL ROMANCES OF MRS. HUMPHRY WARD'S
## MARCELLA (1894) AND SIR GEORGE TRESSADY (1896)

*Judith Wilt*

The niece of Matthew Arnold and wife of the art critic of the *Times* signed most of her many critical, religious, political, and scholarly works "Mary A. Ward," and her 27 novels "Mrs. Humphry Ward": a temperament and a set of achievements both progressive and conservative marked the life of this hard-working, best-selling, and influential writer. During a long Victorian/Edwardian life (1851–1920) Mary Ward carried the torch for liberal humanism, an often heterodox Christian Socialism, and Arnoldian "culture" in a series of extremely popular novels continuing the traditions of George Eliot and George Meredith. Her *Robert Elsmere* (1888) was the blockbuster of the century: the clamored-for quick reprint of her *Marcella* (1894) was, as biographer John Sutherland remarks, "the torpedo that sunk the three-decker and . . . stripped Mudie of his dictatorial powers." *Elsmere* is still in print (U of Nebraska P and others); *Marcella* and her fine tragic romance *Helbeck of Bannisdale* (1898) intermittently so. During the first decade of the twentieth century she was simultaneously raising funds for and organizing important progressive educational and social reforms through the Passmore Edwards Settlement House in London's East End, and heading up the Anti-Suffrage League. She remained steadfastly attached to the "separate spheres" ideology while she served as breadwinner for her family, conversed with prime ministers and presidents, and (in her sixties) became the first woman journalist to visit the Allied Front, in preparation for two books about the war. Her popularity as a novelist declined after 1910 but her reputation remained formidable enough to attract the anxious attacks of a new generation of feminist writers like Rebecca West and Virginia Woolf.

Like the novels of Sir Walter Scott the novels of Mrs. Humphry Ward constitute a Romance of Property[1]—a laying hold on, a defining and transmission of, an endangered national and racial inheritance through the manipulation of sexuality and fertility. Between *Waverley: Tis Sixty Years Since,* begun in 1808, and *Marcella,* published in 1894, the imperatives and formulas of romance have changed little, the definition and character of property, a great deal. And the "inheritor" most of all.

No less than *Waverley, Marcella* and its sequel, *Sir George Tressady,* position themselves deliberately in "the transition time" (*M* 197),[2] the English movement from aristocracy to meritocracy to democracy, looking anxiously past the myth of Divine Right to rationalize new concepts of ownership, stewardship, of land, work, wealth, influence.

In *Marcella* a passionate but wayward girl sets herself in opposition to the political and gender structures of power and ownership pressing her toward marriage with "the Master," but her seriously engaged relationship with socialist and labor theory and its practice with the laboring poor, simply better prepares her for her inevitable final march down the aisle with her still conservative, though enlightened and chastened, aristocrat. In *Sir George Tressady* an intelligent but melancholy young gentleman living upon his coal revenues enters politics out of no conviction, following the pattern of his gender and class, and finds himself fatally entangled with Marcella Boyce Maxwell, who seduces him to political and moral conviction in a relationship which virtually constitutes a Romance.

*Marcella* is the first of Ward's novels clearly designed as a Romance of Property: *Sir George Tressady* her first sequel (the second and last, fifteen years later, is *The Case of Richard Meynell* [1911], sequel to *Elsmere*). The purpose of a sequel, that most primitive form of the desire which Rachel Blau DuPlessis named "writing beyond the ending,"[3] is to break the frame of the composed inheritance, the established marriage, of the parent novel, issuing as its bastard child, its legitimate child, its double, or, as we shall see in *Sir George Tressady,* some combination of these. Writing beyond the ending reflects a desire not only for continuation/development of the established world, for "history," but also for a review, even revision, of issues sublimated in the compositional process of closure.

Both psychologically and socially, closure in traditional narrative tends inevitably to select one powerful strand of narrative, Romance—the finding of the self's goal in another, or in some high social/philosophical purpose—over the other powerful strand of narrative, which is Quest—the self constructed in (and unselfed without) seeking. Mary Ward's novels hew firmly to the traditions of Romance narrative, but we can see in them the outlines of a still contemporary conundrum. In an age when the female psyche presses its claim to the pleasures and the responsibilities of the unresting quest for selfhood, the male psyche, numb under its centuries-long monopoly of the quest, struggles with a crippling doubt of the viability and worth of this essential "property," the self.

Meanwhile, for reformers of all sorts, the concept of "property" now wavers and expands from its feudal locus in the land of the Lord, through places and processes around a globe made intimate through the ideologies of Empire, to the inmost domain of "self realisation." These new meanings of property both allow for the expansion of individuals' rights over newly defined property (like "labor") and, of course, allow the ideology of property itself to survive with relatively little change. Individual and Parliamentary votes, precious property won through the century, can award the sanctity of self-possessed property to the bodies and the work of sweated tailors in London and blackened miners in West Mercia. For Edward Hallin, the prophet of *Marcella,* property is exactly "self-realisation," "the fuller human opportunity"; personal possession of this body and this work is the "discipline" that focuses and brings to birth the soul's "capacity" (*M* 412).[4] As such, he argues, personal possession must be extended more widely in every age by "the pressure of an emancipating legislation" that "strikes off the shackles, one by one," from every form of property until possession itself is redeemed.

How is this to be done? The experiments of peoples are ongoing. The experiment of fiction cleaves closely to the paradoxes of Romance, the finding of freedom in service, self-surrender as self-possession, passion crossing boundaries which return again as "disciplines." In *Marcella* and *Sir George Tressady* it is the female protagonist who makes the "Waverleyan" journey from property, through the alienating camp of the antagonist, Socialism, and back, moderated, to grasp the nettle of property as a discipline, as power and power-sharing. In the first novel the strict formulas of Romance in the tradition of English realistic fiction call for the protagonist's Luciferian interlude of revolt with the book's "dark hero," the socialist leader Henry Wharton, an interlude marked by solitary stretches of self-communing as well as testing in situations of public violence. Settled at the end of the novel in her place of chastened power, Marcella becomes in the sequel herself the dark star to the drifting planet Sir George Tressady, forcing him through stages of revolt, self-loathing and self-surrender, to self-discovery. At the climax he crosses the boundary of class and political party and passion to give her his key property, his vote in Parliament, retiring to his own place of chastened power in possession of a newly fertile marriage and a newly, and finally fatally, shared patrimony with the colliers of West Mercia.

His death scene serves many purposes, sentimental, romantic, trailing clouds of political reconciliation, poetic justice, and religious transcendence. At bottom, though, there is something serious, disturbing, fin de siècle about it. It is a death inevitable from the first pages of the novel, where Mary Ward describes an ironic man cut off from belief in his own sincerity or that of others, holding at bay a "harsh melancholy" (*SGT* I, 114) born of an "inner disgust" (*SGT* I, 62) at the "bunkum" (*SGT* I, 2) talked by those, himself included, who have been rashly trusted with a future they cannot really imagine. Throughout the novel he feels a "moral nausea" (*SGT* I, 210), really a world-nausea at the structure of being he perceives around him, a structure which returns to every action, every enthusiasm, "something hideous— some torture—something that'll make us wish we'd never been born" (*SGT* I, 266). This cry in the male upper class, echoing that of Hardy's worker in *Jude the Obscure*, eventually meets Marcella's resistant feminine "But even so, if the power behind things cares nothing for us, I should only regard it as challenging us to care more for each other" (*SGT* I, 266). By no accident, her next words to Sir George are "Do you know anything personally of the London poor" (*SGT* I, 266). As a girl Marcella Boyce's whole ambition was to see more (*M* 167); as a political reformer, Marcella Maxwell's whole program is to force the governing classes to see more. For "the real making of one's country goes on out of sight in garrets and workshops and coalpits" (*SGT* I, 262). And the seeing, a combination of the new scientific and political research with the old empathetic vision, is the source of Marcella's hope.

It is this fidelity to the country being made "out of sight" that drives the Romance of Property in the fiction of Mary Ward, that integrates its often shrewd and progressive analysis of politics with the post-Miraculous mysticism of late Victorian religious thought. Out of sight, making one's country, are the "hands" of the traditional condition-of-England novel, represented in the rural plaiters and poachers of *Marcella* and the urban garment workers and coal miners of *Sir George Tressady*. The hands are making more than material goods in this transition time: they are also making their politics, the politics of Labor.

Out of sight too is the "new spiritual polity" (*SGT* II, 351) being fashioned, in Ward's Christianized Nietzschean image, within "the Will that asks our will" (*M* 512). This potential polity is figured in the classic biblical story of an "impotent" man too paralyzed to step into the pool of Bethesda after its "troubling" by the healing angel.[5] The heroine of this double novel is characterized by action, movement, though she suffers a period of "impotence" too in the third book of *Marcella*, where the "awful growth of sympathy" for workers caught in the trap of misery and "pain I never can help" (*M* 300) drives her toward paralyzing self-contempt. The sequel novel will supply in *Sir George Tressady* the fully operational image of the paralyzed person, and the occasion for a national drama of immersion and healing.

With passionate empathy, then, but also with trepidation, with duplicitous possessiveness, both the governing classes and the religious thinkers seek a share in the making of these new properties. The genteel writers and readers of fiction seek a share too, and during the decades in which she projected with vigor and range this empathy, this trepidation and this duplicity, Mary Augusta Arnold Ward, "Mrs. Humphry Ward," was the best-selling English writer of fiction.

## I. Conversions: *Marcella*

Mary Ward's novels return again and again to the issue of conversions—religious, sociopolitical, psychological. The thinkers of the 1850s and 1860s had assembled theories of "development" within which to organize elements of stability and change, and the writers of fiction, Eliot and Meredith especially, had consolingly dramatized how that development might animate movement in individuals and in whole communities. But the pace seemed in the 1880s and 1890s to have speeded up drastically. In a time of enforced change, a transition time both hyperconscious and intensely violent, how can one, really, distinguish between true religious sociopolitical and psychological conversion, or growth, and mere egotistical coat-turning or role playing, or worse, violent and uncontrollable metamorphosis? Dark fables of unexpected metamorphosis gripped the popular imagination of the 1890s; tales like *Dr. Jeckyll and Mr. Hyde* and *Dracula* and *The Island of Dr. Moreau* warned of grim reversals or startling splits and jumps in the drama of shape-shifting to which, under the name of development and reform, the human race had committed itself.

Mary Ward's own family contained such a drama. The geographical and ideological "wanderings" of her father, Thomas Arnold, above all his bewildering conversions from Anglican to Roman Catholic Christianity (1856, Mary was 4), and back again (1865), and back to Roman Catholicism (1876), challenged the psychic security of the daughter and produced in her a temperament which combined the willfulness of her driven father and the shrinking and vexed loyalty of her mother. The narrator of *Marcella* describes several changes of "being" during her partly orphaned and rather autobiographical heroine's girlhood, and allows the heroine herself a touch of real anger as well as pride in her description at age 18 of the outcome: "I was not brought up at all: I have had to make myself" (*M* 35).

To such a consciousness the secret terror is that the made self is no more than a string of poses. No wonder, then, that her first adult novel is about an actress (*Miss Bretherton,* 1884), her second about the agonizingly slow remaking of a doubting clergyman's Christianity (the blockbuster *Robert Elsmere,* 1888), and her third about a vehemently "self-made" working-class intellectual (*The History of David Grieve,* 1892). In her fourth and fifth novels, *Marcella* and *Sir George Tressady,* Mary Ward is again at the obsessive heart of her difficult and poignant project, the assertion of an authentic unity in the inevitably "made" self. In *Marcella* the project is to explore the slow knitting together of a true self from the initial felt split of an intelligent young girl—"One half of her was impulsive and passionate; the other half looked on and put in finishing touches" (*M* 35); and to establish the possibility of moral authenticity in a climate of ideological opportunism—"'Think of the sweated women in London.' 'Ah, think of them,' he said in a different tone. There was a pause of silence. 'No!' said Marcella, springing up. 'Don't let's think of them. I get to believe the whole thing a pose in myself and other people'" (*M* 112). In *Sir George Tressady* the project for Marcella is to use the power of passionate persuasion innocently in an atmosphere of political and sexual innuendo—"Suddenly George said, in an odd voice: 'Do you mind my saying it? You know, nobody is ever converted—politically—nowadays'" (*SGT* I 269). To the cynical contemporary consciousness that nobody is ever converted, politically, only in some fashion bribed, that nobody is ever converted religiously, only neurotically gratified, that nobody is ever ripely converted from one idea or work or love to another, only helplessly metamorphosed, Ward opposes her dramas of a redeemed, or at least redeemable conversion.

*Marcella* dazzles with its shrewd and vigorous staging of 1880s debates over land and work reform, the necessary violence of progress and the maneuverings of political parties, but its romantic structure comes from Scott and Austen. Its protagonist's conversion is finally to the middle of the road, politically, socially, and to the conventional mate of birth and wealth, the boy (and the property) next door. Mysteriously alienated from her wellborn parents, Marcella Boyce passes her childhood as "a little spitfire outsider" (*M* 8), at a lonely succession of schools, but the novel opens, as so many of Mary Ward's novels do, with a vista of well-beloved land caught in its possessor's "devouring" (*M* 1), even "covetous" (*M* 2), gaze. Marcella has come back to the ancestral, if neglected, property of the Boyces after a heady conversion to Morrissian communism during a period of desultory study of art and ideas in London's yeasty and penurious student culture. Her conversion, as she herself is aware, was a mixture of youthful self-dramatizing, that tendency to respond as "the prey of the last speaker" (*M* 106) for which the unsympathetic contemporary term is "political correctness," and that genuine capacity both for empathy and for action on behalf of empathy which is the hallmark of the Victorian fictional heroine.[6]

As with the Scott hero or Austen heroine, a waywardness or inadequacy in the parental generation, in this case an episode of speculation and dishonesty and exile in her father's life, has ruptured the protagonist's inheritance, both material and psychological. This has pushed Marcella into the world of opposition, where she is free to make alliance with, champion and identify with, to feel the erotic glamour of, the dispossessed. The dispossessed of *Marcella,* the working poor of the agricultural and commercial depression of the 1880s, are victims of a genuine systemic injustice: they have both their genuine prophets and their devious, half-sincere genteel leaders. The poor of Ward's novel turn out to have their own traditions of self-respect and community politics and cannot simply be "managed" by ideologies, however learned, or idealists, however empathetic. Like Scott's heroes, Marcella's heroine will figure her political conversions in erotic ones; like Austen's heroines, like Scott's dark ladies, she will turn for a time resolutely aside from the eligible parti Maxwell, the (fellow) inheritor, to enter the dynamic thrall of the dispossessed, the George Wickham/Frank Churchill figure through whose skeptical eyes, for a time, she and the reader can see the ponderous imperviousness, hence the risible futility, of the traditional inheritor.

As Marcella looks at her own small property she nurtures small schemes of improvement; as she looks across the boundary to the Maxwell property surrounding it on three sides (as Mr. Knightley's does Emma's), she sees the Maxwell heir, Aldous Raeburn, and recognizes a still greater theater for her still mixed ambition to serve and to rule. He too is experimenting with democracy, in too small a way and at too slow a pace for her; he too has been touched by the socialist philosopher of her early conversion, Edward Hallin, and is now touched again by Marcella's beauty and "freshness of feeling" (*M* 121). He will one day be a cabinet minister: she might do tremendous work from that eminence.

A proposal is inevitable, and Marcella accepts it in book one, repressing a momentary qualm because she recognizes that the "thrill" of liking she feels, of expectant activity, of a life "opened to great issues" (*M* 120), was not, nevertheless, the genuine passion of love. The narrative embodies this repressed qualm immediately, as the newly engaged couple cross paths with "a young and malevolent" presence with bright chestnut curls and eighteenth-century charm (*M* 122), Marcella's nemesis and alter ego, the socialist politician Henry Wharton. He too, as he tells her frankly, is pursuing the "thrill" of activity in "the workmen's war," the best drama in England (*M* 165).

In young Wharton, a kind of dark Will Ladislaw, a well-informed and aggressive intelligence fuels a speaking style both witty in the drawing room—"Nowadays society is trying to get out of doing what [socialists] want, by doing what Carlyle wanted" (M 163), and effective on the hustings—"and as a first step to this new Jerusalem—organisation!, self-sacrifice enough to form and maintain a union, to vote for Radical and Socialist candidates in the teeth of the people who have coals and blankets to give away!" (M 198). In Wharton, Marcella will see her strongest desires and deepest fears flower. He is a defier of the Masters, a defender and champion of the dispossessed, but he is also a showman and an unashamed connoisseur of his own and other people's shows and roles, including Marcella's: "You are a Socialist, and you are going—some day—to be Lady Maxwell. These combinations are only possible to women. They can sustain them, because they are imaginative—not logical" (M 164).

Wharton is a fine creation: the novelist is clearly as fascinated by him as she is resistant. He is a thinker and actor of talent, but his radiance, like Frank Churchill's, is rootless. His brilliant speech—a true analysis of systemic injustice never disowned by the narrative—emerges from emotional aridity. His social confidence is a mask for financial insecurity. He is a gambler, literally, politically, even psychologically: when his social passion turns to erotic desire and he takes a kiss from the half-willing almost-Lady Maxwell, he is a spectator at his own potential conversion: "That was a scene. . . . What did I say?—How much did I mean? My God! how can I tell? I began as an actor, did I finish as a man?" (M 225). The "thrill" of this kind of roll of the dice is not, finally, for Marcella. Wharton, and Wharton's kiss, are useful to her, as she dimly perceives, to cut her off, as she thinks finally, from the Inheritor: where she ended book one engaged to Maxwell, she ends book two, after a post-kiss confrontation with her fiancé, "alone—and free" (M 308).

Marcella began as an actor: to finish as a woman, in Victorian terms, she needs to enter the central Victorian scene for psychological conversion, which is not love, but work. "Alone and free," she has reached a developmental stage which Elizabeth Gaskell had defined in *North and South,* when her heroine Margaret Hale, her relationship with millmaster John Thornton broken off, "took her own life into her hands," gained from her family "the acknowledgement of her right to follow her own ideas of duty," and developed various unspecified "plans" for work that would take her, to the dismay of that family, into "all those places" where a genteel woman would pick up dirt on her clothes (508). Gaskell and Ward both organize the "breaking off" in a long series of carefully worked out chapters of alienation from the "masters." But the world of "plans," self-actualized work, which Mrs. Gaskell sketched in a few paragraphs is given a full book in Ward's novel.

As the newly arrived heiress of Mellors, as the fiancée of the Maxwell Inheritor, Marcella had laid eager but rash hands on the structures of work in the country for which she would be responsible, seeking to recreate women's crafts, getting Maxwell to give construction work to agricultural "hand" Jim Hurd to keep him from winter poaching. But the women resist the scheme of the well-meaning stranger. And Hurd's poaching has deep roots not only in his poverty but in his understandable craving for excitement, independent activity, and sport, the wish of the dispossessed to duplicate at night the licensed daytime play of the game preserving/destroying Inheritors. In pursuit of these sensations he kills a boyhood tormentor who had become one of Maxwell's gamekeepers, and is caught, condemned, and executed for murder. Maxwell's stiff but principled refusal to sign a petition for clemency puts the nail in the coffin of his engagement. Marcella now feels the raw ignorance and futility of her ideas both about other people's work and about the self that, as would-be Lady Bountiful, developed the ideas. More is broken over the Hurd case than Marcella's engagement though; it is of herself that she speaks when she writes to Wharton, "If the tool breaks and blunts, how can the task be done? It can be of no use till it has been reset" (M 328).

Resetting the tool means, for Marcella herself, a hard year's training and several months of action in the physical, intellectual, and sociological work of nursing: "a little honest work for the first time in my life" as she defiantly tells the harlequin Wharton when he accuses her of "masquerading" in her nurse's uniform (M 403). Book three's London scenes move between various sites of work in this key national "transition time," knitting together the microcosm of social stress and social healing, Marcella's activities in the tenements of East London, and the macrocosm of legislative and executive power presided over by the men. In the House of Commons Henry Wharton seeks to fashion the Labor Party out of a heterogeneous group of socialist and liberal interests through sponsorship of a bill to regularize the hours of work in factories. As under-secretary in the Home Office, Aldous Raeburn collects statistics, studies political reality, reaches and executes decisions on the management of the working classes. Marcella meets both men in the streets, tenements, debating halls of the poor, where she attends first hand upon both the origins and the results of the social policies debated and pressed by Wharton and the opposition, modified or carried out by Maxwell and the government. Learned in her new craft, living among her loved but now thoroughly individuated poor, Marcella now has firm ground to reestablish her political identity according to the standard formulas of the Victorian Social Problem novel. Eschewing "mechanical" political systems (M 435), particularizing her thought issue to issue, she retains from her early "Venturist" socialism the passionate faith that individual activity counts for much in the inevitable transfer of the national Property to the new Democratic Inheritors. She is certain, she tells her earlier teachers, that socialism, the political philosophy now catalyzing the "transition time," is creating, not itself, exactly, but something still unnamed, "out of sight," more mysterious, creating it in cooperation with some hidden "motive power" Christians named "grace" (M 376, 386). Marcella's early socialist rejection of religion, like her rather stiffly doctrinaire embrace of "the poor," has undergone some rethinking.

From this new ground of experience, at once denser with material experience and leavened by spiritual suffering, Marcella watches the darker and meaner conversion of the novel's socialist hero, Wharton. Still the scintillating speaker for important pieces of social legislation, Wharton is also increasingly easy in the company of cynical aristocratic kingmakers like Lady Selina Farrell. Is this policy, schizophrenia, or hypocrisy? Wharton himself scarcely knows. In the end, financial pressures from a gambling habit of soul bring him to take a bribe from a manufacturing syndicate to end a strike; his leadership for Labour is irretrievably compromised, and, his proposal of marriage rejected by Marcella, he is captured in marriage and converted in politics by Lady Selina.

Against the increasingly centrifugal disassembling of Wharton's several personae, Marcella learns to value the steady and effective activity of Raeburn. For it is of the essence of Mary Ward's Romance of Property that the traditional inheritor needs no "conversion." He stands for the country itself, a psycho-geographical metonymy of unity, of persistence-with-modification. He feels "the old faiths—economical, social, religious—fermenting within him in different stages of disintegration and reconstruction"; a scholarly leaven of pure speculation is contained in him by the sheer mass and weight of his Inheritance, "a particular individuality with a particular place and label in the world" (M 47).

So Aldous Raeburn, labeled "the Maxwell heir," a cartoon to the young socialist gaze, was first coveted and then scorned by Marcella Boyce, the lady-in-making. In book four Raeburn must—not change, not convert, but rather inhabit his label. With the death of his grandfather he must actually come into, and be humanized within, his inheritance. His own temperament, we are told in an analysis which in some ways prefigures the one Ward will attempt with *Sir George Tressady,* has always been melancholic. His inheritance has been to him "rather a consciousness of weight than of inspiration" (*M* 44), the potentially disabling source of modern "remorses and scruples" (*M* 44) which make it impossible for him either to feel the pleasure of his Maxwell power or exercise it with the feudal "charm" and "effectiveness" of his grandfather (*M* 527). In book four the new Lord Maxwell does his work stolidly, goes impatiently through the required "play at greatness" of his new title. For a brief time, harassed by the same slippage of identity into "poses" that had plagued Marcella, and swallowed Henry Wharton, "he constantly felt himself absurd" (*M* 526). His inheritance, pure mass, awaits aeration, female potency, according to the Romance of Property.

At the same time Marcella enters the last stage of her conversion, an Elizabeth Bennett/Emma Woodhouse–like illumination of her desire for her own final female inheritance, "the power to lose herself—the power to love" (*M* 387). This "transforming" power (*M* 387), less to lose than to consolidate her self, choose an identity, end the quest, and marshal its energy in specific action, is figured in the Romance as heterosexual desire, figured in the Romance of Property as desire for the male inheritor. Only he can compel the admiration that releases this power. And he can compel it only if he has actually entered on his inheritance and proved in character equal to its mass.

In a curious final interlude of great interest to feminist criticism, Marcella may grasp this new desire/power only after establishing a new relationship with her mother. Mrs. Boyce, an enigmatically intelligent and proudly dutiful Victorian wife, had been the spine of the family throughout her husband's feckless dishonesty and exile. Now in book four, freed by Richard Boyce's death and Marcella's work-built independence, the sacrificing mother speaks up boldly for the psychological freedom and emotional self-sufficiency she has always coveted, just at the moment the daughter, her reviving love for Raeburn blocked, as she thinks, by a rival, turns with kindling passion to the mother–daughter bond. Mrs. Boyce, sympathetic, is nevertheless resistant to this return to the womb. Mother and daughter interestingly exchange roles here. In a cool rejection of the "hot" patterns of a male-ascribed maternity which recalls George Eliot's Princess Alcharisi and anticipates E.M. Forster's Mrs. Moore, the woman of forty-five strikes out along the modern path many readers would have preferred for the daughter—"all sorts of crushed powers and desires, mostly of the intellectual sort, had been strangely reviving within her. . . . She wished . . . to travel, to read, to make acquaintances" (*M* 522). Meanwhile the younger woman, whose "rich emotional nature" had "suffered conviction," (M 523) that is, conversion to "the woman's" inheritance of guilt, humiliation, and desire, moves back into the emotional field of the Inheritor.

The closing pages of *Marcella,* a quick escape from the shortest of the novel's four books, are nevertheless packed with those contrarieties and disturbances that often testify to the anxiety of ending, the writing beyond the ending, in the Romance, especially the Romance of Property. As Marcella boldly sends to Aldous the letter that signals her change of heart, readying herself like the letter for the journey "from her own keeping to that of another" (M 553), her imagination of the Inheritor's look taking her into keeping "made her sick and faint with feeling" (M 554). As she assembles her new "conviction" that no system cut and dried can at a stroke change the oppression she had hated, or at a stroke make the human race share her passionate sympathy with the poor, she sees the possibility that "true love" will "deaden in her that hatred" and that sympathy and her soul "cried out in denial" of that possibility (M 555). The moment of her reengagement is filled with narrative gestures of Ruskinian submissiveness.[7] We are told that "she did not look up . . . she had sunk on her knees before him . . . she stooped in a hasty passion and kissed his hand. . . . Piteously, childishly, with seeking eyes, she held out her hand to him" (M 557, 560, 555). But framing these, next to each other on one of the last pages, are the direct question the heroine of the Romance must ask herself, "would marriage fetter her?" and the exhortation that undoes the topos of ending, the prophet Edward Hallin's cry, in bold italics, "Never resign yourself!" (M 555).

## Writing beyond the Ending: *Sir George Tressady*

Five years after the end of *Marcella,* Marcella Boyce Raeburn, now Lady Maxwell, paces her elegant drawing room, stirred by another man, and the property he holds—a vote in Parliament on a bill to improve working conditions in London which she helped her husband draft. Would her marriage fetter her? Must she resign herself to a political power only exercised ventriloqually, through her marriage? Chapter six of the sequel romance, *Sir George Tressady,* climaxes with her double reverie before two "pictures" which together legitimize and energize her personal pursuit of this property, her "attack" upon this man (*SGT* I, 131). The first picture, a photograph of her husband, "relaxes" her face and releases her conscience: "it was for his sake, for his sake only." The second image, her own beautiful face framed in a mirror, brings to full consciousness the independent power she possesses, the beauty which secures that "opening in any game" of political process without which the eloquence, the persistence, experience, and learning which she brings to the conduct of political affairs would be useless. A year or two younger than Marcella Maxwell, Sir George Tressady at twenty-four is a swing member of the small but influential group of Imperialists that is bidding to block the Maxwell Bill. He is a mocker, but of somewhat malleable stuff, ready to engage in witty debate, but refreshingly free of that "quick glance of bold or sensual eye" with which even the English gentleman politician will seek to confine even the passionately "married" and intellectually credentialed Lady Maxwell to her "place" in the mirror (*SGT* I, 132). Talking the campaign over a moment later with her husband, "with a comrade's freedom and vivacity" (*SGT* I, 133) Marcella frees the image from the frame to pursue its project: "No—I don't think after all he's your sort. Suppose I see what can be done!" (*SGT* I, 143).[8]

In a rhythm common to *Marcella* and many of Mary Ward's novels, *Sir George Tressady* establishes its story first in the countryside—still in the 1880s the key locus of political electoral power—interweaving scenes of Great House political life with the world of the working poor which sustains that life. It then moves to London, following the same dialectic, interweaving scenes of urban working-class life and debate about that life with the Parliamentary work of the governing classes, since, "our country being what it is, the plans that are made in Mile End or Shoreditch have to be adopted by Mayfair" (*SGT* I, 149). The sequel novel, like *Marcella,* will return to the countryside for its brief climax, but its main attention is riveted on the dialectic between Mayfair and Mile End in the transition time, a dialectic which Ward is well aware represents the final moment of equipoise between the two powers before the twentieth century renders Mayfair in its current form obsolete.

During this transition time men elected in the countryside must make decisions about the social progress of England's urban industrial masses. Usually they are men like the young Sir George, who grew up protected from contact with the origins of his own wealth in the West Mercian coal fields and is inflamed instead, after a university education in Greek and Roman imperial classicism and a Grand Tour of England's own Empire, to believe that the heroes of imperial conquest, trade, jurisprudence, the (male) builders of systems, states, and great houses, have "made" England. Marcella's own equivalent of a Grand Tour while a nurse in London gave her the competing vision that "the real making of one's country is done out of sight, in garrets and workshops and coalpits, by people who die every minute—forgotten" (*SGT* I, 262). Her political desire is to make Mayfair see the conditions of Mile End and Shoreditch which the exotica of classical studies and Eastern travels have erased for the educated Englishman: "She saw herself, in a kind of despair, driving such persons through streets, and into houses she knew, forcing them to look, and feel" (*SGT* I, 301).

The struggle between Marcella and George is thus rooted in the politics of feeling, though the surface of the struggle, the debate on the Maxwell Bill, is genuinely "a representative contest between two liberties—a true battle of ideas" (*SGT* II, 13). The bill, progressive in early modern terms, is a trio of rules setting up machinery to enforce the shorter day for London male and female sweated workers by making it illegal for individuals to work themselves to death while "making the country . . . out of sight." In meeting after meeting, Marcella presses George on the Maxwell Bill and its liberalizing enforcement (familiar paradox) on workers and proprietors alike of an eight-hour workday, talking of ideas but calling on feeling. In the conversations she is penetrating layer after layer of protective irony and witty fatalism in his psyche, coming closer to stirring the waters of the "black pool" (*SGT* I, 178) of melancholy, suicidal disgust, nihilist dread of the iron laws of an inimical Necessity.

This is what George knows, at bottom, as feeling; this is what he had hoped to distance himself from by marrying the vivacious and pleasure-loving Letty Sewell. To feel with the inevitably trampled individual life is to feel despair and rage, George thinks, and that whether the individual life one is asked to feel for is another's, or one's own. George resists feeling for his own life as much as he does for the colliers' lives of his home estate or the London workers' lives Marcella would show him. In his electoral speeches as in private talk with a bereaved colliery woman, "he found himself growing eloquent at last, yet all the time regarding himself, as it were, from a distance—ironically" (*SGT* I, 173). Irony affirming his own shallowness enables his irony about everyone else's shallowness, including that of the famous reformer Lady Maxwell, friend of the people, whose elegant Mayfair house George approaches with the "amused, investigating look" (*SGT* I, 116) of an epicure in irony.

To give up the security of this irony for the social pity that is Marcella's nature, her political tool and touchstone, is to risk the waters of the black pool. Again and again, in a powerful network of images calling on the story of the pool at Bethesda, the stirring of these waters reveals to George his "moral nausea" (*SGT* II, 325). In the novel's terms this condition bodes well for that moral and political conversion he had adamantly denied as a possibility in the ironical reality necessitated by "the world and its iron conditions" (*SGT* II, 17). His political philosophy—"he was in the mood again tonight to feel it a kind of impertinence, this endless, peering anxiety about a world you never planned and cannot mend" (*SGT* II, 34)—

depends on a resistance to pity, including, and especially, self-pity. At bottom it is built on a masculine fear of/desire for, brute power: "The world can't be run by pity. . . . To be too careful, too gingerly over the separate life, brings it all to a standstill. . . . Then the nation goes to pieces—till some strong ruffian without a scruple puts it together again" (*SGT* I, 210). The breakthrough moment will come when George, recognizing during Marcella's impassioned speech to East End workers the "hunger" of his own heart for her depth of feeling, his hunger for her, puts out his hand, in a kind of angry rivalry with the workers, "to claim his own share of the common pain," revealing the ultimate stirring of the waters, "a hard, reluctant tear" (*SGT* II, 54).

Mary Ward said in the Westmoreland edition's introduction to *Sir George Tressady* that it would have been better for the story had she and her Anglo-Saxon audiences felt able to treat more "earthily" the erotic charge in the relationship between the ironical man and the pitying woman as it moves to its climaxes—Marcella's claiming of George's vote, George's literal and fatal claiming of the common pain.[9] To carry that off, while evading the relegation of the powerful woman to her "place" either framed in the mirror or crushed in the gutter, would have required an uncommon talent indeed. Instead Mary Ward will offer that crushed place to the man. Yet the relationship she does develop has its own fascination, as George braves the dangerous waters of feeling and Marcella the corrupting mazes of Influence, debating all the while the genuine limitations of "pity" as a political force and feeling for the "separate life" as a political principle.

There is no lack of sincerity in Marcella as she argues "the difference between now and twenty years ago is that women work much more, the men less. I can never get away from the thought of the women!" and hears George respond, "Is it reasonable to take all our own poor little joy and drench it in this horrible pain of sympathy?" There is no pose in her resulting tear, or in his quick rueful admission, "You have made one person feel . . . the things you feel. I don't know that I am particularly grateful to you" (*SGT* II, 60, 61). Her look of "wild sweetness and gratitude" (*SGT* II, 61) disturbs her into a quick scene of "weakness, submission, loveliness" (*SGT* II, 68) the next time she meets her husband: that look, an evocation of her "southern" (read sexual) heritage, has its part in producing the excitement with which George continues the talk of the coming Parliamentary votes, "each of them, so he felt in his exaltation, a blow dealt to her—that he must help to deal" (*SGT* II, 62).

George, like Marcella, veers wildly between impulses to deal blows, exert power, and impulses of self-abasement about the raw uses of power.

In their two meetings before the Maxwell Bill comes to its final vote, George feels Marcella's influence politically in "that fatal capacity for sympathy, for the double-seeing of compromise, which takes from a man all the joy of battle" (*SGT* II, 110), and personally in a spiritualized rising passion which readies him for a great deed of passion. Not, clearly, a "French" deed, but an emphatically English one, the transfer of his vote from his own party to Marcella's. The deed enacts the romantic collaboration of an Imperialist Conservative and a Little Englander Conservative in the rewinning of socialist and liberal votes to a socialist cause embodied in the bill of a conservative government, a further transfer—by oh, so deliberate steps, of the property of England, the labor of its people, to the democratic inheritor.

The last irony here is one that links the romantic and political thematic of the two novels. In the novel's most telling scenes of political argument George and Marcella debate the conditions of liberty as they are both compromised and forwarded by the Maxwell Bill. George speaks for the eighteenth-century rationalist point of view, advocating the least possible formal law, and the largest possible increment of personal freedom even if it means the exploiter's freedom to enable his neighbor to survive by working himself nearly to death. Marcella argues for the slow but sure legal enforcement of the community's best social conscience even upon those individuals who actually cannot survive except by their unfairly sweated labor (*SGT* I, 263). There will, she says, be pitying friends like herself to help the individuals caught in the transition time.

Thus Marcella's care for the separate lives of people leads her to support a system of laws which will, at the moment of implementation, cause much individual misery, maybe even death. She is politically and psychologically vulnerable to George's mockery about this until his feeling for her, for his own soul's inchoate hunger, for the separate life which he knows first as his own, makes him vulnerable too to self-contradiction, absurdity. And the only path forward from this condition is conversion, if only to a blind faith in the sincerity of her faith. George holds apart from "conversion" for the votes on the Bill's first two clauses, which the Maxwell forces win by narrowing margins, but on the third clause, which establishes the enforcement mechanism by which the whole edifice stands or falls, he delivers his vote to Marcella. He does this not on rational grounds at all: he is still doubtful in his pessimist's rationalist's classicist's mind, that any law or combination of laws can effect the psycho-social change his dream lady dreams of. He does it out of faith and desire. Simply that the woman who moved him to feel might have her heart's desire, he votes against the stream of his party, momentarily uniting, by his eloquence and the risk of his surprising deed, the forces, socialist, liberal, moderate conservative, needed to carry the bill.

To win that result Marcella put forth her direct power, erotic, maternal, moral, aesthetic and intellectual, as surely as if she had been Maxwell's party whip. From the sanctuary of her marriage, in the freedom of that fetter, she had gone out to Sir George Tressady in argument, she had "driven him through the streets" to see what should make him feel, she had deliberately stirred the waters of the black pool in him and felt her own "excitement" (*SGT* II, 150) at the approach of victory. She had shaken his rationalism and more than proposed, allowed herself literally to embody, ideals of human character. She had become the Angel in his internal House. In an eloquent later flash of identification with George's shallow and forsaken wife she recognizes the effect of this usurpation on his marriage: "How she could have hated—with what fierceness, what flame!—the woman who taught ideal truths to Maxwell" (*SGT* II, 183). She had, in the key moment of her relationship with George, spoken most intimately of her marriage, her "life in another," as the source of her pity, her faith, her hope for the bill, allowed him this intimacy, this "delicious" moment of "privilege" (*SGT* II, 155), this sharing of her marriage. And that was the one moment in all the novel which she cannot share with her husband (*SGT* II, 156). It was an act of political courage, individual enterprise, and emotional adultery for which, in the tangle of late Victorian conventional mores, Marcella and George must both strive and "pay."

For the Victorian faithful, and Mary Ward is their spokesperson, both social and individual freedom pivot in both private and public life, around "the divinest law man serves—that he must 'die to live,' must surrender to obtain" (*SGT* I, 143). Eloquent illustrations of this dynamic crowd the final chapters of this double novel. In homage to the marriage fetter which is her freedom, Marcella must be shown the humiliatingly vicious and understandably angry letter that George's wife Letty writes to Maxwell about the intellectual seduction she had allowed. Marcella must undertake the rescue of the never really enacted, almost destroyed Tressady marriage in a visit to Letty which reenacts Dorothea's visit to Rosamond at the end of *Middlemarch*.

And, cleverly, George's near-adulterous action in the vote must be quickly followed and substituted for by an act reshaping his and Marcella's relationship within the confines of the social maternity with which it began. For this purpose a lengthily contrived subplot involving a sexually irresponsible son and a saintly mother must be brought to climax in an attempted flight of the two to an immoral life on the French (naturally) coast: George follows as the mother's and Marcella's envoy to talk the son, his age-peer, away from his dark seductress and back into the moral fold.

Marcella had suggested this role for George specifically to return him to the fold, to give him an errand delicately expressing the confidence of both Maxwells in his soundness on sexual mores, placing him as a trusted elder son governing a wild younger son, restoring him to comfort and social productivity. Yet though he performs this task well, and the community, including, somewhat pettishly, his wife, stand ready to help him maintain that comfortable place, though "some angel had stirred the pool" (SGT II, 311) of his dread and disgust and offered a faith, rash and partly blinded, to replace it, his energies have been seriously depleted by his conversion, and reversion threatens. The moral nausea of his first election campaign with its poses and roles, returns doubled as he has to fight striking miners on his own property despite his real uncertainty as to "his own place and rights in a world of combat" (SGT II, 325). Once he was a comfortably cynical soldier, then a converted saint: what felt for an hour like conversion now seems another in a series of random and rootless changes.

The last book of the novel shows him surrendering to fatalism again, shrinking from all enthusiasms, alienated from the "triumphs of his own class" (SGT II, 319) in the breaking of the strike, a prey to self-disgust. Disgust, "that enfeebling, paralyzing something which in all directions made him really prefer the half to the whole" (SGT II, 318) realizes itself literally in the last chapter, when George, in a dim reflex both of the traditional inheritor's instinct of possession and the new political instinct to "share" the painful experiences of the coming democratic inheritor, descends with a rescue team to a group of miners injured in an explosion, and is himself paralyzed from the waist down in a second explosion. Two novel-long image networks here become literal. In that crushed body we see the English male psyche paralyzed before its fin de siècle burden of patriarchal government; we also see the "paralytic," or in another translation "the impotent man" of the Pool of Bethesda in John's Gospel, unable to enter the healing angel-stirred pool unless someone bodily puts him into it.

George does take one step toward his fate in an act of brotherhood, joining the rescue team: "Why should you risk more than I?" he says to one of his own workers moving deeper into the mine (SGT II, 339). In the resulting explosion he recognizes one final irony: the pain of his crushed body revives in him that ineluctable sense of the importance of the individual life he could once see only through sharing the passion of Marcella. Once he had comfortably set aside such scenes as the one which now contains him. Workers dying out of sight, bodies broken by inadequately conditioned and compensated work, these were the stuff of vulgar headlines and the carriers of the degenerative disease of pity. Now he is among the pitiable: "What a horrible quickening had overtaken him of that sense for misery, that intolerable compassion. . . . It was as though the old scorn for pity he had once flung at Marcella Maxwell had been but the fruit of some obscure and shrinking foresight that he himself should die drowned and lost in pity" (*SGT* II, 351). But though his fastidious mind shrinks in disgust, his quickened soul welcomes a solemn sense of participation in the common bond of pain: "He, George Tressady, a man of no professions and no enthusiasms, had yet paid his share" (*SGT* II, 351).

In the final paragraph a vision of the water-stirring angel closes George's sightless eyes in the mine, and a kind of nonspecific, part-miraculous world-faith replaces the world nausea of this representative of the governing classes. The vision is nameless and "featureless," but we know it is Marcella because he asks the vision, as he had asked Marcella, to care for his wife and for the child in the womb miraculously granted the Tressady marriage in its final moments: the Romance of Property, widened since Scott to include the democratic inheritor, cannot yet dispense with the symbolic iconography of the fertile aristocrat.

The assumption is that Marcella's influence will move "Socialist experiments" on George's industrial property as it has on her own agricultural inheritance of Mellors, and on Maxwell's lands too, though, of course, "moderately." On the other hand, nothing is clearer to Ward's narrators in both these novels than that the pace of change is no longer in the hands of Mayfair. Though the Romance of Property inevitably dramatizes social change through the passionate "quickening" of a representative genteel individual to the wider social process, to "history," and the establishment of this quickening in a fertile marriage, "history," after a hundred years of the Romance of Property, is not satisfied with this.

Perhaps the most characteristic move of Mrs. Ward's plots, then, is a scene treating the representative hero or prophet of moderate social progress to the genuine and understandable impatience of mass history to the programs and plots of moderation. Both *Marcella* and *Sir George Tressady* contain such a scene, strategically placed both to forward the individual Romance and to compromise it. Toward the end of *Marcella* the teacher of both Marcella and Aldous Raeburn, Edward Hallin, speaks to a large crowd of working people who have moved beyond Hallin's Christian Socialism toward radical land reform ideas: "Somehow Hallin damps you down [when] what you want just now is fight" says one Labor leader (*M* 241). Their hostility evokes in him a desperate religious autobiographical rhapsody which they reject as "damned canting stuff" (*M* 502), and he dies shortly thereafter a broken man, though not before his extremity has brought Marcella and Aldous together on the way to their final reconciliation. The middle of *Sir George Tressady* is dominated by a long scene at an East End meeting where male and female workers supply moving anecdotes of wretched lives while they discuss the immediate hardships and possible long-term benefits of the Maxwell Bill. Marcella's own speech in its favor, full of technical details from her and Aldous's Blue Book studies, is ineffective and ignored, and her exit marred by hostile insults and even stone-throwing—"Look at the bloomin' bloats. . . . Let 'em stop at 'ome and mind their own 'usbands!" (*SGT* II, 56)—though not before Sir George Tressady has had the chance to rescue the lady and resume his fascinated relationship with her.

One of the bloomin' bloats herself by this time, Mary Ward recognizes her own and her class's belatedness in these scenes. She recognizes it in the working class MP Wilson's snarl to his fellows that their attraction to the scintillating Wharton is a sign of a retrograde and finally unworkable desire to have "a gentleman" head their party (*M* 481). Ward has recognized her belatedness, and, I would say, in a way not entirely ignoble, enjoyed it. Belatedness is a way, after all, of sharing responsibility with history: to organize and passionately defend a process (moderation) or project (Christianizing socialism), and then have it remade by the social process, and then to cooperate with good "grace" (as Mary Ward would say) in the remaking. This is a way of taking shares in the ultimate property, social process itself.

Ward herself had submitted to social process in one of her most cherished projects. She had helped start one of the first and longest lasting of the London Settlement Houses, Bloomsbury's University Hall, which was to bring arts, Humanities, and "Christian theism" to the working poor. Raising money on this basis, the indefatigable novelist discovered that what the working poor actually wanted was childcare and youth education facilities, political and social action, and "no preaching." During the years she was writing *Marcella* and *Sir George Tressady* she at first resisted this reorientation, then gamely and actively supported it and raised even more money for it.

Still operating today, the Mary Ward Centre in Queen Square sports a sign describing itself as "the friendly place to learn," advertising both university-affiliated and general educational classes in arts, crafts, and humanities to the working community of London, as well as free counseling in health, legal, and social issues. Among its 1993–1994 offerings in women's studies are a course whose title critiques the psychological premise "She

Never Thinks of Herself" and another course advancing from Christian theism to "Beyond God the Father." The contents of these courses would be no surprise to, would be less uncongenial than we think to, the novelist who created the contradictory Marcella, and who headed the Women's Anti-Suffrage League, in gingerly partnership with the history that she always kept one step behind.

## Notes

1. The influential term is from Alexander Welsh's *The Hero of the Waverley Novels,* rereleased in 1992 with additional essays on the novels of Walter Scott.

2. No modern standard edition exists for the novels of Mrs. Humphry Ward, though she did oversee a sixteen-volume collective reissue of her first dozen works in 1911, called the Autograph Edition in America and the Westmoreland Edition in England. She wrote Introductions for the novels published in this edition, including *Marcella* and *Sir George Tressady.* This essay refers to the modern paperback of *Marcella* (M) issued by Virago Press, Viking Penguin, New York, 1985, and the one-volume edition of *Sir George Tressady* (SGT) issued by Grosset and Dunlap (New York, 1986).

3. Blau DuPlessis's important 1985 study is subtitled "Narrative Strategies of Twentieth-Century Women Writers," but develops its thesis about the stresses between the female quest plot and the heterosexual romance plot in a preface and first chapter about nineteenth-century women writers, though Mary Ward does not figure in it. Ward wrote one other novel–sequel pair: *The Case of Richard Meynell* (1911) took up the story of *Robert Elsmere* a generation later. That sequel resonates interestingly with some current thinking about religious feeling and community as a "property," but was a failure at the time of its publication.

4. A good treatment of Mary Ward's attraction to the Christian social thought of Oxford scholar J.R. Green is given by John Sutherland in his important recent biography, *Mrs. Humphry Ward, Eminent Victorian, Pre-Eminent Edwardian.* Green, like Hallin, strove to put his theology into practice by working much of his life in the East End of London. Sutherland's somewhat Stracheyan treatment of this relationship ("Green's intellectual positions—particularly his rational theism—insidiously became hers," [62]) is typical of the tone of the biography, which veers between respect for and impatience with this most "respectable" of authors.

5. The miracle of the pool is reported in John's Gospel, chapter five: "whoever first stepped into the water after its troubling was made whole of whatsoever disease he had" (*The Holy Bible: King James Version*).

6. *Marcella* and *Sir George Tressady,* like most of Mary Ward's novels, answer interestingly to the analysis of earlier Victorian social problems novels in such influential works as Catherine Gallagher's *The Industrial Reformation of English Fiction* and Rosemarie Bodenheimer's *The Politics of Story in Victorian Social Fiction.* Bodenheimer clarifies the degree to which the "female paternalist" heroine rescues paternal ideology as well as individuals in the empathetic actions allocated to them in social problem plots, and both critics explore the ways in which fiction by middle-class English women writers works to contain working-class "movement" in the circularities and closures of "story" (see especially Bodenheimer's chapter 1, "The Romance of the Female Paternalist," and Gallagher's chapter 9, "The Politics of Culture and the Debate over Representation in the 1860's." By the 1890s Mary Ward's best-selling fictions played a major role in this action, valorizing "transition time" and the mediation of the heroine, as the idea of "completion" inevitably recedes.

7. William Peterson's *Victorian Heretic* describes the strong and continuing influence exerted in Mary Arnold's girlhood by the novels of Christian submissive-

ness of Charlotte Yonge. He sees in Ward's novels "the conservative moral sensibility of a Charlotte Mary Yonge overlaid with the incisive, uncompromising intellect of a Mark Pattison" (60).

8. Examining this mirror scene to excellent effect, feminist critic Anne M. Bindslev notes that the "double consciousness" created in the narrative around Marcella and Sir George allows both the reader, and in some ways Marcella herself, to see Marcella "both as a subject and as a sex object" (85). Bindslev also notes that the doubling in the narrative, representative of so much doubling in the conservative and liberal ideologies in the book, the double desire for the romance plot and the quest plot for feminine consciousness, actually recapitulates "the schism that, in the first place, prompted the writing of the [sequel] novel" (82).

9. Extending the earth metaphor in flirtatious Victorian paradox, she continued: "Had I dragged my heroine through ways of a more commonplace difficulty and miriness, she would have been more appealing" ( SGT I, 1: introduction, xii).

WORKS CITED

Bindslev, Anne M. Mrs. Humphry Ward: A Study in Late-Victorian Feminine Consciousness and Creative Expression. Stockholm: Almqvist and Wiksell International, 1985.

Blau DuPlessis, Rachel. Writing beyond the Ending: Narrative Strategies of Twentieth-Century Women Writers. Bloomington: Indiana UP, 1985.

Bodenheimer, Rosemarie. The Politics of Story in Victorian Social Fiction. Ithaca, N.Y.: Cornell UP, 1988.

Gallagher, Catherine. The Industrial Reformation of English Fiction: 1832–1867. Chicago: U of Chicago P, 1985.

Gaskell, Elizabeth. North and South. 1855. Harmondsworth, Middlesex: Penguin, 1974.

Peterson, William S. Victorian Heretic: Mrs. Humphry Ward's "Robert Elsmere." Leicester UP, 1976.

Sutherland, John. Mrs. Humphry Ward: Eminent Victorian, Pre-Eminent Edwardian. New York: Oxford UP, 1991.

Ward, Mrs. Humphry. Marcella. 1894. New York: Viking Penguin, 1985.

———. Sir George Tressady. New York: Grosset and Dunlap, 1896.

Welsh, Alexander. The Hero of the Waverley Novels. 1963. 2nd ed. Princeton: Princeton UP, 1992.

SELECTED SECONDARY SOURCES

Anne M. Bindslev, Mrs. Humphry Ward: A Study in Late Victorian Feminine Consciousness and Creative Expression (Stockholm: Almqvist and Wiksell International, 1985); William S. Peterson, Victorian Heretic: Mrs. Humphry Ward's "Robert Elsmere" (Leicester: Leicester UP, 1976); John Sutherland, Mrs. Humphry Ward: Eminent Victorian, Pre-Eminent Edwardian (New York: Oxford UP, 1991).

# Mobilizing Chivalry

### Rape in Flora Annie Steel's *On the Face of the Waters* (1896) and Other British Novels about the Indian Uprising of 1857

*Nancy L. Paxton*

This essay surveys novels by five lesser-known popular Victorian writers. James Grant (1822–1887), after serving in the army, wrote military histories and more than seventy novels, mostly boys' adventures with military themes, including *The Adventures of Rob Roy* (1864) and *First Love and Last Love: A Tale of the Indian Mutiny* (1868). G.A. Henty (1832–1902) wrote over 120 novels, mostly boys' adventures, his best known work being *With Clive in India* (1884). *Rujub the Juggler* (1893) is one of the few novels Henty wrote ostensibly for adults. George Chesney lived for many years in India, where he had a distinguished career as an officer in the Indian Army, as a civil engineer, and an administrator, eventually holding a seat as the military member on the Governor-General's Council. He is the author of *The Battle of Dorking: Reminiscences of a Volunteer* (1871) and *Indian Polity: A View of the System of Administration in India* (1868) as well as two novels, *The Dilemma* being better known. Meadows Taylor (1808–1876), who served for many years in the Indian Army in the service of the nizam, is author of six novels, including his influential *Confessions of a Thug* (1839). *Seeta* is the last volume in a series of three novels focusing on major political changes in India in 1657, 1757, and 1857; the two earlier volumes are *Tara* and *Ralph Darnell*. Finally, Flora Annie Steel (1847–1929), married an Indian civil servant and went to India in 1868, living and working there during his twenty-two year tour of duty. She is the author of more than thirty works, including novels, historical romances, short story collections, translations, and a cookbook called *The Complete Indian Housekeeper and Cook*. *On the Face of the Waters* is her best-known novel.

All of the novels discussed in this essay are out of print. Grant's *First Love and Last Love* was originally published by Routledge; Henty's *Rujub the Juggler* by Chatto and Windus; Chesney's *The Dilemma* by Blackwood and Sons; Taylor's *Seeta* by K. Paul, Trench Trübner; and Steel's *On the Face of the Waters* by Heinemann.

Edmund Burke was the first, indisputably the most eloquent, and, as Sara Suleri reminds us, "certainly the most widely read member of Parliament to debate the question of India" in the last three decades of the eighteenth century, when the foundations for the British empire in India were laid (Suleri 26). Burke was also the first British statesman to exploit the rhetorical power of the metaphor of rape to criticize the policies of the East India Company. For example, in "A Letter to a Member of the National Assembly," he declared that 1767 marked the year when:

> administration discovered, that the East India Company were guardians to a very handsome and rich lady in Hindostan. Accordingly, they set parliament in motion: and parliament . . . directly became a suitor, and took the lady into its tender, fond, grasping arms, pretending all the while that it meant nothing but what was fair and honorable; that no rape or violence was intended; that its sole aim was to rescue her and her fortune out of the pilfering hands of a set of rapacious stewards, who had let her estate run to waste, and had committed various depredations.[1]

By 1787, Burke had succeeded in convincing his colleagues in the Commons to initiate proceedings to remove Warren Hastings, ex-Governor-General of India, from the seat he then occupied in the House of Lords. In his opening statements at Hastings's trial, Burke insisted that rape was more than a metaphor, that it literally characterized the sexual violence that Hastings countenanced and personally practiced during his rise and rule as Governor-General (1774–1785). Burke charged that Hastings not only designed policies that destroyed "the honour of the whole female race" of India, but that he had personally "undone women of the first rank," noting especially his humiliation of the Princesses of Oude in 1772–1773. Burke vividly catalogued Hastings's barbaric treatment of Indian women: "Virgins . . . publicly were violated by the lowest and wickedest of the human race" and "wives were torn from the arms of their husbands, and suffered the same flagitious wrongs. . . . But it did not end there. Growing from crime to crime, ripened by cruelty for cruelty, these fiends . . . these infernal furies planted death in the source of life" and "there they exercised and glutted their unnatural, monstrous, and nefarious cruelty" (10: 88–89).

Burke's powerful allegations about Hastings's unspeakable colonial acts inspired apparent agitation in the large audiences he attracted, but he failed, nonetheless, to persuade the House of Lords (Suleri 61). After a trial that lasted seven years, Hastings was acquitted in 1795. Burke's criticism of the rapaciousness of British colonial policy in India was a minority voice at the time, and, with his death in 1797, his inimitable and inflammatory rhetoric about the rape of India by the lawless agents of the East India Company was silenced.

Historians have offered various explanations for the complex political and economic causes for the muting of the criticism of Indian colonial policy that Burke so forcefully articulated between 1772 and 1795.[2] The use of rape as a metaphor to describe the English colonizer's violent relation to the colonized has, by contrast, a strange and unexamined history. The very familiarity of the trope of rape has obscured the changing ideological work that it has performed in colonial discourse. In fact, Dominique Mannoni, Frantz Fanon, and other postcolonial critics have ignored Burke's sensational deployment of rape to describe colonial relations; they have argued, on the contrary, that colonial discourse has always been haunted by the figure of a white woman raped by a dark man.[3] This version of the colonial rape narrative, then, often appears as the master text of imperialism and a symptom of the colonizers' bad faith.

In British colonial discourse about India, however, the story of English women raped by Indian men was not the original or the only rape narrative in circulation; instead, it emerged at a particular crisis point in the British rule of India and performed specific ideological work. This familiar version of the colonial rape narrative became popular after the Indian Uprising of 1857 when dozens of British and Anglo-Indian novelists began to write and rewrite narratives about the Mutiny which hinged on the rape of English women by Indian men. By rereading five representative novels about the Indian Uprising in this larger historical context, I will show how this version of the colonial rape narrative performed double duty. Novels written after 1857 which were organized around this narrative naturalized British colonizers' dominance by asserting the lawlessness of Indian men and, at the same time, shored up traditional gender roles by assigning British women the role of victim, countering British feminist demands for women's greater political and social equality. In short, texts which focus on the rape of English women by Indian men were used to mobilize literary traditions about chivalry in service to the Raj.

I.

Stories about interracial rape were especially susceptible to redefinition by many of the technologies of gender at work in the nineteenth century. The trope of the colonizing English man raping Indian women went through two major transformations between 1770 and 1857. First, the figure of the English man as rapist disappeared from nineteenth-century discourse, which points to a more general silencing of both the word and the metaphor that was occurring in English culture in the last two decades of the eighteenth century. Around 1795, transcripts of London rape trials, for example, were no longer printed because they were considered "too 'indecent' to expose to the eyes of the public" (Clark 75). Likewise, though rape had been one of the major organizing metaphors in serious eighteenth-century English novels, Gothic conventions in the 1790s acted to shift the scene of rape farther and farther away from England and to redefine the rapist as a foreigner.[4]

By the 1830s, then, Gothic conventions had restructured English romances about India in such a way that Indian men were usually assigned the role of the villain-rapist while Indian women remained in the victim's position that Burke so graphically described.[5] Parliamentary reports in the 1820s about the incidence of suttee, the ritual immolation of a Hindu woman after the death of her husband, and British attempts to eradicate it, did much, no doubt, to sensationalize the domestic violence faced by high-caste Indian women and, among the more literary minded, to reinforce the association of the Indian male with the Gothic villain. Popular translations of *The Arabian Nights,* as Ali has shown, also reinforced this pattern. Edward Lane's translation, for example, presents Scheherazade as taking up her heroic performance as story-teller in order to prevent King Shahrir from raping and murdering any more of her countrywomen, though Lane decorously talks about this virgin sacrifice as "marriage."

After the Indian Uprising of 1857, there is a second more abrupt transformation in the trope of rape in British novels about India as English women replace Indian women as the victims of threatened or actual sexual violence. In other words, by 1857 all the actors in Burke's scenario had changed places and races so that innocent English women are depicted as abducted, imprisoned, and threatened with rape and torture by violent and lawless Indian men.

Rape narratives about English women raped by Indian men are familiar, in part, because of the popularity of British novels about what British historians usually call the Indian Mutiny of 1857. Between 1857 and 1900, more than fifty English novels about the Uprising were published and more than thirty more appeared before World War II (Brantlinger 199; see also Gupta and the less reliable survey by Singh). Patrick Brantlinger and other literary critics have argued that novels about the Indian Uprising drew heavily on popular British histories about it, but they have not adequately described the ideological and symbolic work performed by these texts.

While English novels about the Uprising claim the authority of history, they increasingly contradict authoritative historical accounts of the Mutiny. British and Anglo-Indian[6] fiction about the Indian Uprising thus displays, I would argue, what Mikhail Bakhtin has identified as the unique "dialogical" capacities of the novel which allowed it to accommodate competing contemporary voices (11–12). These novels were able to incorporate not only the more sensationalized public accounts of the Mutiny repeated in British newspaper reports and stage melodramas, but also the private versions of it heard in diaries, letters, and returning soldiers' tales which express the deepest fears and fantasies of English colonizers in India (see Sharpe).

As early as 1865, the distinguished historian George Trevelyan argued in *Cawnpore* that there was no evidence that English women were actually raped during the Uprising of 1857. The most famous victims of the Mutiny, the English women imprisoned and killed at Cawnpore had, he claimed, died "without apprehension of dishonour" (305). Anglo-Indian magistrates assigned to investigate rumors that English women had been raped similarly could find "no evidence of systematic mutilation, rape, and torture at Cawnpore or anyplace else" (Sharpe 32). Trevelyan reported that only one woman, the youngest daughter of Sir Hugh Wheeler, was abducted at Cawnpore. Disputing the accuracy of several popular London melodramas that represented her as killing her Indian attacker in order to save her honor, Trevelyan reported that Miss Wheeler and her abductor survived the fighting at Cawnpore; she was discovered, several years later, living quietly with her "master under a Mohammedan name" (255).

Nonetheless, Trevelyan's conclusions about the only surviving English rape victim whose case he could substantiate demonstrate how the Victorian notion that a grown woman could not be raped "against her will" insinuated itself into the history of the Mutiny. Trevelyan assumed that Miss Wheeler's survival and marriage either proved that she had consented to sex or that she was not a true English woman because a "pure" woman would have died to protect her honor or committed suicide afterward. Indicating how rape, as early as 1865, became entangled with emerging ideas about racial purity, later authorized by social Darwinism, Trevelyan concluded that Miss Wheeler's survival proved she "was by no means of pure English blood" (255). Trevelyan's treatment of Miss Wheeler's case demonstrates why any English woman who was actually raped during the Mutiny and survived would probably never tell her story.

II.

Mutiny novels written by British men and women who lived in India, in contrast to novels written by writers in the metropolis, reflected more of the tension and heat of life in this colonial "contact zone" (Pratt 5–6). Though Anglo-Indian novels about the Mutiny bear the traces of metropolitan colonial discourse, they were potentially open to a much wider variety of voices and often contest the language, ideologies, and assumptions of Orientalist constructions of India.

Both British and Anglo-Indian novels about the Mutiny show the writers' difficulties in reconciling contradictions generated by at least two conflicting ideologies: one which asserted the racial superiority of British men and women in India, and a second which demonstrated the necessity of male domination in both the public and private sphere (this second premise, by definition, included Indian as well as English men). Mutiny novelists usually obscured these conflicts by presenting their narratives as "national epics" which typically valorized the heroic sacrifices of English men and women during this colonial crisis by alluding to Roman and Greek epics. References to the rape of Lucrece were especially common because they established parallels between the establishment of the Roman Empire and the founding of the British Raj.

In attempting to present their narratives as epics about a heroic national past, Mutiny novelists tried to project very recent events into the distant, absolute epic past. Mutiny novels are consequently marked by efforts to fashion what Bakhtin calls a "world of 'beginnings' and 'peak times' in the national history, a world of fathers and of founders of families, a world of 'firsts' and 'bests'" (14). As a result, many Mutiny novels conform to what Bakhtin calls the "chronotype" of the chivalric romance (154). This symbolic organization of space and time in the novel endeavors to fuse the formal features of the epic with those of the Greek romance. While the hero and heroine in the chivalric romance face a hectic series of adventures which test their "chastity and mutual fidelity," they remain virtually unchanged and the result of the "whole lengthy novel is that the hero marries his sweetheart. . . . The hammer of events shatters nothing and forges nothing—it merely tries the durability of an already finished product" (106–7).

Likewise in the chivalric romance, Bakhtin explains, "heroic deeds are performed by which the heroes glorify themselves and glorify others (their liege lord, their lady)," and this attention to "glory and glorification," he claims, "heightens the similarity between the chivalric romance and epic" (153). However, the hero of the novel, in contrast to the hero of the epic, inhabits an imaginary world that is ideologically contested. As Bakhtin reminds us, "In the epic, there is one unitary and singular belief system. In the novel, there are many such systems, with the hero generally acting within his own system" (334).

When Anglo-Indian novels about the Mutiny are compared with romances written by writers in the metropolis, they reveal greater structural tension created especially by discursive technologies of race and gender that operated differently in the colonial "contact zone." By the 1890s, for example, as more Indian men were educated in English universities and as the Indian nationalist movement increasingly asserted the rights of the colonized, the English in India faced civil as well as military challenges to their authority: in the courts, in the civil service, in the political arena, in journalism, and in literature. Highly educated Indian women also began to dispute the authority of English feminists and Indian men who presumed to speak for them (see Sangari and Vaid). It became increasingly more difficult, then, for Anglo-Indian novelists to contain this rising chorus of Indian voices.

Moreover, by the 1890s, many prolific Anglo-Indian women also competed directly with male novelists, and several women in this generation wrote novels about the Mutiny (see Gregg). While some female novelists published their work under sexually ambiguous names like Maxwell Grey, others signed their texts with frankly feminine names like Hilda Gregg and Flora Annie Steel. The presence of a significant number of Anglo-Indian women writing in this period suggests in itself how traditional gender roles were unraveling by the end of the nineteenth century. As more and more English women went out to India, to work outside as well as inside the home, and as more of them represented their own versions of colonial life, they challenged Victorian social conventions equating domestic seclusion with modesty and female honor with silence.

By looking in more detail at the symbolic structure of five nineteenth-century novels about the Indian Uprising of 1857, we can begin to understand why the figure of the English woman raped by the Indian man became such an important icon in British "epics" about the Mutiny. By comparing two novels about the Mutiny by metropolitan writers, James Grant's *First Love and Last Love: A Tale of the Indian Mutiny* (1868) and G.A. Henty's *Rujub the Juggler* (1893), with three Anglo-Indian novels, George Chesney's *The Dilemma* (1876), Meadows Taylor's *Seeta* (1872), and Flora Annie Steel's *On the Face of the Waters* (1896), we can see why this particular rape narrative was so unstable, why it had to be repeated again and again. All five novels demonstrate in their particular ways that British India was contested ideological territory where Victorian technologies of gender worked to redefine honor, identity, sexuality, marriage, parenthood, and duty in service to the Raj. Ultimately, they also show how narratives about rape act, as Patricia Joplin has argued, to conceal the ways that "political hierarchy built upon male sexual dominance requires the violent appropriation of woman's power to speak" (41).

The most extraordinary feature of Grant's *First Love and Last Love*, one of the earliest novels about the Mutiny, is that it violates perhaps the most powerful literary taboo of the Victorian era which prohibited the description of the naked (white) female body and silenced mentions of rape in polite literature.[7] In describing the English women lost or left behind in the chaos that followed the retreat of the British forces from Delhi on 11 May 1857, Grant graphically details how English women became the victims of "every indignity that the singularly fiendish invention of the Oriental mind could suggest" (133). Defenseless English women, he reports, were driven into the streets:

> always stripped of their clothing, treated with every indignity, and then slowly tortured to death, or hacked at once to pieces, according to the fancy of their captors. . . . "No mercy was shown to age or sex. Delicate women were stripped to the skin, turned thus into the streets, beaten with bamboos, pelted with filth, and abandoned to the vile lusts of blood-stained miscreants until death or madness terminated their unutterable woe." (157–58)

In assigning English women this spectacular place as victims of the Mutiny, Grant uncannily, and probably inadvertently, repeats many of the details of the torture and rape that Burke described, but he assigns English rather than Indian women to the victim's place while the Indian rabble replaces Hastings and his men.

Grant justifies his violation of Victorian literary decorum and underscores the "epic" dimensions of this human sacrifice by alluding to the rape of Lucrece. The gap Grant attempts to span in linking England with Rome by this allusion is, needless to say, a wide one. Grant's difficulties are suggested by one surreal image of two English women caught in the streets of Delhi who were "stripped perfectly nude" and "bound by their tender limbs with ropes to two nine-pounder gun-carriages, on which, with their dishevelled hair sweeping the streets, they were drawn away towards the market place, amid the jeers and mockery of the lowest ruffians in Delhi" (198). In describing these anonymous women as rendered speechless by "unutterable woe," Grant explicitly alludes to Shakespeare's famous poem about Lucrece, which suggests how these women will reenact Lucrece's final sacrifice to the power of the phallus.

By providing this epic frame for his narrative about love and war, Grant also attempts to make his novel conform to the chronotype of the chivalric romance. Grant's novel recounts the careers of two young British officers, Rowley Thompson and Jack Harrower, and dramatizes their heroic efforts during the fall and recapture of Delhi in 1857, to defend and protect Kate and Madelena Weston, two beautiful English sisters whom they love. The insurrection interrupts Rowley's and Kate's wedding ceremony, and nearly three hundred pages of heroic military self-sacrifice and hectic adventure stand between the ritual and its erotic consummation, a pattern which is typical, according to Bakhtin, of the chivalric romance (151). Grant, however, multiplies his heroes and heroines, and the intertwined narratives about Kate and her sisters also demonstrate his response to the technologies of gender at work in Victorian England. It is important to note that the three Weston sisters do not claim Lucrece's power of speech or imitate her heroic resolve in killing herself. By the 1850s, Victorian social conventions restrained "pure" women from recognizing or speaking about rape, severely restricted their movement in public spaces by insisting they needed male protection outside the home, and blurred the distinctions between rape and seduction (Clark 128). The fates of the Weston sisters disclose Grant's allegiance to a conservative gender ideology which would transfer this Victorian view of rape to British India.

Madelena Weston, the eldest sister, has been courted by Jack Harrower but has rejected him, preferring a dashing cavalry officer with more status and sex appeal. During the crisis caused by the Uprising, Madelena escapes from a fate worse than death by assuming native dress and hiding for several weeks in the "wilderness" outside of Delhi with Jack as her chivalrous protector (or maybe a witness to prove she is not dishonored by her move into undomesticated space). Chastened by her ordeal, Madelena eventually agrees to marry Jack out of gratitude for his protection. This is one of the ways that rape policed female desire in British novels about India.

Grant faces an even more difficult problem in representing Kate Weston's fate since he apparently wished to conform to the chronotype of the chivalric romance which required that the heroine's virginity be preserved so that she could be happily reunited with her husband. When Kate is abducted by one of the Indian insurgents and imprisoned in her own home, Grant must provide some plausible reason why her captor does not simply rape her, an outrage the typical Oriental villain should, almost by definition, attempt. Grant's narrator explains that her abductor is caught in a dispute with his superiors as to who has the right to "possess" Kate, so he contents himself with humiliating her by forcing her to act as his servant before his "leering" male friends. In this way, Grant displays how rape threatens English women with a loss of class status as well as bodily violation.

The fate of the youngest, sixteen-year-old and "immaculately blond" Weston sister is perhaps the most illustrative of this transfer of Victorian politics of rape to India. Polly Weston is seized by one of the princes of Delhi and imprisoned in the royal harem. The aristocratic Muslim prince wants to enjoy Polly's love before he possesses her body, but because she resists all his advances, he finally loses patience and sends her into the streets where she is raped and tortured by the rabble. In this way Grant endorses Victorian presumptions that while upper-class men may seduce, only lower-class men rape (Edwards 141–43).

When the British retake Delhi, Jack Harrower discovers what the rabble has done to Polly Weston:

> There against the palace wall, which was shattered by cannon shot, and thickly starred by rifle bullets, was the body of a girl, snowy white, sorely emaciated and nailed by her hands and feet against the masonry, with her golden hair—'that mute ornament which God has given to woman'—waving in ripples on the wind. (412)

In representing the rape and murder of English women in such spectacular terms—in fact, in Polly's case as a crucifixion—Grant compares English women's ultimate sacrifice with that of Lucrece in order to emphasize how their deaths contributed to the greater glory of the empire. In short, Grant's novel indicates that the only rapes that count are those of white golden-haired English women, but these innocent victims cannot survive or describe their rape and so are violently reduced to silence.

III.

Writing about the Mutiny from the safe distance of the Mother Country, James Grant apparently was untroubled by the ways that the myth of Lucrece challenged Christian prohibitions about sex and suicide. George Chesney, who lived in India for many years (Lyall 132–34), focuses on these contradictions in his Mutiny novel, *The Dilemma* (1876). Chesney's title alludes to the moral "dilemma" that St. Augustine located in Lucrece's rape and suicide. Augustine asked, if Lucrece is "adulterous, why is she praised? If chaste, why put to death?" (Donaldson 29). By his allusions to Lucrece's rape, Chesney exposes moral problems that Grant ignores, a conflict Patrick Brantlinger misses in his brief exegesis of this novel. *The Dilemma* ultimately discloses how the heroine is destroyed by the conflicting premises of imperial and Christian duty that underlie colonial life and by the assumptions about male and female honor that distinguish the gender arrangements in British India from those in the metropolis.

Unlike most Mutiny novels, *The Dilemma* does not conform to the chronotype of the chivalric romance. Instead, Chesney exposes the ideological conflicts in colonial life that are generated by imperialism. While Chesney clearly respects the Christian fortitude shown by Anglo-Indian men and women during the Mutiny, he also criticizes the hypocrisy of Christian evangelicals who imagine all Indians as unregenerate heathens and who overlook the evils produced by repressive class and gender systems at home as well as abroad. Likewise, though he asserts the moral superiority of British colonizers as the legitimate source of their power over the colonized, Chesney nonetheless questions a laissez-faire capitalism that imposes severe duties on the colonizers in India in order to support lives of luxurious self-indulgence in England.

Like the typical hero of the chivalric romance, Chesney's hero, Arthur Yorke, falls in love at first sight with the heroine, Olivia Cunningham, but he stands by helplessly as she marries a much older man, Colonel Falkland, the District Commissioner of Mustaphabad. Olivia plays to perfection the part of the beautiful, chaste, and self-possessed memsahib. After the Mutiny erupts, Olivia acts as nurse with exemplary coolness, selflessness, and courage. When her husband falls and is carried off during the siege of the Residency, Olivia, like Lucrece, sternly represses her personal grief.

Like Polly Weston, Olivia also eventually becomes a sacrificial victim but only after she remarries and returns to England to live in poverty, having been abandoned by her dishonorable second husband. Exiled in a culture that no longer values her labor or her self-sacrifice, Olivia is forced to live out Lucrece's dilemma and is martyred by her sexual guilt. The colonial moral code that required her patriotic self-sacrifice and sexual repression in India becomes the cause of her shame at home. Olivia's moral crisis is caused not by rape but by bigamy, when, ten years after her first husband's reported death, she discovers that he did not actually die in battle. Maimed and deformed, Falkland escaped from captivity too late to prevent Olivia's second marriage. Following her to England, he heroically, but implausibly, rescues her and her children but is killed when their burning house collapses around him.

Realizing that Falkland's appearance means she has innocently committed bigamy, Olivia subsequently regards herself as adulterous—in other words, she sees herself in Augustine's terms, as an unchaste woman. Identifying the children she has borne by her second marriage as "wretched little bastard brat[s]" (423), Olivia sees herself as no "better than a street-walker" (423). Overcome by guilt about her violation of the sexual code that equates chastity with female honor, Olivia is driven to madness and drowns herself. But her insanity clears her of the charge of willful suicide that Augustine identified as Lucrece's worst sin. Chesney's narrative, in contrast to Grant's, shows that Victorian moral standards premised on female asexuality and animated by the ethics of shame could not discriminate between women who had been raped and those who committed bigamy or consensual adultery. Given this moral training, Victorian women like Olivia could not understand, much less imitate, Lucrece's heroic resistance.

Chesney reveals paradoxes that are usually repressed in chivalric romances about the India Mutiny not only in his representation of his heroine's pathetic sacrifice to a sexual ideology which defined female honor only in terms of chastity, but in his treatment of his hero as well. In India, Yorke recognizes the dilemma that marriage posed for a young British colonial soldier: "He could not help thinking that although the hope of winning the fair prize now before him was a source of strength and courage at present, it would be a hard wrench to leave her side to go campaigning again" (243–44). Because marriageable white women are rare in British India and Yorke's junior officer's pay prevents him from being recognized as an appropriate suitor, he does not have to face this moral test.

Similarly, Chesney challenges emerging stereotypes defining Anglo-Indian women like Madelena Weston as vain, frivolous, idle, status seekers when his hero compares the leisure of upper-class English women with the self-sacrifice of their colonial counterparts. When the unmarried Yorke returns to England as a decorated colonel, he ruefully observes that his rank and military honors have dramatically improved his stock in the marriage market. Approached by the father of a rich young heiress who seeks him as a partner for his daughter, Yorke notes with disapproval that his intended, Lucy Peevor, unlike the women of colonial India, has lived in a "hot bed of luxury" all her life. "How many hundred girls in England," Yorke wonders, "were spending just the same dawdling, useless, unprofitable lives, who would never be missed outside the home circle, and hardly within it?" (365). Lucy nonetheless earns Yorke's love and proves she would be a good colonial wife when she shows her courage and physical strength by rescuing him from drowning. In this marriage which finally unites Yorke with one of England's "new women," Chesney acknowledges how nineteenth-century feminism rendered obsolete many of the conventions of the chivalric romance.

Chesney also reexamines the ostensible glory at the center of the chivalric romance by challenging the imperial ethics which usually valorized "fathers and founders of families" in Mutiny novels (Donaldson 103–8). While Yorke admires Falkland's old-fashioned chivalry, he recognizes that his commanding officer's assumptions about duty and authority are no longer functional. Recognizing that the Enfield rifle that ignited the Mutiny also made war more fatal, Yorke offers technical advice which Falkland fails to implement in planning the fortifications for the defense of the Residency, and many die as a consequence.

Likewise, Chesney shows what happens when the aggressive individualism fostered by English laissez-faire capitalism is imported to British India where it acted to undermine the chivalric code of honor in the rising generation of younger officers. Serving under Olivia's second husband, Yorke observes first hand how Colonel Kirke's brutality and passion for self-advancement destroy all pretense of honorable conduct in the British campaign to reestablish control after the Mutiny. Kirke murders defenseless Indian civilians, condones looting, and steals at least one wealthy prisoner's jewels rather than turning them over to the "prize agent," as army regulations required (259–60). Kirke's court-martial thus anticipates his private dishonor when he abandons Olivia and their two daughters. By exposing these conflicts between colonial and metropolitan ethics, Chesney demonstrates that chivalry is effectively dead and shows how the Roman formulations of glory and honor imbedded in the chivalric romance often act to hide a lust for conquest.

## IV.

Meadows Taylor's *Seeta* (1872) is even more open to the heteroglossia of colonial life and more perceptive about the conflicts generated by the racist and sexist ideologies at work in the "contact zone" of British India. Taylor rejected altogether the dominant trope of the rape of white women by Indian men which usually structures "national epics" about the Mutiny and displays, instead, how racial prejudices are inflamed by sensational rape narratives like Grant's. *Seeta* reasserts interracial marriage as an alternative to rape and revenge by recalling the marriages in Indian epics where daughters are exchanged to establish stronger and more peaceful political alliances between conquering and conquered warriors.

Taylor's title, of course, suggests the importance of rape in this novel by inviting comparison with Sita, the female heroine of the popular Indian epic, the *Ramayana;* in most versions of this epic, Sita was herself a victim of rumors about rape rather than rape itself. Unlike Grant, Taylor recognized the ambiguity that allowed rape to be confused with seduction, making it what Patricia Joplin calls an "equivocal sign" (46). In colonial societies, this ambiguity generates dangerous suspicions, for imperialism itself breeds mutual betrayal, suspicion, violence, and revenge, feelings that Taylor shows are experienced by both the colonizer and the colonized. *Seeta* offers an implicit criticism of British colonizers who saw their religion and race as undisputed evidence of their moral superiority. In rejecting the racial imperative implicit in the "chivalric romance," Taylor presents a narrative that reasserts the earlier Gothic model of rape, which assigned the Indian rather than the English woman to the position of victim.

In his transparently truthful autobiography, Taylor asks the question that most Mutiny novels would repress when he writes: "[English] people ask me what I found in the natives to like so much. Could I help loving them when they loved me so? Why should I not love them?" (*Life* 445; see also Manusukhani; Amur). Perhaps because it is infused by this sympathy, Taylor's *Seeta* presents the least racist and most optimistic representation of interracial marriage in any Mutiny novel that I know, which is not to say it escapes racism altogether.

The autobiographical traces that appear in *Seeta* mitigate against epic distancing. Cyril Brandon, the novel's hero, violates the unspoken racial premises of most Mutiny romances because he falls in love and marries Seeta, a rich and beautiful Indian widow. Taylor's description of Seeta's physical appearance and personality also reveals some autobiographical traces for she resembles Mary Palmer, Taylor's beloved wife.[8] Some of Taylor's English acquaintances felt that he, like Brandon, had crossed over the color barrier in marrying Mary Palmer whose grandfather was Warren Hastings's secretary and whose grandmother was one of the Princesses of Delhi. During a visit to London in 1838–1840, one bigoted English matron disparaged Mary's "blackness" and ridiculed Taylor's apparent devotion to his "little Indian queen" (Taylor, *Letters* x). Taylor's sharp critique of the deployment of British ideologies of race and gender in colonial India is evidently informed by this experience.

In representing the mutual love that Seeta and Brandon share, Taylor reasserts a more Romantic perspective on the power of sympathy and sexual passion to overcome racial prejudice and accommodate cultural difference. Taylor's Romanticism is also evident in his feminist assessment of the potential of Indian and English women. Believing in companionate marriage, his hero wants a wife who is more intellectually and morally compatible than the poorly educated English women he meets in India. Dismayed by Brandon's Shelleyan idealism, his more conventional male companion protests, "If all men in India were as aesthetic . . . as you we should have flights of blue stockings coming out by every mail" (74).

Seeta also presents a dramatic contrast to the silent and passive victim epitomized by Polly Weston and Olivia Cunningham. Unlike most English heroines in Mutiny novels, Seeta claims Lucrece's original power of eloquent speech early in the novel when she testifies in court about the details of her first husband's murder, her near-rape, and her other injuries. Brandon, who acts as magistrate in this hearing, marvels over "evidence given so clearly, so firmly . . . so minutely" (66). He falls in love with Seeta not only because of her power with words but also because she is "a good Sanscrit scholar" (86), with an inquiring mind, an expansive imagination, a high spirit, and a generous heart.

In contrast to most British and Anglo-Indian novelists of the post-Mutiny period, Taylor does not represent this interracial union as biologically doomed. Married to a man who publicly espouses and privately practices his feminist principles, Seeta escapes from those Indian—and Victorian—proprieties that would keep her silent and confine her to the domestic sphere. In contrast to those "delicate women who had never in their lives known hardships" (314) whose victimization Grant describes, Seeta displays extraordinary physical as well as moral courage during the Uprising. Assuming the "simple boy's dress" (286) that allows her to ride astride and armed with a small revolver, Seeta takes a "strange delight" in sharing her husband's dangerous "duty" (318) as he travels around the district in his effort to maintain (English) law and order.

Taylor's novel also differs dramatically from Grant's because it does not represent the Mutiny in epic terms where the past is "absolute and complete . . . as closed as a circle" (Bakhtin 16). On the contrary, *Seeta* describes a world which reaches into "the present day with all its inconclusiveness, its indecision, its openness, its potential for re-thinking and re-evaluating" (Bakhtin 16). Though Taylor's narrator occasionally mentions the historical events at Lucknow, Cawnpore, Delhi, and Jhansi in the "red year" of 1857, he focuses instead on colonial life elsewhere, fictionalizing his own experience as a District-Commissioner in West Berar in 1857–1858 where he maintained order by force of his personality alone, without the aid of any British troops.

In contrast to both Grant and Chesney, Taylor identifies the causes of the Uprising of 1857 not by depicting the rebelling Sepoys as interchangeable "Oriental fiends" who are driven mad by their lust to rape white women, but by particularizing the somewhat more comprehensible motives of Azrael Pande, a discharged Indian sepoy. Pande is presented as a brilliant demagogue, a skillful politician, and a potential Indian nationalist, but he also reveals the irrationality typical of the Gothic villain in his fascination with Thuggee and witchcraft. Taylor insists, though, that Pande is ultimately driven mad not by his balked desire for English women but rather because he wants to possess the rich and beautiful Indian woman Brandon has married. In this way, Taylor exposes the sexual rivalry between English and Indian men who vie for the attention of Indian women, a conflict that is nearly always obscured in other English Mutiny novels and histories.

In contrasting Brandon's love for Seeta with Pande's desire to abduct, humiliate, and exploit her, Taylor also violates Victorian literary decorum by drawing clear distinctions between the motives of the lover and those of the rapist. Azrael Pande exploits rumors of rape in order to excite both Hindus and Moslems to take revenge upon the English, transforming the news of Seeta's and Cyril's marriage into a story about Seeta's abduction and rape by this powerful English man (135).

Pande's retelling of the colonial rape narrative not only harkens back to Burke's version of the colonial rape narrative but also exploits resentment over the increasing institutionalization of racism in the civil and religious laws defining colonial relations in British India in the 1850s. Pande is not the only member of the colonized group to see the ambiguities in Cyril's and Seeta's union. Before their marriage, Seeta's aunt fears that Cyril has taken advantage of his superior position in the colonial hierarchy and has seduced her niece, since, as the representative of justice in this district, Cyril could rape Seeta without fear of reprisal (120).

Moreover, the colonizing English men who are Brandon's superiors in the colonial bureaucracy also see the politically dangerous consequences of interracial unions and refuse to recognize Cyril's marriage as permanent. Likewise, the English matrons in Cyril's home station of Noorpoor are affronted because he has chosen to marry an Indian woman and not one of their daughters. Inflamed by envy, ignorant racial bigotry, sexual hunger, and boredom, they imagine Seeta as the agent and Cyril as the victim of her seduction (213). The Anglo-Indian women at Brandon's station are able to take revenge on Seeta and assert their moral superiority by explaining how the laws of the Church of England prohibiting the marriage of Christians and non-Christians would therefore refuse to recognize the children of Seeta's and Brandon's union as legally legitimate.

Dispirited by this news, Seeta, ultimately, repeats Lucrece's sacrifice; she is fatally wounded when she interposes her body to protect Brandon from Pande and receives the sword thrust meant to kill her husband. Taylor apparently could not imagine how Seeta's union with Brandon [9] could be sustained after the Mutiny when, as many of these novels attest, colonizers confused racial bigotry with patriotic zeal.

Finally, though Taylor's novel shows his efforts to reject both the racism of British culture and the patriarchal habits of mind which define women as a species of property to be valued only for their chastity, it shows nonetheless his inability to question English property laws concerning legitimacy, inheritance, land tenure, and taxation, laws he was employed to impose upon the Indians. Because Seeta dies before she bears any children, Taylor is able to avoid the deeper psychological issues that Flora Annie Steel explores in her treatment of the "mystery" of fatherhood and motherhood in *On the Face of the Waters*. With Seeta conveniently eliminated, Brandon returns to England, claims his estate, marries a liberal, well-educated English woman who also knew and loved Seeta, and produces an heir who will be more easily accepted in English society.

## V.

One of the most extraordinary features of novels about the Indian Uprising of 1857 is their sameness and persistence. The 1890s witnessed a new wave of novels about the Mutiny which invites us to ask what prompted the obsessive repetition of this symbolic narrative? With the Mutiny more than thirty years in the past, epic distance became easier to create, and many British novelists continued to produce novels that conformed to the formula of the "chivalric romance."

By the 1890s most professional British historians of the Mutiny agreed that English women were not raped during the Mutiny, but most British and Anglo-Indian novels about it continued to repeat these disputed stories about the torture and rape of English women. Ann L. Stoler has argued that "concern over protection of white women" existed in colonies throughout Southeast Asia at this time, and this concern "intensified during real and perceived crises of control—provoked by threats to the internal cohesion of European communities or by infringements on their borders" (641). Stoler has shown that there was no correlation between the actual incidence of interracial rape and the passage of race-specific laws that imposed severe penalties on native men who assaulted—or even touched—European women.

The controversy surrounding the Ilbert Bill in British India in 1883 appears as just such a crisis of control. Mrinalini Sinha has demonstrated that Gladstone's Liberal government ignited a "white mutiny" when it sponsored a reform measure which would have removed a "racially discriminatory clause," introduced in 1872, preventing Indian judges from "exercising jurisdiction over European British subjects living outside the chief Presidency towns" (Sinha 98; see also Hirschmann). Three to five thousand Anglo-Indian civilians and governmental officials, planters, and soldiers joined in mass protests which eventually forced India's Viceroy, Marquis of Ripon, to modify the Ilbert Bill.

Some of the most hysterical objections to the Ilbert Bill concerned the imagined spectacle of an English woman who brought charges of rape or sexual assault against an Indian man in a court with an Indian judge presiding. Sinha reports that "there were numerous . . . cases of assaults or attempted assaults on white women reported in the Anglo-Indian press" but "there was no evidence that these 'vile offenses' against white women were exceptional to the time" (103). Breaking strong social taboos which usually confined them to silence on public issues and prevented them from speaking about rape, many Anglo-Indian women organized protests and vehemently denounced this bill. Yet, as Sinha argues, "the mobilization of white women on their own initiative . . . threatened the edifice on which colonial society was built" (106). As Mutiny novels of the 1890s show, the "image of the pure and passionless white woman as the helpless victim of a lascivious native male" (105) performed its ideological work best when the victim remained passive and silent.

The controversy surrounding the Ilbert Bill widened the political and social gap between metropolitan and Anglo-Indian culture, and assigned further ideological work to Anglo-Indian novelists. Mutiny novels of the 1890s written by metropolitan writers also suggest that this crisis of control was precipitated not only by anxiety about increasing racial conflict in India but also by a profound crisis in definitions of gender roles and sexual identity at home. Even the most conventional Mutiny novels of the 1890s indicate how changing gender roles undermined the chronotype of the chivalric romance.

The hero, for example, in G.A. Henty's *Rujub the Juggler* (1893) still plunges "headfirst into adventures" and inhabits a world of adventure time where "the unexpected is what is expected," and where chance prevails (Bakhtin 151). But Henty's heroine, Isobel Hanney, participates more fully in the hero's adventures. The threat of rape, then, functions as a check and reminder of the heroine's sexual difference.

Like most Mutiny novels, *Rujub the Juggler* combines a story about love with a story about war, and the narrative hinges on the near rape of the heroine. When the orphaned Isobel Hanney comes to India to act as hostess for her uncle who is stationed in Cawnpore, the notorious historical site for the rumored rapes and murder of English women, she attracts the unwanted attentions of the Indian leader, Nana Sahib because of her beauty and grace. During the Mutiny, he captures her and imprisons her in his harem and threatens to rape her. When the hero devises a bizarre strategy to "save" Isobel which identifies self-mutilation as her best defense, she wordlessly acquiesces; she does not even consider asking him to bring her a weapon to defend herself or poison to kill Nana Sahib. Following the hero's scientifically precise directions, Isobel spreads acid all over her face and shoulders to blister her skin, making herself so unattractive to Nana Sahib that he releases her from the harem and allows her to rejoin the other captured English women. One English matron laments Isobel's defacement but applauds her courage, saying: "'Bravely done, girl! Bravely and nobly done'" (3: 135). In this exchange Henty indicates how Victorian women were encouraged to police their own self-destructive responses to the threat of rape.[10]

The real problem in this novel is that the hero, Ralph Bathurst, has questions about his manhood; he suffers from a "nervous" complaint that causes him to tremble and shake "like a girl at the sound of firearms" (1: 33). When the Mutiny erupts, Bathurst's secret is forced into the open, and he is humiliated because he cannot take his place with the other marksmen shooting at the mutineers and is forced to "play the part of a woman rather than a man" (3: 25). It is the Indian guru, Rujub—the embodiment of all the mystical secrets of Eastern philosophy—who cures Bathurst and helps him finally to perform adequately on the battlefield (and as it turns out in the bedroom). Only a hack like Henty could disclose the powerful secrets of Rujub's "magic" with such symbolic—and hilarious—naiveté, for Rujub's most marvelous trick involves a telescoping pole that extends itself more than one hundred feet in the air, bearing his daughter aloft, and then slowly deflates, causing her to vanish magically. The trick of the monumental telescoping phallus is performed twice, and confounds even the most scientific Englishmen in this novel, who subsequently show a studied respect for Rujub's inexplicable prowess. In describing this trick, Henty inadvertently exposes the heterosexual rivalry (and homosexual desire) that colonizing English men were expected to repress.

Rujub and his daughter, like many servants in Anglo-Indian novels, prove their loyalty to the Raj when they later cooperate with Bathurst to help Isobel escape from Nana Sahib. When Isobel and Ralph reach safety many pages later, they declare their love and their desire to marry, but Bathurst must first prove his manhood by surviving in battle. Their marriage ceremony is conducted just minutes before Bathurst's volunteer company departs, so the consummation of this marriage, like Kate Weston's in *First Love and Last Love,* is delayed by a long wartime campaign. In most novels of the 1890s, this is how the warrior's code of ethics is represented and mobilized.

VI.

While Flora Annie Steel explicitly identifies her novel, *On the Face of the Waters,* as an "epic of the race" (Steel, *Garden* 226), it is remarkable because it reflects many of the new ideological tensions in colonial discourse of the 1890s.[11] Like Taylor's *Seeta,* Steel's novel is far more open to the heteroglossia of colonial life than the novels of Grant or Henty. In *On the Face of the Waters,* Steel emphasizes the multiplicity of colonial voices by contrasting, for example, the mutinous sepoy with the Indian soldier who remained true to his salt, the treacherous household servant with the loyal Indian ayah, and the duplicitous wife of the king of Delhi with the devout Moghul Princess who remained aloof from the plotting against the English. Moreover, as these polarities suggest, Steel saw gender as a determining factor in the experiences of both the Indians and the British caught up in the drama of the Mutiny. While English characters remain at the center of her novel, Steel challenged the gender paradigm of earlier chivalric romances about the Indian Uprising by refusing, like Taylor, to write a narrative which hinged on the rape of an English woman. In rejecting the "chronotype" of the chivalric romance and the allusions to Lucrece which allowed writers like Grant and Henty to establish symbolic parallels between the birth of the Roman Republic and the British Raj, Steel attempted to create a national epic that allowed English women to be heroes without becoming sacrificial victims. In order to satisfy this objective, Steel naturalized the institutional racism that Taylor's novel contests.

One cause of Steel's resistance to the basic formula of the "chivalric romance" can perhaps be found in her experience of colonial life in India and her endorsement of many of the goals of British feminism. During her twenty-year stay in India, Steel studied several Indian languages and worked outside as well as inside the home, superintending several Indian girls' schools, for a time. When she returned to live permanently in England in 1889, Steel defied the Victorian conventions that would keep her silent; she joined with the conservative branch of the "suffragette" movement to fight for women's vote and wrote more than twenty popular novels before her death in 1929. Steel's experience of colonial life in India apparently convinced her that the private realm of home and family could not be separated from the public realm of work and war. Because both men and women were called to work in service to the Raj, she wished to judge them by the same code of honor, and so rejected the gender-specific ethics that are exalted in Grant's and Henty's novels and that prove fatal to the heroines in Chesney's and Taylor's work.[12]

Unlike chivalric romances about the Mutiny, Steel's *On the Face of the Waters* interrogates the definitions of "honor" and "glory" that prevail in other Mutiny novels which culminate in the presumably happy marriage of the English hero and heroine. While most Mutiny novels insist on the sexual rapaciousness of Indian men, Steel's novel discloses instead the sexual hypocrisy imbedded in most chivalric romances about British India by displaying the sexual lawlessness of English men who freely transgress the boundaries set by marriage and by the color bar. Major Erlton, the heroine's husband, suffers no censure from his military superiors even though he flaunts his adulterous relationship with the pretty, adventurous English-woman, Alice Gissing (See Saunders). Married to a man who fails to behave "like a gentleman" by showing proper sexual restraint, and who, in fact, neither respects nor loves her, Kate Erlton experiences sexual relations, even in marriage, as rape. Likewise, Jim Douglas, who plays the role of the hero in this novel, has been ostracized from polite British society because he was caught in an adulterous alliance with his superior officer's wife which re-sulted in his court-martial. Douglas subsequently places himself beyond the pale by "buying" and living for seven years with a Muslim woman. Like many feminists of her generation, Steel thought the best way to eliminate these sexual double standards was by subjecting English men to the same "repressive standard of sexual morality" as was applied to respectable En-glish women (Holton 22).

Steel's most audacious gesture in her national epic is that she refuses conventions of female heroism that define rape as the fatal test of an Englishwoman's morality and virtue. Kate Erlton escapes from a fate worse than death by only pretending to be a victim of rape. During the fall of Delhi, Kate is separated from her husband. She is rescued when Jim Douglas, dis-guised as a marauding Afghani, throws her across his saddlebow, and she, disguised as a native woman, screams as if she expected to be raped. Dou-glas then offers Kate shelter in the native quarter of Delhi, but she must save herself from detection by passing as Douglas's new Indian paramour, wear-ing eastern veils and adjusting to life in seclusion. (Now this is imprison-ment in the harem with a difference.) Steel thus turns inside out the Orientalist harem tales that Grant and Henty invoke and uses the occasion, instead, to teach her morally rebellious hero to better appreciate the English values of companionate marriage.

Steel's national epic also differs from the other Mutiny novels because it imagines the revolutionary potential of an international and interracial sisterhood that emerged from feminist critiques of male sexuality and vio-lence in both English and Indian culture. Kate eventually escapes from Delhi by establishing sisterly bonds with Indian women. She is protected both by a Muslim princess who lives in a neighboring house and by her Hindu servant, Tara, who shelters her in an ashram. Kate remains in hiding for nearly a week in this religious retreat, where, for a brief time, she is able to see war as the "primitive art" of a "primitive people" (393) and to imagine the possibility of a world without war, a paradoxical discovery when war is raging all around her.

In the end, though, this fragile sisterly alliance between English and Indian women is sabotaged by Kate's—and Steel's—unqualified belief in the superiority of English culture and by her individualism and unacknowledged sexual competitiveness. Steel translated and published an English version of the *Ramayana* for children, so she was well aware that this epic presented Sita's trial by fire as the ultimate test of her heroism and purity. Faced with this idealized example of Sita's courage, chastity, and devotion, Steel labored to show why her English heroine was morally superior to Tara, the Indian woman who plans to perform suttee earlier in the novel and sacrifices so much to save Kate.

Steel signals the moral inferiority of her Indian heroine by including a shocking display of Tara's nearly naked body, as she parades through the streets of Delhi in preparation for the ritual of suttee:

> She was naked to the waist, and the scanty ochre-tinted cloth folded about her middle was raised so as to show the scars upon her lower limbs. The sunlight gleaming on the magnificent bronze curves showed a seam or two upon her breast also. . . . Her face, full of wild spiritual exaltation, was unmarred and, with the shaven head, stood out bold and clear as a cameo. (112)

In willingly exposing her body, Tara betrays what Steel regarded as unwomanly indelicacy. Shortly afterward, Tara abandons her plans to enact the ritual and returns to domestic service, at Douglas's request, in order to take care of Kate. Douglas saved Tara from the pyre once before and the high-caste Hindu woman conformed to conventions in Anglo-Indian romances by falling in love with him. In this way, Steel suggests the moral inferiority of upper class Indian women by showing how they are easily persuaded to abandon religious vows because of appeals to their passion and sexual desire.

The ideological conflict between international feminism and nationalism is most obvious when Tara sacrifices everything in order to lead Kate out of the city to be reunited with her husband and countrymen on the Ridge above Delhi. Though Tara is still in love with Jim Douglas, she passively concedes that Kate is a more worthy mate. She subsequently surrenders her love for Douglas, cuts herself off from her brother, defiles her caste, violates her religious integrity, and betrays what in another novel could be defined as the cause of Indian nationalism to save Kate. After performing this service, Tara enacts a suttee-like suicide when she remains in a house that is burned when the British soldiers retake the city. Thus Steel presents Tara's death, which could be seen as uncomfortably close to Lucrece's, as an expression of Hindu fanaticism rather than a laudable act of courage and self-mastery. Steel provides no plausible motive for this generous sacrifice since Kate enters into only the most superficial and patronizing relationship with Tara, an implausibility evident in Henty's treatment of Rujub and in many other British novels as well.

The conclusion of Steel's novel is also deformed by her desire to legitimize the preeminence of English men as conquerors and English women as wives and mothers of their children, even though she was willing to criticize the patriarchal foundations of epics about British "fathers and founders of families." Steel restores her heroine to her place in history when she is briefly reunited with her husband and lives among the English soldiers before their final assault on Delhi. Forced to face the reality of war and violence, Kate renounces her desire for "healing and atonement" and "forgets" the female vision of world beyond war that once united her with Indian women. In the British war camp, Kate admits that she can "imagine a world without women . . . but not a world without men" (432). She consequently learns to reimagine the causes of the Mutiny in orthodox patriarchal terms: as one of Steel's characters puts it earlier, "Delhi had been lost to save women; the trouble begun to please them" (286). Earlier in the novel, Kate recognized the power of revenge when she feels "a pride, almost a pleasure in the thought of the revenge which would surely be taken sooner or later . . . for every woman, every child killed, wounded,—even touched. She was conscious of it, even though she stood aghast before a vision of the years stretching away into an eternity of division and mutual hate" (251–52). Restored to her place in the patriarchy, Kate accepts her complicity in promoting the heroics of revenge.

In recounting the English assault on Delhi, Steel also reveals her endorsement of English hero worship and dramatizes her own allegiance to the Conservative imperial politics of force. She presents John Nicholson, a famous and brutal British officer who died of wounds sustained in the final attack on Delhi, as a compelling and attractive figure "full of passion, energy, vitality" (440) (see Wurgaft). Likewise, Kate's husband almost recovers his lost honor by displaying courage on the battlefield, though he dies unheroically enough in the random gunfire before the final attack on the city. Major Erlton's death thus frees Kate to marry Jim Douglas, the man who has learned to love her during their captivity. Yet, Douglas must prove he has the same heroic vitality as Nicholson by joining in the campaign to subdue Indian insurgents in the countryside after Delhi is retaken. Like all the other heroes described above, Douglas survives many battles, a long sickness, and eventually returns to England, where, in a postscript, he marries Kate.

Thus, Steel allowed herself to be "used to silence" the voice of the Other and succumbed to that amnesia, that pressure to "not-see, to not-know, to not-name what is true" (Joplin 55) about the violence suffered by those whose bodies and minds are colonized. In this way, Steel revealed the privilege of the English woman who, whether she writes or not, had many inducements to forget her own experience of colonialization and the insight it gave her into the lives of multiply colonized Indian men and women.

In designing this conclusion for her novel, Steel preserved the power that the chivalric romance granted to English women by valorizing their class and race prerogatives as memsahib and mother. Though Steel recognized the "exchange of violence" that underlay the "exchange of women" in marriage (Joplin 45), she nevertheless endorsed new evolutionary theories of race which enhanced the power of white women as mothers. In her novel, interracial marriages like Cyril's and Seeta's are imagined as impossibly painful and the fates of the children of these racially mixed marriages are envisioned as unavoidably tragic. Jim Douglas feels relief, rather than grief, when his racially mixed son, that "little morsel of flesh" (357), dies. Setting aside the guilty memories of his Indian mistress and their son, Douglas goes to war hoping to prove himself worthy of a pure English woman like Kate who will allow him to father a son he would be "proud of possessing," a boy who would go to school and be "fagged and flogged and inherit familiar virtues and vices instead of strange ones" (357). Despite her resistances, Steel's novel finally confirms an ideology of nationalism that defines chastity and social purity as signs of the evolutionary superiority of English men and women.

In its conclusion, Steel's novel reflects two conflicts in the feminisms of her time, conflicts which persist today. First it suggests the power of cultural as well as political imperialism to redefine not only feminism but national identity itself through its representation of motherhood and fatherhood; that is, through its emphasis on the heterosexual couple. Steel's heroine is given a second chance in life because of an Indian woman's vision and self-sacrifice, but Kate finds no permanent escape from the patriarchal logic defining her sexuality, gender, race, and nationality.

Second, Steel's novel shows the conflicts that are part of the history of nineteenth-century feminism by showing the difficulties she faced in reconciling emancipationist feminist discourse which would justify elite women's participation in the public sphere with late-nineteenth-century feminist discourse about female sexuality which stressed all women's sexual victimization by men. Thus, Steel authorized British women's emancipation by silencing stories about rape and sexual desire. This gesture is not unexpected, as Patricia Joplin reminds us. Writing about sexuality was—and is—profoundly threatening to the woman writer because "coming into language, especially into language about her body, has entailed the risk of a hidden but felt sexual anxiety, a premonition of violence" directed at women who try to tell unconventional truths about rape (Joplin 39).

In turning her back on her feminist vision of interracial sisterhood, Steel achieves closure in her novel by invoking the authority not only of social Darwinism but of history as well, which, as Bakhtin argues, "demands that we acknowledge it, that we make it our own." In conforming to the most authoritative accounts of the Mutiny written in the 1890s, Steel submits to "the authoritative word . . . located in a distanced zone, organically connected with a past that is felt to be hierarchically higher. It is, so to speak, the word of the fathers" (Bakhtin 342).

While Steel, like Taylor, resists repeating the sensational stories about the rape of English women during the Mutiny, her novel nonetheless remains haunted by the ghost of Miss Wheeler, by the part of the story about rape under the Raj that always threatened to break through the narratives which would deny it. Finally, even feminist efforts less conflicted than Steel's must fail if their authors desire to legitimize their texts by reference to women's history, part of which remains irretrievably lost (Spivak). Certainly, there were other English women whose stories were censored by historians like Trevelyan in order to shore up conflict-ridden Victorian interpretations of the warrior code which redeemed or justified violence by reference to rape. And though official British records do not acknowledge it, there certainly were many other stories, like the one Edmund Burke described, about Indian women raped by English men drunk on power, violence, and revenge. Because novels about the Mutiny could explore the symbolic territory that Victorian history would deny, they retained their popularity long after the chivalric romance was dead.

*Notes*

Earlier drafts of this essay were originally presented at the Nationalisms and Sexualities Conference, Harvard University, Cambridge, Massachusetts, on 17 June

1989, and at the Bunting Institute, Radcliffe College, 31 October 1990. Special thanks to Florence Ladd, Director of the Bunting Institute, and to Beverly Grier, Bina Agarwal, Lynn Wilson, Mary Carpenter, and all the other Institute fellows. Thanks also to Joe Boone, Roger Rouse, Ann L. Stoler, and Martha Vicinus for their insightful comments about this project.

1. See *The Complete Works of Edmund Burke* 2: 535. See also Kramnick, 136. Percival Spear identifies Hastings as the "real founder of the British domination in India" (2: 92).

2. I have been most influenced by accounts offered by Thomas Metcalf and Chandra, 94–97. *In Crisis of the Raj: The Revolt of 1857, Through British Lieutenants' Eyes*, Wayne Broehl argues that news of the massacre at Cawnpore "inflamed" British ferocity and retribution as no other event in the Mutiny; he reports that many officers, including John Nicholson, "firmly believed" that Englishwomen had been raped and "dishonored" in this war (141).

3. While eighteenth-century and Romantic Orientalist discourse did include narratives about white women imprisoned in harems, I would argue that these stories were not specific to Indian colonial discourse. See Melman; Lowe. This essay is part of a larger project which surveys the representation of rape and gender in British novels on India between 1830 and 1947; it has been made possible by excellent recent scholarship on rape. See collections by Tomaselli and Porter; Higgins and Silver; Clark; and Edwards.

4. See useful discussions of the role of rape in eighteenth-century English novels, in Eagleton; Ferguson; and Jacobus.

5. In M. Mainwaring, *The Suttee: Or the Hindu Converts* (London: Newman, 1830) and Sydney Owenson's *The Missionary* (London: Stockdale, 1811), the villains are sultans. Likewise, in James Henry Lawrence's strange Indian fantasy, *The Empire of the Nairs*, India is presented as an erotic playground where the sultans alone are depicted as lawless sexual aggressors who want to imprison beautiful white women in their harems.

6. I use this term in its nineteenth-century sense to describe the British residents in British colonies in India; I do not intend this term to denote mixed race peoples. Like Lisa Lowe and B.J. Moore-Gilbert, I see Orientalist discourse as far more contested than is often argued.

7. Helena Michie argues that women's bodies could not be mentioned in Victorian novels. I would argue that this generalization does not apply to the bodies of nonwhite women.

8. Compare Seeta's description with Taylor's portrait of Mary Palmer, painted a few years after their marriage. The painting is reproduced in Taylor, *Letters*.

9. Perhaps this failure of imagination can be explained personally since Taylor's wife died in 1844. Some critics have claimed that Taylor later established a permanent alliance with one or more Indian women but he never remarried (see Amur 1–12).

10. Patrick Brantlinger sees the acid defense as "nonsense" and diagnoses Bathurst's problem, somewhat dismissively, by saying that he is "gun shy" (217). Both these implausibilities display, it seems to me, the increasing pressure on the conservative and patriarchal definitions of female honor that Henty wanted to valorize.

11. Flora Annie Steel in *On the Face of the Waters* notes that English women at home were more threatened by rape and by efforts to police it than were Indian women; her heroine is "comforted" when she veils herself and remembers: "it was not England where a lonely woman might be challenged all the more for her loneliness. In this heathen land, that down-dropped veil hedged even a poor grass-cutter's wife about with respect" (268).

12. I discuss Steel's ambivalent feminism in more detail in "Disembodied Subjects: English Women's Autobiography under the Raj," and "Feminism under the Raj: Complicity and Resistance in the Writings of Flora Annie Steel and Annie Besant."

Ali, Muhsin Jassim. *Scheherezade in England: A Study of Nineteenth-Century English Criticism of the 'Arabian Nights.'* Washington: Three Continents, 1981.

Amur, G.S. "Meadows Taylor and the Three Cultures." *The Image of India in Western Creative Writing.* Edited by M.K. Naik, S.K. Desai, and S. T. Kallapur. Madras: Macmillan, 1971. 1–12.

Bakhtin, M.M. *The Dialogic Imagination: Four Essays.* Austin: U of Texas P, 1981.

Brantlinger, Patrick. *Rule of Darkness: British Colonial Literature and Imperialism, 1830–1914.* Ithaca, N.Y.: Cornell UP, 1988.

Broehl, Wayne. *Crisis of the Raj: The Revolt of 1857, Through British Lieutenants' Eyes.* Hanover, N.H.: UP of New England, 1986.

Burke, Edmund. *The Complete Works of the Right Honourable Edmund Burke.* 10 vols. Boston: Little, Brown, 1866–1869.

Chandra, Bipan. *Modern India.* New Delhi: National Council of Educational Training and Research, 1976.

Chesney, George. *The Dilemma.* 1876. New York: Abbatt, 1908.

Clark, Anna. *Women's Silence, Men's Violence: Sexual Assault in England, 1770–1845.* London: Pandora, 1987.

Donaldson, Ian. *The Rape of Lucrece: A Myth and Its Transformation.* Oxford: Clarendon, 1982.

Eagleton, Terry. *The Rape of Clarissa: Writing, Sexuality, and Class Struggle in Samuel Richardson.* Oxford: Blackwell, 1982.

Edwards, Susan. *Female Sexuality and the Law: A Study of Constructs of Female Sexuality As They Inform Statute and Legal Procedure.* Oxford: Robertson, 1981.

Ellis, Kate Ferguson. *The Contested Castle: Gothic Novels and the Subversion of Domestic Economy.* Urbana: U of Illinois P, 1989.

Fanon, Frantz. *Black Skin, White Masks.* New York: Grove, 1967.

Ferguson, Frances. "Rape and the Rise of the Novel." *Representations* 20 (1987): 88–112.

Grant, James. *First Love and Last Love: A Tale of the Indian Mutiny.* London: Routledge, 1868. Reprint. *Grant's Novels.* London: Routledge, n.d.

Gregg, Hilda. "The Indian Mutiny in Fiction." *Blackwood's Magazine* 161 (February 1897): 218–31.

Gupta, Brijen Krishore. *India in English Fiction, 1800–1970.* Metuchen, N.J.: Scarecrow, 1973.

Henty, G.A. *Rujub the Juggler.* London: Chatto and Windus, 1893.

Higgins, Lynn A., and Brenda R. Silver, eds. *Rape and Representation.* New York: Columbia UP, 1991.

Hirschmann, Edwin. *The White Mutiny: The Ilbert Bill Crisis in India and the Genesis of the Indian National Congress.* Delhi: Heritage, 1980.

Holton, Sandra Stanley. *Feminism and Democracy: Women's Suffrage and Reform Politics in Britain, 1900–1918.* Cambridge: Cambridge UP, 1986.

Jacobus, Mary. "In Parenthesis: Immaculate Conceptions and Feminine Desire." *Body/Politics: Women and the Discourse of Science.* Edited by Mary Jacobus, Evelyn Fox Keller, and Sally Shuttleworth. London: Routledge, 1990. 11–28.

Joplin, Patricia Klindienst. "The Voice of the Shuttle is Ours." *Rape and Representation.* Edited by Lynn Higgins and Brenda Silver. New York: Columbia UP, 1991. 33–64.

Kramnick, Isaac. *The Rage of Edmund Burke: A Portrait of an Ambivalent Conservative.* New York: Basic, 1977.

Lawrence, James Henry. *The Empire of the Nairs.* 1811. Edited by Janet Todd. Delmar, N.Y.: Scholar's Facsimiles, 1976.

Lowe, Lisa. *Critical Terrains: French and British Orientalisms.* Ithaca, N.Y.: Cornell UP, 1991.

Lyall, Alfred C. *Studies in Literature and History*. Freeport, N.J.: Books for Libraries, 1968.

Mainwaring, M. *The Suttee: Or the Hindu Converts*. London: Newman, 1830.

Mannoni, Dominique O. *Prospero and Caliban: The Psychology of Colonization*. New York: Praeger, 1964.

Manusukhani, G.S. *Philip Meadows Taylor: A Critical Study*. Bombay: New Books, 1951.

Melman, Billie. *Women's Orients: English Women and the Middle East, 1718–1918. Sexuality, Religion, and Work*. Ann Arbor: U of Michigan P, 1992.

Metcalf, Thomas. *The Aftermath of Revolt: India, 1857–1870*. Princeton: Princeton UP, l964.

Michie, Helena. *The Flesh Made Word: Female Figures and Women's Bodies*. New York: Oxford UP, 1987.

Moore-Gilbert, B.J. *Kipling and "Orientalism."* New York: St. Martin's, 1986.

Musselwhite, David. "The Trial of Warren Hastings." *Literature, Politics and Theory*. Edited by Francis Barker et al. London: Methuen, 1986. 77–103.

Owenson, Sydney. *The Missionary*. London: Stockdale, 1811.

Paxton, Nancy L. "Disembodied Subjects: English Women's Autobiography under the Raj." *De/Colonizing the Subject: Gender and the Politics of Women's Autobiography*. Edited by Sidonie Smith and Julia Watson. Minneapolis: U of Minnesota P, 1991. 387–409.

———. "Feminism under the Raj: Complicity and Resistance in the Writings of Flora Annie Steel and Annie Besant." *Women's Studies International Forum* 13 (1990): 333–46.

Pratt, Mary Louise. *Imperial Eyes: Travel Writing and Transculturation*. London: Routledge, 1992.

Sangari, Kumkum, and Sudesh Vaid, eds. *Recasting Women: Essays in Indian Colonial History*. New Brunswick: Rutgers UP, 1990. 88–126.

Saunders, Rebecca. "Gender, Colonialism, and Exile: Flora Annie Steel and Sara Jeannette Duncan in India." *Women's Writing in Exile*. Edited by Mary Lynn Broe and Angela Ingram. Chapel Hill: U of North Carolina P, 1989. 303–24.

Sharpe, Jenny. "The Unspeakable Limits of Rape: Colonial Violence and Counter-Insurgency." *Genders* 10 (1991): 25–46.

Singh, Shailendra Dhari. *Novels on the Indian Mutiny*. New Delhi: Arnold-Heinemann, 1973.

Sinha, Mrinalini. "'Chattams, Pitts, and Gladstones in Petticoats':The Politics of Gender and Race in the Ilbert Bill Controversy, 1883–84." *Western Women and Imperialism: Complicity and Resistance*. Edited by Nurpur Chaudhuri and Margaret Strobel. Bloomington: Indiana UP, 1992. 98–116.

Spear, Percival. *A History of India*. 2 vols. Harmondsworth: Penguin, 1973.

Spivak, Gayatri Chakravorty. "Can the Subaltern Speak?" *Marxism and the Interpretation of Culture*. Edited by Cary Nelson and Lawrence Grossberg. Urbana: U of Illinois P, 1988. 271–313.

Steel, Flora Annie. *The Garden of Fidelity: The Autobiography of Flora Annie Steel, 1847–1929*. London: Macmillan, 1930.

———. *On the Face of the Waters*. London: Heinemann, 1896.

Stoler, Ann L. "Making Empire Respectable: The Politics of Race and Sexual Morality in 20th-Century Colonial Cultures." *American Ethnologist* 16 (1989): 634–60.

Suleri, Sara. *The Rhetoric of English India*. Chicago: U of Chicago P, 1992.

Taylor, [Philip] Meadows. *The Letters of Philip Meadows Taylor to Henry Reeve*. Edited by Patrick Caddell. London: Oxford UP, 1947.

———. *Seeta*. 1872. London: Kegan Paul, 1881.

———. *The Story of My Life*. Edited by Alice M. Taylor London: Blackwood, 1878.

Tomaselli, Sylvia, and Roy Porter, eds. *Rape: An Historical and Social Enquiry*. London: Routledge, 1986.

Trevelyan, George O. *Cawnpore*. 1865. London: Macmillan, 1910.

Wurgaft, Lewis. *The Imperial Imagination: Magic and Myth in Kipling's India.* Middletown, Conn.: Wesleyan UP, 1983.

## SELECTED SECONDARY SOURCES

Important secondary sources analyzing the novels of James Grant, George Chesney, G.A. Henty, and Meadows Taylor include Patrick Brantlinger's *Rule of Darkness: British Colonial Literature and Imperialism, 1830–1914* (Ithaca, N.Y.: Cornell UP, 1988); B.J. Moore-Gilbert, *Kipling and "Orientalism"* (New York: St. Martin's, 1986); and Misra Udayon, *The Raj in Fiction: A Study of Nineteenth-Century British Attitudes toward India* (New Delhi: B.R. Publishing, 1987). Recent studies providing general background on literary trends influencing these novels include Lisa Lowe's *Critical Terrains: French and British Orientalisms* (Ithaca, N.Y.: Cornell UP, 1991); Sara Suleri's *The Rhetoric of English India* (Chicago: U of Chicago P, 1992); Margaret Strobel's *European Women and the Second British Empire* (Bloomington: Indiana UP, 1991); Vron Ware's *Beyond the Pale: White Women, Racism, and History* (London: Verso, 1992); and Susie Tharu and K. Lalita's *Women Writing in India: 600 B.C. to the Present.* Vol. 1 (New York: Feminist Press, 1991). On Steel's novels, see also Benita Parry's *Delusions and Discoveries: Studies on India in the British Imagination 1880–1930* (Berkeley: U of Calif. P, 1972) and Jenny Sharpe, *Allegories of Empire: The Figure of Woman in the Colonial Text* (Minneapolis: U of Minnesota P, 1993). Two biographies include: Daya Patwardhan, *A Star of India: Flora Annie Steel: Her Works and Times* (Poona: Prakashan, 1963); and Violet Powell, *Flora Annie Steel: Novelist of India* (London: Heinemann, 1981).

# CONTRIBUTORS

**Nancy Fix Anderson** is associate professor of history at Loyola University in New Orleans. She has published *Woman against Women in Victorian England: A Life of Eliza Lynn Linton* (Indiana UP, 1987) and many articles on Victorian women and the family. She is currently at work on a book about Annie Besant and the dilemmas of cross-cultural feminism.

**Deirdre David**, professor of English at Temple University, is the author of *Fictions of Resolution in Three Victorian Novels* (1981) and *Intellectual Women and Victorian Patriarchy: Harriet Martineau, Elizabeth Barrett Browning, George Eliot* (1987). *Rule Britannia: Women, Empire, and Victorian Writing* is forthcoming from Cornell UP.

**Jasmine Yong Hall** is assistant professor of English and director of women's studies at Elms College, Chicopee, Massachusetts. Her work on narratives of investigation in Victorian literature has appeared in *Studies in Short Fiction* and *Dickens Studies Annual*. She is currently working on a study of the interplay between professionalism, consumerism, and gender identity in the Victorian and modern British novel.

**Barbara Leah Harman** is professor of English at Wellesley College. She is the author of *Costly Monuments: Representations of the Self in George Herbert's Poetry* (Harvard, 1982) and, more recently, of articles on Gaskell, Gissing, and Charlotte Brontë in such journals as *Victorian Studies* and *Texas Studies in Literature and Language*, as well as in the collection *Making Feminist History* (1994). She is completing a book entitled *In Promiscuous Company: Female Public Appearance and the Nineteenth-Century English Novel*, and is coeditor of this volume.

Tamar Heller, who teaches at the University of Louisville, is the author of *Dead Secrets: Wilkie Collins and the Female Gothic* (Yale UP, 1992). Her current research is on the representation of female sexuality and orality in late-nineteenth- and twentieth-century women's writing.

Laura Hanft Korobkin is visiting assistant professor of English at Williams College. A graduate of Harvard Law School, she was a litigator in Boston before obtaining her Ph.D. in English at Harvard.

John Kucich is professor of English at the University of Michigan. He is the author of *Excess and Restraint in the Novels of Charles Dickens* (U of Georgia P, 1981), *Repression in Victorian Fiction: Charlotte Brontë, George Eliot, and Charles Dickens* (U of California P, 1987), and *The Power of Lies: Transgression in Victorian Fiction* (Cornell UP, 1994). He has also written numerous articles on Victorian fiction in such journals as *PMLA, ELH, Nineteenth-Century Fiction,* and *Victorian Studies.*

Kate McCullough is assistant professor of English and women's studies at Miami University, Ohio. She has published on Louisa May Alcott and is completing a book about turn-of-the-century (19th/20th) American women writers, gendered genre construction, and the making of American national identity.

Susan Meyer is associate professor of English at Wellesley College. She is the author of *Imperialism at Home: Race and Victorian Women's Fiction* (Cornell UP, 1996.) Her articles on Victorian literature and on American literature and culture have appeared in various essay collections and in such journals as *Victorian Studies, ELH,* and *Prospects.* She is also coeditor of this volume.

Judith Mitchell is associate professor at the University of Victoria, British Columbia, Canada. She has published numerous articles on George Moore and the nineteenth-century novel and is the author of *The Stone and The Scorpion: The Female Subject of Desire in the Novels of Charlotte Brontë, George Eliot and Thomas Hardy* (Greenwood Press, 1994).

Wim Neetens teaches English at the University of Ghent and at the East-Flanders College for Interpreters and Translators. He has edited two collections of gender-oriented criticism, and is the author of *Writing and Democracy: Literature, Politics and Culture in Transition* (Harvester Wheatsheaf,

1991) as well as numerous scholarly articles both in English and Dutch. His most recent publication is a collection of short stories in Dutch. Address: Varenlaan 13, 2610 Wilrijk, Antwerp, Belgium.

**Joseph H. O'Mealy** is associate professor of English at the University of Hawaii at Manoa. He has published essays on Dickens, Conrad, and Mrs. Oliphant in such journals as *Victorian Newsletter, Studies in the Novel, Dickens Quarterly,* and *Studies in Short Fiction.*

**Nancy L. Paxton** is associate professor of English at Northern Arizona University. She is the author of *George Eliot and Herbert Spencer: Feminism, Evolutionism, and the Reconstruction of Gender* (Princeton, 1991). She is currently completing a book on British novels about India entitled *Writing under the Raj: Gender, Race, and Rape in the British Imagination, 1830-1930,* as well as an essay entitled "Secrets of the Colonial Harem: Kipling's Indian Novels" to appear in B.J. Moore-Gilbert's forthcoming *Writing India, 1754–1930* (U of Manchester P, 1995).

**Judith Rosen** is assistant professor of English at the University of California, Los Angeles. She has published articles on nineteenth-century British conduct books and penny-press fiction, and is currently writing a book on theatricality and female identity in Victorian culture.

**John Sutherland** teaches at University College London and at the California Institute of Technology. He is the author of numerous books and articles on the publishing industry, including *Victorian Novelists and Publishers* (1976), *Fiction and the Fiction Industry* (1980), and *Victorian Fiction Writers, Publishers, Readers* (forthcoming). He is also a biographer—of Mrs. Humphry Ward (1990) and Walter Scott (1995)—as well as a bibliographer in *The Stanford Companion to Victorian Fiction* (1989). Sutherland has written extensively on Thackeray, as well as on other Victorian novelists, and has edited several volumes of Oxford's World's Classics Series (on Trollope). He is also a regular contributor to the *TLS* and the *London Review of Books.*

**Judith Wilt** is professor of English at Boston College, cofounder of its Women's Studies Program and chair of the English Department. She writes on nineteenth- and twentieth-century English fiction; her most recent books are *Secret Leaves: The Novels of Walter Scott* (1985) and *Abortion, Choice and Contemporary Fiction: The Armageddon of the Maternal Instinct* (1990).

# INDEX